D1549550

JAMES BARR
AND THE BIBLE

CRITIQUE OF A NEW LIBERALISM

PAUL RONALD WELLS

Presbyterian and Reformed Publishing Company
Phillipsburg, New Jersey 08865
1980

PRINTED IN THE UNITED STATES OF AMERICA

ISBN 0-87552-546-6

Acknowledgements

My debt of gratitude for help in accomplishing this work extends to several institutions and many individuals. Thanks must be expressed first of all to the Conseil de la Faculté libre de Théologie Réformée d'Aix-en-Provence for granting a semester leave to write the work. Particularly I must mention my colleagues Pierre Courthial, Pierre Berthoud, and Peter Jones, who encouraged me at various times; also Bill Edgar, who read sections of the text and discussed the issues with me. And thanks goes to M. Mailloux for reading the proofs.

To another seminary, geographically distant but theologically close, Westminster Seminary in Philadelphia, my gratitude is extended for the instruction I received there as a student. There an interest in Biblical theology was first fostered in the classes of E. P. Clowney, R. B. Gaffin, M. G. Kline, and O. P. Robertson.

I would also like to thank Professor Barr for his interest in this project, expressed in correspondence and conversation. I would also apologise for the times, and surely there will be plenty, when I have failed to represent his thought adequately or have not done him justice because of my lack of knowledge of the latest developments of biblical studies, which is a field that lies beyond my own domain of specialisation.

Professor J. Veenhof, who has helped and encouraged me throughout my cursus of doctoral studies at the Vrije Universiteit, Amsterdam, has been an ever enthusiastic advisor. I want to thank him for his kindness and the depth of understanding he always shows on the personal and the academic level.

Finally and above all, my thanks can hardly find words to express my gratitude to Alison, who at all times helped and supported with loving sympathy, was many times a sticker when I was a quitter, and who managed to correct the manuscript at the end of days with the children.

ACKNOWLEDGEMENTS

This thesis is dedicated to Professeur Pierre Courthial and to Dr. Pierre Marcel, who have both been defenders of the Reformed doctrine of Scripture in their ministries of more than 25 years as pastors of the Eglise Réformée de France. May their faithful witness stand as an encouragement to many others.

Paul Wells
Aix-en-Provence
1 February 1979

Abbreviations of Sources

BJRL	*Bulletin of the John Rylands Library.*
BMW	James Barr, *The Bible in the Modern World,* London, 1973.
BWT	————, *Biblical Words for Time,* London, 1969 (revised edition).
CBQ	*Catholic Bible Quarterly.*
CP	James Barr, *Comparative Philology and the Text of the Old Testament,* Oxford, 1968.
ER	*Ecumenical Review.*
ET	*Expository Times.*
F	James Barr, *Fundamentalism,* London, 1977.
IDB(S)	*Interpreter's Dictionary of the Bible,* New York/Nashville, 1962; (S)—Supplementary Volume.
Int	*Interpretation.*
JBL	*Journal of Biblical Literature.*
JR	*Journal of Religion.*
JSS	*Journal of Semitic Studies.*
JTS	*Journal of Theological Studies.*
ONI	James Barr, *Old and New in Interpretation,* London, 1966.
SBL	————, *The Semantics of Biblical Language,* Oxford, 1961.
SJT	*Scottish Journal of Theology.*
TDNT	*Theological Dictionary of the New Testament,* ed. G. Kittel and G. Friedrich, trans. and ed. G. W. Bromiley, Grand Rapids, 1964ff.
ThL	*Theologische Literaturzeitung.*
ThS	*Theological Studies.*
ThZ	*Theologische Zeitschrift.*
VT(S)	*Vetus Testamentum;* (S)—Supplement.
WTJ	*Westminster Theological Journal.*

Contents

I

A Problematic Analogy:
The Person of Christ and the Nature of Scripture

The history of Protestant theology, church life, and social thinking has been marked by a firm adherence to the Scripture principle. The *sola Scriptura* of the Reformers has often been referred to as the norm governing questions of faith and practice. Even when the practice fell far short of the high principle it claimed to apply, the material inadequacies were not the result of criticism of the formal principle itself. Divergences of opinion remained within the pale of the reference to Scripture as supreme authority, and judgments were expected to be made by application of the principle as ultimate.

More recently a change of climate is to be noted in both the principles governing theological research and church practice. Even if the origins of this contemporary modification of attitudes can be historically traced to long before our present day, it is today that we are faced with this radically different way of looking at Scripture. For we are witnessing now not only a great diversity of opinion through the application of a principle, but the crisis of the formerly revered principle itself. *Sola Scriptura* is no longer widely considered the basis for theological reflexion. Sometimes it seems to enter very little into the preoccupations of theologians, and whenever detailed examination is made of it, the result is usually one which places it in the context of several other religious authorities. Or rather, with perfect consistency, "authorities" are no longer spoken of, but one refers to "sources" or "formative factors" of theology. It is quite natural that in this climate it is frequently affirmed that Scripture is not to be taken as itself being revelation.[1] Thus when the unique

---

1. See, for example, J. Macquarrie, *Principles of Christian Theology* (London, 1966), pp. 4ff.

1

correlation of Scripture and revelation passes out of consideration, the normativity of the Scripture principle also fades from view. No longer does Scripture stand in isolation, but in theology or practice it takes its place in continuity with other factors. The authority of Scripture, if one still cares to speak of it, stands alongside other authorities.

When this modern attitude is adopted and Scripture is placed in continuity with other authorities, the problem remains very acute. It is not at all obvious that there is any easy point of contact between the various formative factors of theology. Since there is no apparent unitive principle common to the several factors, the question of their integral relationship is perplexing. Is it to be considered in egalitarian or hierarchical fashion? Does Scripture determine one's attitude to experience, tradition, historical research, or reason, or does any one of these have preeminence over any others one might care to name? Or perhaps they are to be held in some sort of creative tension, to use a popular expression? These simple questions should make it clear that the crisis of the Scripture principle makes the search for "common horizons" and their fusion no easy matter.[2] In fact, the difference between the Scripture and any other factor one might wish to name raises a series of questions, not merely because of the gap "then and now" but because of the way in which the claim to authority made by the Scripture impresses itself on us as Christian believers.

Some of these difficulties will be touched upon in the course of this study. The examination of the theological development in the thought of James Barr which we plan to make is placed in the context of the erosion of the authority of Scripture defined in previous decades of this century in the Barthian and Biblical theology movements. Barr's work can essentially be seen as a reaction against the authority structures of these modern attempts to revive the principle of the normativity of Scripture and the effect which this had upon biblical interpretation. This is not to say that the reaction is a radical one at all points, although some of its consequences could be considered quite radical. In very broad terms, it might be said that in reference to the work of Barr we are witnesses of an evolution of

---

2. W. Pannenberg, "The Crisis of the Scripture Principle," in *Basic Questions in Theology* (London, 1970), I:10ff.

theological thought from an authority-centred structure to one which is much less concerned with authorising statements by means of a prior norm. This latter state is commonly known now as a pluralistic situation. In such a situation the normative principle of *sola Scriptura* is no longer applied as a test at the outset of a theological process for judging the validity of a particular enterprise. To be sure, such a process must include criteria for itself which can be internally validated, and Scripture will enter into consideration at some point of the total description. However, there is no compelling consideration which would dictate that this point must be the start of the theological reflexion, granted the correlativity of the Scripture principle with other possible factors.[3] So it is that S. M. Ogden remarks: "not even the highly qualified senses in which neo-orthodox theologians have typically understood the scriptural principle warrant the certainty that it can still be maintained."[4]

Barr himself expresses this slightly differently when he affirms in his inaugural lecture, delivered before the University of Oxford in the spring of 1977, that the viewpoint of a biblical scholar stands or falls not by consideration of his presuppositions, but by the relation between his opinion and the evidence.[5] He elucidates this idea in the following paragraph of central importance:

> It is in the interest of theology that it should allow and encourage the scripture to speak freely to the church and to theology. It must be able to say something other than what current theological and interpretative fashion would have it say. But it cannot do this if theology controls the presuppositions with which it may be approached. It is thus in the interests of theology itself that the meaning of scripture should be allowed an adequate measure of independence; and that must mean that the discipline of biblical study also should be recognised to have a fitting independence.[6]

3. D. H. Kelsey, *The Uses of Scripture in Recent Theology* (London, 1975), particularly chaps. 8-10. Cf. from an evangelical point of view, S. T. Davis, *The Debate about the Bible* (Philadelphia, 1977), pp. 71ff.

4. S. M. Ogden, *Int* 30:243.

5. J. Barr, "Does Biblical Study Still Belong to Theology?" (1977), p. 15. A complete bibliography of the works of Professor Barr referred to in this study is appended to the work. James Barr is now professor of Hebrew at Oxford, having previously held posts at Montreal, Edinburgh, Princeton, and Manchester.

6. Ibid. On the freedom of exegesis in theology see also B. J. Oosterhoff, *De vrijheid van de exegese* (Kampen, 1976).

One could hardly wish for a clearer statement regarding exegetical method by a biblical scholar. Whether the aim stated in this passage is realisable in practical terms is, of course, another question and will subsequently retain our attention. For the present it is sufficient to define the perspective, which is quite lucid. Perhaps it should be retained firstly that Barr is speaking with respect to British universities and their approach to biblical studies. These remarks are broadened to apply to the relation of biblical studies and theology in general. The distinction which Barr sees between the two lies in that the one gives a purely descriptive statement of the evidence, whereas the other involves the theologian in a statement of personal faith, either individual or ecclesial.[7] Biblical studies then involve assertions about human relations, which, even should they provide material for theological affirmation in the proper sense of the word, do not themselves transcend the descriptive by venturing into the domain of faith-statements oriented to the divine. Biblical studies in the academic sense are therefore largely descriptive, and no common methodology covers all aspects of this study, to say nothing of such a methodology including also the properly theological, which is on a different level.[8]

Thus Barr's statement becomes rather clear. Theological presuppositions, church beliefs, and traditional beliefs should not crowd in to stifle the interpretation of Scripture. Only when there is freedom from preconceived ideas of what the text *must* mean in the realm of descriptive study can the Scripture speak *freely*. Barr's prescription for a vigorous theology and a church not dominated by traditions is that theology as such practice a "hands off" attitude as far as descriptive biblical study is concerned. In turn, it will itself benefit from the freedom of the Scripture.

This concise statement provides an insight into the work of James Barr as a whole and permits us to map out the contours of the intention in many of his theological contributions. The continuing effort of Barr is directed to seeking the freedom of Scripture from dogmas concerning its status and preconceived ideas imposing upon its interpretation. The critique which can be traced through the de-

---

7. Ibid., pp. 7, 8.
8. Ibid., p. 4; cf. pp. 14, 16.

veloping stages is profoundly anti-authoritarian. Barr is an exegetical pilgrim who has struggled through the slough of false authorities with the hope in view of the free exegesis of an open Bible.[9]

At this point, we may do well to realise that Barr's plea for the freedom of the Bible may well need some clarification in the context of recent theology. Did not neo-orthodoxy and earlier Biblical theology claim to let Scripture speak from the "inside," for itself? Was there not during that generation also a certain reserve about dogmatics or at least about the presuppositions of dogmatics? If this is indeed the case, it is surely appropriate to ask what difference lies between the two moments in the history of contemporary theology.

The aim of Barr to let the Scripture speak freely is one which has certain points in common with the thought of his predecessors, particularly Karl Barth, to whom Barr seems not a little concerned to relate his reflexion in some of his early work. However, if Barr has profited from his forerunners in listening to their desire to revalorise the message of Scripture, as far as the best way of doing this is concerned, the divergences will be quite notable. In this study of the thought of Barr and its development we shall therefore be concerned with indicating these aspects of continuity and discontinuity as the work progresses.

Widening this perspective a little more, the elements of continuity and opposition we find in the study of James Barr, as far as neo-orthodoxy is concerned, may lead to some reflexion as to the strengths and weaknesses of that theology itself in the presence of a continuing liberalism. Barr is conscious of this presence as a valid theological option, particularly in connection with the decline of the vitality of neo-orthodox Biblical theology. This broader contextual consideration regarding the work of Barr indicates the parenthetic nature of Barthian theology, which some scholars claim is to be seen as a critical movement in the continuing liberal tradition.[10] The question which might be raised here is whether Barr, in advocating the

---

9. The freedom which Barr seeks for the Scripture and its interpretation is something other than the traditional notion of the self-interpretation of Scripture, as we shall presently see.

10. For a concise definition of what we mean in this section by "neo-orthodoxy" see Barr's own account in *BMW*, pp. 1ff. It is, says Barr, "best exemplified in Karl Barth. Taking its rise soon after the First World War, by the end of the Second this movement had made a great impact. Its emphasis

freedom of Scripture, in continuity with one of the aims of Barthian theology, is not rather more in line with the liberal tradition in carrying the aim through in concrete terms. To put it slightly differently, we might ask if Barr's fundamental desire to continue in the Barthian tradition does not at some points oblige him to break with it in order to maintain theological consistency. At these points Barr might in fact be found to be more in the liberal line. The problem is thus one concerning the inner consistency of the kerygmatic, evangelical neo-orthodoxy which sought and seeks to expound the Scripture in the sphere of a certain concept of theological authority. Is not this conservatism, Barr might well ask, an obstacle to the free speaking of the Scripture, which in some cases at least approaches the fundamentalism which paralyses the real apprehension of its message?

At one point Barr is apparently more in continuation with the liberal tradition than the Barthian, although he may well not choose to frame it himself in these terms. He affirms in the citation above that descriptive biblical studies can be independent of theological concerns. This is brought out in quite striking fashion when Barr says: "If theology in the strict sense makes assertions about the divine, biblical study seems a great deal of the time to make assertions about human relations."[11] Although Barr is not here saying how things should be but how they are, he has an obvious sympathy for this approach. In it biblical study can get on with its job uncluttered by considerations of theological normativity. On this level they do not enter into the rules of the game. Biblical study, then, aims at this objective description which largely concerns human relations.

Conceding that my presentation here might well be a little more emphasized and less nuanced than Barr's description in his lecture, it remains quite plain that this account is a good deal more than a Sabbath day's journey away from what a Barthian might be expected to say on the same subject. This brings us to the main point

---

was strongly biblical. . . . It rejected the 'liberal' types of theology which were . . . rather a human attempt to see and understand God in the image of man. . . ." On this see also D. Tracy, *Blessed Rage for Order: The New Pluralism in Theology* (New York, 1975), pp. 9f., 15n7, 22, 237-50, and passim. C. Van Til denied much earlier that neo-orthodoxy could simply be considered reformational, *The New Modernism* (Philadelphia, 1946), 1972[2], p. vii.

11. Barr, art. cit., p. 8.

of this introduction, namely, the nature of the Scripture considered as divine and human. The separation of the biblical-descriptive and the theological-normative which we have considered may be seen as a refusal on the part of Barr to make a conjunction of the divine and human elements of Scripture an integral factor in the understanding of Scripture. Scripture must be examined as a human document quite apart from an immediate consideration of its divine origin or the revelation it may contain or witness to. The risk of considering Scripture in terms of a christological analogy is that of falsifying the truly human character of the Scripture. Thus in establishing the analogy between the two natures of Christ and the divine and human with respect to Scripture the temptation is to underemphasize the human character of the Scripture by holding it in tension with the divine. The danger is that in spite of assertions to the contrary, there takes place an implicit transfer of the hypostatic union of Christ to the Bible. When the divine and human of Scripture are discussed in the sphere of the notion of verbal inspiration, it is possible, thinks T. F. Torrance, to come close to what amounts to an "incarnation of the Holy Spirit."[12]

In the neo-orthodox revival of biblical authority, reference was quite often made to the christological analogy with respect to Scripture. However, there was little really detailed discussion of the analogy, or so it would seem, and one has the impression it was rather mentioned in passing, being taken for granted.[13] To be sure, there were strong words about Docetism from many of those who wrote about Scripture at this time, often in connection with the refutation of a mechanical view of inspiration.[14] Occasionally, by way of riposte, more conservative theologians criticized neo-orthodoxy

---

12. T. F. Torrance, *SJT* 7:107, in his review of B. B. Warfield's *Inspiration and Authority of the Bible.*

13. See H. Vogel, *Gott in Christo* (Berlin, 1951), pp. 99-156; E. Brunner, *Revelation and Reason* (London, 1947), pp. 12, 276; L. S. Thornton, *Revelation and the Modern World* (London, 1950), pp. 130, 248ff.; the analogy also has an important place in certain Catholic works, see, e.g., J. Levie, *The Bible, Word of God in Words of Men* (London, 1961), pp. 203-301, and P. Grelot, "L'inspiration scripturaire," *Recherches de science religieuse* 51:365ff. Criticisms have been advanced, among others, by Markus Barth, *Conversation with the Bible* (New York, 1964), pp. 151ff., and G. C. Berkouwer, *Holy Scripture* (Grand Rapids, 1975), chap. 7.

14. J. K. S. Reid, *The Authority of Scripture* (London, 1957), p. 217ff.

as being Nestorian in its doctrine of Scripture.[15] In this fashion
the terminology of the christological disputes of the first centuries
was transplanted to the discussion of the doctrine of Scripture.[16]

In spite of the protestations against Docetism and the criticism
of fundamentalism's fear that the human element will overshadow the
"divinity" of Scripture, neo-orthodoxy had its own problems. In
particular, once a christological analogy is used to speak of Scripture
there is the problem of indicating how the divine and human are related in this case. Being fundamentally a reassertion of biblical
authority but not wishing to neglect the humanity of Scripture, neo-
orthodoxy was involved in the difficulty of relating the normativity
it wished to accord Scripture and its specifically human character.
Within the context of an authority-centred theology it is more apparent that this authority can be established with the divine aspect
predominant than by appealing to the specifically human character
of the texts. By implication, the seduction of relating authority and
the divine element places the human in a merely preliminary role.
Instead of being central to the understanding of the nature of Scripture, in spite of protestations to the contrary, the human stands in
constant possibility of being relegated to the realm of a preamble.
In terms of the interpretation of the text, historical criticism becomes
a stage to be gotten over by paying cursory lip service.

Similar considerations appear in the criticism Barr makes of the
christological analogy, as we hope shortly to show. For the Scripture
to speak freely, it is important that the human aspect be considered
in its own right, as something other than merely a preparatory stage
which exists only because of what lies beyond it. Interpretation must
be free in the sense that its methods must have some justification
other than an impulse to move from the human to the divine-
normative, with as little difficulty as possible. Exegetical method
must not be overpowered by the needs of an imposed christological
analogy. The Scripture is honoured and speaks freely through our

---

15. J. I. Packer, *'Fundamentalism' and the Word of God* (London, 1958),
pp. 83ff.

16. This in itself is not anything new; see the remarks of H. D. McDonald in
Theories of Revelation (London, 1963), pp. 257f.; also A. G. Hebert, *Int* 11:
194. On the church fathers and the use of the analogy see J. H. Crehan,
JTS 6:87-90.

interpretation when we consider it for what it really is—a human document.

The interpretation of Barr's work that we propose is that as a whole it can be considered as an ongoing critique of the christological analogy as imposing on interpretation and on views of the status of Scripture. As the critique of Barr progresses, we shall see that it applies to the two movements where interpretation and the doctrine of Scripture have been most influenced by considering the divine and human in Scripture, namely, the neo-orthodox "Biblical theology movement" and the conservative Fundamentalist position. For both of these cases the character of the human element in Scripture in relation to the divine is problematic. Both place certainty and faith in the divine aspect of revelation, or might at first seem to, and create the difficulty of relating this faith to the human witness of Scripture.[17] This will in turn raise the question of where certainty is to be localized when the humanity of Scripture is stated out of the context of a christological analogy.

We do not wish to claim that this particular presentation of the work of Barr is the only one possible. Other interpretations may be equally valid. Nor do I wish to suggest that Barr might think of his theological work as related to the christological analogy and criticism of it in a self-conscious way. What I do claim is that Barr's work, which starts, as we shall see, with a vigorous critique of the christological analogy, continues in a polemic against authoritarian impositions upon interpretation in Biblical theology, and discusses weaknesses in present views of Scripture, can quite suitably be treated in this way. Positively considered, this criticism represents a continued seeking after a freedom in explaining and listening to the message of Scripture.

However, before we come to these points of detail, we must enquire after the meaning of this christological analogy by seeing how it might function in Barr's theological background.

1.1. *The basis of the analogy in the two natures of Christ.*

The criticism which Barr makes of the christological analogy must be understood as a prolongation of christological elements in his

---

17. On this generally see G. C. Berkouwer, op. cit., pp. 18ff.

early thinking. Although the sources for this in terms of published material are slight, being limited to two articles and several dictionary articles, two significant points can be discerned which have bearing on the question of the two "natures" of Scripture.[18] The first of these concerns the nature of the humanity in which Christ partakes; the second a certain tendency in the christological discussion to emphasize the dynamic aspect of the union of the two natures of Christ. Both of these aspects reveal the impress of Karl Barth's dogmatics on Barr's early thinking.

In speaking of the incarnational theme in Paul[19] Barr remarks on the association of "flesh" with law, sin, and death. This does not necessarily imply that fleshly existence is *ipso facto* evil. It is the present flesh of sinful man which is involved with sin and hence mortal. Flesh can be neutral in the sense of the human constitution or oppositional in that of enmity with God. Barr affirms that "the double sense is held in one term" by Paul.[20] This fact is important as it reveals Christ to have been assimilated to fallen human flesh and not merely to flesh in a neutral sense. Christ participates in sinful flesh, although this does not mean Paul thinks Christ to have been a sinner. Galatians 4:4 indicates the participation of Jesus not just in human life, but his submission to its essential weaknesses. The influence of Barth is quite clear in this discussion. Even Barr's choice of title for his article is quite reminiscent of the tone of the well-known section in Barth's *Dogmatics*.[21] In this passage Barth first treats *sarx* as a description of neutral human nature and then goes on to affirm that "flesh is the concrete form of human nature marked by Adam's fall. . . ."[22] This means, as T. F. Torrance comments, that the Word "appropriated human form . . . in such a way as to take up the frail and finite conditions of the creature into Himself not merely as the earthen vessel of the Word of God but as His actual

---

18. See "Christ in Gospel and Creed," *SJT* 8:225-37, "The Word Became Flesh: The Incarnation in the New Testament," *Int* 10:16-23, and the articles in Hastings' *Dictionary of the Bible* (rev. ed., 1963), indicated in the bibliography.

19. *Int* 10:21.

20. This remark is indeed interesting in the light of Barr's later semantic criticisms and reveals in this early stage the sort of theological misuse of language which he was later to denounce.

21. K. Barth, *Church Dogmatics* (Edinburgh, 1956), I.2, 149ff.

22. Ibid., p. 151.

speaking of it to us."[23] The Word becomes flesh not just in terms of
appropriation but also in terms of participation. Although this man
Jesus exists only in appropriation to the Word, as man he stands in
a relation of participation with men, yet with the dissimilarity of sinlessness. This fact Barth insists upon quite outspokenly a little
further on in the section referred to: "How can God sin, deny Himself to Himself . . . ?"[24] Yet in the same few lines we also hear that
the Word "exists in the state and position, amid the conditions, under
the curse and punishment of sinful man."

We will not enquire as to the theological orthodoxy of this statement; our intention in this section is simply to outline some points in
Barr's early thinking for establishing the analogy between Christ and
Scripture.[25] One of the determinative factors with respect to Christ's
assumption of fallen human nature as far as the analogy with Scripture is concerned, would seem to lie in the consideration that since it is
this nature that is assumed, the human character is not itself revelatory.
Barth refuses the idea that Christ assumes human-nature-in-general.
This would throw a shadow of Docetism over Christology; Christ is
not "an ideal man" but "a man as we are, equal to us as a creature,
as a human individual, but also equal to us in the state and condition
into which our disobedience has brought us."[26] We can consider the
Word of God only in the mystery of his *Welthaftigheit*. The human
nature of the Word is not in itself revelatory, since God hides himself
in his revelation. The flesh is object of the Subject-Word's sovereign
divine act, albeit in an abiding manner. So it is that God appropriates
to himself human existence, by "assuming" flesh. Yet all is not
simply limitation. The Word assumes the restrictions and lowness of

23. T. F. Torrance, *God and Rationality* (London, 1971), p. 142. See also
H. Chavannes, *L'analogie entre Dieu et le monde selon Saint Thomas et selon
Karl Barth* (Paris, 1969), pp. 195ff.

24. Barth, ibid., pp. 195ff.

25. J. Hamer in his work *Karl Barth* (London and Glasgow, 1962), p. 44,
thinks Barth sees in Christ's taking our place a "purely material substitution"
which loses sight of God's holiness and the finality proper to the incarnation.
He also speaks of certain aspects of Barth's thought coming close to an un-
conscious Nestorianism. R. Swanton, "Scottish Theology and Karl Barth," *The
Reformed Theological Review* 33:17-25, notes the lack of support for the view
that Christ assumed *natura vitiata* in the fathers and the confessions and compares Barth's view with that of Edward Irving (1792–1834).

26. Barth, op. cit., p. 151.

human condition, yet it is the *Word* which does so. Barth affirms that the "Son of God is the same in quite a different way from us."[27] The Word in assuming flesh incorporates the human being into the unity of his divine being. The Word does not cease to be himself as the Word in the full sense. "He takes over human being into unity with Himself."[28] There is no becoming of the Word or third element between Word and flesh, but the assumption of the flesh by the Word. The manhood is the predicate of his Godhead, the predicate of the acting of the Word.

The possibility of an analogy between the Word-incarnation and the word-inscripturation is present in the general structure of Barth's description. In taking on human flesh the Logos assumes also the form of human language relations. In the word preached, man's speech is bound to God and real through God. But this does not mean that man's speech or the sacrament is identical with God. The man Jesus is identical with God because of the way the Word assumes flesh. The Word remains Subject of the appropriation, and it is in this sense that identity can be spoken of. It cannot be attributed to the predicate of the divine action apart from consideration of its relatedness to the sovereign divine will.[29] Concerning this G. Wingren says: "God 'assumes' flesh, just as the divine Word clothes itself in human words; although the distance between the divine and the human is greater in the word of Scripture than in the person of the incarnate Word."[30] The parallel is perhaps well drawn, in that it points out a similarity and a distinction between incarnation and in-scripturation. Both the human nature of Christ and the word of Scripture are objects of a divine action which assimilates them to the Word, in a more abiding sense in the case of incarnation. In neither instance is the human as such to be considered in itself revelatory. Revelation is something which occurs only in reference to the Word's action. Yet as a result of this divine action, identification does take place; the Word becomes flesh, the word becomes Word of God.

---

27. Ibid., p. 155.
28. Ibid., pp. 160-61.
29. Ibid., p. 162.
30. G. Wingren, *Theology in Conflict* (Edinburgh, 1958), p. 115. J. Hamer, op. cit., pp. 40ff., points out that the association has an abiding character in the case of the humanity of Christ and speaks of successive manifestations in the case of other forms of the Word of God.

However, this is not all, for beyond this comparison of a formal nature between Christ and Scripture it is possible to attempt to found it in a more integral way with respect to the incarnation itself. This is what T. F. Torrance would appear to do in his work referred to above. The Word, he states, came to *dwell* among us. This includes the fact that the Word, to be heard as such, had to enter the speaker-hearer relationships within humanity and become speech to man through the medium of human language.[31] This is prepared for in Israel, the community formed by the address of the Word of God to man through the medium of human words, so creating a reciprocity between God and man. Israel is a community of this reciprocity within human society and as such is the appropriate medium for the continuing communication of the Word to man. Israel is prepared for the incarnation. Through Jesus "God's Word has become speech to man through the medium of human words and speaks to men as man to man, for in Him God has graciously assumed our human speech into union with His own, effecting it as the human expression of the divine Word, and giving it as such an essential place in His revelation to man."[32] The union takes place not only on the level of humanity but in particular with respect to the speech aspect of that humanity. This effects not only a union between Word and flesh, but also an integration of the Word of God and the word of man.

The ramifications of these propositions may well be legion. Suffice it to say here that they illustrate rather well the reason for the forcefulness of the christological analogy in the Barthian theology of which Barr's early works are tributary in some measure. For the possibility of an analogy here rests not on a purely formal induction from Christ to Scripture but can claim a basis in the incarnation itself in the speech aspect of the humanity of Christ.

However, there is another aspect to these considerations which may well be brought out. In Jesus Christ we have not only the speech of God to man, but because of the union of the human word to the divine, we find man's obedient response to God "incorporated into God's Word as an essential part of it."[33] Christ is not the Word of God in an abstract way, but the Word made flesh and as such the

---

31. See Torrance's discussion, *op. cit.*, pp. 146ff.
32. Ibid., p. 149.
33. Ibid., p. 151.

Word of God from within our humanity. He helps us by existing "in the place where we exist."[34] The Word is then also one of faithful response to God on the part of man, and so that this should be efficacious the Word accepts the limitations of the human condition as the Word made flesh.

Some of these notions must now be grouped concisely, to indicate their relevance for the christological analogy.[35] The general drift of our remarks may be summarized thus: as in the case of the person of Christ, with respect to Scripture God in his revelation appropriates human words which are not themselves different from other human words. There is a necessary limitation in this mode of revelation. However, because of the integration of the Word of God and the word of man in Christ, the human word which witnesses to this, with its necessary limitations, is appropriated by God in his act of revelation. Scripture partakes in the fallen condition of all language, and to seek inherent divinity in it is to ignore its truly human character and err in the way of monophysitism. On the other hand, one might speak of the revelatory potential of this word as witness to revelation, which lies in the act of appropriation of this word by God.

The point of contention, of course, lies in the application to Scripture of the idea that the Son of God is the same as us in quite a different way from us. Christ participates in our fallen human nature yet without sin, but can one conclude from this that the inscripturation of the Bible is without error? Barth is apparently not willing to carry the analogy this far and seems to think that although true humanity need not involve sin in the case of the incarnate Word, the humanity of the inscripturated word involves fallibility.[36] To be totally logical here it would seem that Barth would have to argue that fallibility is not sinful. K. Runia thinks this is the Achilles heel of the analogy in

---

34. Barth, *op. cit.,* p. 155. This aspect of Barth's thought is climaxed in his teaching concerning the reconciliation in Christ. See the discussion by Berkouwer, *The Triumph of Grace in the Theology of Karl Barth* (Grand Rapids, 1956), particularly pp. 125ff.

35. Klaas Runia has already discussed the analogy in the thought of Barth in detailed fashion in his book, *Karl Barth's Doctrine of Holy Scripture* (Grand Rapids, 1962), pp. 65-78. It is not our intention at this point to discuss the analogy fully but to indicate some salient aspects contributing to the understanding of Barr's critique.

36. Barth, op. cit., pp. 506ff., speaks of the witnesses as "fallible, erring men like ourselves."

the case of Barth: "To insist upon biblical fallibility along with its humanity is actually to destroy the whole parallel with the incarnation. The only thing that is left is a purely human book which can be used of God to communicate his divine message, but which as such *is* not this message."[37] The point of Runia is well taken, and it would appear that Barth's equivalence between humanity in the true sense and fallibility does in fact destroy the possibility of the union of the divine and the human in Scripture.

Nevertheless, it may well be doubted that Barth's thought ever ran on such logical lines. It may even surprise us, with a little reflexion, that given the activistic character of Barth's Christology, he bothered to construct such an analogy at all. As G. Ebeling has indicated, the view which establishes a parallel incarnation-inscripturation is bound up with an ontological interpretation of the event of revelation. This view, according to Ebeling, was modified by the Reformers, who, however, did not in principle surrender to it.[38] If this is indeed so (and we state this with some reserve), it is just at such points that we might expect the Barthian synthesis to dissolve under the pressure of a more consistent approach to Scripture along some of the lines suggested by Barth himself. Moreover, it could be argued that should we say that Barth ought to have carried through the analogy in a more thoroughgoing way, we are in fact doing so by paying insufficient attention to the "occasionalism" of Barth's theology of the Word."[39]

At this point we can turn back to James Barr and mention two passages in his latest work, *Fundamentalism.* In one of these he speaks of the analogy between Christ and Scripture in a critical way. Barr comments in passing on the function of the analogy in the thought of Barth, insisting on the humanity of the Bible which is "subject to the strains and weaknesses of any human product" and "that the revelatory content is not the Bible, its words and sentences. . . . what God reveals is himself, not books and verses."[40] In the course of this description of neo-orthodoxy, we see that something troubles Barr, namely, the fact that the Barthian heritage in the English-

37. Runia, op. cit., p. 77.
38. G. Ebeling, *Word and Faith* (London, 1963), pp. 30ff.
39. Hamer and Wingren in particular put a great emphasis on this aspect of Barth's thought, as does also Cornelius Van Til.
40. Barr, *F,* pp. 214ff.

speaking world has fallen into the hands of people who are a great deal more conservative.[41] In the outcome a christological analogy such as Barth used, with minor modification, becomes a gun in the arsenal of conservatism. Barr does not explicitly state so, of course, but this may well be a factor in his sharp criticism of the use of the analogy by the likes of B. B. Warfield and J. I. Packer.[42]

About these two representatives of fundamentalism Barr remarks, concerning the basis of their use of the analogy, that he doubts whether their Christology is orthodox. It seeks to delimit the humanity of Christ's person within the recognition of his Person as a divine unity. Perhaps Barr considers this to be docetic, but he does not say so. It matters little, in any case, whether this is orthodox in terms of ancient discussions, as any formulation which would satisfy present understanding might well be heterodox in those terms. In the second place, the problem is the application of this Christology, which may or may not be correct, to Scripture, so as to make the Bible a divine book, its human character being one aspect of the divine. Since Barr is discussing questions relating to literary matters in this passage, one wonders why the question of the christological analogy is introduced at this point. His analysis of the situation amounts to this: in order to secure the fundamentalist view of the Bible as inerrant in matters of fact and literary authorship, the authority of Jesus as a divine teacher is used to authenticate these facts. In other words, Barr seems to be saying that the authority of Jesus is being used to prove what is already known about the Bible in fundamentalist tradition—that the Bible is a divine production. By a strange kind of inversion Christ is seen in analogy with the Scripture. Barr affirms as much thus:

> . . . I do not believe that either Packer or Warfield would have taken this stand about the person of Christ but for the pressure of the issue of biblical inerrancy. That is the obvious and only motivating power for the argument they present. . . . Christological doctrine has to be so defined as to give the maximum possible shelter to inerrancy.[43]

This has taken us away from our main subject somewhat, but this

---

41. Ibid., p. 218.
42. Ibid., pp. 171f. See J. I. Packer, op cit., pp. 82f., and B. B. Warfield, *Inspiration and Authority of the Bible* (Philadelphia, 1948), pp. 162f.
43. Ibid., p. 172.

recent illustration serves to show what may motivate a certain re-
luctance about analogies on the part of Barr. According to his
analysis, the Barthian analogy of Christ and Scripture becomes in
the hands of theological conservatism a boomerang in which Christ
actually becomes analogous to inerrant Scripture, as the divinity of
Christ is appealed to in settling questions relating to the minutiae in
the text. In serving this need, Jesus, says Barr, is separated from the
limitations of his time and made into "a superhuman and inhuman
person." In doing this we ignore the functional character of Jesus'
teaching.[44] Nothing could be more killing to the freedom of biblical
interpretation than this authoritarian appeal to a superhuman knowledge of a divine person to assure the divinity of a text.

When considering the christological aspects of Barr's early thought,
which contribute to his understanding and subsequent criticism of the
christological analogy, we can discuss, as well as the humanity of
Christ, the issue of the nature of the union of the divine and human.
Already something has been said of this in terms of the appropriation
of humanity by the Word. Now it is fitting to say a little more about
the specifically dynamic character of this act.

In 1955 Barr published an article touching on this subject entitled,
significantly, "Christ in Gospel and Creed." Barr indicates the inten-

---

44. Whether one concedes the rightness of Barr's interpretation of the
christological analogy in fundamentalism will depend largely on whether
one accepts the main point of his book concerning the function of inerrancy
in that tradition. Nothing affirmed by Packer and Warfield, it seems, would
tend to support Barr's argument at this specific point. Firstly, it is not clear,
as Barr would have it, that Packer is actually following Warfield at this point,
although he does refer to him in a note. Secondly, the specific remarks of
Packer with regard to the method of Christology are in reply to the words of
R. H. Fuller about seeing the divinity in Christ's humanity and the Word of
God in fallible words of man (Packer, op. cit., p. 82). Packer is not intend-
ing a full doctrinal statement; his affirmation is circumstantial. Moreover, Barr
gives the impression of a good deal of inflexibility concerning the analogy in the
two mentioned. This is in stark contrast to the reserve they show in actually
stating the analogy. Warfield spends half the page where he refers to it in
stating its limitations. We read: "Between such diverse things there can exist
only a remote analogy; . . . it amounts to no more than that in both cases
Divine and human factors are involved, though very differently" (Warfield,
loc. cit.). Nor is there any evidence to prove conclusively that in this case
the motivation is provided by inerrancy, as Barr affirms. Certainly, there is
no more than could be provided to prove that Barth argued that the Word
participated in fallen human nature because he believed Scripture fallible.

tions of the two-nature Chalcedonian Christology and the attempt
to shield against misunderstanding the confession that in Jesus Christ
the two natures are united.[45] The question is as to whether or not the
Scriptures in fact speak this way. Even though it has been suggested
that the NT "points towards" this doctrine, Barr does not find it
satisfactory just to say that Scripture raises questions to which the
creeds give answers.[46] The complication arises from the fact that
modern historical research is hindered by dogmatic influences, and
we must have our minds free to approach the Bible without these presuppositions: "we have to allow the historical material of the Bible
freedom to criticise our dogma."[47] This does not mean that Barr is
adopting a position which advocates radical criticism of the creeds
and their relegation to insignificance. Far from this, Barr asserts
that we must see a sort of complementarity between gospel and creed,
which does not mean that they are of equal stature. What he rejects
is the approach which naively rejects the traditional theology in
search of a "non-theological picture" of Jesus. There never was
one, says Barr, and where the traditional formulations have been
swept aside they have been replaced not "by a pure and unbiased
directness of approach but rather by another system of axiomatic
prejudices . . . which has obscured the Biblical material. . . ." In the
same paragraph we read that biblical exegesis can be assisted by the
understanding of the traditional christological concepts.[48]

What is striking in these formulations is the moderation of the
general approach, which appreciates the creedal formulations for not
seeking to give an explanation of the mystery of the incarnation and
for doing all that can be done in "constructing a fence" to limit
"certain constructions . . . false to Biblical authority."[49] However,
this does not mean we can simply read back elements of the traditional
Christology into the Gospels and, for example, take the Son of God
and Son of Man ideas as representing elements in the union of the
divine and human natures. When we study the Gospel narratives we

---

45. Barr, "Christ in Gospel and Creed," *SJT* 8:225.
46. Ibid., p. 226. An example of this basic approach is found in A. W.
Wainwright's work on *The Trinity in the New Testament* (London, 1962),
where he also argues that the beginnings of the answers are found in the NT.
47. Ibid.
48. Ibid., p. 227.
49. Ibid., p. 228.

are confronted with something rather different, which is highlighted in the way Jesus presents himself to men. This is done through "His word in a situation." This word is not a universal truth but a statement in context, which by its enigmatic ambiguity provokes decision in reply to the fundamental puzzle of the person of Jesus.[50] Contrasting gospel and creed, Barr produces a nice image which is illustrative of his approach: "Later theology with its two-nature doctrine was in fact attempting to produce a still form of [a] moving picture, something static and fixed which was fully true and equally true at every moment."[51] Likewise, if the Gospels are dynamic, so is Paul, who expresses his Christology dynamically in terms of the progress of Christ through his life.[52]

How does Barr then propose to reconcile these two approaches? Surely there is some difficulty, not to say an improbability of producing a still picture from a moving one. Barr affirms that the still form does represent faithfully what is disclosed in movement, and that "both types of Christological statement are true."[53] It is not therefore a case of either/or as far as Christology is concerned. What the exegete has to be able to do is to maintain the equilibrium of the two forces, realising that the ontological approach of the creeds has something to contribute to the integration of exegesis since the question of who Jesus *was* cannot be separated from the interests of the NT. History cannot be separated from theology, as the historical Jesus was the ontological Jesus, and to work with such a dichotomy is to fail to be historical in the true way. Barr thinks that modern historical research fails just at this point.[54] To consider the ontological in continuity with the historical "moving picture" of the Gospels is not to impose a foreign notion on the text but to let the text "speak for itself" in so far as it is concerned with "what He *was.*"

This early article of Barr's is of great interest in retrospect, as in it we see held together certain elements which will in fact in later works

---

50. Ibid., p. 231.
51. Ibid., p. 233.
52. Ibid. Barr says Paul "refuses to make a purely static statement." This seems to go a little too far. For this to be the case one would have to show, among other things, that Paul envisaged the possibility of such a statement and rejected it.
53. Ibid., p. 234.
54. Ibid., pp. 235-37.

stand in opposition to a much greater extent. Here we have the complementarity of the ontological approach and the historical which in terms of the two natures of Christ and the union of his person means a holding together of the dynamic picture and the static formulation. Barr manages to hold these together in his exposition by proposing that this is not the imposition of foreign presuppositions on the biblical picture, but an important element for an understanding of the Scripture's own approach. This itself implies that the Bible is in "some way the foundation and criterion of Christian teaching."[55] However, this does not mean that Scripture is the only consideration in the theological process, for Barr affirms quite clearly that "It is impossible for us today, and indeed always was impossible, to derive a true theology by simple deduction from the Biblical texts."[56]

Our description serves, therefore, to indicate some points of tension at this stage in Barr's development, between the ontological and the historical and between what might be termed the self-witness of Scripture in interpretation and other factors which demand attention. The equilibrium is maintained by tracing the ontological within the historical-dynamic and reconciling dogmatico-theological concerns with the witness of Scripture in such a way as to claim that these considerations do not prejudice proper interpretation of the text, being concordant with that aim. In spite of these tensions which later tend to become oppositional, at this point there would appear to be in the thought of Barr an adequate basis for the formulation of the analogy between the divine and human in Christ and the two aspects of Scripture, perhaps with an accent on the fallibility of Scripture by way of consideration of the "flesh," as in the analogy of Karl Barth.

A short time after these two articles Barr made several central contributions to the revised edition of Hastings' *Dictionary of the Bible*. These reveal a certain change of emphasis in Barr's approach to christological problems and a much greater preoccupation with the functional-dynamic side of the gospel portrayal.[57] Firstly, there is

55. Ibid., p. 226.
56. Ibid., p. 228.
57. Although the fact must not be lost from view that these are dictionary articles and not therefore personal statements of Barr's theological position, they are important nevertheless as statements of what Barr considers a reasonable account of the biblical material.

an article entitled "God" in which Barr reviews the scope of the biblical materials, terminating with a section on "the place of Christology."[58] Here we read that the NT does not conceive of the relation between God and Christ in a static way "which could be once stated and would then be unchangeably valid and fitting in all situations." This relation "has its being only in, and not apart from" the mission of Jesus. It is messianological and eschatological, to use Barr's expressions. There is therefore no possibility of extracting the relation from this context which is that of the mission of Jesus and petrifying it as an independent formulation. This is so not only of the Gospels but also of the Epistles, as in Romans 1:3f. Barr goes further again than this and applies this to the doctrine of the Trinity. Thus, the fatherhood of God is not a "universal fact" but a relation to the messianic Son. "The relation of Father and Son appears therefore as it is connected with the mission of Jesus." Likewise, the Spirit "confirms that mission." No "trinitarianism" or "three-in-one" formulas are found in the NT.

The clarity of this article demands our gratitude. Its fundamental perspectives can be confirmed from other contributions to this volume, particularly that on "Messiah."[59] Why did Jesus not identify himself as such? Surely, says Barr, this cannot be accounted for by political convenience. The reason lies elsewhere. Trust which Jesus seeks to elicit is inconsistent with a straightforward assertion of messiahship. So the messianic presentation of Jesus is not through particular affirmations "but in the total series of the events of the gospel." This culminates only in the passion and resurrection of Jesus. If there is no reason to doubt that Jesus was conscious of being the Christ of the OT promise, it is hardly the interest of the NT writers to penetrate the inner consciousness of Jesus. Their specific genius lies in weaving together the richness of messianic manifestation and the reserve of Jesus as to direct affirmation. In the same vein in the article on "Revelation"[60] we read in connection with Matthew 16:17 that Jesus Christ is not "evident and unmistakable" when he does not declare his identity, but is a "secret which must be broken through."

58. *Dictionary of the Bible,* revised by F. C. Grant and H. H. Rowley (Edinburgh, 1963), p. 338.

59. Ibid., pp. 646-55, above all, pp. 654-55.

60. Ibid., p. 848.

The source of the disclosure is not "within humanity," but is the Father in heaven. In a nutshell, there is no revelation of the Son as such apart from the relation with the Father. Nor can this be generalized as divine revelation, since it is only significant in terms of the relation.

A further indication is furnished where Barr treats the notion of "Atonement."[61] Jesus does not just state the truths of Christology and act them out. The messianic claim, the atonement, and the making-known of these unfold together in the mission of Jesus. This mission can be understood with respect to atonement in the OT, where its ultimate ground is the "faithful will of God to sustain his covenant with man." Christ then is the living embodiment of the covenant, "as One who in His body holds together by His faithfulness God and man."[62]

At a risk of squeezing the lemon too hard, these statements can be contrasted with what Barr says about fundamentalism's view of God. Fundamentalism has assimilated the Greek idea of God existing in a kind of static perfection.[63] In turning its back on a historical approach to reality as exemplified in biblical criticism and history-oriented theology it has turned its back on liberating movements. So it gets stuck with a static view of God and defines the relation between God and Christ in terms of essences. Thus fundamentalism misses the functional or dynamic character of Jesus' ministry and the atonement and finds it above all necessary to insist that Jesus is *God*.[64] So if a Christology starts with a consideration of Jesus as man, it is a highly suspicious sign. The important thing is not the relation of Christ and God but the deity of Christ. This ties in with the whole orientation to the inerrancy of Scripture. We must, thinks Barr, seize the functional character of Jesus' ministry and see it not in terms

---

61. Ibid., pp. 76-78.

62. This statement applies the general structure of a Barthian theology of the Word, Christ being at once God's Word to man and man's response of obedience to God, to the doctrine of reconciliation. It might be said that in Christ man's obedience and God's are incorporated, just as in the Word man's response is appropriated to the Word of God as part of it. See the references in notes 32-34.

63. Barr, *F*, p. 277. Barr does add that this idea is endemic throughout many other strains of modern Christianity.

64. Ibid., pp. 169ff.

of divine and human or eternal truth but against the situations of Jesus' own life. Only this can "loosen the logjam."

What, then, does all this add up to? May it be possible to suggest, with some circumspection, that there is a shift discernible even within the confines of the limited evidence we have examined? In this the main feature is the movement away from traditional christological interpretation based on ontological questions. If, in the first article we mentioned, dating from 1955, there is a sustained effort to relate a dynamic NT-centred Christology and traditional ontological formulations, in the later dictionary articles this concern is not so evident. In *Fundamentalism,* it is openly rejected. It would appear that Barr finds it more fruitful to think through christological questions in functional terms and even if this does not imply a total unconcern for questions concerning the divine and human in Christ or Scripture, it certainly does show a preference as to the way of approach. This may well point to an increasing difficulty in holding together the static, two-nature approach and the dynamic view which redefines christological doctrine in relational terms. Jesus' sonship, messianity, atoning work, rather than being developed in terms of divine and human natures, are defined in terms of Christ's relation with the Father worked out through the concrete situations of his life and death. Such a christological shift spells change for the christological analogy, which depends on an ontological approach in matters of Christology. This in turn opens the way to the criticism of methods of interpretation which treat Scripture in one way or another as a divine book having its unity of meaning in the divine mind and owing its existence to revelation. Open too, when the ontological structure of the traditional Christology is eclipsed, is the way to a critique of Scripture as a document connected with revelation, as inspired and authoritative Word of God. A functional view of the person of Christ, which relies for its foundations on a dynamic relational approach, will require also a dynamic history-centred doctrine of Scripture, not a static one appealing to the divine and human in Scripture. In fact, it might not be going too deeply into speculation to indicate that the present questions about the nature of Scripture may well be related on a deeper level to problems connected with the nature of the incarnation. But here we have run ahead of ourselves, and must now turn again to the criticism of the christological analogy in the work of Barr.

1.2. *Making the analogy with Scripture*

Some attempt has been made by those who adopted this view of incarnation as appropriation and participation to found the possibility of theological discourse on the incarnation. Only the fact that communion is restored in Christ can valorise theological language as analogical to the reality of God. On this view, theological statements have their validity in so far as they refer to the ultimate Truth of Christ in an analogic fashion, but in their human character their truthfulness is in continuity with this-worldly experience and criteria applicable to it.[65] This approach can be understood in the light that the Scripture is analogous to the incarnation, bearing special reference to the revelation of God in Christ while being continuous with other human speech.

Karl Barth himself puts this in a very pointed way when he writes: "That the Word has become Scripture is not one and the same thing as its becoming flesh. But the uniqueness and at the same time general relevance of its becoming flesh necessarily involved its becoming Scripture. The Divine Word became the word of the prophets and apostles by becoming flesh."[66] This quotation is remarkably concise and indicates at the same time the distinction between incarnation and inscripturation and their continuity. It is the same Word involved in both cases and the Scripture is "necessarily" the implicate of the incarnate Word. The possibility of a christological analogy is inherent in the nature of the incarnation as act of God.

Hitherto we have noted some parallels between the Christology of Karl Barth and that of James Barr in the few early illustrative sources of his thinking which we have. Going beyond this, we can now trace some of the applications of this Christology to the doctrine of Scripture in the development of Barr's thought. In the Preface to *ONI,* Barr relates his work on Scripture to the thought of Barth in a very exact way:

> . . . there is in my work a very decided striving for reappraisal of the work of Karl Barth. This has a sort of biographical explana-

---

65. T. F. Torrance, *Theological Science* (London, 1969), pp. 186, 190ff. For a criticism of this approach see J. Macquarrie, *God-Talk* (London, 1967), pp. 40ff., particularly p. 49.

66. Barth, op. cit., p. 500.

tion through the great influence of Barth on my earlier theological formation. Though I still feel that it is Barth's God whom I seek to worship, the intellectual framework of Barth's theology has in my consciousness to a very great extent collapsed in ruins. . . . Barth's theology forms for me one of the chief areas in which I hope to find lines of thought. Sometimes it has afforded me suggestions for fresh construction; sometimes it has made clear for me a point to which we must go back if certain dilemmas of modern discussion are to be overcome.[67]

This relatedness to Karl Barth and the desire to find new directions from within his thought is clear above all in the substantial review which Barr wrote on J. K. S. Reid's *The Authority of Scripture*. In this short critique a concise evaluation of certain canons of recent discussion of Scripture is given, together with some positive suggestion. In the scope of a few pages Barr confronts some of the weaknesses of the received views and states some possibilities which will unfold as definite theological statements in his later works. To be sure, it is quite uncommon that a book review should occupy an important place in the understanding of a writer's thinking, but in this case it is of great significance in the development of the whole, as comment on Reid's work acts as a sort of mirror for Barr's reflexion.

Barr notes at the outset the centrality of the christological analogy for the understanding of Scripture and compares statements by Reid and Barth to this effect.[68] Reid affirms that the imperfection of the Bible is located in the human and not the divine element, in the recording and not in the revelation itself.[69] "It is men in their finitude, and more exactly in their sinfulness, that introduce perversion into God's self-disclosure, or rather into the record they make of it." Reid has clearly learned in Barth's school—the drawing together of

---

67. *ONI*, p. 12. The title of this book is also related to the intention of Barr with regard to the work of Barth as expressed here, cf. p. 11. It refers not only to the problem of the relation of the OT and NT, but also to what is "old, traditional, and given" in interpretation and what is "new, fresh, and surprising." Thus Barr relates the question of OT and NT to that of Scripture and tradition in a general sense. In this context Barr's understanding of his work can be pointed to as something new arising in the context of a reconsideration of the Barthian tradition.

68. *SJT* 11:86.

69. See J. K. S. Reid, op. cit., pp. 184-85.

finitude and sinfulness, and the contrast of self-disclosure and Scripture as record of revelation are fairly typical, to say nothing of the structure of this thought which tends to contrast the divine and human.

What, then, does Barr think about all this? Firstly, he recognises the central significance of the analogy "which more than any other single factor assisted the revival of biblical authority in the Church." The analogy has been a powerful weapon against fundamentalism with its infallibility mentality and liberalism which saw little in Scripture beyond human religiosity. However, the last word has not been said. What lacks in Reid's book is a criticism of the Theology of the Word; Barr wonders whether with Barth's formulation we have really reached a terminus, or if "a new period of restatement must now begin."[70] Barr suggests that "considerable modification" must be made because of an "important inadequacy" in the Theology of the Word. Nor is it possible to advance by a return to fundamentalism or liberalism but by carrying through an insight of that theology.

The point at issue here concerns the role of the human response "behind" the Scripture.[71] Although the Bible is the word of man, an evaluation destructive of bibliolatry, this insight remains undeveloped in Barthian theology for the reason that it is built into a system in which the Word characterises a movement from God to man.[72] In the *Church Dogmatics* Barth does insist on the witness, writtenness, and humanity of Scripture. The Bible is everywhere a human word and must be understood as such in its historical dimensions. But this is not all, for if humanness implies a necessary limitation and distinction from revelation, it is precisely here that we shall find also its divinity. Thus we can no more ignore the humanness of Scripture than we can the humanity of Christ. Taking the Bible in a true historical way, we must go beyond the humanity as such and see God's revelation.[73] To understand the Bible we must not only consider its humanity but press beyond this to the unity of the Scripture with God's revelation. If Scripture and Word of God stand

---

70. Barr, art. cit., p. 87.
71. Ibid. The use of the word "behind" is rather strange in this context, but is perhaps indicative of Barr's appreciation of its subsidiary character.
72. Ibid., p. 88.
73. Barth, op. cit., pp. 462ff., particularly pp. 468-69.

in a relation of disjunction on one level, they are not totally irrelevant to each other. Their relation not being coincidental as in the traditional theology of Protestantism, Barth seeks to establish it in a new way. God has at once limited himself by providing a witness to his Word in the form of a text, but this word as object of his free sovereign action can become revelatory.[74] "As the Bible and proclamation become God's Word in virtue of the actuality of revelation they are God's Word; the one Word of God within which there can be neither a more nor a less."[75]

In terms of the christological analogy this structure has been described by Barr's fellow Scot in detail:

> If Christ is the Word of God become Man, then He is not only the Word of God come to men, but as Man He bears, He is the Word of God. In Him our weakness and unprofitableness have been taken up, so that our human word in spite of its weakness . . . may be not only the frame and the earthen vessel of the Word, but the speaking of that Word. Jesus Christ . . . is not only the Word as God utters it, but the same Word heard and uttered and lived out by Man. That is the Word we hear in the Holy Scriptures, the Word of God in human form, which can be uttered by human lips, so that . . . the Word of God may also be God's own speech to men. . . . It is because the Word of God is not only God in His self-revelation, but Man . . . that it can be received by man . . . and yet remain God's very Word.[76]

How are we to understand what Torrance calls "the Word of God in human form"? Barr does not think that theologies which insist on Scripture as witness and speak of its "pointing away from itself" do justice to the human form of the text. For we must, says Barr, take into consideration the facts of the formation of the Bible. In respect to the relation of the word in its God-to-man and its man-to-God aspect, Barr says that the second is at least as important, if not more constitutive of Scripture than the first. For in the making of the Scripture-tradition the Word/Act of God and the human response are entwined together, having worked on one another in the tradition. "The moulding of the tradition is a continual response to the divine

---

74. See on this J. Hamer, op. cit., pp. 17-24.
75. Barth, op. cit., I.1, 121.
76. T. F. Torrance, *Karl Barth: An Introduction to His Early Theology, 1910–1931* (London, 1962), pp. 104-5.

Act or Word."[77] This amounts to saying that as there is interaction of both elements within the tradition their relation must be seen in terms of the process of tradition. It is not so much a case of revelation and response, the one being divine and the other human, but both the divine and the human element exist within the context of an historical unfolding of tradition in Israel and the church.

The difference between Barr and Barth opens at this point. Barr puts it very precisely. In Barth's structure the prophetic/apostolic response "is a response of further transmission of the Word *to* Man, not a response of answer to God from Man." What Barr envisages is that even if there be divine revelation, this Act/Word takes its place in the tradition as an element of the developing human response of man to God. So although Barr does not want to deny the function of the Bible as witness to God's revelation, we cannot consider this unilaterally. "Scripture is answer as well as address." Referring to one of Barth's images Barr says with some wit: "The finger of John the Baptist should be given a rest; he is simply not an adequate analogue for the whole range of biblical statement."

How are we to consider this suggestion of Barr's in relation to the thought of Barth? It seems possible that this can be seen as the radicalisation of one of the aspects which entered into the finely balanced dialectic of revelation and Scripture in Barth. In Barth the negative distinction between human and divine and the emphasis on the limitation of the Word existed nevertheless with a positive aim— that of pointing beyond to the ultimate unity of the Word in the actuality of revelation. Even should Barth affirm the total character of the humanity of Scripture as witness, to the point of declaring it to be "everywhere a human word"[78] in the overall structure, the human could function only as preliminary to the divine, rather than something of value for itself. So for Barr, this humanity remains neglected as being only a moment in the movement from God to man, which remains dominant. On the other hand, Barr would like to see something really positive in the human aspect for itself, and in the wake of re-

---

77. Barr, loc. cit. In this quotation, Barr begins to show an OT scholar's concern for historical interpretation over against dogmatic formulations. The reference to the "tradition" can probably be attributed to an awareness of the importance of Von Rad's *Theology,* published in German in 1957 (vol. I), reviewed by Barr in *JSS* 4:173-75, 286-88 (1959).

78. Barth, op. cit., I.2, 464.

cent developments in the field of OT studies, suggests a radicalisation of the human aspect indicated by Barth. Thus the Scripture is seen as a tradition process which entwines the divine Act and the response as man's answer to God. If one regrets a slight lack of focus in the exposition of these ideas and the absence of a more explicit development, the rectification is to be expected in subsequent developments.

Barr applies his criticism of the Bible as witness to the specific question of the relation between Christ and Scripture.[79] According to Barr the distinction Word of God/Word of Man must undergo modification. The lack of clarity of this distinction is a longstanding thorn in the flesh, and one is accustomed to complaints concerning games of theological hide-and-seek for the Word of God. As H. Cunliffe-Jones said, "for many reasons, the Christian Church is uncertain at the present time, how to treat the Bible as the Word of God."[80] It is not amazing therefore that Barr should add his fuel to the fire in the light of his remarks about "witness." For witness and word of God have in recent decades been held in correlation. Pursuing his remarks about tradition, Barr thinks it incorrect simply to describe Scripture as "Word of Man." It may indeed be this, but it is more. It is the word of Israel and the church. As such it is the word of a covenanted community which bears the "stigmata of divine action." As word of the community "it moves both from God to Man and from Man to God."[81] Put more specifically in terms of the christological analogy, this means that Scripture should not be thought of merely in terms of the incarnation but also as related to the human obedience of Christ in his priestly mission and ascension. Barr wonders whether Barth would give greater place to the human response of obedience if he were to be writing his doctrine of Scripture today.

As far as the traditional way of speaking of the "elements" of

---

79. Barr, loc. cit., pp. 88-89.

80. H. Cunliffe-Jones, *The Authority of the Biblical Revelation* (London, 1948), p. 132. Paul Tillich thinks that calling the Bible "Word of God" results in many confusions, *Systematic Theology* (Chicago, 1967), I:158-59.

81. There is, I think, a lack of clarity in Barr's formulations at this point. It is by no means certain what Barr means when he speaks of the word of the community as moving from God to man and from man to God. In what sense this word could really be a word from God is not explained.

Scripture goes, Barr reckons it to have broken down. For if we make the act of revelation the divine aspect and the recording the human function, then it is clear that the divine act is simply depicted in a human story. The divine act itself is not a part of the Bible. Or, alternatively, if we speak of the divine and human as mingled in Scripture the "two elements" fall from view. Therefore it is better to affirm, says Barr, that "there is in fact only one 'element,' the human," in Scripture.

A further advantage exists in this way of approaching the Bible, according to Barr. The christological analogy as used by Barth and followers implied that to "true God" there corresponded the "witness of the revelation"; to "true man" the "historical literary document of a definite humanity."[82] The problem with this is that the revelation and authority of Scripture are implied to be in the divine character. The human word falls on a different level, that of the historical and the literary. Although Barr is reserved as to whether or not this would really constitute a representation of Barth's thought, he discerns a tendency to seek the divine Word away from the human word of Scripture. "And here, says Barr, it needs to be said emphatically—the *human* character is the bearer of revelation, the *human* word is the word that has authority." This is another way of insisting on the Scripture as the product of the covenant community bearing witness to and responding to revelation in its texts.

At a later date, Barr sums up his reservations about the analogy in these terms:

> There is . . . no good reason why the relationship between God and man in the person of Christ should be supposed to hold good also for the relationship of divine and human in the Bible; even if one accepts in the fullest way a formula like the Chalcedonian . . . there is no reason why it should be applicable also to the Bible. . . .[83]

Equally doubtful are views of Scripture patterned around a theory of the three forms of the Word of God. Barr does not deny that such patterns can be constructed, but contests the idea they must be mandatory for theological reflexion.

In résumé: the "inadequacy" of the Theology of the Word is that

---

82. Barr, art. cit., p. 90.
83. *BMW*, p. 22.

although the human is acknowledged it does not really come into its own. Barr thinks this must be criticized, but at the same time this insight of Barth's theology must be carried to its proper conclusion. All the Scripture is human; revelation and authority cannot be placed beyond human tradition which itself includes witness and answer. The text as answer of man to God is totally human and includes in response the understanding of revelation. We can see in these propositions, which are no doubt somewhat tentative at this stage, an application of Barr's dynamic emphasis in Christology to the doctrine of Scripture. Just as Jesus' messianity and sonship are not considered in ontological terms but rather under a functional bias from the standpoint of the relation between the Father and the Son, so also Scripture is seen as expressing human relationships and particularly the community reply to God. There is a certain parallel in this respect between Barr's way of speaking of Jesus as Christ, following Barth, and his way of speaking of Scripture as a human word. This need not be taken to mean that Barr totally rejects ontological considerations, although certain of Barr's assertions do point in that direction. Probably it is better to see this as a question of perspective. Barr finds it more illuminating to speak functionally of these issues; the dynamic approach opens us to historical questions, and this fully allows us to value the human. It avoids what has been called the danger of unconsciously putting the Bible in the place of God.[84] It may also place the emphasis on what Markus Barth calls "what is said" in the Bible, rather than on those who speak.[85]

As well as this, Barr's proposals would pare away the knotty problem of reconciling the errors of Scripture and the fundamental revelatory nature of the Bible. If it is possible in terms of the christological analogy to explain the errors or fallibility of Scripture with reference to the humanity of Christ, this parallel was not necessarily accepted by non-Barthians. It depended on Barth's particular idea of the relation of Word and flesh. Catholic versions of the analogy or those of Warfield and Packer were more likely to say "without sin" and "without error."[86] While the analogy is in use there remains the

84. L. Hodgson, in *On the Authority of the Bible* (London, 1960), pp. 5, 6.

85. M. Barth, op. cit., pp. 144ff.

86. On this point see J. Baillie, *The Idea of Revelation in Recent Thought* (New York, 1967), pp. 109ff.; Reid, op. cit., p. 149; Torrance's review of Warfield in *SJT* 7:104-8, and J. McIntyre, "Analogy," in *SJT* 12:12, 13.

possibility of transferring to a thing statements appropriate only to a person.[87]

Barr's position at this early stage is already drawing away from that of his mentor. Yet, even though there is discontinuity with Barth, these new aspects can be regarded as the blossoming of seeds already present in Barth's work. Two elements in Barth's thought in particular would seem to foster this movement. The insistence on biblical fallibility along with humanity really undermines the christological analogy and leaves us with a purely human book. This aspect is taken up in the ideas of Barr we have examined and reworked in terms of seeing the Scripture as a process of human tradition.[88] The second element favouring this change of perspective can be located in Barth's view of revelation itself. When Barr suggests that Scripture should be seen as a covenanted response, the answer of the community, what he is really doing is prolonging Barth's idea that revelation and Scripture stand in an indirect relation. God is the Wholly Other and there is no natural unity between God and man. Even in the case of Christ it is not possible to speak of a direct identity between God and man; at the most it can be an assumed identity, willed by God and effected by Him and to that extent indirect.[89] This assumed identity rests not in the essence of God or man, according to Barth, but in the decision and act of God.

So it is also with Scripture. Except in Scripture the nonidentity is greater: there is no unity of person between God and the prophets and apostles.[90] In this case the indirect identity can only be effected by the decision and act of God. Scripture, says Barth in the same place, is "the Word of God in the sign of the word of man." Scripture is described in terms of signs, tokens, witnesses, testimonies, or reminders, for its relation to the Word is indirect. Thus, "It is neither divine only nor human only. Nor is it a mixture of the two nor a *tertium quid* between them."[91] God alone establishes the identity in

---

87. This is the basic criticism of M. Barth in op. cit., p. 162, also by J. Baillie of L. Thornton's ideas in *Revelation and the Modern World,* see op. cit., pp. 121ff.

88. See Runia's remarks already referred to, op. cit., p. 77.

89. Barth, op. cit., p. 499.

90. Ibid., p. 500.

91. Ibid., p. 501; cf. I.1, 133-35, and the article in J. Baillie and H. Martin, eds., *Revelation* (London, 1937), pp. 46-51.

His act. The absence of any direct identity is the factor which in Barr's reworking of the character of Scripture leads very promptly to his judgment that the "two element" view has broken down and that Scripture must be a "one element" document. This undoubtedly breaks a certain equilibrium in the thought of Barth, and may not be "orthodox" in terms of Barthian orthodoxy, but it is certainly a logical and a not-unwarranted development of a Barthian theme.

In conclusion to this section we can remark on an aspect we referred to concerning the person of Christ, namely, the tension created in any attempt to synthesise an ontological and a dynamic approach in theology. The fragility of Barth's efforts at mediation between divine and human in the two cases under discussion accrues from this ambiguity of method: the dynamic tends to eclipse the ontological. Without wishing to infer that this is a case of a thin kine eating a fat one, it remains to be seen when the functional aspect is emphasised in Christology and bibliology what real link can be forged with *divine* revelation. Barr veers strongly in this direction by wishing to describe Christ in relational/situational terms and Scripture in the light of the relation between God and the covenant community. Is there any *objective* revelation left, related to Christ or to Scripture? These are connected and might be said to constitute the real theological problem of our era.

1.3. *Analogy and interpretation.*

So far we have spoken of the doctrine of Scripture as such. Now we must say a word about the christological analogy and its implications for interpretation, as this question is the one which concerns Barr in his early criticisms of the Biblical theology movement.

If it is possible to speak originally on every subject in the world, says Karl Barth, as far as revelation is concerned here "it is possible only to speak faithfully, that is exegetically."[92] This does not mean that some kind of neutral method can be developed.[93] Exegetical method is to be adapted to the subject-matter in view. Exegesis, according to Barth, must take into consideration the reality beyond the text in order to constitute a proper means to understanding. Scripture

92. Barth, *God in Action* (Edinburgh, 1936), p. 7.
93. For Barth's view of the presupposition question, see *Church Dogmatics*, I.2, 469-70.

being considered a human witness to revelation, interpretation must seek to go beyond the humanity to see God's revelation.[94] This is at the heart of Barth's well-known remarks concerning historical criticism and interpretation in his Preface to *Romans*.[95] In this Barth states that "the question of the true nature of interpretation is the supreme question." An historical understanding of the human text of Scripture is not in itself sufficient. We cannot forget that the Bible is witness; a true historical understanding cannot ignore this. The Bible does not speak of itself, but of God's revelation. Interpretation, if it is to achieve its goal, must seek not only the human and historic, but in order to understand these, must see them as witness pointing beyond to the divine revelation.

It may not be necessary to belabour the point here, as it should be fairly clear that this orientation fits hand in glove with what Barth says of the christological analogy in the context of his Theology of the Word. Exegesis must take into account the structure of appropriation and participation which characterises incarnation and inscripturation. Just as humanity is taken up into the revelation of Christ in the Word made flesh, and human words are taken into service in the biblical witness, so also interpretation cannot ignore that the text, if a human word, belongs with revelation. So it has to look beyond the text itself, to the act of revelation. If the divinity of Christ is concealed in his humanity, as is the witness to revelation in fallible human words, and if a free sovereign act is required in order for the revelation to be accomplished, so also interpretation is open to error and must ever bear in mind the revelation to which the text points. It is only "by revelation that revelation can be spoken in the Bible," says Barth, and just as there is only one Word of God, not three, so also in exegesis "there is only one truth."[96]

It is in this sense that Barth speaks of "open exegesis," in a passage which has attracted the interest of Barr. This expression is used of an interpretation which is "open and ready" to meet the mystery of the subject-matter, not by mastering it but by being gripped by it. Exegesis cannot lose sight of the fact that this subject-matter

94. Ibid., p. 466.

95. See the remarks of J. M. Robinson in *The New Hermeneutic,* ed. J. M. Robinson and J. B. Cobb (New York, 1964), pp. 22ff.

96. Barth, op. cit., pp. 469-70.

is sovereign and free both with respect to the word before us and to us ourselves. It cannot then be confused with the humanity of the speakers or our own humanity.[97] In a similar passage[98] Barth makes the same plea for this perspective. Exegesis is in danger of being taken captive by the church; the free power of the Bible ever runs the risk of being transformed into the authority of the church. This happens when correct exposition is made dependent on the judgment of the "teaching office of the Church or on the judgment of a historico-critical scholarship which comports itself with equal infallibility." In this instance exegesis is interposition not exposition. The subject-matter of the text is lost to view, being no longer sovereign in its freedom before the text. This sort of exegesis would be, no doubt, closed. The Bible is self-imposing by virtue of its content,[99] and when the Bible "grasps us" this is an event which is "God's affair and not ours. . . ." "His decision and not ours." We must demand, says Barth, "free exegesis for the sake of a free Bible." And again: "the exegesis of the Bible should be . . . left open on all sides, not for the sake of free thought as Liberalism would demand, but for the sake of a free Bible."[100]

This approach has caught the attention of Barr, the exegete. In his review of Reid's book, he refers to the above passage and adds— "Do we not need more guidance what this means, and how the working minister may put it into practice?"[101] That this question has continued to preoccupy Barr is seen in another such affirmation some 15 years later:

> My own position is in every respect in favour of a greater and freer use of the Bible by the church, and I believe that many of the troubles of modern Christianity are self-inflicted burdens which would be much lightened if the message of the Bible were more highly regarded.[102]

Barr's concern as stated here has obvious Barthian undertones. However, if Barr has taken this basic concern for an "open" Bible and its "free" use from him, this is by no means an indication that his

---

97. Ibid., pp. 470-71.
98. Barth, op. cit., I.1, 106-7.
99. Ibid., p. 109.
100. Ibid., p. 106. Cf. Reid, op. cit., pp. 199ff.
101. Barr, art. cit., p. 93.
102. *BMW*, p. 112.

way of achieving this freedom will necessarily coincide. As we have sought to point out, in Barth's case this freedom is concerned with a recognition of the threefold structure of the Word of God. The relation of the divine and human in Christ applied to Scripture, with the necessary modifications, gives the essential structure which exegesis must bear in mind. For exegesis does not exist for itself, but in seeking an understanding of the subject-matter of the text must envisage proclamation and the freedom of the event of God. It is a preparation for being grasped by the subject-matter of the text which lies beyond the human aspects of the text.

However, we have already seen that for Barr there is a breakdown of the divine-human as far as the consideration of Scripture is concerned. Would not this mean also that Barth's view of the goal of exegesis is also to be called into question as too quickly passing over the human conditions of the text to encounter with the Subject beyond? And if this is the case, has Barth really achieved a free-speaking of the Bible as a human response? This is obviously a much controversed issue. Some would see Barth's way of being "more critical" than the historical method as a neglect of the essential control of exegesis in theological constructions.[103] Others might see Barth's value as lying precisely in the way he puts historico-critical questions in their place.[104] Barr is conscious of this difficulty quite early in his work. Modern scientific exegesis, he remarks in his comments on Reid's book, has as its starting point the Bible as the Word of Israel or the church. From here "it is able to penetrate not only to historical-critical results but to the real biblical theology."[105] The problem with the double-nature approach, complains Barr, is that it leads to a dualism in exegesis, one line working with the human in a scientific fashion and the other making a "theological" approach to the divine Word. The difficulty is that of establishing contact between the two, in such a way as to make exegetes aware of the theological issues involved in their work and dogmaticians of the procedures of modern exegetical practice. Barr does not here

---

103. See Oscar Cullmann's criticism in *The Early Church* (London, 1956), pp. 15, 16. He sees Barth's danger as treating "philological and historical explanation as too preliminary in character."

104. See Alan Richardson in the *Cambridge History of the Bible,* ed. S. L. Greenslade (1963), III:322-23.

105. Barr, art. cit., p. 90.

go any further into the relation of exegesis and dogmatics beyond these brief remarks. Nevertheless, it is obvious that for him the dualism of the approaches is based on a now defunct understanding of the nature of Scripture. In his restatement the freedom of exegesis will be no longer, as with Barth, the freedom of the Subject related to a construal of the text in terms of the divine and human. It will rather be an openness based on the interpretation of Scripture on a totally human level, unencumbered by the interjection of theological authority.[106]

Barr's approach to exegetical questions here is in correlation with his criticism of the structure of the christological analogy. Just as this inhibits our discernment of the true humanity of Scripture by the contact with the divine, so in the realm of interpretation considerations of theological normativity connected with the divine aspect will inhibit true freedom in exegesis. This again is a consequence of the tension between an ontological approach and a functional one in theological methodology. Exegesis is not concerned primarily with questions of theological normativity but with an account of *human* relations.[107] It is concerned with the dynamics of history, and ontological questions should not impede it in this pursuit. This is not to say it will never be concerned with this sort of question, but such considerations are not its aim. It seeks above all the opening of the meaning of a human text in freedom from considerations of authority.

Thus Barr refers to the christological analogy in another article, saying that in the thought of Barth the Bible has authority as witness to revelation: ". . . on one side it is entirely word of man, on another side it is entirely Word of God." Barr remarks the decrease of importance of this in recent years and says that "though theologically impressive, it has seemed to offer little help in solving actual interpretative problems within biblical scholarship; also, the focus of study has moved from the difference between divine and human to the difference between ancient and modern, between biblical times and our own."[108] With the reserve one would expect in such an article, Barr notes the incompatibility of perspective between the

---

106. As we have seen in Barr's inaugural lecture, referred to in notes 5-8.
107. Barr, "Does Biblical Study Still Belong to Theology?," p. 8.
108. "Scripture, Authority of," in *IDB* (S), p. 795.

two positions. The thinking which centres interpretation on divine
and human has been replaced by an historical approach in which
the question of the divine does not enter, but only that of "then and
now" in a human context. Conversely, we have to see as well, argues Barr, that the christological formulations of the early centuries
probably would never have "emerged in this form had the historical
mode of reading then been in fashion."[109] Orthodox brethren may
breathe a sigh of relief that it was not the mode then, but this is
beside the question. The fact is that the historical mode is the present
way and that formulations relying on consideration of essence are
somewhat incompatible with its dynamic. In Barr's criticism, functional Christology, Scripture as a human document and historical
thinking are correlates. Or, to put it another way, a functional
Christology is out of joint with a passive view of inspiration of
Scripture[110] which insists on the divine origination of the writings
and considers the human aspect in this context.

All this sets the scene for Barr's critique of methods of biblical
interpretation, which we shall review in chapter 2. If this is to be
free and the Bible is to be really open, then interpretation must be
liberated from norms other than its own historical methods. The
success of much of Barr's writing and its effectiveness must be
attributed to its having touched chords agreeable to the ears of many
exegetes. In fact, Barr's call for freedom of exegesis has been a
perennial concern of Biblical theologians. Speaking of those of the
time of the Enlightenment who considered Biblical theology as the
historical study of biblical religion, R. C. Dentan remarks: "No
biblical theology in the modern sense of the term was possible until
scholarship generally had abandoned the old hermeneutic principles of
analogia scripturae and *analogia fidei,* which assumed both the uni-
formity of religious ideas in the Scriptures and their identity with
the doctrines of the orthodox churches."[111] History tends to repeat
itself. Barr might well be seen as standing in a tradition of critical

109. "Reading the Bible as Literature," *BJRL* 56: 20.
110. Warfield, op. cit., pp. 245-96. See also the remarks of Berkouwer,
op. cit., pp. 139ff.
111. R. C. Dentan in *Preface to Old Testament Theology* (New Haven,
1950), p. 6, cited by E. P. Clowney, *Preaching and Biblical Theology* (London, 1962), p. 11.

reflexion which struggles to have freedom from dogmatic prejudices.[112] One of these prejudices of the previous generation is the
interpretation of Scripture in terms of the christological analogy.
Barr would doubtless agree with Markus Barth on this when he says
that the analogy cannot solve the problem of Scripture's authority
and affirms that "this analogy is but another yoke fabricated by
those who want to impose the Bible on its readers."[113]

That leaves us with the leading question of theological work—when
is exegesis really free and Scripture genuinely open? The question
is vital for Christian life too, as H. M. Kuitert says. "The freedom
of a Christian man stands or falls with the free Bible—the Bible that is
not bound by authoritative interpretations of yesterday."[114] That
is the sort of statement one could almost hear Barr making! Our
particular question with respect to all this is as to whether freedom
from the traditional does not also involve submission to some other
kind of authority. This must subsequently be borne in mind.

1.4. *Christ and Scripture or Spirit and people of God?*

Barr's own contribution to the debate on the christological analogy
is not only the emphasis on the human aspect of the Bible text. It
is a little more adventurous than this, and quite original, in its way.
Leading on from his assertion that there is only one element in the
Bible, the human, Barr seeks to formulate the consequences of this
for the doctrine of Scripture. His suggestion is as follows: ". . . the
true analogy for the Scripture as Word of God is *not* the unity of
God and Man in the Incarnation; it is the relation of the Spirit of God
to the People of God."[115] This, Barr admits, does itself have certain
analogies with the incarnation, but this does not obscure its differences. The difference is that it cuts away the doctrine of inspiration

---

112. W. Wrede saw the history of biblical studies in the nineteenth century
in this perspective. See I. H. Marshall, ed., *New Testament Interpretation*
(Exeter, 1977), pp. 62-63.

113. M. Barth, op. cit., p. 170. The judgment of Barth seems a little pre-
cipitous, as he admits on the same page that a full development of a Chalce-
donian-type analogy does not exist in theological literature.

114. H. M. Kuitert, *Do You Understand What You Read?* (Grand Rapids,
1970), p. 49.

115. Barr's review of Reid, p. 89.

from the question of the divine and human in Scripture and permits us to rework the notion of inspiration in a purely human sense. So Barr adds: ". . . inasmuch as the Scripture is strictly not of two 'elements' but of one, an incarnational analogy is not an adequate substitute for a doctrine of inspiration."[116]

These propositions can be understood in the context of the modification of Barth's analysis of the threefold form of the Word of God. Once the analogy between Christ and Scripture is removed from this structure, the third form of revelation, not Scripture, becomes the mediacy where the Word is actualised. No longer is mediacy sought on the level of Scripture as a divine-human analogue to revelation in Christ, but in the form of the continuing people of God in relation to the Spirit. This shift is already prepared for in Barth's own work, where Scripture and proclamation are two aspects of the same genus. Scripture is a church-document, written proclamation, which present-day preaching continues. Jeremiah and Paul are at the beginning and the modern preacher nearer the end of one and the same series.[117] If there is also dissimilarity, related to the constitutive significance of Scripture, the continuities are very profound.

These statements of Barth are capital for contextualising Barr's remarks. The removal of the analogy between Christ and Scripture in terms of divine and human means that the Scripture has its place along a line of human development of the people of God. Scripture becomes part of a tradition-process which develops. Thus rather than analogy between the nature of Christ and the writings of the OT and NT there is a relation of continuity in the life of the people of God through contact with the Spirit. Christ and Scripture are not related in terms of divine-human *revelation* but as part of the same ongoing process of the people of God in history.

How can this tradition-process be related to the will of God for history and his act of revelation? Is inspiration, somewhat secondary in a theology of the Word, useful? We must remember, says Barr, that the Scripture is a totally *human* document, and if we are to use

---

116. Ibid., pp. 89-90. In the article referred to from *IDB* (S) in note 108 Barr remarks that in Karl Barth the emphasis was more on "Word of God" than on inspiration., loc. cit.

117. Barth, op. cit., I.1, 101-2.

inspiration "it must be purified from all suggestion of inerrancy and infallibility, and from all teaching that identified the production of the Bible with the revelation of God."[118] Inspiration is to be defined in totally human terms. This means that the inspiration of Scripture is in the response of the people of God which has an authentic relation to the divine action; it is obedience in forming tradition and recognising this in canonisation; it is the guidance of the people of God. In this view inspiration fits in with election, for it is this tradition God "elects into existence." Inspiration, in conclusion, "must lie distinctly in the realm of the communion of the Spirit with the People of God, as the means by which the divine action is both lighted up and is made to be a source of light in time following."[119]

The Barthian superstructure has crumbled, but one element does remain, or so it would appear, in this formulation. The relation between Spirit and people of God is indirect. We recall Barth to have said: "Encounter with the Word of God is genuine, irrevocable encounter, i.e., encounter that can never be dissolved in union."[120] There is no mixing of divine and human. Spirit may be more volatile than Word, but in our review of this idea we can see that there is no union of people and Spirit of God, their relation at best is indirect. And even if we talk of the inspiring of the fallible human tradition, how can we describe this inspiring in the context of indirectness? What is the *work* of the Spirit, and can we say anything more about it than Barth could say about the mysterious encounter with the Word?[121]

One conclusion which can be drawn from these reflexions is that it is clear that the centrality of revelation in the traditional sense becomes very susceptible in Barr's proposal. The development of this will unfold as Barr's work continues. The question which will reappear later is the following: With the disappearance of the mediacy of the christological analogy and its replacement by a dynamic mediacy between people and Spirit of God, are we faced with the problem of a *deus absconditus,* out of contact with history, revela-

---

118. Barr, art. cit., pp. 90-91.
119. Ibid.
120. Barth, op. cit., I.1, 141; cf. I.2, 499-501.
121. For a critique of contemporary trends on this point see C. Henry, *God, Revelation and Authority* (Waco, 1976), II:143ff.

tion, inspiration, as over against a dynamic of contingency in the growth of the people of God?[122]

*   *   *   *   *

The general perspective of this study should now be clear. It concerns the carrying through of the criticism of the christological analogy as outlined in this chapter. This will be described in the three following chapters. Firstly, the critique of the analogy leads from the evaluation of Scripture in connection with divine and human aspects to a consideration of the Scripture as human. As far as interpretation goes, this means the Scripture will be considered as any other text. No longer are we "looking through" the human to the divine. The meaning of the text is on the level of the human. This opens up on the critique of language in interpretation which we have in Barr and the refusal of the imposition on the text of authority structures foreign to the text itself.

Secondly, from interpretation which considers the text on a human level there arise questions about the authoritarian views of the status of the text which have imposed on the exegesis of the text. Barr reconsiders the accepted ways of handling the Scripture as connected with revelation and finds these insufficient. This is an application of Barr's critique of the christological analogy to the status of Scripture itself.

Thirdly, there is Barr's own attempt to formulate a doctrine of

---

122. Some comparison might be made between the views of Barr on the relation of people and the Spirit of God and inspiration and aspects of Pannenberg's thought, as expressed in his article, "Analogy and Doxology," in op. cit., pp. 211-38. Analogy is attained here not in terms of being, but in doxological language on the basis of God's acts (pp. 215ff.). Doxological language is a form of mediacy as it turns us to the sublimity of God in the abandonment of "conceptual univocity." This is a more dogmatic way of stating Barr's point about the inspiration of worship in the response of the people of God. Pannenberg also refers to God "making our metaphorical speech his own through his revelation" giving it its "ultimately valid content" (p. 237). This approaches Barr's idea that the tradition becomes "a source of light in time following" (art. cit., p. 91) because of the communion with the Spirit of God of the people. A further comparison might be indicated, not without significance, between Barr's view of this communion and C. H. Dodd's view that "God is the Author not of the Bible, but of the life in which the authors of the Bible partake, and of which they tell in such imperfect human words as they could command"—*The Authority of the Bible* (London, 1960), p. 27.

Scripture apart from the conditions of revelation and normativity of criticised models. Scripture is seen in the light of a developing tradition and is itself "pluralist."

Finally, some evaluation of Barr's work and importance will be attempted, together with some final remarks on the christological analogy.

2

James Barr: Critic
Of Methods of Biblical Interpretation

A sizable part of James Barr's work is devoted to a detailed examination of questions relating to the interpretation of the Bible. Two particular aspects of this critique will be referred to at different stages of this description. Firstly, as an implication of the *human* character of the Bible, a sustained effort is made to align methods of interpretation of this text with those used presently in parallel disciplines. Biblical semantics must learn from modern linguistics; historical research must be practised without according any special privileges to this text. There is an effort here to put biblical research back in contact with other fields of learning. Secondly, there is an equally sustained effort to maintain the freedom of these methods against the entry of considerations of normativity which hamper their efficacity. The humanity of Scripture must be accorded a full recognition in interpretation. To appeal too rapidly to the authority of the text as revelation can involve the risk of imposing a predetermined idea of what it might be expected to say. Consequently, the Bible would not have its real freedom of expression.

In the field of interpretation, Barr is above all concerned with the methods of interpretation which were used in what came to be known as the Biblical theology movement.[1] However, fundamentalism also illustrates in a more extreme fashion some of the conservative features of the BTM, and Barr also engages a vigorous polemic with its interpretative practices. In this chapter it is largely with these two influential varieties of modern Protestantism that we shall be occupied.

---

1. The Biblical theology movement will be abbreviated BTM in the text.

2.1. Naming a culprit—the Biblical theology movement

Professor Barr has written extensively about Biblical theology, particularly in criticism of that modern revival of biblical authority called the BTM. As far as its general identity goes, we shall limit ourselves to two of the recent concise indications given by Barr, before describing some general characteristics.[2]

2.1.1. Identifying the BTM

There might be some temptation to question today, in view of our present situation, whether there was ever such a thing as the BTM. It would be easy for one to think that this designation is a label for conveniently grouping a number of theologians who had similar aims but who formed no plan of common approach. If it is true that there was no school as such, no common platform or manifesto, this does not eliminate the possibility of the BTM having existed in a spontaneous way. Barr is quite definite about the existence of such a movement. At a certain time, many theologians working in biblical studies were pursuing common aims with a similar perspective on the methods to be used to achieve these aims. Although the term "Biblical theology" can simply be used in the sense of a theological appreciation of the Bible, it is "normally used in the English-speaking theological world to indicate a new distinctive approach, which had its modern beginning in the 1930s. . . ."[3] Barr remarks that the term "Biblical theology" is not a derogatory designation, but that it was used by the practitioners themselves. As a movement it stood over against the previous trends of liberal theology and represented a reaction against its analytic approach, evolutionism, and tendency to interpret the Bible in terms of its surrounding milieu.[4] In contrast with liberalism, H. H. Rowley noted in the heyday of the BTM a "growing recognition that only a biblical religion founded on and

---

2. Found in Barr's works *BWT,* p. 12, and *IDB*(S), p. 105.

3. *BWT,* ad loc. For a detailed bibliography, see G. Eldon Ladd, *Int* 25: 41-44. In general see also section 1 of H.-J. Kraus, *Die biblische Theologie, ihre Geschichte und Problematik* (Neukirchen-Vluyn, 1970); G. Ebeling in *Word and Faith* (London, 1963), pp. 79-97, and B. S. Childs, *Biblical Theology in Crisis* (Philadelphia, 1970), chaps. 1-4. Barr thinks that Childs exaggerates the extent to which the movement was specifically American in *IDB*(S), p. 105.

4. *IDB*(S), ad. loc.

nourished by the Bible can suffice for this or any other day."[5] This relevance of the Bible is considered an alternative to the atomism and historicism of liberal theology, which was incapable of doing justice to the unity and the revelational content of the Bible. If in the decades following the 1930s the movement was strong, it was partly because of a widespread dissatisfaction with the results of liberal theology. In particular the objective stance of the historicism of liberalism rendered synthesis and assessment of the data difficult.[6] As A. N. Wilder said, "The analytical historian kills the soul and retains the corpse."[7]

The fault of liberalism in its analytical evolutionary historicism is its compromise with humanism and natural science.[8] Great care was taken to distinguish the BTM from liberalism, which imposes modern ideas on the Bible and fundamentalism with its mania for "literalness." By way of reaction, then, it sought to view the Bible from "inside out" and in so doing to do justice to both the "deity" and the "humanity" of Scripture.[9]

2.1.2. Characteristics of the BTM

Barr defines the distinctive aspects of the BTM in many places, but nowhere more concisely than his article in *IDB*(S) on Biblical theology, where he lists eight characteristic features. We shall indicate the main features here, seeking to show their relations and giving some illustrations.[10]

What has been already pointed out about the opposition to liberalism in the BTM gives us the lie of the land for understanding its main characteristics. Together with the distrust of foreign elements

---

5. H. H. Rowley, *Int* 1:3.

6. D. H. Wallace, *ThZ* 19:94.

7. A. N. Wilder, quoted by Wallace in ibid.

8. See Wallace, ibid., pp. 90f.; T. W. Manson on "The Failure of Liberalism to Interpret the Bible as the Word of God" in C. W. Dugmore, ed., *The Interpretation of the Bible* (London, 1944), pp. 101ff.; also D. E. Nineham, *The Use and Abuse of the Bible* (London, 1976), pp. 73ff.

9. B. W. Anderson, *Rediscovering the Bible* (New York, 1951), chap. 1, particularly pp. 20f.; Nineham, op. cit., p. 74.

10. *IDB*(S), p. 105. Examples of the characteristics which Barr describes are seen in works such as C. H. Dodd's *The Bible Today* (Cambridge, 1947), H. H. Rowley's *The Relevance of the Bible* (London, 1941), and A. Richardson's *A Preface to Bible Study* (London, 1943).

went a healthy respect for the Scripture itself. Biblical thought was contrasted with "philosophical" ways of thinking and Biblical theology was opposed to philosophical theology. The same attitude prevailed toward dogmatics, which reduced the "living organism" of biblical thought to a system.[11] A quotation from the work of L. S. Thornton will depict well the feeling that was in the air:

> Instead of making his own mind, with its modern stand-point, the centre round which a theological unity is to be built, the biblical theologian of the coming time will bend his thoughts down to the mental habits of the inspired writers.[12]

So when the BTM was at its zenith, it was widely considered that the Bible was a rallying point for ecumenical renewal in face of the diverse traditions of the particular Christian confessions.[13] The Bible was thought of as the final authority in theological discussion. The church must have an authority outside and above itself; the Bible is that over which nothing else can take precedence. It was even said that "the final authority over the Christian is a *book,*" not because of what it is itself "but rather by virtue of the God to whom it witnesses and who speaks in its pages."[14] On this basis, "People spoke without hesitation about *the* biblical message and *the* concept of the Bible"[15] while referring to a whole gamut of topics, some of which seem startlingly remote from the universe of Scripture.

The authority of the biblical concepts was sustained by reference to their distinctive nature; Hebrew thought is different from Greek and also the Bible is distinctive in comparison with other environing cultures.[16] Though by no means representative of the BTM, Paul Van Buren expresses an opinion commonly held in it when he declares that "biblical theology has given modern theology a fresh appreciation of the distinctive thought world of the Bible and of the

---

11. Barr, loc. cit., points i and ii in his exposition.
12. L. S. Thornton, *Revelation and the Modern World* (London, 1950), p. 50.
13. See Barr's study outline on "The Authority of the Bible," *ER* 21:138, point iv on this.
14. J. Bright, *The Authority of the Old Testament* (London, 1967), p. 31.
15. E. Flesseman van Leer, "Biblical Interpretation in the World Council of Churches," *Study Encounter* 8, 2 (1972):2. See Barr, art. cit., *ER* 21:137, point ii.
16. Barr, *IBD*(S), loc. cit., points ii, vi.

categories which were central for the biblical authors."[17] In its turn
this distinctiveness of the biblical way of thinking implied the unity
of the Bible, a unity which was found not only in the Bible itself but
was to be reproduced in theology and applied as the biblical message
to the modern world. In the BTM, says Barr, "an attempt was made
to develop not only a biblical basis for theology but also a biblical
design for its construction, a mandatory biblical pattern for its
thinking."[18]

The BTM drew much of its power from appeal to these two attributes of Scripture—its authority and its unity—both of which referred to the idea of the distinctiveness of the Bible for support. Both
were considered indispensable for theology. As Barr states in his
analysis: "In neo-orthodoxy it was taken as axiomatic that the Bible
was authoritative and that for this purpose 'the Bible' meant both
Old and New Testaments."[19] Barr goes on to add that there was
room for discussion of *how* this was so, but to ask *whether* it was so
would have been to "place oneself immediately outside the bounds
of true Christian belief." It was of the essence of this theology then,
according to Barr, to speak of the Bible as a *whole*. Putting it another way, Barr says that "the unity was thought of as the theologically positive factor and the diversity as the theologically negative."[20]
This goal of unity placed a high value on studies of the relation of the
testaments[21] and studies which ranged across the great divide to establish the message of the whole Bible. Of particular interest is the
fact that the OT, which lay rather inert in the wake of liberalism,
received a breath of new life from the Elijahs of the BTM. The
movement which began in the '30s, comments Barr, gave the OT such
an intelligibility that it became the very foundation of the Christian
faith.[22] As such, the OT became, in the context of the idea of the
distinctiveness of Hebrew thought, *the* authority for thinking about

17. P. Van Buren, *The Secular Meaning of the Gospel* (London, 1963),
p. 45.
18. Barr, "Trends and Prospects in Biblical Theology," *JTS* 29:265.
19. Barr, "The Old Testament and the New Crisis of Biblical Authority,"
Int 25:25.
20. Barr, *ER* 21:137; also *IDB*(S), loc. cit., point iv. See also the extensive review in Childs, op. cit., pp. 36ff.
21. Cf. G. Ebeling, op. cit., pp. 94, 96.
22. Barr, *Int* 25:26.

the NT. Promise and fulfilment were the orders of the day.

All this added up, in the BTM, to a renewed attention to the purpose of the biblical writers and a semi-eclipse of historical criticism. The keynote was the coherence of the biblical material rather than the analytic methods of criticism.[23] There was a greater insight that there was something beyond the text which historical criticism could not grasp, in the realm of the theological consciousness of the writers and the unity of that consciousness—that is, in what B. S. Childs has called the "theological dimension" of the Bible.[24] This coherence in the theological realm came to be discerned in the BTM as the distinctive character of the biblical corpus and was related to the unique events of revelation to which that corpus bore witness. The theological unity of OT and NT was found in the single redemptive process which constitutes its uniqueness.[25] The key to Scripture lies in redemptive events or, in some cases, in their interpretation. One way or the other, these are seen as giving rise to a special historical consciousness in Hebrew thinking. Barr comments that when this is phrased to mean that "history" itself belonged to Israel rather than the Greeks or Romans, this constitutes one of the "more bizarre aberrations from reason within the older biblical theology."[26] Elsewhere he affirms that for the BTM revelation in history was "common to the entire Bible and the basis of its inner unity, unintelligible to philosophy, and poorly appreciated by dogmatics."[27] The concern with history in the BTM is expressed by John Bright when he says that "the unity of the Testaments within a single redemptive history must at all times be affirmed."[28] In contrast to non-biblical thought the inner coherence of the Bible based on redemptive events appears in its conceptual structure.[29] Inner coherence and distinctiveness are

---

23. *BWT*, p. 11.

24. Childs, op. cit., pp. 33ff.

25. J. Bright, op. cit., pp. 110ff., gives a full description of the nature, authority, and unity envisaged by the BTM with reference to the OT. The unity is on the divine side rather than the human as in later attempts to state the unity in the context of the development of a tradition.

26. Barr, "Story and History in Biblical Theology," *JR* 56:12.

27. *IDB*(S), loc. cit. Cf. Childs, op. cit., pp. 39ff.

28. J. Bright, op. cit., p. 200. Also A. Richardson in *Cambridge History of the Bible,* III, ed. S. L. Greenslade (1963), pp. 329ff.

29. *BWT*, loc. cit. D. H. Kelsey in *The Uses of Scripture in Recent Theology* (London, 1975), p. 37, makes the point that G. E. Wright, in spite of his

correlated and work together as the principle purpose of the method of Biblical theology.[30]

In contrast with the positivism of historical criticism, the literalist approach of fundamentalism or the ethical distillation of earlier liberalism, the ultimate unitive factor in the BTM is its Christocentricity. Progressive revelation culminates on Christ and thus is relevant for modern man as Christian revelation.[31] This is the reflection in biblical studies of the principle of the christological analogy in dogmatics. What the analogy is in formal discussions of the nature of Scripture, the idea of "revelation in history" is in the material description of that unity in the diachronic study of the progressive redemption. In dogmatics the nature of the Bible was defined in terms of the nature of Christ at once *kata pneuma* and *kata sarka;* christocentric interpretation permitted the texts to be placed in their historical milieu and retain an eschatological significance in the plan of God in their Christian reference. With Christocentricity assured by revelation in history on the material front and by analogy on the formal front, the unity and authority of the Scripture seemed sure in the fortifications erected by the neo-orthodox BTM.

2.1.3. The BTM and neo-orthodoxy

The above reflexions on Christ-centred thinking in dogmatics and biblical studies provoke us to think of the relation of the BTM and Barthian dogmatics.

Barr sees a similarity but also a dissimilarity between these two. Positively, the BTM represents, in the characteristics described, many of the concerns of neo-orthodox dogmatics. If the level of work was different, the course was a parallel one.[32] The opposition to liberalism, the centrality of the Bible with the stress on revelation, the unity

event-centred approach, lands back at "biblical concept theology." Narrative qua narrative cannot authorise proposals about God, but only give grounds for defining biblical concepts which the modern Christian is to restate.

30. See E. Burnier, "Restauration de la théologie biblique et sa signification epistémologique," in his *Bible et Theologie* (Lausanne, 1943), pp. 15-61. Here we read of the rich lines of coherence in modern Biblical theology and the stability of results of this synthesis of concepts in contrast with the "criticist period" (pp. 32-34).

31. Cf. H. F. Hahn, *The Old Testament in Modern Research* (London, 1956), p. 240.

32. Barr, *F,* pp. 214, 217.

and distinctiveness illustrated in biblical concepts, all indicate a common concern. Thus Barr esteems the BTM to be "the biblical companion and parallel to the neo-orthodox movement in general theology"[33] and that it "represented a pressure in the same general direction as neo-orthodox theology." Just as Karl Barth reacted to liberalism's analytic study and natural theology and sought a Theology of the Word, so in its own way the BTM represented a "weariness with a merely analytic approach; it sought to establish a synthesis."[34] Both showed a compromise with critical methods and without rejecting them outright accorded them a propaedeutic significance. This role of criticism together with the emphasis on the coherence of the Bible assured the central place of the Scripture in theological work.

In the introduction to *BWT* we have a concise expression of what Barr determines to be the general character of the BTM. Speaking of the search for distinctiveness and coherence of biblical thought he states that this "is not only a necessary part of the method; it is also a principle purpose of the method."[35] In other words, in the BTM we have a case of theological procedure being influenced by that which it wishes to prove. Method is not an end in itself, but is a means to a predetermined end, namely, the goal of setting forth the specific character of the Bible. It is here overruled in its concerns by the need of demonstrating the authority of the Bible. This is characteristic of an authority-centred theology and creates the sort of conditions in which the Bible can hardly speak in freedom. Barr thinks that the more conservative side of Barth's theology bears this same tendency and in *Fundamentalism* discusses neo-orthodoxy's influence on conservatism. The more conservative side of Barthianism comes to a "conservative evangelical kind of position."[36] On this same point J. M. Robinson has remarked that "Barthianism consists in America, as in Europe, of a meeting of the later Barth's move to the right with conservatism's opening itself to influence from the center."[37]

---

33. *IDB*(S), loc. cit., cf. *BWT*, pp. 11f.
34. *F*, p. 218.
35. *BWT*, loc cit.
36. *F*, p. 219.
37. J. M. Robinson, *The Beginnings of Dialectic Theology* (Richmond, 1968), I:28. Thus Robinson thinks that the early possibilities of dialectic

However, should Barr discern certain common aims in these two, and even an overall common character, there is no way to ignore their differences. In spite of the "pressure in the same general direction" in neo-orthodoxy and the BTM, Biblical theologians did not have the massive understanding of Barth in philosophy or theological problems. Nor did they share his concern for the tradition of theology as a whole. If common ground is shared with Barth, it must not be overlooked that the BTM is essentially the intellectual side of a more crass reaction against liberalism. Barr is very hard in describing this and refers to "a certain Philistinism" and "a typical pietistic reaction" which is seen in the "amusing illusion" of the rejection of the systematizing of dogmatics. The word-study method of Biblical theology seemed to provide a way in which the biblical languages could be used by those whose ability to handle texts in the languages was "exiguous."[38] The BTM represents, then, in Barr's analysis, some continuity with Barthianism, but it is above all the intellectual side of a more general religious reaction. Thus its strength and passing success came from a grassroots reaction against liberal theology. Along similar lines B. S. Childs has remarked on the misunderstanding of Karl Barth's exegesis by the BTM. He thinks that, although some attention has been paid to Barth's theology in mediated form in the BTM, there was not much attention paid to his exegesis. Even though this was sometimes criticised by Biblical theologians as "pre-critical," Childs points out that Barth remained "invulnerable to the weaknesses that beset the BTM." In particular he would have nothing to do with *Heilsgeschichte,* Hebrew mentality, or unity and diversity in the Bible.[39]

These remarks are important for situating James Barr's critique of the BTM. It is not simply a case of a reaction against Barthianism on the part of Barr. If the two do have in common a certain way of approaching the Bible in the context of revelation and therefore in

theology have not been carried through in the later Barth's work or in Barthianism. B. S. Childs refers to several works which comment on the uncongeniality of the "theology of crisis" for the British temperament, op. cit., p. 23, n. 16.

   38. *IDB*(S), loc. cit.

   39. Childs, op. cit., pp. 110f. Childs thinks that when Barr speaks of the "great theologian's alienation from the world of Biblical scholarship" as "painful" (*ONI,* p. 96), Barr shares a similar misunderstanding as other Biblical theologians.

terms of a structure of relations characterised by authority, Barr sees the BTM as much less refined and as the intellectual arm of a more general religious mood. As such, it is no doubt more susceptible to making interpretation the servant of a particular religious goal. Thus certain methods of interpretation are central as they are "the only way in which the biblical material could appear to answer a given problem. . . ."[40] To wring answers from the Bible to questions which were not in the minds of the biblical writers does not "honour the Bible."

At this point it is time to ask what Barr's intention is in his critique of the methods of interpretation.

2.1.4. The perspective of James Barr's critique of interpretation

The BTM asked a lot of the Bible. It asked such questions that it was led, in seeking answers, to the use of methods which in fact injured the real sense of Scripture. Barr's intention in his early books on language is not to criticise the BTM itself or its theology, but to make a rigid scrutiny of the acceptability of its methods of interpretation. A misunderstanding has often arisen at this point about Barr's work. Many reviews of *SBL* that one can read in the journals were from those who were associated with the BTM and did not always react kindly to the confrontational criticism. So we often read of Barr's "formalism" or the "negativism" of his criticism. This rebuff of Barr's work really misses the point, particularly in the general context we have tried to depict. If Barr's criticism is of a negative nature, this is because it is above all corrective. Many critics, one feels now, when considering the linguistic work in the global development of Barr's thought, missed the fact that positively he wanted to bring out the humanness of biblical language. This language must be evaluated in systematic relations with language in general. The dissatisfaction which many critics showed with Barr's book can be attributed to their ignorance of structural linguistics, which proves what Barr was saying all along.[41]

---

40. *BWT*, p. 14.

41. The main reviews of *SBL* are by Childs, *JBL* 80:374-77; Alonso Schökel in *Biblica* 63:217-23; S. H. Hooke, *JTS* 13:128-30; N. T. Porteous, *ET* 75:70-74; and a vituperative article by Boman in *SJT* 15:319-24. Other major comments were contributed by G. Friedrich, *ThL* 94:802-16; C. Payot, *Revue de Théologie et de Philosophie* (1968), pp. 218-35; K. A. Tangberg,

Barr's purpose is set forth with clarity in the opening pages of *SBL*.[42] Here he states that his aim is not "to criticize biblical theology or any other kind of theology as such, but to criticize certain methods in the handling of linguistic evidence in theological discussion." By this Barr hopes to "clear the way for a re-assessment of biblical language,"[43] its use, and the possibility of understanding the Bible today. At this stage Barr thinks that invalid use of linguistic evidence does not involve the wrongness of theology. The theological argument would be better sustained by evidence other than the linguistic. However, faulty linguistic arguments do reveal "a wrong understanding of biblical interpretation in general."[44] They show weaknesses in certain "fundamental procedures of interpretation." Again at this juncture, which is a critical one in Barr's work, it is implied that the theological end should not dictate the means to that end. To do this is to foster errors in the basic procedures of interpretation. At this stage Barr does not accuse Biblical theology of being the sort of theology which necessarily falls into this mistake because of its character; this criticism appears later when the linguistic method and the theological dogmas of the BTM are seen as in some way related. At the early stage Barr criticizes the linguistics but leaves the theology untouched.

So he comments that, while E. Jacob's linguistic method is very dubious, he "has not led us far astray in his treatment of the Hebrew idea of man."[45] Barr does at some places venture in the direction of connecting linguistic abuse and theological opinion, when he says, for example, that the type of argument used by Jacob "tends to bring linguistic material under the domination of systematic theological method."[46] Here interpretation succumbs to theological authority. But at this time Barr does not negate the possibility of isolating biblical concepts as long as they are brought out of the Bible in a proper

---

The Bible Translator 24:3-21; N. Ridderbos, *Gereformeerd Theologische Tijdschrift* 64:209-29; B. Salomonsen, *Dansk Teologisk Tidsskrift* 31:35-59; D. Ritschl, *Int* 17:206-9 (on *BWT*); E. Dinkler, *ThL* 94:482-90. D. Hill has made some detailed criticisms in two parts of his *Greek Words and Hebrew Meanings* (Cambridge, 1967), and Barr has replied in *Biblica* 49:377-87.

42. *SBL*, p. 6. See Hill, op. cit., pp. 1f.
43. Ibid., p. 4.
44. Ibid., p. 6.
45. Ibid., p. 147. See similar statement, p. 194, and *BWT*, pp. 16, 18, 45.
46. Ibid.

way. So when he speaks of Von Rad's criticism of biblical "concepts" as generalizing and abstracting, Barr comments that this is not really the problem. It lies rather in the faulty use of linguistic evidence; because Von Rad fails to see this, he sometimes falls into the same pit. Tracing a Hebrew concept can be "of basic theological importance," when it is done properly.[47] Even at a much later stage, in spite of his criticisms of a certain form of authoritarianism which expressed itself in the BTM, Barr remains quite appreciative of certain of its achievements. Given the weaknesses of approach, "some solid results seem to have emerged from all the energetic work. . . . It is at least in principle possible that principles of structure and order may be identified from the Bible itself. . . ."[48] The main stress lines can be mapped out, as the Bible is not an "uncharted sea" or a "trackless chaos."

If in this last quotation from *BMW* (1973) the confidence of Barr as to biblical unity is somewhat rejuvenated, during the middle '60s, following the critique of language, Barr does seem to have passed through a considerably more sceptical period. This doubt, if not the fruit of the linguistic critique itself, is related to it. Even if at the start Barr's remarks touch only language, they tend to spill over into theological considerations, when he asks what kind of theology is championing these views of language. The semantic work pointed up the insecurity of the seemingly imposing theological structure of the neo-orthodox BTM. In effect, what the linguistic arguments did was to take away the foundations of a theology which was left with a view of biblical unity and authority lacking in exegetical support. This early work destroys a theological edifice by undermining its unity and authority. Conversely, because the exegetical support is removed, the theology appears in its real relation to exegesis as an authoritarian one which had perversely influenced the methods of interpretation. In so far as this was the case, the Bible's humanity and diversity had been lost to view; the biblical materials had not been disposed of in such a way as to promote the freedom of the Bible message. As Barr remarks with regard to his discussion of Jacob's view, the Bible is under the domination of systematic theol-

---

47. Barr's review of Von Rad in *ET* 73:143.
48. *BMW*, p. 159.

ogy in its interpretation. However, in spite of the inferences of some critics, Barr's intention is not to destroy theology or to propose a purely formal approach to language. The best way to bring out the Bible's message is by honouring its language with the methods of interpretation used in general. This will allow the real message of the Bible to appear.

We now feel able, this clarification having been stated, to examine some ways in which the unity and authority of the BTM were maintained and the methodological slackness Barr uncovers in his critique.

2.2. *The illusion of the distinctiveness of biblical language*

The attack launched on the methods of interpretation used in the BTM has been called by B. S. Childs an offensive so devastating "that the defences appeared like a Maginot line facing a new form of Blitzkreig. . . . Seldom has one book brought down so much superstructure with such effectiveness."[49] Childs, in reviewing *SBL,* shows sound judgment when he remarks that this book ends a too easy-going attitude toward interpretation upon which much theology has been built. In particular, he points out that an indisciplined use of language has supported preconceived ideas.[50] True, the fault did not entirely lie with the BTM if modern linguistic methods had not been incorporated into its procedures. As J. L. Moreau has observed, the field of semantics is difficult to penetrate for the outsider, and some of the "language employed by semanticists appears to be a proper subject for semantic analysis."[51] Barr himself has made a similar observation when, following E. Ullendorff, he speaks of the "distrust and neglect of general linguistics . . . endemic in Semitic scholarship."[52] One reason for this distrust, according to Barr, is that modern linguistics have made little contact with biblical studies in terms of method. This is no doubt abetted by the new areas of

---

49. Childs, op. cit., p. 72; see also his review of *SBL.*
50. Childs, *JBL* 80:374.
51. J. L. Moreau, *Language and Religious Language* (Philadelphia, 1967), p. 89.
52. Barr, "The Ancient Semitic Languages—The Conflict Between Philology and Linguistics," *Transactions of the Philological Society* (1968), quotation of E. Ullendorff, p. 45.

biblical research opened through discoveries in which comparative studies are encouraged. In addition, wishing to avoid entanglement with theological questions, biblical studies adopted a purely historical approach which tended to separate them from the synchronic orientation of modern linguistics.[53] These factors contribute to an estrangement between the approach to language of the BTM and that which is often practised today in the linguistic branch of semantics.[54]

This can, however, constitute no reason for ignorance. If there is a certain independence of theology from linguistics, so that an OT theology does not depend on semantic study in selecting elements for its constructions, it does have to decide what use to make of semantics. Also where it appeals to semantics it has to submit to the structures imposed by the modern study of language.[55] It is at this point that the question arises: Which account of the modern study of language is to be followed? In reply Barr does not propose any esoteric solution tied to a particular *école,* nor does he offer a theory of language which could be a part of a universal hermeneutic. His remarks and criticisms remain in the context of the broad principles of the structuralist method advocated by de Saussure.[56] This simplicity is at once the strength of Barr's criticism and a possible weakness.[57] The structuralist approach to literature and linguistics Barr contrasts with the traditional methods. These focus on meaning by interpreting a text in terms of what the author meant to say, or by understanding words in relation to the objects to which they refer.[58] Of the traditional approach Max Black writes: "Until comparatively recently the prevailing conception of the nature of language was straightforward and simple. It stressed communication of thought to the neglect of feeling and attitude, emphasized words rather than speech-acts in context, and assumed a sharp contrast between

---

53. Ibid., pp. 45-51.
54. A brief approach to the question of semantics in relation to biblical language is found in Barr's article, "Semantics," in *A Dictionary of Christian Theology,* ed. A. Richardson (London, 1969).
55. See Barr's article, "Semantics and Biblical Theology," *VT*(S) 22:11ff.
56. The affirmation of A. C. Thiselton seems correct to us: ". . . in spite of his obvious knowledge of more recent writers, the fundamental inspiration behind Barr's contribution is the figure of Ferdinand de Saussure," in *New Testament Interpretation,* ed. I. H. Marshall (Exeter, 1977), p. 75.
57. As suggested by Payot in his art. cit., p. 230. See sec. 5.4. of this study.
58. "Reading the Bible as Literature," *BJRL* 56:21, 26, 27.

thought and its symbolic expression."[59] Barr calls this way of studying language atomistic in that it separates elements of language and
relates them to other elements in the same or another language,[60]
rather than seeing them as part of a system.[61] This is obviously the
case with etymology and comparative philology. Christianity has a
history of fascination with the first of these in particular.[62] The
traditional grammar was founded on a word-centred approach in
which "the form of a word signified 'things' by virtue of the 'concept' associated with the form of the word in the minds of the speakers
of the language; the 'concept' . . . was the meaning of the word."[63]
This view formulated by the medieval grammarians, was completed
later by the hypothesis that logical and grammatical structures are
isomorphic and that differences of thought can be seen in grammatical structure. Thus language reflected and conditioned "the ways of
thought and expression of the people using it."[64]

Barr terms this approach to meaning as weak[65] and outdated.[66]
Language must be seen as a system, in which the elements sustain
relations of similarity and opposition with each other. These relations constitute the structure within the system at any one time and
thus language must be considered synchronically. Barr is at this
stage simply using the basic ideas of de Saussure.[67] The perspective
of his semantic critique is to see the question of meaning in terms
of the structure of language as a system of signs. What the author
meant is removed from a position of central concern. The aim of
the structuralist way is to see meaning in the context of the system
of language. Thus it concentrates on the structures of the text, not

---

59. M. Black, *The Labyrinth of Language* (London, 1968), p. 9.

60. Barr, art. cit., p. 27.

61. On structuralism in exegesis see D. Patte, *What Is Structural Exegesis?*
(Philadelphia, 1976), pp. 1ff.; also P. Ricoeur, in the collective work, *Exégèse et herméneutique,* R. Barthes et al. (Paris, 1971), pp. 305ff. These bring
out the contrast between the traditional approach and structuralism.

62. See Barr's article in Richardson, ed., op. cit., pp. 311-12.

63. J. Lyons, *Introduction to Theoretical Linguists* (Cambridge, 1968),
p. 404.

64. Ibid., p. 24. This view is associated with the thought of W. von Humboldt. The development of this idea has held great sway in the BTM as seen
in the influence of the work of T. Boman.

65. Barr, art. cit., loc. cit.

66. *BJRL* 56:27.

67. See Thiselton, art. cit., pp. 80ff. Cf. Payot, art. cit., p. 219.

what the words mean or the object to which they refer.[68] The linguistic methods of the BTM are in opposition to the more recent advances of structural linguistics. Following the traditional grammar, they revolve around the study of the meaning of words, are often diachronic in their perspective, as in the use of etymology, seek to relate the words to concepts, which in the context of logico-grammatical parallelism makes language the correlate of a cultural mentality.[69] Particularly prominent is the tracing of biblical concepts via the study of certain words, which is often taken to reveal a Hebrew mentality. Barr criticises these efforts as linguistic fantasy and as failing in two ways. They fail, firstly, to do justice to the examination of the relevant languages and, secondly, to "relate what is said . . . to a general semantic method related to general linguistics."[70] How Barr is indebted to structural linguistics for his criticism will become apparent as the individual weaknesses are noted in the interpretation practiced in the BTM and also in Kittel's *TDNT*.

2.2.1. Hebrew and Greek thought

A point which appears with almost monotonous regularity in Barr's earlier books is that which concerns the distinction between Hebrew and Greek thought as used in modern Biblical theology.[71] Although a dogma of the BTM, the distinction has been influential beyond the pale of those interested in Biblical theology. Its theological import has been to back up a view of the unity of Scripture based on the idea of a common Hebraic mentality lying behind the linguistic structures of the Bible. As far as the NT is concerned, this means that the Greek of the NT has been moulded by the dynamic Hebrew thought it conveys.[72] Barr's discussion of this point constitutes a

---

68. D. Patte, op. cit., pp. 14ff.
69. B. Siertsema, "Language and World View," *The Bible Translator* 20: 3, 4.
70. Barr, *SBL*, p. 21.
71. *SBL, chap.* 2; *ONI,* chap. 2; *BWT*, pp. 14-18.
72. For example, even following Barr's detailed refutations of the distinction of Hebrew/Greek as applied to the study of biblical words, N. Turner maintains that in the realm of syntax Dr. Barr will find that "Semitic influence on Christian language and the same process of Christian transformation of speech are even clearer than in the realm of vocabulary." *Grammatical Insights into the New Testament* (Edinburgh, 1965), p. 2. Cf. also C. F. D. Moule, *An Idiom Book of New Testament Greek* (Cambridge, 1959), pp. 3f.

refutation of the distinction between Hebrew and Greek thought
and the idea that biblical language is distinctive in some way because
of its content. In this section we shall resume Barr's main criticisms
and try to discern their theological significance. It is not our intention to give a detailed outline of the ramifications of the theory
itself. It suffices to give a few indications relative to Barr's critique.[73]

In spite of the sustained critique of Barr, the contrast continues
to crop up very widely in different domains of theological reflexion,
which is some measure of its pervasiveness.[74] Christianity is said to
be essentially Jewish. The NT words are de-hellenised and receive
a new content from the contact with Hebrew mentality—"they are
washed clean, elevated and baptized with new meaning."[75] Thus the
distinctiveness of Christianity is made possible over against Greek
religion. It is time-related, dynamic and concrete, and implies a
certain conception of man.[76] The unity of the OT and NT is guaranteed by this regeneration of Greek which creates a common biblical
way of thinking describably in terms of concepts.

In an early article Barr describes the contrast between Hebrew
and Greek thought as subtle, but seems to accept it as a matter of
course.[77] In *SBL* he is above all preoccupied by what the acceptance
of this contrast implies for the interpretation of biblical language.
As Barr sees it, the contrast has been aided in modern biblical
studies by two wider influences. The reaction against liberal analytical criticism with its divisive techniques has enhanced the at-
tractiveness of an opinion which seems to sustain the idea of a
common Hebrew mind. In addition there is a reaction against "natural theology" and philosophy which can be assimilated to the "Greek

73. See T. Boman, *Hebrew Thought Compared with Greek* (London, 1960),
and his contribution to *Current Issues in New Testament Interpretation,* ed.
K. Klassen and G. F. Snyder (London, 1962), pp. 1-22.
74. See the remarks of J. Macquarrie, *Thinking about God* (London, 1975),
pp. 80ff. In spite of the remarks of Childs about Karl Barth and the weaknesses
of the BTM (see note 39 above, this chap.), Barth affirmed that the Bible is
tied up with the Jewish spirit and that to understand it we must be prepared to
become "Jews with the Jews." *Church Dogmatics,* 1.2, 510-11.
75. B. M. Metzger, "The Language of the New Testament," in *IDB* 7:56.
Barr treats this as romanticisation, *SBL,* pp. 247f.
76. T. Torrance sees the contrast in terms of one between dualist and non-
dualist thought, *Space, Time and Resurrection* (Grand Rapids, 1976), pp. 40ff.
77. Barr, "Tradition and Expectation in Ancient Israel," *SJT* 10:28.

mind" as over against the Hebrew way. Such factors favoured a way of looking at the Bible as distinctive from its milieu and as forming a unity owing to the Hebrew way of thinking. The Bible was to be understood free from external influences; if the critics were incapable of seeing the distinctiveness of biblical language, it was that they were impregnated with the hellenic spirit themselves.[78] The main contrasts between Hebrew and Greek are seen in the polarities dynamic-static, concrete-abstract, totality-duality in man and totality-analytic in thought. Thus the static abstract Greek way was productive of fine distinctions unknown to the Hebrew mind which viewed the totality.[79] The distinctiveness of the Bible lies in its dynamic thought. One can even read as an illustration of this view that the rabbis were right to refuse the canonicity of books later than Ezra, as after this the "Hebrew genius became tempered with the spirit of the larger world and no longer appeared in its pristine purity."[80]

It is a short step, where the traditional grammar is unreflectingly accepted, from the thought itself to the language related to that way of thought. A fairly typical comment is the following: "The language of the Hebrew and his manner of expressing himself is *concrete,* reflecting, as it does, his thinking. He grasps things, men and their actions, the way they are in concrete reality. Even when he has a part of something in mind, he sees it *in relation to the whole. . . .*"[81] Barr is above all interested in the way linguistic evidence has been handled in accordance with this conception and how it has functioned to illustrate the contrast.[82] *SBL* deals with the way this relates to questions of grammatical and lexical structure, while *BWT* carries on this with relation to a particular example, to show how the structure of lexical stock has been used to yield a theology.[83]

---

78. *SBL,* pp. 5, 6, 9f.
79. Ibid., pp. 10-13. Cf. *ONI,* p. 34.
80. R. C. Dentan, "The Unity of the Old Testament," *Int* 5:155. Although the same writer is not willing to reduce the unity of the OT merely to the distinctiveness of the Hebrew against the Greek mentality, cf. p. 156.
81. B. J. LeFrois, "Semitic Totality Thinking," *CBQ* 17:195. See also the quote from J. Schildenberger (*Vom Geheimnis des Gottesworts* [Heidelberg, 1950], p. 149), "One of the characteristics of the Semitic mind is that it thinks in totalities and expresses itself accordingly."
82. *SBL,* p. 14.
83. *BWT,* p. 16.

There is no need to go into the byways of Barr's argument here. This is readily accessible in his books, and few could preach Barr's message better than he himself. It suffices to note the standpoint of his criticism. Having reviewed the ways the verb and nouns in Hebrew are said to reveal the dynamic of the Hebrew mind, Barr remarks that the way this parallelism is being used in theology "may well be regarded as wholly outmoded and a survival from the time before the scientific study of language began."[84] It is linguistically naive, then, to argue for a correspondence between a mentality and the structure of a language. Correlation between language and worldview, as one reviewer remarks, "disregards the fundamental law of descriptive (synchronic) linguistics in failing to recognise the arbitrary character of words."[85] B. Siertsema, discussing this question, has put a finger on the problem Barr evokes in his criticism.[86] The deduction of a worldview from the *how* of a language, its vocabulary and sentences involves a form of circular reasoning. Linguistic data in themselves can prove nothing of a link between two things, the language and the worldview.

The linguistic evidence turned over by Barr in the case of the nominal phrase, the construct state and the verbal system in Hebrew in no way substantiates the claim for the distinctiveness of the Hebrew mind. Rather it shows the impossibility of ignoring the fact that the linguistic contexts show otherwise. The unjustified correlation between Hebrew language and mentality is the result of a facile acceptance by the BTM of the idealistic philosophy of language of W. von Humboldt. This proposed that the moving force in language was "the spiritual force of *Geisteskraft* active in human life and culture."[87] The Hebrew/Greek contrast works, then, not at the level of the texts but "on the level of basic philosophy and psychology."[88] Owing to this false orientation, the linguistic evidence is distorted to fit in with certain views presupposed in the logico-

---

84. *SBL,* p. 33. Cf. pp. 14ff., and *BWT,* pp. 82f., 135-58.
85. B. S. Childs, *JBL* 80:374.
86. B. Siertsema, art. cit., p. 18.
87. *SBL,* p. 48, in a discussion of the views of T. Boman.
88. *ONI,* p. 48. It is of significance that some Biblical theologians proposed that biblical research take on a more psychological interest in the Hebrew mind "as the channel through which God spoke." See, e.g., L. Thornton, *Revelation and the Modern World* (London, 1950), p. 52.

grammatical parallelism.[89] This encourages the taking of words from their context and evaluating them in the structure of this parallel, so ignoring their sociological and historical reality.

To the specifically linguistic criticism, Barr adds his reflexion of a more general nature. The contrast applies mainly to the NT, but it is of little help for the study of the OT, where distinctiveness cannot be gauged with reference to Greeks but only to Semites.[90] In addition to this, the distinction does not seem to be corroborated by the usage of the church fathers, in whom there is no discernible reaction for Hebrew against Greek thought, nor in the NT itself, where suspicion of Greek thought is absent.[91] In short, the distinction is often a pretext for those who wish to avoid involvement in modern culture in favour of what is termed by Barr a "purist" ideal.[92] Finally, a point taken up elsewhere: It is the intelligible content of what we say that counts. In the church of the apostles, it was not so much the question of thought structures, Hebrew or Greek, that mattered, but the relation of the persons to the people of God. The real struggle is not between Hebrew and Greek thought but is a conflict within Israel and the church.[93]

These last remarks bear development. Barr's refusal of the contrast between Hebrew and Greek thought is not motivated by purely linguistic considerations, but is tied in with his idea of the human character of Scripture. The "purist" ideal wishes to protect Scripture from external influences which would mitigate its message. This ideal "is that the interpretation of the Bible must be 'from within' rather than 'from without.' It is from outside that error and misunderstanding come. . . ."[94] This shows how for Barr the purist ideal ties in with the view of the Scripture in the context of a God-to-man movement which he has criticized in his review of Reid's book. This considers the content of Scripture as related to revelation, and it is important to uphold the purity of its concepts, even if this cannot be stretched to the fundamentalist idea of verbal inspiration. Barr on the contrary argues for a view of inspiration which allows for fallibility. In this sense it is no longer necessary to maintain an idea of the purity of the content of the Bible. The Spirit is related to the people

89. *SBL*, p. 43.
90. *Ibid.*, pp. 19ff.
91. *ONI*, pp. 42, 55.
92. Ibid., pp. 40-59.
93. Ibid., pp. 59-64.
94. Ibid., p. 40.

of God also in its struggles, Scripture bearing witness to these. There is therefore no need to maintain that the language of the Bible, which reflects these conflicts, is any different from other human language. To link this language to the Hebrew mind, which itself is formed in accord with the mind of God, comes close to absolutising this language. It is not without cause that John Macquarrie has said that "the more extreme exponents of biblical theology . . . have tended to absolutize the language of the Bible and what they suppose to be the conceptuality of the Hebrew mind, as expressed in the Semitic linguistic forms. In doing this, they have come near to setting up a new kind of 'verbal inspiration.' "[95] This is a well-taken comparison, and it is above all of interest to note that Barr's linguistic criticism is not without some theological motivation.

A little later in *ONI* Barr becomes a good deal more expressive. This is one of the tantalizing things about his work: We get the whole picture progressively. In this case he returns to the Hebrew/Greek contrast while talking of revelation. The contrast, argues Barr, is one of the ways the BTM has been forced to identify structures on the historical-cultural, evidential level which support a revelation-based Bible exegesis. So "in the deutero-Barthian tradition there has been an immense amount of striving to assemble detailed evidences and proofs which will work on the normal scholarly level and provide support . . . for the positions dear to revelational theology."[96]

Now the jigsaw pieces have fallen a little more into place. It is not only linguistics which has driven Barr to criticise a certain form of theology, on account of its handling of the evidence. It is apparently the theology Barr is beginning to formulate which also opens the way to a critique of the linguistics of the BTM. Perhaps there is just a little more here than might have first met the eye, or than we might have been led by Barr to believe.

All this brings us back to a central affirmation by Barr earlier in *ONI* to the effect that the contrast is essentially a modern one. It can be argued that it "serves as the historical-cultural projection of a particular ideal in theological interpretation."[97] It is typical of an

---

95. J. Macquarrie, *God-Talk* (London, 1967), p. 44. It is interesting to note that Macquarrie, like Childs, notes the difference between the BTM and Karl Barth, who "avoids giving the biblical language a monopoly."

96. *ONI*, pp. 96-97.

97. Ibid., pp. 40, 43.

approach to Scripture that wishes to seize the message of the Bible "from within." This at once involves a contradiction, as the NT materials do not have this perspective, and a form of obscurantism which renders its revision impossible. Interpretation is closed off by this contrast from any influence of materials outside the text. Theological argument here obstructs any possible modification of this historical-cultural picture, and the linguistic methods used to exegete the text are controlled by the cultural picture. This is contrary to an open Bible and a free interpretation; rather it is exegesis in a vacuum. Thus the fields of revelation and non-revelation are correlated with Hebrew and Greek thought and by implication with Hebrew and Greek language.[98] The attitude which seeks the meaning of the Bible from within opposes also Biblical theology and dogmatics, which has fallen under the influence of the static formulations of Greek thought. Thus G. E. Wright, to take an example, has contrasted the biblical manner of revealing truth with the Greek, which has provided the basic style for Christian theology. This rests on a view of reality as a permanent rational structure indicated by nouns whose semantic fields have their reference in the unmoving rational scheme. "Universals are not declined; they are not in historical movement; they are defined and related to one another as nouns and adjectives, chiefly by the copula 'is.' "[99]

If Barr can affirm with relish that today the "intellectual status" of this procedure has collapsed,[100] this is not only because of its misuse of language, but because it is part of a view of revelation which has lost credence. The Hebrew mentality can no longer be seen as correlating the distinctiveness and unity of the Bible in the context of revelation.[101] The appeals to language which it makes for its support look like linguistic evidence, but this is deceptive: They are really general logical arguments based on "hoary pieces of traditional pseudo-logic."[102] Thus Barr thinks that the effort of the BTM to find a unity of the Bible other than the prediction or the typology of

98. Ibid., p. 59.
99. G. E. Wright, *The Old Testament and Theology* (New York, 1969), p. 45. See also his article in *Studia Biblica et Semitica*, T. H. Vriesen Dedicata (Wageningen, 1966), pp. 382-84.
100. *ONI*, p. 46.
101. Ibid., p. 63.
102. *SBL*, p. 79; cf. pp. 53, 55, 57, 68; *ONI*, p. 48.

the older methods has failed. The supposition that there is one great system of biblical language related to the distinctiveness of the Hebrew mind in the context of revelation is not tenable.[103] This contact with revelation makes for interpretation in a closed system. Sometimes this unity of mentality was also referred to the innate conservatism of the Hebrew people related to their custodianship of the divine revelation.[104] However, it may be nearer the mark to say that appeals to the Hebrew mentality as unitive may indicate rather the innate conservatism of certain participants in the BTM. Krister Stendahl makes this point by referring to the failure of the Biblical theologians to distinguish between the descriptive "what it meant" and the systematic-normative "what it means" in their study. The result was to take what the text meant as authority, and this, according to Stendahl, plays into the hands of historical romanticism about a Semitic "biblical" way of thought. This confusion of authority creates a "kind of evolutionism in reverse," the primitive being the theologically chic.[105] The Hebrew-Greek structure fits in with a pattern which tends to make Biblical theology more than descriptive and therefore seeks to place authority within the discernible characters of the text itself. It is, to use Stendahl's expression, an "arrogant imperialism" for Biblical theology to pretend to bring out the distinctiveness of the biblical corpus through arguments such as this contrast of Hebrew and Greek thought. A descriptive Biblical theology must protect the church from this "imperialism."[106] Although Barr[107] has not become as explicit as this in his own analysis— he merely says that it is difficult to ascertain whether the Hebrew thought is taken as a valid option for today, or whether it simply seeks to avoid misinterpretation—he obviously does conceive of the contrast as a way of putting exegesis in the context of a theological authority structure. This explains his polemic in many places. It is essentially a struggle for the freedom of the text in interpretation.

These arguments in their cumulative effect shake the foundations

---

103. *SBL,* p. 9; cf. *BWT,* pp. 14ff.

104. See, for example, the reference of Porteous to Köhler's *Der Hebräische Mensch,* p. 125 in *SJT* 7:156.

105. K. Stendahl, "Method in the Study of Biblical Theology," in *The Bible in Modern Scholarship,* ed. J. P. Hyatt (Nashville/New York, 1965), p. 199.

106. Ibid., pp. 204-5.

107. *SBL,* p. 13.

of the temple of theological orthodoxy erected by the BTM, constructed on the supposition of the unity of the testaments and their distinctive authority as records of revelatory events. In this particular case, as we have seen, the argument is directed against the confusion engendered by an *a priori* in the treatment of empirical linguistic evidence.

2.2.2. The correlation of language and thought patterns

The question of the relation of language and thought has already been approached in so far as it concerns the distinction between Hebrew and Greek thought. It is now the moment to engage ourselves with Barr's more detailed discussion of this problem and the ways it applies to some other aspects of the handling of linguistic evidence such as the relation of lexical stocks and theological structure, the methods of etymology and comparative philology and the questions raised by Kittel's *TDNT*.

(a) The relation of language and thought
      and interpretation in the BTM

The discussion of the relation of thought and language is an extremely complex and controversial one, and it is not the subject of this section. What interests us is the more approachable question of Barr's criticism of the way the relation was envisaged in the BTM. Barr thinks that the relation of the two has been assumed by theologians who base their linguistic descriptions on ethno-psychological connections. They fail to examine the languages as a whole, and their use of evidence is highly selective and haphazard.[108] The theological viewpoint is dominated by the theory which says that language and thought must be related. The argument runs like this, satirizes Barr: "You *know* how distinctive the Hebrew mind is, and surely this distinctiveness in concepts and in thought *must somehow* be manifested in the linguistic phenomena."[109] The theory is "presumptive evidence for the interpretation of facts that are doubtful." So one way the relation is approached is by selecting evidence to illustrate it. From the opposite direction, lexical stocks can be outlined which are supposed to tally with thought structure. This produces arguments of

108. Ibid., pp. 21ff.
109. Ibid., p. 22.

the type "the Greeks had a word for it," except in this case it is "usually the Jews who have a word for it rather than the Greeks."[110] Or alternatively, the work is done from the morphological structure or the syntax which is taken to reflect thought patterns. But no one, jibes Barr, will think the Turks are ignorant of sex differences because their language has no genders, or that the Hittites who have a neuter but no feminine, saw no essential difference between man and woman![111] Barr therefore refutes that Semitic thought can be "read off" Semitic grammar.[112]

The tone of these quotations gives a good indication of what Barr thinks of these constructions, which appear worthy of *reductio ad absurdum*. Yet the surprising thing was, as with the Hebrew-Greek contrast, their widespread acceptance. Thus we find H. W. Robinson, for example, telling us that a Hebrew sentence is like the Hebrew idea of personality, or Frank Michaeli affirming that the Hebrew language is the source of Biblical theology, for grammar expresses the genius of a people and is a window by which we can look on the soul.[113] From the point of interpretation the problem lies in the fact that the parallelism which is a presupposition of these procedures is never justified. It is never called into question, but the peculiarity of Hebrew thought and language is presupposed. Even von Humboldt, says Barr, knew enough about languages not to be overly impressed by the character of Hebrew! The use of this parallelism is not in the interests of Biblical theology, and it would do better to abandon this prejudice.[114]

What, then, does Barr propose on this subject? Certain reviewers have not been slow to criticize Barr of positivism or formalism in

---

110. Ibid., p. 35.

111. Ibid., pp. 39, 45n.

112. Ibid., p. 41. B. S. Childs has sought to reply to Barr's attack of J. Pedersen on this score. Childs thinks the issue is more complicated than a mere relation between language and thought. (Pedersen finds signs in the use of words which pointed to a mythopoeic view of the world.) But he concedes that Barr is essentially correct in his criticism. See *Memory and Tradition in Israel* (London, 1962), pp. 20f., 30.

113. See H. W. Robinson in *The People and the Book,* ed. A. S. Peake (Oxford, 1925), p. 380; F. Michaeli, in *Maqqél Shâqédh, Hommage à W. Vischer* (Montpellier, 1960), pp. 146ff.; W. Vischer in *Etudes Théologiques et Religieuses,* 21:318-26; also from a critical angle A. C. Thiselton, *JTS* 25:283-99.

114. *SBL,* pp. 47, 49, 84.

his approach to linguistics.[115] However, it should not be ignored that Barr is not primarily interested in questions of philosophical semantics, but with biblical interpretation. His aim is not to affirm or deny the relations which might exist between language and thought, and he leaves this question open.[116] There is a clear statement of Barr's perspective in his article on "Semantics and Biblical Theology,"[117] in which Barr affirms that language and thought are related, but in a haphazard way. He denies that the position he adopts in *SBL* involves necessarily a separation between thought and language. Language, argues Barr, has many different levels, and these are not uniformly related to thought and culture. Two levels which must be related are those of the language as a system or stock and the body of literary or spoken complexes created by this stock. But the relation is not the same one. Biblical theology does not stand in the same relation to the OT as it does to the Hebrew language. There is no direct way from the grammatical structures of Hebrew to OT thought.

Thus Barr uses the well-known Saussurian distinction between *langue* and *parole*.[118] This distinction points to the fact that the linguist in his study works with instances of *parole* from which he draws evidence for a description of the language system underlying the *parole*. The *langue* or underlying structure is an inherited convention of the social body. *Parole* is the speech act in which the user concretises or gives a "sample" of the *langue* which is the whole system of conventions recognised. The performance is therefore also in terms of the system, and some linguists speak of the user being "used" by the *langue*.[119] In using this distinction Barr is not affirming

115. See the postscript to *BWT,* where Barr discusses this, pp. 194ff.

116. Ibid., p. 197. Barr does not shrink, for instance, from agreeing with L. Spitzer that the entirety of cultural history is relevant to the understanding of semantic change. The history of an idea is important for understanding the history of semantics. *SBL,* p. 217.

117. In *VT*(S), 22:12ff.

118. See F. de Saussure, *Course in General Linguistics* (London, 1960), pp. 9, 13, 14; Ducrot, Todorov, op. cit., pp. 29ff.; Ricoeur, art. cit., pp. 302ff.; Lyons, op. cit., pp. 51f.; as applied to recent interpretation in theology see Thiselton in op. cit., ed. Marshall, and the articles in *Int* 28; particularly Culley, pp. 166ff. Also French works referred to in the Bibliography under Barthes, Antoine, and Ricoeur.

119. See Lyons, op. cit., 51, 139, who refers to Chomsky's distinction between competence and performance. Some theologians have pushed this idea quite far: e.g., B. Vawter, *Biblical Inspiration* (London, 1972), pp. 116,

that there is no relation between language and thought, but simply that as levels of language exist no one uniform relation can be established. This is made clear in *BWT*, where Barr replies to the charge of "nominalism."

> My own position is not that there is no relation between language and thought (or culture), but that this relation is logically haphazard, so that detailed word-meanings cannot be plotted from a knowledge of thoughts entertained . . . nor can a system of concepts or ideas be read off from a structure of lexical elements.[120]

Thus Barr advocates a practical separation of the linguistic study of the grammar of the text from questions of study of the meaning of the text.[121] Identity and differences in grammatical structure are not to be simply matched with the same features in meaning. Even if both *langue* and *parole* could be related to culture or thought, this does not mean they are related in a similar way. It is for this reason that Barr says that the language *as used* is the thought and that the study for the meaning of the OT must be centred on the sentences and longer units of the text.[122] For the same reason, Barr refuses theological arguments such as those of T. F. Torrance which relate directly theological judgments and the inherent structure of the language.[123] But the problem is that not all speakers of the Hebrew language "thought the same way."[124] In the OT there is no uniform culture, and the linguistic patterns were the arena of theological conflict with idolatry and might as well be said to lead to an anti-theology of the OT, if one adopts a strict correlation between thought and language patterns.

These points are well illustrated in the exchange between D. Hill and Barr over Hill's defence of Kittel's *TDNT* in his work on the semantics of soteriological terms. Hill takes the position of those "linguists who maintain that the difference between the thought and culture of peoples is reflected in the vocabulary stocks of their lan-

---

119, 128. "Most Biblical language . . . responded to literary conventions and it was these rather than the Biblical authors that chose the words of the text" (p. 119).
120. *BWT*, p. 205.
121. Lyons, op. cit., pp. 134f.
122. *BWT*, loc. cit.
123. *SBL*, pp. 177ff.
124. *VT*(S), 22:13.

guages."[125] This difference applies also to the level of semantic studies, although Hill would not wish to push this as far as a contrast between Hebrew and Greek thinking. To Hill, Barr's position seems formalistic and excludes sociological and psychological factors. Barr refuses these criticisms.[126] He reaffirms that it is not his intention to criticise these factors in themselves, but to show how they lead to false construction of linguistic evidence. Thus when Hill affirms against Barr that words have a "kernel" of meaning and are not solely dependent on context, Barr replies that he does not deny the existence of a psychological reality corresponding to words like "truth." This may be so, but it is not the central approach to meaning, nor would identifying this kernel give us a theology.[127]

These few remarks should be sufficient to clarify the purpose of Barr's criticism of the relation of thought and language seen in the practice of the BTM. Barr is not wishing here to argue the general philosophical question, "What is meaning?," nor even the linguist's more specific concern of how meaning is encoded in language. He does argue that a certain view of the relation of thought or culture and language presents obstacles to interpretation. Moreover, this view is naive in terms of modern linguistics, in which it is proposed that meaning is related not to the *langue* in a direct way by an examination of its structures, but to actual usage. Meaning is related more directly to what is said, the *parole,* and it might be preferable for the linguist to examine questions of grammar independently of their meaning. This explains Barr's affirmation that OT theology cannot be related to the grammar of Hebrew.

Here again, within this complicated linguistic discussion, we may discern the concern of Barr for the freedom of biblical interpretation. His interest in linguistic questions, if wide ranging, can be traced to the fact that these questions are important for exegesis. Barr's arguments attack linguistic views which misuse the evidence and prevent correct interpretation. This critique must be placed in the sphere of Barr's theological concerns. These views have not only been incorrect on the linguistic level, but in the context of the BTM they have acquired a certain authority because of their theological

125. D. Hill, op. cit., p. 294.
126. See ibid., pp. 10, 294ff., and Barr's reply in *Biblica* 49:378.
127. Barr, art. cit., p. 382.

connections. Hebrew grammar is supposed to give access to the dynamic thought of those in contact with revelation. Barr refers to this in his reply to Hill:

> Used in theology . . . I fear that such points of view will not be taken as hypotheses to be proved linguistically, but as ammunition in support of philosophical and theological views already traditional.[128]

In other words, this particular relation between language and thought has been used in the BTM in support of an authoritarian structure based on revelation. The linguistic evidence then is distorted to make it more univocal theologically than it is.[129]

In terms of our previous discussion of the christological analogy we could perhaps put the matter in a slightly different way. In the neo-orthodox revival of biblical authority the text of Scripture is thought of as divine and human in parallel with Christ. The character of the text is related directly to an external reality to which the text bears witness. The human character of the text leads us to a divine reality behind it. In this context it was possible for the grammar of the text to be thought of as relating directly to theology. As part of a movement from the divine to the human it is quite normal to accept the possibility of returning the direction from the human character of the text to the revelational thought it envelops. Barr refuses this whole revelational scenario, and when one no longer thinks along these lines it is possible to approach the text as a totally human document. It is basically this theological consciousness that opens up the way for Barr to look afresh at interpretation. Thus when Barr says that the language of the text *as used* is the thought, he is affirming something which corresponds to one of the premises of modern linguistics, but also tallies with his affirmation concerning the inspiration of the Scripture as being a human character. Far from digging a trench between language and psychology and culture, Barr is in fact affirming their continuity in the matrix of human history.[130] Thus language is seen not as revelatory, but (and perhaps this contrast is a little abrupt) as based on the social conventions of communication.[131]

---

128. Ibid.
129. *BWT*, p. 207.
130. Art. cit., pp. 378-79.
131. *SBL*, pp. 113, 159.

(b) Lexical stocks and theological structure

In connection with this correlation of thought and language there arises another feature of the BTM which Barr finds reprehensible. One of the faulty procedures mentioned in *SBL* and expanded at length in *BWT* is that of building up a thought-structure or pattern of theology from a consideration of the lexical stock and its structure. In this case it is assumed that the layout of the lexical stock of a language is symmorphous with a pattern of thought, and that variations in the structure represent cultural differences.[132] The theological import of this procedure lies in the fact that "an interest in the unity and the distinctiveness of the Old Testament has been widely linked with lexical procedures." Barr adds the following clarification:

> My criticism of this lexical approach does not intend or imply any attack on the idea of the coherence or distinctiveness of the Bible, except where such coherence or distinctiveness is understood in a sense inextricable from involvement in the lexical procedures which have sometimes been allied with it.[133]

Barr's criticism is motivated by his understanding of the relation of semantics and Biblical theology. Sympathy for Biblical theology is not a prerequisite for sound semantic study of the OT. Likewise, Biblical theology goes beyond the area of semantics and is not tied to it. The structure of theology cannot be determined from the patterns discerned in lexical stocks which yield a pattern of "biblical thinking."[134] So in *BWT* Barr seeks to demonstrate how the "biblical view" of time cannot be developed from a consideration of the distinction between *kairos* and *chronos* as in Marsh or J. A. T. Robinson or that of *kairos* and *aiōn* as Cullmann has argued.

If one tries to see theological differences in connection with the use of certain words, in such a way as to trace in the choice of a word the articulation of a certain theological view, several problems of linguistics appear. Barr admits that within a language certain words may be arranged in such a way as to indicate a contrast of thought. These are technical in nature and are arranged so as to express a way of looking at reality. But as a whole, language is not organized

---

132. *BWT,* p. 110.
133. Ibid., p. 16.
134. Barr, *VT*(S), 22:11-12.

in this way. If differences exist between certain words, this need not indicate a difference in thought. In fact, the stock of words is inherited and therefore precedes any technical distinctions applied to it, which will happen in a small number of cases. To trace differences in thought to the structures of vocabulary is to ignore the conventionality of language. Most important of all is the fact that argument about thought structures on the basis of linguistic layout ignores the synchronic character of language. A word has its meaning in its context in a particular time. It is not an idea independent of usage which remains constant at different stages of its usage. Barr's criticism is that this ignores the synchronic study of lexical stocks by means of word substitution to test meaning. A true historical study of language is one which pays attention to a series of synchronic states of the language as a whole. A word must not be thought of as a concept in the way which has been normal in the BTM. This ignores that vocabulary is not a system in the way grammar or phonology is and does not take into account the context. It leads to desyntacticisation of words and the danger of seeing the concept in each occurrence.[135] If the knowledge of lexical stocks is important, no meaning can be attributed to this distribution which varies between languages and even according to the habits of speakers of one language.

This practice of relating words to concepts is the backbone of a theological method which seeks to relate the distribution of lexical stocks and theological meaning. One result of this correspondence between linguistic patterns and theological structures is illustrated in what Barr calls the hypostasis of words. Some forms of hypostasis are normal types of linguistic activity, such as quotations and words used out of their normal distribution. In these cases, abstraction is used to bring special attention to a unit outside its normal context.[136] What Barr refers to by this term is another form of hypostasis, which, for example, studies the verb "to be" (*hayah*), supposing that it will reveal a concept of being in Hebrew thought.

---

135. *BWT*, pp. 110, 114f., 154; *CP*, p. 94.
136. For a general description, see K. L. Pike, *Language in Relation to a Unified Theory of the Structure of Human Behavior* (The Hague, 1967), pp. 107ff., Barr's article, "Hypostatization of Linguistic Phenomena in Modern Theological Interpretation," *JSS* 7:85-94; *SBL*, pp. 38, 71, 130; *BWT*, pp. 61f.

Barr points out that T. Boman "tends to pass from a treatment of a word which has meaning in sentences into a treatment of an aspect of ultimate reality."[137] Thus *hayah* ceases to be a word, but becomes an aspect of ultimate reality. In this false hypostatisation words begin to appear as supra-linguistic entities, the normal linguistic function is forgotten, and characteristics are attributed to the word which are inconsistent with this function. Thus a false hypostatisation is discerned by the non-conformity with the use of the words in normal syntactical contexts. The meaning of certain words is predetermined by a conceptual meaning irrespective of their usage in context.[138] Thus a theological content is seen as inherent in each usage and is imputed to the word in its varying occurrences. So one hears of the *kairos* concept or of the *dabar* of God. So heavily laden are these with content that they become impossible to translate and are thus transliterated. On this score Barr criticizes Cullmann, but also a host of others.[139]

All this rests on the supposition that a word can be placed in direct relation with the reality to which it is said to refer. Against this Barr considers that the meaning of the text can only be attained by means of interpretation which is governed by the rules of semantic description. In this respect Barr's evaluation of Cullmann's method is interesting. He views Cullmann's way of working with words thus:

1. Cullmann repudiates philosophy and theology based on it in favour of the biblical material;
2. by his lexical method he hypostatises and conceptualises words;
3. words are thus assimilated to mental concepts and their linguistic function in usage is obscured;
4. this de-syntacticisation produces a structure out of words giving the biblical view [of time].

Barr claims the implicit idealism of this procedure. Cullmann, he

137. T. Boman, *Hebrew Thought Compared with Greek* (London, 1960), pp. 38-49. Barr's criticisms are in art. cit., p. 86, and *SBL,* p. 71.
138. Barr, art. cit., pp. 87-89, considers that two tendencies in modern biblical interpretation make this danger great: a) the linguistic method which suggests that the lexical stock corresponds to the theological relations obtainable, and b) the importance of etymology.
139. See re Cullmann, *BWT,* p. 63; Boman, art. cit., p. 86; Torrance, *SBL,* pp. 129ff.; Delling, *BWT,* pp. 57ff.; Jacob, *SBL,* pp. 144ff.; Snaith, pp. 115ff.

thinks, rejects philosophy for biblical categories, but really smuggles in under the cover of this claim the supposition that there is a real relation between words and concepts. In fact, by hypostatisation biblical concept theology forces a dogmatic and philosophical scheme on the text of Scripture.[140] At this point, Barr does not wish to carry his views about Cullmann's faulty linguistics through onto the level of a theological criticism. This is often the case at this stage of his work. He allows that Cullmann's assertions about time may be right, as they may have theological justification apart from the linguistic argument. But Barr is reserved about this—it may be preferable to adopt Eichrodt's view that there is no specifically biblical view of time. At least this would avoid the appeal to founding a biblical view on a notion of a language having a distinctive content.[141] If we accept this possibility, we may still be able to find a starting point in the Bible without succumbing to the danger of creating a structure of hypostatised words. Cullmann's good intentions boomerang on themselves, deems Barr: "That some kind of authoritative value in teaching, similar in some respect to the authority of the statements and communications of the Bible, should be conceded to lexical structures of the terminology, must be very dubious doctrine within any currently accepted view of biblical authority."[142] To be theologically credible, a doctrine must be semantically viable. Its foundations, rather than in words conceptualized to yield structure, must be found in the units of sense and in the meaning of the statements of Scripture.

---

140. *BWT,* pp. 139ff., 143. Compare Cullmann's reply in *Christ and Time,* 3rd ed. (London, 1967), pp. xxx f. In this addendum Cullmann does little to defend his exegetical method. He does not think that Barr's critique modifies the basic thesis of his book. In any case, Barr allows for this possibility in *BWT,* p. 152. I must admit in this addendum of Cullmann's to be perplexed by the affirmation: "[Barr] does not criticize my method as such, only in so far as it is based on a lexicography similar to the principles of Kittel's *Wörterbuch.*" Cullmann in this statement seems to misunderstand the implications of Barr's critique for theological method in general and so protects his own thesis by inferring Barr has exaggerated (xxxi). The remarks of D. H. Wallace, "Oscar Cullmann," in *Creative Minds in Contemporary Theology,* ed. P. E. Hughes (Grand Rapids, 1969), pp. 189ff., in defence of Cullmann contra Barr seem to be based on a misunderstanding of Barr's view of language.

141. *BWT,* p. 150.

142. Ibid., p. 143.

The great weakness of the concept method used in the BTM is that it disregards polysemy, the fact that a word can have several different senses. When the link between language and concepts is made in the way described, the sense of any one word is maximised by the relation it is thought to bear with the concept. In the case of a word with uncertain meaning, the cumulative effect of the other examples bearing relation to the concept is overwhelming; the word is taken to fit in with the general pattern. Thus the word is laden with a burden of meaning which can hardly be related to the context. This disregards what the linguist M. Joos terms "semantic axiom no. one": that in defining a word it must be made to contribute least to the total context. Likewise, E. A. Nida states that "Words do not carry with them all the meanings which they may have in other sets of co-occurrences."[143] These rules would allow for the different meanings of words to appear. This must be accounted for, thinks Barr, in relating words and meanings. It must not be thought, however, that Barr is denying that a word can be related to a concept or affirming that the word is just a "cipher or counter." He explicitly states that his desire is to leave this question open, although it does seem wrong to him to speak of a word as if it were a concept.[144] N. W. Porteous seems to have made an accurate evaluation on this point when he remarked that Barr does not deny that words can be related to concepts, but they may be related to "meanings" or "translation substitutes."[145] The thrust of Barr's statement is that meanings cannot be collated into a single unitary concept which is omnipresent when the Bible writers use the word.

If the method under discussion is as faulty as Barr would have it, why, it might be asked, were the errors not seen sooner? Barr gives four reasons for this.[146] It could be that the evidence of Hellenistic usage is either ignored or passed over as irrelevant; that the im-

---

143. M. Joos, "Semantic Axiom Number One," *Language* 48:257; E. A. Nida, in *JBL* 91:86, quoted by Thiselton in Marshall, ed., op. cit., p. 84.

144. On this see Barr's reply to D. Hill's criticism in *Biblica* 49:385. Here Barr says he would be prepared to say for practical purposes that a word indicates a concept, although he does not much like it. What he rejects is Kittel's way of treating words as concepts.

145. N. W. Porteous, in *ET* 75:71f.; cf. Barr's reply, "Did Isaiah know about Hebrew 'Root Meanings'?," *ET* 75:242. Also the remarks of J. F. A. Sawyer, *Semantics in Biblical Research* (London, 1972), pp. 9, 90.

146. *BWT*, p. 56.

portance accorded to events in Biblical theology might predispose theologians to accept linguistic evidence establishing an idea of "decisive time"; that words such as *kairos* used in a certain way in modern philosophy or theology might lead one to expect that the ancient usage is similar; finally, such subjects as that of "time" are rather vague, and this general intangibility may prevent the realisation of the weakness of the linguistic arguments. But most pervasive is the supposition that language must reveal thought. The evidence then falls under this light, that it must be possible to conceptualise words. This fallacy involves the idea that the word is the unit of meaning and to this unit there will correspond a concept.

On this subject, once again, Barr is conscious of the connection between misuse of linguistic evidence and the motivation in the BTM to hold up the unity and authority of the Bible. Therefore:

> The misuse of language in recent "biblical theology" is nowhere more evident than where the judgments of careful scholarship are . . . thrown aside because they do not fit the lexical-theological web woven by recent fashions.[147]

The BTM with its emphasis on biblical authority found lexical studies congenial, as they fit in easily with the approach of dogmatics.[148] The study of the text in this context becomes the servant of the need to get a normative teaching from the text. To find the "biblical view" is possible and necessary. The concepts of the Bible, when unravelled, reveal the unity of Scripture and provide something normative. This is one of the quirks of the BTM, which did not want to accept the authority of Scripture in the inspired Word, as in fundamentalism. Yet it sought the authority of Scripture in connection with the text, on another level.

Barr's criticism of biblical concept theology is really a continuation of a question raised earlier by Karl Barth with regard to the project of a biblico-theological dictionary. Barth indicated the need to go beyond the "selection of arbitrary themes" to the coherent exposition of Scripture itself. This must be carried through on the basis that "the revelation which they attest does not stand or occur, and is not to be sought, behind or above the texts but in them."[149] In the same pas-

---

147. Ibid., p. 42.
148. Ibid., p. 162.
149. K. Barth, op. cit., I.2, 494.

sage, Barth affirms that the insights of the historical method must not be forgotten. These two aspects of the interpretation of Scripture have found their echo in Barr's work, namely, the necessity of a critical approach (appealing to "common sense"—see the debate with D. Hill), and a concentration on the text of Scripture itself. When biblical concepts are sought, the danger is to select them so as to fit in with a dogmatic structure. This method assumes that there is a tissue of concepts in the Bible, proceeds on the basis of a form of linguistic harmonisation through hypostasis, and creates a kind of second degree canon from the Bible canon.[150] The result borders on an obsession with certain themes and texts and leaves sections of the biblical materials untouched. This explains the observation of B. S. Childs that Biblical theology has failed to give sufficient attention to the biblical canon in its work.[151]

In résumé: The search for biblical concepts is motivated by the impulsion to find the biblical message—the normative revelation of Scripture. This theological motivation places the means used to attain this in a secondary position. The words of the text are linked with their revelatory content, and this occasions the distortion of linguistic evidence. Barr's criticism is a very clear warning to those who see the Bible in some relation with revelation not to yield to the temptation of putting into the Scripture what they want to get out of it. This is not a good use of Scripture. Does Barr himself at the time of writing *SBL* and *BTM* still hold any view of the unity and authority of Scripture? This question may well be irrelevant at this stage, but its answer would seem to depend on the extent these attributes depend on faulty linguistics in the BTM. Can they survive without

---

150. These observations are made by G. Crespy (and modified somewhat by me) in *Parole et Dogmatique* (Paris, 1971), pp. 104f. D. Kelsey, in *The Uses of Scripture in Recent Theology* (London, 1975), pp. 29f., compares the biblical concept theology of H. W. Bartsch with the conservative position of B. B. Warfield. In the case of Bartsch, theological proposals are founded on "the distinctiveness of the Bible's quasi-technical concepts." For Warfield it is inerrancy that matters. Both views hold Scripture to be authority because of some intrinsic property of the text. It seems that Kelsey's analysis goes too far in comparison. There is a great difference in the area of revelation of which the text, for Warfield, forms a part. The concepts of Bartsch are not in the same way evident on the surface of the text but are connected with revelation away from it, unlike Warfield's inerrancy, which is a consequence of inspiration of the text.

151. B. S. Childs, *Biblical Theology in Crisis,* pp. 99ff.

these methods? If these linguistics cannot be substituted by a more satisfactory way of showing the Bible to possess these attributes, do not they themselves cease to be valid? If no categorical answer can be given to this question at this time in Barr's theological development, it is obvious what the problem is, and what are the factors which will lead him to formulate a view of Scripture more consistent with what he considers to be the exigencies of interpretation.

(c) Kittel's *TDNT* and "inner lexicography"

On the same issue, Barr assaults the leviathan of contemporary theological achievement, Kittel's *TDNT,* to which he devotes a chapter in *SBL.* This is tantamount to eating the show bread on the tables of modern Biblical theology, and Barr's profanation has drawn more than a little condemnation from irate clerics.

The essence of Barr's discontent with the method of Kittel (as exemplified by certain articles) is adequately expressed in this remark:

> . . . the articles in *TWNT,* while apparently organized under a Greek word (like *agapao* or *hamartia*) have a tendency to be an essay on the biblical conception of Love or of Sin; and in difficult cases to leave it somewhat uncertain whether that whole conception can be taken to be indicated in a particular passage by the word which is the subject of the article.[152]

According to Barr the problem is that it is difficult to know whether we are talking about words or concepts; it is less a question of word history than idea history. This confusion leads to two dubious methodological procedures. In some cases the semantic identity of a word is transferred to another context, where it does not bear the same semantic value. In the second place the meaning of a word is read into each particular occurrence of the word as being its specific sense in each case.[153]   Barr sees a rather close relation between the

---

152. *SBL,* pp. 217. See the discussion of Barr's critique in S. Neill, *The Interpretation of the New Testament 1861–1961* (London, 1964), pp. 322ff.; P. Grech, "Problèmes methodologiques contemporains dans la théologie du NT," *Bulletin de Théologie Biblique* 2:275ff.; D. Hill, op. cit., pp. 5ff.; Burnier, op. cit., pp. 55ff.; and the articles by G. Friedrich in *ThZ* 94:802-16 and *TDNT,* X, 613-661.

153. Ibid., p. 218; Barr calls these illegitimate identity transfer and illegitimate totality transfer.

way words have been confused with concepts both by Kittel and in
the BTM in general. Underlying this procedure is the supposition
that words as semantic units are more or less autonomous and that
language is in character polysynthetic rather than synthetic.[154] For
Barr, it is a mistake, not so much to speak of the psychological content of language or its "inner" lexicography as Kittel does, but to
suppose that "all such content is already present in the 'external lexicography.' "[155] The formal structure of language when studied in its
formal relations cannot be thought of as a direct indicator of psychological mentality. There is not necessarily a split between the formal
and the psychological relation in language, but their relation is haphazard. J. F. A. Sawyer sums up the reason of Barr's unease with
Kittel: ". . . what is quite inadmissible, and the deserving target of
so much criticism since Barr's *Semantics,* is the assumption that because a word has a particular meaning in one context, it automatically
has the same meaning in another quite different context a couple of
thousand years earlier."[156] It does seem quite true to say, being
careful not to generalise the judgment to include the totality of Kittel's
TDNT, that certain of the articles neglect the social convention of
the significance of words and the fact that "semantic statements must
be based on the social conscience" because of the social nature of
language as a means of communication. When this is lost from view,
the Bible can be man-handled as a system of quasi-technical concepts, bolstered up by a diachronic method which creates a structure
of biblical concepts.[157]

David Hill is quite correct when he describes Barr's major criticisms
against *TDNT* as being against the confusion of words and concepts
and the attempt to build up general concepts from words. Barr's
criticism is in fact very pointed about this: The work of the dictionary
is in the realm of concept history, but it is a dictionary of *words.*
The relation between the lexical stock and the concept stock is not

---

154. "Synthetic" being taken to mean that words exist embedded in their
syntactic contexts. G. Friedrich has rejected Barr's criticism of *TDNT* for
identifying Kittel and the *BTM, art. cit.,* p. 813. He accuses Barr of adopting
a positivistic attitude (p. 816), and maintains against Barr the autonomy of
the word. See also Tangberg, art. cit., p. 305.
155. Barr, *Biblica* 49:378, as in *SBL,* p. 245.
156. J. F. A. Sawyer, op. cit., p. 9.
157. *SBL,* pp. 13, 113, 159.

clarified. In fact Barr thinks that the problem is even further increased by the ambiguity of the word "concept," claiming to have
found four different senses. Such confusions lead to a crop of weak
interpretations which fail to discover *what was meant* and rely on
etymology and the remote associations of words.[158]

However, Hill criticizes Barr on the grounds that he does not take
into sufficient account the non-linguistic context of interpretation
and also that he makes too little of the idea of the relative autonomy
of the word. In this Hill sees the possibility of relating a word and
an idea. Thus Hill thinks it must be allowed that words can have
theological meaning. Barr has too often given the impression that
there is no connection between words and concepts. He also thinks
it is possible, while recognizing some of Barr's criticism, to maintain
the basic approach of the *TDNT*. It cannot be considered invalid
on the basis that a dictionary cannot pass from the linguistic material to the inner world of thought. Words can be considered as
semantic "markers" related to fields of meaning.[159] Barr in reply to
Hill states that these remarks by-pass the question. He has not
denied the existence of contact between formal and psychological
questions in language. What Barr is criticizing is in fact a neglect of
the formal study of the language itself, as potentially revelatory of
psychological operations, in favour of a form of language study
which works out psychological relations from another source and
brings them to bear upon the formal linguistic evidence.[160] Barr's
argument is not in fact against the relation of language and thought,
but against the determining of the meaning of words by supposed in-
variable concepts of the human mind.[161] If Hill is correct in seeing

---

158. Ibid., pp. 207ff.
159. D. Hill, op. cit., pp. 5-11.
160. Barr, art. cit., pp. 378f. Thus Hill's criticisms seem misplaced, particularly that of formalism. In reply, Barr accuses Hill of idealism which is
espoused in such a way as to deal a blow to the Biblical theology he seeks to
defend, cf. p. 386.
161. On the alleged universality of semantic components, see Lyons, op. cit.,
pp. 472f. Barr admits that he was not totally clear in *SBL* as to the relation
of words and concepts and tried to leave it open. But affirms that it should
have been clear that he was not denying any possible relation, art. cit., p. 385.
It is interesting to note that J. Macquarrie sees Barr's criticism in an entirely
different light from Hill. He sees Barr's criticism against Kittel as touching
the neglect of the logical function of words and the kind of discourse they are

Barr's criticism of Kittel as lying in the confusion of words and concepts, he goes too far when he affirms that Barr is arguing against the idea that a word can indicate a concept.

Some mutterings have been heard to the effect that Barr has capitalised on a few of the weaker articles in *TDNT* to cast opprobrium on the totality of the work. G. E. Wright, for example, suggested that generalisations regarding all lexical attempts were made from a few weak points and thinks Barr steps behind "linguistics" when positive statement is needed.[162] Barr has replied to these criticisms. Contrary to what is suggested, his criticism is not levelled at a few samples, but at the *philosophy* behind Kittel. Even though his points are widely drawn from early volumes only, Barr thinks there would have been no problem in extending the critique to the remainder, except in the cases where the express philosophy of the work was ignored.[163] This general philosophy is what, for Barr, mars the handling of linguistic evidence in *TDNT*. The relation between language and thought is predetermined on grounds other than the linguistic and in fact means that the evidence is slotted into this scheme. In particular Barr places the methodology of Kittel in the context of the old debate as to the character of the NT Greek. In the seventeenth-century orthodoxy there was a tendency to insist on the purity of the NT Greek. While recognising the existence of Hebraisms in the NT, there was a refusal to admit the presence of barbarisms or solecisms in Scripture.[164] The idea of the "language of the Holy Spirit" has remained influential, though passing through various modifications as to the exact nature of the inspiration. N. Turner, among others, is not averse to reconsidering this view. G. Friedrich asserts: "Today

---

found in. In other words, he sees in Barr's criticism precisely what Hill accuses Barr of not seeing. In stressing the sentence Barr is saying in linguistics "precisely what Wittgenstein has said" (*God Talk*, p. 120).

162. G. E. Wright, *The Old Testament and Theology* (New York, 1969) p. 45, n. 15; cf. Hill, op. cit., pp. 5f.; Langevin in *Laval*, 29:94.

163. Barr, *IDB*(S), p. 107.

164. See R. Preus, *The Inspiration of Scripture* (Edinburgh, 1955), pp. 64ff. Preus says this desire to maintain the purity of the language is related to inspiration; the inspired Word cannot be judged by the laws of pagan literature. A. Lecerf, "Inspiration et grammaire d'après les théologiens protestants du XVIIᵉ siècle," thinks it not to be a case of verbal inspiration as such, with regard to the purity of Bible language, but of God not using what is troubled by sin. *Etudes Calvinistes* (Neuchâtel, 1949), pp. 140-46.

. . . one must agree that not merely the content of the NT is unique but also the language. . . ."[165]

Barr situates the methodology of *TDNT* in continuity with the previous work in this field by H. Cremer and J. Kögel. Their perspective was that of a more thorough appreciation of the influence of the Holy Spirit on language, discerned through the special nature of of biblical Greek. The influence of Christianity on the Greek language has been to give it a new power and meaning, renewing it through this transformation. This view of the "language-moulding power of Christianity" was attacked by Deissmann, who saw the NT as being written in the normal *Koine*. Barr sympathizes strongly with the position of Deissmann. The lexicographical method of Kittel can be traced in the development of the idea of the language-moulding power of Christianity. There was, thinks Barr, a certain original effort to see this in the stock of new words in the NT. When advances in language study revealed that this was not unique and that the notion could not be substantiated in the area of morphology and syntax, the interest was moved over into the lexical department. Barr affirms that first Cremer and later Kittel consider the new content of the Greek of the NT in relation to the Hebraic content and its impact on the Greek language. Kögel introduced the distinction of "outer" and "inner" expression of words and proposed that the task of theological lexica was to restore the connection between the word and the special inner meaning given to it by the writer. In the case of the NT, this is related to the question of revelation. The NT writers used such words as were available; yet these words indicated a new experience and were new as well as old. Thus the word in its outer form is Greek, "old"; but in its inner form is Hebraic-Christan, "new."[166]

Such is Barr's analysis, in very brief form, of the parentage of the concept method used in modern Biblical theology. Whether this analysis is in fact correct need not detain us here. But what is important is the fact that this method can claim better than anything else the distinctive character of biblical language. This distinctiveness is related to revelation and is constituted by the overlaying of a new

---

165. N. Turner in J. H. Moulton, *A Grammar of NT Greek*, III:4; G. Friedrich, *TDNT*, X:653.

166. For Barr's development of this whole argument see *SBL*, pp. 238ff.

content on the Greek words. One has to look through the externalities to see the inner meaning of the words in the structure of revelation. Barr is unequivocal in his denial of this method: It is erroneous. The reason for this is that words on the external level are already functioning semantically; as words have no more than their semantic function, there can be no inner depth.[167] Barr infers that the inner lexicography of Kittel results in the formalisation of semantic study and over-emphasis on the relation between the word and the inner depth meaning. He sees this as a reaction against taking the proposition as the carrier of religious truth. The word study method seeks to penetrate from the words to the world of thought of the writers. In the case of biblical words this means also penetrating the world of revelation connected with the thought of the writers. To this Barr adds his doubt that the "activity of the Holy Spirit can be legitimately listed among the causes of semantic change."[168]

Is it simply for linguistic reasons that Barr rejects the lexical approach to Biblical theology suggested in this tradition? I suspect that the reasons for Barr's rejection lie deeper than the linguistic level, although this is obviously a central factor. It is the idea of justifying the distinctiveness of Christian language in the sphere of revelation that Barr rebuts. This involves the reference to a God-to-man movement and some special historical pleading for the Greek of the NT. Can the true humanness of biblical language be maintained if we are involved in theories about the inner meaning of words in this connection? In addition, this method is, for Barr, an open door to abuses. The *TDNT* has been "idolized" in the BTM.[169] "I find it faintly comic or ridiculous, intones Barr, to think of (say) the preacher whose text contains the word 'terror' turning solemnly to the article *'êmah* and reading up the theology of terror in the Old Testament."[170] Under this tone of badinage there is a serious criticism. The danger of a theological dictionary such as Kittel is that of becoming a subsidiary norm. Barr comments on the first volume of the *TDNT* that its "tone is set by a desire to inform rather than in-

---

167. Barr's criticisms are in ibid., pp. 244ff. When Barr affirms as here that words signify on the "external" level, "emotional suggestion, reference to traditional patterns and ideas," are also included in this signifying.

168. Ibid., p. 248.

169. *IDBS*(S), loc. cit. Other references to abuses in *SBL*, pp. 219ff.

170. *Int* 30:187.

culcate."[171] Barr seems to be hinting something here about the *TDNT*
which was "idolized." A theological dictionary, particularly one that
trades in normative biblical concepts, runs the risk of becoming a
leader of men. It entails the loss of a certain objectivity in that it
selects the evidence; the non-specialist has little way of construing the
material in another way. Barr's advice: Learn Hebrew thoroughly
and do your theological evaluation for yourself.

Barr's attack on Kittel's *TDNT* is therefore not merely a linguistic
sally, but is more deeply motivated by a concern for the freedom of
the text. The *TDNT* was a part of the authority complex of the BTM.

(d) Etymology in interpretation

The close correlation between lexical stock and thought structure,
the notions of "inner" meaning and taking the word as the unit of
meaning, contribute to make etymology an important factor in interpretation. To lay bare the origin of a word is to open its real
meaning.[172] Added to this, etymology is a great temptation, as it
has always figured in the tradition of Christian interpretation sometimes in quite a central way. It goes hand-in-glove with the approach
of the *TDNT,* which tends to separate Hebrew words from others
in the same semantic field.[173]

Concerning the use of etymology in the BTM, Barr is most scath-
ing. His broadsides against etymologizing make his criticisms already
described look like mere grapeshot. It has been said that in these
criticisms Barr has "to some extent underplayed the positive value of
diachronic semantics."[174] If this is so, it is largely for the reason that
at the time of publication of *SBL,* some strong antidotes were necessary to dispel the bewitching character of illegitimate etymologizing,
which is highly alluring not only on the level of academic studies
(where it permits the specialist to do a command performance), but

171. Ibid., p. 186.
172. Lyons, op. cit., p. 4, says that the term itself, formed on the Greek
stem *etymo-* signifying true or real, betrays its philosophical origin!
173. See "Etymology and the Old Testament," *Oudtestamentische Studien*
19:2, 27. Also re etymology and theological dictionaries *Int* 30:188. Barr
thinks a better approach would group several Hebrew words under one English
one.
174. Sawyer, op. cit. p. 88.

also in the homiletic field (where it serves as an introduction or a piece of local colour).

Barr rejects the use of etymology made oft-times in Biblical theology as being anti-contextual and involving speculation.[175] The origin of the word can only ever be a secondary consideration after consideration of the meaning of the word in context. It is not a means of making statements about meaning, but only about history. Nor can the existence of etymology within the Bible itself justify etymological study as a sort of modern midrash: ". . . etymology within the Bible does not in itself justify a concern with modern etymology as a proper semantic concern of the modern scholar."[176]

What is semantically unacceptable to Barr is the idea that etymology is a profitable way of finding a core of meaning which inheres the word itself. An example of this is found in a quotation of Snaith when he claims:

> While it must be recognised that words can change their meaning in strange and unexpected ways through the centuries, yet in all languages there is a fundamental motif in a word which tends to endure, whatever other changes the years may bring.[177]

This is highly questionable in itself, but as far as the interpretation of the text goes, it is really beside the point. The meaning of words is in the present linguistic units of the communicator and not in the linguistic word of his ancestor.[178] However, what is merely doubtful becomes positively unlawful when the etymologizing approach is connected to the conceptual matrix of the Hebrew/Greek thought distinction. Etymology becomes another argument for positing the

---

175. *SBL, chap.* 6.
176. "Etymology and the Old Testament," p. 27.
177. N. H. Snaith, "The Language of the Old Testament," in *IDB,* I:224.
178. The danger of another kind of "etymologizing" is present in philological research which is trans-language but is tangential to etymology in so far as philologists sometimes think of themselves as working in one Semitic world. This is the background for Barr's critique of Dahood's work. Cf. "Philology and Exegesis" in *Questions disputées d'Ancien Testament* (Grembloux, 1974), p. 42. Also Barr's suggestions in *CP,* pp. 172ff., 190, 290. Barr thinks that comparative philology develops an etymologizing approach in seeking the meaning of a word in different languages and in downplaying the function of the (biblical) word in the context of a sacred tradition (pp. 217ff.). A sharp rejoinder has been proffered by Mendenhall in *Int* 25:358-62. More positive evaluations of Barr's views in *CP* are those of Terrien in *Union Seminary Quarterly Review* 33:391, and Nicholas, *WTJ* 34:127ff.

distinctiveness of biblical thought based on the "inner life" or "depth meaning" of Hebrew words. These have a different historical weight behind them than Greek words and consequently characterise a different mental approach to reality.[179] The risk of this approach is that etymology, which is a precise science, is in danger of becoming the handmaid of "concepts," with the result that it becomes a hazard for interpretation. Barr argues that when the semantics of the words, within the period of the texts and their language, are neglected, the interpreter arrogates a large power of selectivity. Etymologies are adopted because they fit in—and how convincingly!—with an overall pattern of concepts.[180] Barr's argument and examples adduced seek to demonstrate that "the idea of bringing out the uniqueness of Hebrew psychology through emphasizing the etymological relations of words is not only wrong in principle but certain to fail in practice."[181]

What is achieved by etymologizing is in fact illusory, if this method is seeking to confer a sort of regularity on semantic change. It is incapable of reducing the arbitrariness of language. One of the fundamental facts about human language is the arbitrariness of the relation between sign and the thing signified, between word and thing designated. Although etymological study may give the appearance of regularity and order, all it really achieves is to remove the problem backwards in an historical sense.[182] The distribution of lexical stocks, Barr wishes to say, is haphazard, and the practice of translation is a good precautionary element in a proper linguistic examination of lexical stocks. By this means the exaggerations of etymologizing can be avoided.[183]

Etymology, when practiced in a selective way, with the intention of buttressing the stained-glass patterns of biblical concept theology, does not function in an acceptable way. The diachronic comes to eliminate the synchronic aspects of semantics. Thereby it supports preconceived conceptions of authority. Etymology in recent Biblical theology has often functioned as an element which purports to dis-

---

179. *SBL,* pp. 117f.
180. Ibid., pp. 139f.
181. Ibid., p. 118.
182. "Etymology and the Old Testament," p. 21.
183. *BWT,* p. 122. Barr warns against etymologizing in *CP:* "The meaning of a word is its meaning in its own language, not its meaning in some other," pp. 89ff.

close the coherence and distinctiveness of biblical concepts. As such, study which is properly historical has become the lackey of an authority. It gives a false appearance of reducing the arbitrariness of language; fitted into a dogmatic pattern, it receives an authority it does not properly have. Barr's criticism is once again that this procedure distorts the evaluation of linguistic evidence. Concluding his discussion on this procedure in the case of *qahal* and *dabar,* Barr jibes: "If these arguments have any validity at all, you can make the Scripture mean anything you like at all. . . . The interpreter twists the material in any way he likes."[184] The word yields a meaning "for today" from the etymological dispenser.

2.2.3. Idealism and diachronic linguistics

The common element in these various methods is the supposition of the correlation between the structures of language and those of the reality beyond the verbal representations. Allied with the traditional linguistics, this approach makes it possible to move from the word or syntax to the realities to which they point. Barr sees in this approach the influence of idealist philosophy. One must seize the irony of this: The enigma of biblical concept theology is that it puts the prime on the event-character of revelation and Hebraic dynamism against Greek abstractionism and claims to extirpate philosophy from theology. Yet it falls prey itself to trafficking illicitly in idealism. So after this philosophy itself has become part of history, it continues to exercise in the BTM a powerful, if indirect, influence on linguistic practice.

This is one of the more controversed points in Barr's work, and it is no doubt this reference which has merited Barr's classification with the opposing philosophical position.[185] However, the question for Barr does not really lie on the level of a philosophical debate for one opinion or another. It is perhaps rather typical of an idealist ap-

---

184. *SBL,* pp. 138f., 147, 159. Cf. art. cit., p. 20. Barr makes similar criticisms of philology in *Questions disputées,* p. 58.

185. Tangberg, art. cit., pp. 307ff., discusses this point. In *Biblica* 49:382, Barr expresses his doubt as to the usefulness of the Sapir-Whorf hypothesis for theology (i.e., the idea that individual languages have their own "metaphysics" and different languages have different world views. Cf. Lyons, op. cit., p. 433). Barr fears that in theology this would be used in support of views already traditional.

proach to wish to relate Barr's linguistic observations to a certain form of philosophy. Barr is not attacking a philosophical position as such, but those who "regarded idealism as worse than the plague," yet were dependent on it for their treatment of biblical language.[186] Barr sees this as one of the tension points in the BTM; its view of revelation was certainly not that of Schleiermacher, but it still worked with a view of language influenced by him.[187] In particular, the circularity of Schleiermacher's hermeneutic process, which moves from the part to the whole and yet needs the whole to interpret the part, shows the influence of idealism, as T. F. Torrance and Barr point out. Thus Barr quotes Schleiermacher to the effect that an assembly of the elements in the NT where the language-moulding power of Christianity is at work would present the skeleton of a dogmatics of the NT. This process is double, having a grammatical form and an inner psychological form. The mystery is, to Barr, why the theory of Schleiermacher should be such a welcome guide to the Cremer-Kittel tradition. Barr does not solve this one, but simply points to a possible congruence in the area of the circularity of the interpretative process. Biblical theology has a similar method as that of the relation of the part and the whole in Schleiermacher. It moves from particulars to Christ as the centre of Scripture and then imposes the pattern of the whole on the details. The unity of the whole is found in the salvation history, of which Christ is the centre, presented in terms of Hebraic mentality.

This would seem to be another piece to add to our mosaic of the christological analogy in the interpretative processes of Biblical theology. The analogy is not simply in terms of the divine and human natures as in the older dogmatics, but over-laid on this is a layer of idealism in which the "outer" and "inner" correspond to the former distinction of elements. Interpretation moves to the divine content conveyed by the Hebraic concepts, which reveal Christ, and then back to the human to align it with the core of revelation. Theology and linguistics in this system are implicated in each other. This is a special

---

186. Barr, ibid., p. 383, *BWT*, pp. 194ff.

187. Barr identifies several cases in *SBL*, pp. 257ff. On the influence of idealism in Schleiermacher's hermeneutics see T. F. Torrance, "Hermeneutics according to Schleiermacher," *SJT* 21:257ff., and also in *Canadian Journal of Theology* 2:129f. See Barr's comments on Torrance's interpretation in *SBL*, p. 259n.

way in modern theology of maintaining the idea of the self-witness of the Scripture without reference to verbal inspiration. Not only is this an "essentially idealist programme," but Barr thinks it "equivalent to an attempt of the systematic theological consciousness to dominate biblical exegesis."[188] Such a theory is bound to amount to a gagging of the message of the Bible. The claim to the distinctiveness of biblical language is detrimental to free interpretation. The idea of the language-moulding power of Christianity is an obstacle to scientific investigation. It introduces into Biblical theology a confusion between theology and linguistics which leads to the misuse of linguistic evidence.[189]

What is the cause of dissatisfaction on the part of Barr with regard to the linguistic methods of Biblical theology? Underlying the several points discussed here is that these all represent a diachronic approach to the nature of linguistic meaning. Biblical thought concepts are established in a diachronic way by inferring that a word has a similar meaning in its autonomy, irrespective of context; etymology typifies an approach to meaning which features derivation over against synchronic considerations; the distinctiveness of OT and NT is demonstrated diachronically by reference to concept-history. The arch error of this descriptive Biblical theology is to accord preeminence to diachronic study. Thus Barr criticises an exaggerated use of root meanings, the lack of attention given to semantic evolution in the diachronic process, the establishment of statistics without reference to context, and so on. Such an emphasis on diachronic study leads to the misuse of evidence in the four cases we have studied. The danger and fault of the BTM, to use a word Barr dislikes, is *eisegesis,* "that ugly campus word . . . which . . . is doubtful Greek anyway, betraying a failure to understand how the word 'exegesis' was formed."[190]

---

188. *SBL,* pp. 259-60.

189. Ibid., p. 247. Also Barr's article in *JSS* 7:90ff. Barr criticises Hill's work and its defence of Kittel by appeal to idealism by maintaining that precisely this approach will be unacceptable to many of the contributors to *TDNT,* *Biblica* 49:386. For further remarks by Barr see *SBL,* p. 204. On the subject in general see K. Hamilton, *Words and the Word* (Grand Rapids, 1971), chap. 1.

190. *ONI,* p. 189. On the diachronic aspects of the BTM see J. Harvey, "La théologie biblique aujourd' hui," *Bulletin de Théologie Biblique* 1:25ff.

The methods of the BTM were, it would seem, characteristic of a form of world-maintenance in which the distinctiveness of the language of the Bible was used to demonstrate the unity and authority of the Scripture as witness to revelation. This distinctiveness is above all an aspect of the divine content of the Bible which must be seen through the external appearance of the human language. The incisiveness of Barr's critique undermines the foundation of this theology and tolls the death-knell of the revival of biblical authority in this form. A decade later B. S. Childs wrote of "Biblical Theology in Crisis."

2.3 Heilsgeschichte *and the unity of Scripture*

In addition to the problems of language and their bearing on theology, James Barr has devoted a good deal of his time to the criticism of another *lieu commun* of the BTM, the question of history. Barr sees this emphasis on history as an apologetic reaction to the threat this notion posed to Christianity in the last century. Moreover, when revelation is said to be in history, this also constitutes in the BTM a reaction to liberal views of revelation. Choosing to stand with history, Christian theology has made it central; practically all theological approaches this century doff their caps to it in one way or another. "Nothing," Barr says, "takes history so seriously as does true Christian faith. . . . revelation in history forms a basis for a kind of unity in theology today; and above all, it is the response to the apologetic needs of the nineteenth century."[191] If non-biblical religion is nature-centred and timeless, revelation through history is dynamic and a unifying factor in the Scripture. It is not only central in biblical thinking, but in the BTM it is central in theology. It is the "conventional wisdom" of modern theology and to deny its regulative place would render one "heretical in the eyes of almost all schools of thought," as well as irrelevant.[192]

Before examining Barr's criticisms of revelation in history, the contiguity of the linguistic method of the BTM and its construction of a "holy history" must be commented on. This similarity of ap-

---

191. Barr, "Revelation through History in the Old Testament and in Modern Theology," in *New Theology No. 1* (1964), p. 63. See also Barr's article, "Revelation in History," *IDB*(S), p. 746.

192. Ibid., p. 61.

proach has often been overlooked, yet it is essential for situating the hermeneutical processes of neo-orthodoxy. As with the distinction between "outer" and "inner" linguistics, *Heilsgeschichte* seeks the unity of Scripture in a history behind the text of Scripture. An example might illustrate this. Pierre Barthel, commenting on the method of Cullmann's theology, says that Cullmann thinks it possible to pass from the line of history to the reality represented beyond this. The history of salvation is constituted by the discernment of the relation between the witnesses of the NT which are of objective historical character, and the intuitive apprehension of the religious "object" beyond these.[193] There is a similar movement in historical method in the constitution of a "holy history" as in the establishment of concepts by means of "inner lexicography." The passing from given to not given as a means of understanding is essential to the process.

Barr has seen this point quite clearly. Concept history and the christocentric *Heilsgeschichte* are complementary. The purpose of "inner lexicography" is to pinpoint the concept related to the event or to Christ himself. These underlie the biblical text. Another common factor here is that inner lexicography replaces the old notion of inspiration; the idea of a holy history, beyond the texts' representations, eases the burden of the need of historical accuracy in the text. The search of concepts related to saving events in the BTM is a compensation for the rejection of verbal inspiration. We can do no better than quote Barr's incisive remark here:

> In general it seems true that with the loss of stress on the historical accuracy and doctrinal perfection of Scriptural statements in modern times, there has gone an effort to emphasize the inner coherence of the Bible in some way, and that the importance placed on this inner coherence by some theologians, in respect both of lexicography and of synthetic biblical theology, is perhaps a compensation for the apparent thinning down of biblical inspiration.[194]

Proof *words* replace proof *texts;* holy history replaces biblical nar-

---

193. P. Barthel, *Interprétation du Langage mythique et théologie biblique* (Leiden, 1967), p. 130.
194. *SBL,* p. 271n.; cf. pp. 208-9; *BWT,* p. 162; *IDB*(S), p. 795.

rative.[195] This determines the importance of the study of words in
the BTM, which are deemed to be filled with eschatological content.
These remarks indicate something of the importance of *Heilsgeschichte*
as the foundation in neo-orthodoxy of the unity and authority of the
Bible.

There is, in the development of Barr's criticism of the notion of
history in interpretation, a continuing attack on the distortion of the
evidence of the text by a theological notion which functions as a
control on exegesis. Barr's work points to the weaknesses of views
which seek to establish the authority of Scripture in connection with
the distinctive events of revelation in history. In his early article in
New Theology already quoted, Barr argues that history is a category
forced on the text of Scripture. We cannot from the text attribute a
revelatory character to history in itself. This insight is broadened
in *ONI,* where the multiplex character of the OT tradition is stated;
revelation in history is a form of reductionism which is imposed on
the text and involves antinomies. Later, in *BMW,* Barr discusses
more fully the problems connected with the notion of "event." Several constants remain in the deepening of this criticism; the ambiguity
of the association of revelation and history in an exclusive way; the
centrality of the speaking of God in the tradition; the authoritarianism
implied in using this category as an interpretative principle which
demonstrates the unity of Scripture. Some description of this must be
briefly given.

2.3.1. The ambiguity of revelation in history

Barr discerns a series of ambiguities in the notion of revelation in
history used in interpretation. The problems lie in the areas of the
sense of history, how revelation is said to be connected with history,
the relation of the two to the biblical text and the whole question of
"acts" of God.[196]

---

195. See H. W. Frei, *The Eclipse of Biblical Narrative* (New Haven, 1974),
pp. 180ff. Frei contrasts the outlook of salvation history with that of realistic
narrative interpretation. In the first, meaning is not a function of the narrative
but of a sequence of events and the interpretative tradition. This view of Scripture as witness has been inherited by neo-orthodoxy, with all its ambiguities.
196. The thought of Barr is concisely resumed in his articles in *IDB*(S)
on "Revelation in History," pp. 746ff., and "Scripture, Authority of," p. 795.

Modern theology is characterised by the inflation of the notion of history. It is the modern problem which replaces former discussions about the relation of revelation and reason with the question of revelation and history.[197] "Biblical revelation as saving truth is also historical truth, historically mediated, with narrative as the manner in which its variously employed literary forms are knit together."[198] Barr is not alone in thinking that such affirmations go beyond demonstration. B. S. Childs has also noted the diversity of views enclosed in the notion of revelation in history, which seemed to seek a solution in a synthesis above the individual problems of what constitutes revelation and what history is.[199] More recently, B. J. Albrektson has joined Barr in the criticism of the exclusivity of the biblical notion of history and states that a hard and fast distinction between Israel and the surrounding cultures is not afforded by the evidence.[200] Barr criticizes an exclusive concentration on history as an organisational category for biblical reflection. This is not just an attack on *Heilsgeschichte,* but goes further than this to bring out the ambiguous nature of the notion "history" itself in relation to biblical interpretation:

> The Bible has no linguistic term corresponding to "history." . . . its narrative passages are not constant but variable in their relation to what we . . . call "history." . . . The relation which the Old Testament stories bear to history itself varies in relation to a number of variables, . . . the chronological remoteness of the event being described, the nature of that event, . . . the stage of historiographical technique at the time of writing.[201]

Barr precedes this remark with the assurance that history cannot be used as a classifying bracket for the biblical material; it is not a biblical category.[202] If part of the appeal to "history" lies in its am-

---

197. C. Geffré in *La Révélation,* by P. Ricoeur et al. (Bruxelles, 1977), p. 189, and C. Braaten, *History and Hermeneutics* (Philadelphia, 1966), chap. 1.

198. G. E. Wright, in *Translating and Understanding the Old Testament,* ed. H. T. Frank and W. L. Reid (Nashville, 1970), p. 291.

199. B. S. Childs, op. cit., pp. 40ff.

200. See B. Albrektson, *History and the Gods* (Lund, 1967), passim, and Barr's remarks in *IDB*(S), p. 748.

201. *ONI,* pp. 69, 70.

202. F. Filson has made similar remarks to this effect in *JBL* 69:1ff., though in a different sense. He is denouncing the idea that "pure history" can be identified with the special history of Christianity. Had this notion been known to the writers of the NT, they would have rejected it.

biguity, this can also be a cause of tension.[203] P. Minear thinks that
positively it is not a very useful notion, and had it been available to
the NT writers, they would not have relied on it heavily. The problem today is the assumption that we know what history is.[204] Barr
too sees this assumption as a cause of ambiguity when the idea of
history is applied to the biblical evidence. The fact that history is a
non-biblical category means that when it is applied to the biblical
evidence it is stretched to fit the various cases. History cannot be
applied uniformly to the texts of the OT in any normal sense of the
word. When it is used, its normal sense is abandoned and artificial
distinctions have to be made to maintain its intelligibility. Barr says
exegesis has forced him to this conclusion.[205]

The ambiguity involved in the centrality of history is no more apparent than where history is identified as a kind of holy history.
Is the latter *history* in any normal sense of the term? Barr thinks not,
and points out the tension in the *Heilsgeschichte* approach which
maintains that this is a real history, which is, however, not accessible
to critical historical enquiry. If this is the case, in what sense can
this be called history? Yet if critical historical research were to con-
firm the realness of this history, how could it then be claimed to be
a special instance of revelation? The problem is that when examined
in terms of normal historical investigation, either the historical character or the revelatory sense seems to fall away. Here we have an
example in historiography of the special pleading which Barr has
criticised in linguistics. What happens in fact is that in neo-orthodoxy
theologians tend to limp along under the tension of two pictures of
Israel's history, one being the biblical salvation-historical interpretation, and the other the modern positivistic reconstruction of what
happened.[206] What fellowship can there be, one wonders, between
the confessional description and the modern historiography without
God and without revelation?

---

203. D. G. Spriggs in *Two Old Testament Theologies* (London, 1974),
maintains that for Von Rad history does not have any uniform meaning and
is used in a variety of senses (p. 38). G. E. Wright defends Von Rad's approach contra Barr in *The Old Testament and Theology,* pp. 47ff.

204. P. S. Minear, *Int* 5:35, 36.

205. Barr, in *New Theology,* pp. 66f.

206. *IDB*(S), pp. 746-47, and *ONI,* pp. 66ff. Also C. Braaten, op. cit., pp.
108ff.; O. Cullmann, *The Early Church* (London, 1956), pp. 8f.; Van A. Harvey, *The Historian and the Believer* (Toronto, 1969), chap. 5.

Therefore Barr maintains that when the concept of "history" is made mandatory for a concept of revelation, contradictions and antinomies ensue. What happens very often on his understanding is that these tensions about history cause a movement away from history as such in the "real" sense. What actually becomes central is an historical perception of life. Barr relishes pointing this out in one of his constant critics, G. E. Wright, who has, as much as any-one, insisted on revelation in history and the mighty acts of God. Barr thinks Wright's later thought moves from events to Israelite mental patterns. In any case, Barr says that Wright, while talking of the "mighty acts of God," always considered their character in naturalistic terms with a bent for archeology rather than the exegesis of the text.[207] This is significative of the weakness of the approach.

Various efforts have been made to synthesise above the dichotomy created in *Heilsgeschichte*. A recent reaction has been to reject the separation of redemptive happening and history as exemplified by the neo-orthodox BTM. Meaning is said to inhere the event so that there is no separation in essence between event and interpretation. Rather than defining revelation as the acts of God apprehended in faith, there is an attempt to reunite history and kerygma. God's act is no longer thought of as a private event or word of special significance. Rather it is the totality of Israel's progress in history. In this sense R. Rendtorff says:

> In speaking of God's activity in the history of Israel we cannot be satisfied with the alternative between two versions of history, the one produced by historical critical research and the other portrayed by the Old Testament. For Israel's history occurred both in the outer events which are customarily the object of the critical study of history *and* in the various, stratified inner events which we bring together in the concept of tradition.[208]

Traditions and history therefore cannot be divorced. Israel's real history is accessible to us only through her traditions, which are at once influenced by and a part of her history. This synthesis beyond the duality of *Heilsgeshichte* maximises history. Barr acknowl-

---

207. Ibid., pp. 747-48.
208. R. Rendtorff, in *Studien zur Theologie der alttestamentlichen Über-lieferung* (Neukirchen, 1961), p. 89, quoted by Braaten, p. 116.

edges this tradition or transmission history approach proposed by
Pannenberg and his associates. Although he does not meet it with
head-on criticism, the vision of Barr goes along another path. Rather
than maximising history and making revelation commensurate with
the totality of history, in such a way that the antinomies of the *Heilsgeschichte* method are obliterated, Barr proposes to draw other
morals from these antinomies. The lesson he learns from the short-
comings of the BTM as far as history is concerned, is that it cannot be
central and its significance must be minimised. Just as in the field
of linguistics we are obliged to recognise the arbitrary relation between thought and language, so also here we must accept a certain
arbitrariness in the relation between history (what happened) and
the representations of it. No special key moulded by Barth, Von
Rad, or Pannenberg can relativise this arbitrariness. Nor can the
"true biblical view" of history solve the problem, as no such view
exists which could tally with history in the modern sense, or command
general agreement. We must accept that history is not a biblical
category; the most we can say is that the biblical narratives are
history-like.[209] For Barr there is no special biblical language; nor is
there any special view of history.

Barr discerns ambiguity not only in the notion of history but also
in the appeal to the events specified as being revelatory. This follows
on from the ambiguities of the idea of history. If *Heilsgeschichte* is
involved in ambiguities as to the nature of the history being referred
to, it follows that questions arise about the character of true events
seen as revelatory. However, it is not with the formal question of the
possibility of redemptive events in themselves that Barr is concerned;
rather it is the legitimacy of seeing Scripture in terms of a framework
built on the foundation of events of revelation or the mighty acts of
God in history. Is it possible in interpretation to bring everything
under the aegis of revelation in history through events as a controlling category? In such a schema is there not a grave danger that
other elements will be distorted to fit in with this system of interpretation? Speaking of this, D. E. Nineham has also said: "I feel
that only by something of a *tour de force* can all the biblical literature

---

209. See *ONI*, pp. 69, 81. Also Barr's article in *JR* 56:1-17, and his comments on "Samuel" in *Hastings Dictionary of the Bible,* pp. 883-84. Further
discussion on story and history in Barr's thought in 4.2.1.

be brought under this viewpoint and I am not sure that the biblical writers themselves saw things in terms of a series of 'mighty acts of God in history' to anything like the extent that is often suggested nowadays."[210]

Barr shares the reserve of Nineham on this question: ". . . to say that . . . mighty acts are the centre of revelation in the Old Testament . . . would seem . . . incongruous with actual usage." Again, in a chapter in *ONI* Barr states that to make this notion central in interpretation involves certain anomalies.[211] In fact, the whole idea of mighty acts of God as being constitutive of revelation through history is a notion about which theology has been growing more uncertain.[212] Barr's own uncertainty stems from the unworkability of the notion in exegesis. Considerable portions of the OT corpus do not fit in with the idea of revelation in history connected with certain events. If this matrix of interpretation is made central, the problem is the devaluation of the sections of the tradition which do not fit in with it. Barr cites the prime example of the wisdom literature, but even texts which have an historical character cannot be integrated to a *salvation* history scheme in every case. Efforts to fit the creation story into a redemptive-event pattern can end up by doing violence to the way the texts speak. Barr is unconvinced by the idea that the exodus event has precedence over the creation narrative. The reverse might be more probable. The act of salvation is not the origin of historical understanding, but itself has meaning set within a framework in which events are understood:

> The "historical" acts of God make sense only because they are set within a framework of conceptions, stories and conversations which cannot be expressed by any normal use of the term "history."[213]

---

210. D. E. Nineham, "The Use of the Bible in Modern Theology," *BJRL* 52:186.

211. Barr, "Revelation," para. 6, in *Hastings Dictionary of the Bible,* cf. *ONI,* pp. 65ff.

212. See G. Kaufman in *Harvard Theological Review* 61:175-202, and *Int* 25:110; W. Pannenberg, in *Basic Questions in Theology,* I:15-80; S. M. Ogden in *JR* 43:1-20; Kelsey, op. cit., chap. 3, p. 179, n. 15; J. Peter in *SJT* 23:1-12. Perhaps the most important contribution is that of L. Gilkey, "Cosmology, Ontology and the Travail of Biblical Language," *JR* 41:194-205.

213. *ONI,* p. 18. Cf. pp. 72ff., and *New Theology* 1:64f.

If there is a starting-point in the OT, it is the creation story, and from here onwards "the story is cumulative."

Beyond this difficulty with regard to passages of the OT which do not conform to a salvation-historical model, what of those which do speak of redemptive events? Even here Barr discerns a difficulty. In this case it lies in the nature of the events spoken of. Barr thinks one of the reasons for the popularity of the "mighty acts" formula is that it permits talk about these while evading altogether the question of their reality. The discussion slides over quite easily from the miraculous character of the events in the text to an affirmation of divine providence which is quite different.[214] Barr states that the emphasis on the mighty acts of God has concealed the logical issue; the rhetoric of pulpit realism has hidden an attitude of underlying naturalism. A more viable approach to the whole question is to drop the emphasis on history and events and contextualise the events in the cumulative story of the OT. This leaves the interpreter the possibility of a more flexible position for doing justice to the OT itself and seeing the elements of the story as having variable relations to actual history.[215] Thus it might be concluded that certain elements in the OT bear relation to transcendent events, others to immanent ones and, still further, other features of the story might refer to no event at all, but function as an aspect of the narrative form. Such an approach would do more justice to the actual state of the text by breaking the monopoly of the model of "mighty acts."

In the history-like narratives of the OT the participation of God varies in the stories. This variability cannot be simply reduced to the way in which the act of God is interpreted in the theological reflexion which takes place on the act-base itself.[216] It must be understood in relation to the other elements of the tradition. The "act" or "event" cannot be isolated from the tradition and then made a hermeneutical key for the evaluation of the other elements. Even if proximity to the historical events can be shown, this is a mixed blessing, as it remains possible to confuse historical proximity and

214. Ibid., pp. 80f.
215. "Story and History in Biblical Theology," *JR* 56:3ff., 9, 10.
216. *New Theology* 1:65; *ONI*, p. 77. See also *Faith and Order* (Louvain, 1971), pp. 15ff.

theological normativity.[217]   The acts of God do not have their significance in that we can refer them to an historical reality external to the text in a direct way and in doing so constitute them an interpretative principle.   Barr rejects this referential approach which is the twin of a referentialism in linguistics.   Rather the events described in the text have their significance in the relations they sustain with the other elements in the text.   Our understanding of the mighty acts of God must be formulated in terms of these relations. The acts of God are not strictly revelatory; as part of a progressive story they are further instances in the story of God who is already known.[218]   In particular, Barr insists in all his writings on this subject on the complementarity of word and deed of God in the tradition of the OT.   "We cannot attribute to history a revelatory character, in the sense of having substantial priority over the particular divine, spoken communications with particular men, without doing violence to the way in which the biblical traditions in fact speak." If we want to speak of priority, it might well be that the word emphasis of spoken communication is more important than the tradition.[219]

In his early article on revelation through history Barr sounds quite distant from the BTM in the emphasis he places on the aspect of spoken communication in divine revelation.   Direct verbal communication is an inescapable part of the OT message.   But Biblical theology has avoided this, probably out of concern to steer far away from the reefs of propositionalism in revelation.   Barr notes that this "scandal" has been avoided by claiming the "scandalous" nature of revelation in acts.   But really this is bluff and there was nothing about the notion of acts of revelation which troubled the sensibilities of the accepted theological stance very greatly.[220]   The importance of these verbal elements is such that if acts of revelation are made the central element of the biblical witness, an inevitable distortion results.   Later, in *ONI,* Barr reworks these original insights to a much greater degree in the context of his view of the OT texts as a developing tradition.   The central place he accords here to the verbal communication can be seen as a development of the relation

217. *BMW,* p. 81; *ONI,* pp. 17f.   219. Ibid., p. 23.
218. *ONI,* p. 82.   220. *New Theology* 1:70.

between Spirit of God and people of God already proposed in the review of J. K. S. Reid's book. This point is important and prevents us from thinking that for Barr the speaking God is merely an element within the tradition. It is the precondition of the tradition. This quotation should make this clear:

> The speeches and conversations are not a commentary on, or an interpretation of, or an inference from, or a literary mode of presentation of the divine acts. Far from being any of these, the speeches and conversations are a pre-condition of the divine acts to just as great an extent as they are a consequence of them. If God had not talked with Moses . . . there would have been no divine act of deliverance.[221]

The continuity in the OT is not found in a series of acts but in the sequence of divine acts and divine words which bear relation to human acts and human words. If we want to speak of the personal nature of God, it resides precisely in this: that God meets man on his own level, that of his speech. The acts of God are meaningful because of this verbal communication.

This critique of Barr's which brings out the importance of the aspects of verbal "revelation" in the OT, destroys the idea widely held in the BTM that a distinctive biblical history can be founded on the "acts of God in history." However, before the fundamentalists start rubbing their hands about this, it must be made clear that the position Barr is advocating is not theirs. Barr is not saying that the words recorded in the Bible are the actual words which God spoke, as those who maintain verbal inspiration might think.[222] When we speak about the verbal communication of God to the prophets, we are not actually affirming what happened in the first place. Barr thinks we are simply giving an historical-literary ac-

---

221. *ONI*, p. 77. This position was also advocated by C. Westermann in *Essays in Old Testament Interpretation* (London, 1963), pp. 47ff., where he says that "one can only speak meaningfully about this intervention of God in history if it is connected with the word." See also Albrektson, op. cit., pp. 119ff.

222. See G. Vos, *Biblical Theology* (Edinburgh, 1975), pp. 6f., who applies a word-act-word structure to scriptural revelation in general. J. I. Packer has also criticised neo-orthodoxy for ignoring the inter-relatedness of word and act, *Fundamentalism and the Word of God* (London, 1958), p. 92, and *Themelios* 1:10. Also P. K. Jewett, in *Revelation and the Bible,* ed. C. Henry (Grand Rapids, 1959), pp. 48ff., and G. C. Berkouwer, *General Revelation* (Grand Rapids, 1965), p. 100.

count of the form which the text displays. If as scholars we cannot give an adequate account of these phenomena by imagining what
this verbal communication could be like, we can state how the writers
of the ancient literature understood it to be and how it formed the
patterns of their writing. A correct evaluation of the prophetic message "has to be an evaluation of the prophets as men who understood
themselves in the way in which they did understand themselves."[223]
This does not mean that we must believe the message to originate in
the same way as they thought it did. What we believe about its
precise nature may well be different. The prophets thought of it in
terms of hearing. We need not have recourse to a crude idea of
this verbal communication as implying audible noises. It is sufficient
to understand that the hearing of the prophet was of the same dis-
criminatory expression as verbal communication. Barr suggests
that this can be thought of in analogy with human prayer, which is
communication in the other direction; it does not detract from the
reality of prayer to think that this is in our own language, audible or
not. It remains evident, whatever the answer to these reflexions,
that in the OT the content of the contact with God crystallizes in
verbal expressions which are the articulate form of the way God has
related himself to his people.

In defence of this critique of revelation in history through events,
Barr says that all the same problems which apply to verbal communication apply to ideas of revelational history. It may be wondered if this defence is a little too hasty.[224] Barr has criticized the
BTM's *Heilsgeschichte* with respect to its ambiguities tied to the
idea of salvation history being real yet distinct from other history.
He has reaffirmed the importance of the element of verbal communication in Scripture. But has he escaped the antinomies he has
criticized in the case of history? The question might well be asked
in reversing Barr's defence above: Do not all the problems of reve-

---

223. *ONI*, p. 22; the remarks in this paragraph are taken from this passage
and pp. 79f.
224. G. E. Wright certainly thought so in his review of *ONI, Int* 22:85ff.
He says that the point is not that God speaks as well as acts, but it lies in the
peculiar relation of the two. An event of revelation is not happening in time
and space, but one where the Word of God is present, interpreting and giving
it significance. Wright seems to simply restate here the basic ambiguities Barr
has criticised.

lational history apply also to Barr's view of verbal communication? It seems as difficult to affirm that the communication Barr speaks about is real communication as it is to affirm the real historic nature of the mighty acts of God. We cannot, it seems, be more sure on these grounds, that the prophets did say the words of God to man than we can be sure that the events the writers wrote about were really "mighty acts of God."

The problem in both formulations, that of the BTM centred on events and that of Barr making place for verbal communication, is not really as to which element may be central, but whether there is really a revelation of God in history. The answer of the BTM regarding history seemed to be at once yes and no. It was real and yet it is not observable to critical investigation. Barr has changed the pattern a little. He wishes to speak of the communication of God not just in terms of a God-to-man movement following a revelational structure, but in terms of a communion or analogy between God and his people. This will allow for the humanity of Scripture. But this leaves us with the problem of whether the divine word in the writings is really such. Does Barr's rejection of the christological analogy and the correlation of Scripture and revelation not make it difficult for him to do justice to the "thus saith the Lord" of the texts? So Barr speaks of divine verbal communication and affirms the reality of this, but the texts are totally human. There is the same will-o'-the-wisp character in what Barr says about the words of God as there is in what the BTM says about revelation in history. The divine word is a precondition of the tradition; yet in the tradition there is no word which is divine; all are the words of man, and the divine communication functions as an element in the cumulative story. As with the events of the BTM, the communication is real and yet distinct from the text of Scripture. Was Barr's rejection of the christological analogy over-precipitous?

The final point we can bring out briefly with respect to the appeal to events as being of redemptive historical significance in the BTM, is Barr's *coup de grace*. Historical events construed as "mighty acts of God" sought to establish the unity and authority of the Bible as witness to these distinctive interventions. Nothing of the sort is accomplished. An argument about events cannot lead to the 66 books of our Bible. Much of the Bible does not report events, nor is its theology formed by events. The argument about events is not up to the conclusion it is supposed to demonstrate.[225]

This reflexion brings us to the heart of Barr's whole critique of the revelation in history approach. As a method of biblical interpretation it affirms the authority of Scripture in its witness to revelatory events, because it *supposes* the Scripture to have authority: ". . . this position seemed convincing only because most people were biased in favour of some kind of 'biblical authority' anyway."[226] In the "theology as recital" constructions the relation between the method of interpretation and the status of the Bible can be stated in this way: The Bible is to be interpreted in terms of saving events which give access to its meaning as witness to revelation; conversely, this meaning indicates the nature of biblical authority. Barr sees this circularity as imposing a foreign construction on the biblical texts; also, their various elements are lost to view because of the concentration on one aspect. In particular the verbal character of the divine communication is pushed into the background. The correlation of text and saving event in an exclusive way is as detrimental to exegesis as is the correlation of language and culture in linguistics. Both distort the sense of the texts. The evidence is thought to point to biblical authority through distinctive concepts related to history as saving. However, neither concepts behind the text nor events behind the witness can actually demonstrate the authority of Scripture in the way desired. The essence of Barr's criticism is directed against the circularity of this procedure. The biblical texts are related to revelation in history because it is assumed that history is the medium of revelation.[227] Barr criticises Von Rad for not treating the notion of *Heilsgeschichte* more critically; he lets it take complete charge in the elaboration of his theology. Barr makes no bones about this: ". . . by doing the very utmost to make *Heilsgeschichte* control everything, it may only prove the impossibility of letting *Heilsgeschichte* control anything."[228] Barr doubts that history in this sense can be validated

225. See *IDB*(S), p. 796; *BMW*, pp. 79ff.
226. *BMW*, loc. cit.
227. *ONI*, p. 65; *BMW*, pp. 86-88.
228. Review of Von Rad in ET 73:144-45. N. W. Porteous in *Probleme Biblische Theologie*, ed. H. W. Wolff (München, 1971), pp. 419f., argues that Barr has exaggerated this point although he admits that the emphasis on the acts of God is more difficult to work out than it seemed.

by the Bible as a reliable guide to the interpretation of the Bible. It is a source of weakness in exegesis as it not only exists under the compulsion of finding a uniform way of approaching Scripture, but it straitjackets the biblical material which does not conform to it and so eliminates the diversity of the Bible. The biblical evidence, says Barr, should incline us to caution. "How do we know that this history-centred apologetic is not yet another case of cultural imperialism from the West . . . guiding the Biblical material into its own patterns?"[229] Like the Hebrew-Greek distinction, revelation in history is not characteristic of biblical thinking, but rather of modern thinking.

In conclusion here, we can note the similarity of direction in Barr's critique of language and that of history. Both claim distinctiveness and unity for Scripture by appealing to factors beyond the text itself in the context of revelation. This constitutes a structure of authority for the interpretation of Scripture. Unified biblical concepts reveal the one divine mind expressed in revelation; the tissue of saving events reveals the one divine will of salvation. The reason for Barr's critique is that he doubts that the humanity of Scripture in its diversity can be accounted for within this scheme. It is his rejection of the christological analogy in terms of interpretation.

2.3.2. History and typological interpretation

Barr devotes a lengthy chapter to an examination of typology and allegory in *ONI*. It is not our intention to describe this in detail, but simply to indicate how Barr discerns typology to function in interpretation in recent Biblical theology.

Two aspects of Barr's description can be pointed to in connection with the preceding discussion, namely, the relation of typology and interpretation centred on events and the question of the unity of Scripture seen through the typology of such events. The attempt to rehabilitate typology as a method of exegesis depends on the centrality of history; the unity of Scripture achieved in this fashion supposes a common view of history running through the whole

---

229. *New Theology* 1:73. K. Stendahl, art. cit., pp. 200f., has made a similar point. The distinction Geschichte/Historie is an apologetic device, a gimmick, forced on biblical studies by faith's search for normativity.

Bible.[230] Thus typology is said to be between events rather than between persons and institutions and is to be distinguished from allegory, which is non-historical in character. Typology is therefore a valid method of exegesis in contrast with allegory; since it relies on relations of historical correspondence, it recognises the Bible's own emphasis.[231]

It should be immediately evident that Barr's critique of the idea of history has profound repercussions on the possibility of a typological method related to events. Barr doubts that a distinction can be made between typology and allegory as historical and anti-historical. This smacks of the Hebrew-Greek thought contrast. Barr expends a good deal of energy showing that allegory is not always anti-historical and that this cannot be made an ultimate distinction with typology. He suggests that the difference is not one of method with reference to history. It is rather a difference in the relation between the text and the system to which the text is related in interpretation. In the case of the NT the resultant system is the christological kerygma which shows a concentration on events. For this reason, the OT passages interpreted as typical of this resultant system will be in large measure ones which centre on events. This is necessary for the OT types to fit in with the NT situation in a really typical fashion. Two problems are raised by Barr concerning this event-typology widely used in the exegesis of the OT. The first of these touches what Barr has determined to be the ambiguity of the redemptive event, which it is difficult to separate from its context in the biblical material. Secondly the trend, as in Von Rad, to insist on typology with respect to events, not persons and institutions, does not exactly conform to the use of the NT itself where typology moves beyond this narrow category[232]

Even should it be possible to make a distinction between typology and allegory, this would not necessarily imply a particular relation

---

230. *ONI*, pp. 103ff. Barr refers to the works of Lampe, Von Rad, and Eichrodt. See D. L. Baker, *Two Testaments One Bible* (London, 1976), pp. 239ff., 292ff.

231. Ibid., pp. 108f.

232. See Von Rad's essay, "Typological Interpretation of the Old Testament," in C. Westermann, op. cit., pp. 17-39; also A. A. van Ruler's reactions in *The Christian Church and the Old Testament* (Grand Rapids, 1971), pp. 62ff.

between the OT and NT. A simple distinction could not cope adequately with the number of ways the two might be related. For Barr
the relation between the testaments must be extremely complex.
Typology based on revelation history is then too simple and unitary
to do justice to a complex phenomenon, which Barr seeks to describe.[233] Barr regards such a perspective as having other dangers.
To appeal uniquely to events for the unity of the testaments leads to
the elimination of a positive evaluation of the inter-testamental
literature.[234]

Barr's rejection of typology as a key to the interpretation of the
OT is tied up with his critique of the revelational character of events
to which the text is said to witness. Barr doubts that this synthesis
over and above the historical method can do justice to the texts themselves.[235] Above all, the effort to see relations in Scripture founded
on the divine redemptive activity is the reason why Barr has reserves
about a typological method:

> In the achievement of salvation for men we do not see the Bible
> functioning in relation to history done by God only, but also to
> history which is the history of the interpretation of the Bible.
> . . . if we speak of a history of salvation, the history of biblical
> interpretation is as much a source of continuity in that history as
> the sequence of the acts of God are; indeed it might be possible
> that the continuity shifts back and forward between the two.[236]

Typological exegesis which centres on the acts of God as typical of
the act of God in the incarnation tends to find a unity in Scripture and
a principle of interpretation based only on the consideration of the
divine activity of revelation. This neglects the human character of
the biblical interpretation of history and its variable relation with that
history.

---

233. *ONI*, pp. 134ff. It must be noted that Von Rad himself does not define
the relation in terms of typology alone. Cf. Baker, loc. cit.

234. Barr, "Le judaisme postbiblique," *Revue de Theologie et de Philosophie*
(1968), p. 212. Cf. W. Pannenberg, op. cit., pp. 28f.

235. *BMW*, p. 63.

236. *ONI*, p. 147. Van Ruler has brought out the relation between typology
and revelation in op. cit., p. 63, and particularly the relation of the ideas of
Barth (p. 67) to the recent views. Even though Barr is critical of typology
stated in the context of a revelational model, his rejection of typology is not
general, and he is prepared to consider its utility in a literary context, *ONI*,
p. 148, *BJRL* 56:23.

2.3.3. *Heilsgeschichte* and theology

The ambiguities of *Heilsgeschichte* involve not only problems in the interpretation of specific passages, but also on the more general level of articulating an OT theology. In this sphere Barr has above all related his thought to the theological work of G. Von Rad. Barr notes the difference of approach between Eichrodt and Von Rad and the claim of the latter that his theological method corresponds to the nature of the OT itself. This method seeks to give the maximum control to *Heilsgeschichte* by concentrating not on the religion of Israel but on the history of God's acts on Israel. The basis of the theological witness of the OT is in the history of salvation, and the aim of an OT theology is to re-tell this history. OT theology must have an historical form.[237] Barr has also contrasted this approach with that of G. E. Wright in that the *kerygma* is seen in various strata of texts through a literary analysis. Barr considers this method exegetically fertile for the way it relates Israel's confession of historic events to their reinterpretation in the tradition.[238]

The claim of Von Rad to have a method for theology which corresponds to the OT witness is the one which retains Barr's attention. Barr recognises the difference of Von Rad's suggestions and says "he is very conscious of having found the one and only way to do this task properly. . . ."[239] The advantages of Von Rad's method, as over against that of Eichrodt, are connected with the fact that since the theology seeks to describe Israel's witness to God's salvation it avoids the danger of turning into a description of the Israelite mental world. In addition, by concentrating on what Israel directly enunciates about Yahweh the OT theology avoids becoming a static picture or systematised theology of the "religion of Israel." Barr thinks this method is attractive in the way it integrates the historical aspect within a theological treatment without losing the historical perspective. Also this method avoids the approach to the theology of the OT through the study of concepts which are abstracted from the text. The specific character of Von Rad's perspective has been not

---

237. Barr's review in *ET* 73:142f.; cf. *JSS* 4:286-88. Also Barr's comments in *IDB*(S), p. 748, and in *The Church Quarterly* 2:1f.

238. *IDB*(S), loc. cit. In a review in *ET* Barr had compared the salvation historical perspective of Von Rad with that of Wright.

239. *ET,* loc. cit.

only a discernment of the historical character of Israel's faith, but also an effort to conform OT theological method to this as a representation of the material in its historical form.

These gratulatory remarks are followed by the "however" of Barr's reservations. Barr does not think that Von Rad has been successful in observing the canons of his own approach. In certain sections he does not seem to avoid a description of the "world of faith" of Israel. Barr's principal "however" concerns the way in which Von Rad's theology has poorly articulated its relations with dogmatics. Barr is correct in raising this question, as it is one which is often neglected by Biblical theologians.[240] Barr fears that in Von Rad's case, as with Bultmann, a concern for hermeneutics has pushed dogmatics into the background with the possibility that certain dogmatic assumptions have been built into the hermeneutic method. This, if the case, will have affected the description of Israel's traditions.

This criticism of Barr's is a worthy one, as many theologians have commented on the "two histories" in Von Rad's work, without situating the problem in this way. Barr does in fact imply that the controlling position of *Heilsgeschichte* in Von Rad suggests such an integration of a dogmatic assumption into the hermeneutical method. Von Rad claims too much for the principle of *Heilsgeschichte,* which cannot integrate the OT materials successfully in the theology on its own terms. Barr gives some examples of this as showing how a prejudice in favour of this picture has influenced some of the critical work.[241] This leaves the possibility open for a distortion of the exegesis in order to bring about the relation of certain texts with the principle of *Heilsgeschichte.* At this stage in his development, this is the point which concerns Barr. He does not here show a great deal of interest in the problems relative to the history involved, but concentrates on the way in which this principle is taken as ultimate in interpretation.[242]

---

240. Barr refers to Jacob, who has been more precise in stating relations with dogmatics, ibid., p. 144. Elsewhere Barr has made other criticisms of Jacob in a similar vein, particularly with respect to his use of the word *history*. *JSS* 5:167f.

241. Ibid., p. 145.

242. This review was published in 1962, the earlier one in *JSS* in 1959. Both show the preoccupation with the distortion of textual evidence found in *SBL* which must have been in formation at the same time.

Barr remarks the "authoritarian tone" of Von Rad's work, the lack of dialogue with other scholars, the almost total rejection of the principle of selection of materials from the OT, the confidence that *Heilsgeschichte* can iron out all problems, and Von Rad's naive belief that he is simply letting the OT speak for itself. He is not convinced by this last claim. It needs to assume the validity of form and tradition criticism to make it work and to suppose the efficacy of the controlling principle of *Heilsgeschichte*. Barr reproaches Von Rad for not discussing criteria which might be generally accepted but "simply telling us what is right."[243] This review more than any of Barr's early works reveals most clearly the anti-authoritarian character of Barr's critique of interpretation. However, it is not a simple case of iconoclasm; Barr wants to make clear how the text of Scripture can be interpreted in such a way as to do justice to its specific character. In this case *Heilsgeschichte* is deemed to be a controlling principle. This does not work out. Barr thinks that more exegesis of individual passages is needed rather than the writing of "theologies," and more attention needs to be given to the logic of the subject.[244] Later, as we have seen, Barr criticises the idea of salvation history itself. Von Rad's definitions of what constituted salvation history are artificial. Barr notes that Von Rad fails to tell us how this history relates to the version of history in the OT: ". . . in what sense is it revelation in history if the confession is not to events as they took place?" This leaves us with an enormous range of problems.[245] The history of the OT debate has indicated that Barr was not far off the mark in his early criticisms.

J. M. Robinson has resumed the problem well in his review of the question of history. Attempts have been made to give "the past history of the Old Testament [relevance] by distilling from it a con-

---

243. Ibid.,
244. Ibid., p. 146.
245. *IDB*(S), p. 748; cf. *ONI*, pp. 66ff. Also on the problem of the "two" histories, D G. Spriggs, op. cit., pp. 34ff.; Baker, op. cit., 274ff., 291ff.; J. M. Robinson, in *The Old Testament and the Christian Faith*, ed. B. W. Anderson (London, 1964), pp. 124ff.; G. Wenham, in *History, Criticism and Faith*, ed. C. Brown (London, 1976), pp. 17ff.; Braaten, op. cit., pp. 108ff.; B. J. Oosterhoff, *Feit of Interpretatie* (Kampen, 1967), passim; C. Henry, *God, Revelation and Authority* (Waco, 1976), II:268ff.; R. de Vaux, *The Bible and the Ancient Near East* (London, 1972), pp. 56ff., and W. Eichrodt, *Theology of the Old Testament* (London, 1961), I:512ff.

cept which ultimately replaces that history instead of preserving it."[246] This is basically what Barr is getting at in his criticisms of history and language. When the text of Scripture, in its words and the events it recounts, is no longer taken as inspired revelation, the need is to go behind the text to find concepts and "saving events" which are connected with revelation, giving a key to the thought and action of God. These elements become henceforth criteria in the interpretation of other elements of the text. Typology of events and concepts is a consequence of thinking of Scripture in connection with revelation as a God-to-man movement.[247] The danger for interpretation is the need to find a unity and an authority in the patterns of Scripture in the expression of the revelatory movement. This need was endemic in the BTM.

2.4. *Presuppositions and the freedom of interpretation*

The common denominator in these criticisms of interpretation is that the textual evidence has been evaluated in the light of certain untested assumptions. The exegete has found in Scripture what he supposed to be there in the first place. This is detrimental for the free-speaking of the text in its diversity. Perhaps the most telling criticism that Barr makes of the BTM is that in it exegesis has been controlled by certain assumptions. It claims not to be influenced by considerations external to biblical ones, yet in certain cases works in a way which characterises idealism. This factor motivates a lengthy discussion of the question in *ONI*.

The peculiarity of the BTM was that in its stance concerning interpretation it denied the possibility of a complete objectivity. A purely historical, neutral reading of the Bible was thought impossible. All interpretation involves presuppositions. This claim, Barr thinks, involved the BTM in a dilemma: The choice lies between presuppositions coming from the Bible itself and the possibility that they are determined prior to the study of the Bible. In the first case what is presupposed should be obvious from the study of the text; the second possibility bears the implication that Biblical theology is not an independent discipline, but works with assumptions derived from

---

246. J. M. Robinson, art. cit., p. 129.
247. C. Evans, *Is Holy Scripture Christian?* (London, 1971), pp. 32f.

some other source. These approaches Barr calls "purism" and "externalism" as indicating not persons or schools of thought but certain types of argument.[248] Barr is aware of the dangers involved in discussing presuppositions in this way. He regards it as being unethical as well as ruinous for scholarship to judge opinions not for what they say, but on the basis of what their presuppositions are determined to be.[249] His discussion of these two approaches raises doubts as to whether it is useful to refer to presuppositions when evaluating theological statements. The weakness of both is that they place the presuppositional question in a controlling position in interpretation; both involve a search for valid interpretative methods in conformity with the presupposition. Barr states his desire to avoid these emphases which are involved in both purism and externalism.[250]

Barr's critique of presuppositions seems to be motivated by the function of such assumptions in the purism of the BTM. The contrast between Hebrew and Greek mentalities is a purist position which involves the interpreter in the search of "biblical" concepts and "biblical" history and affirms the unity of these as distinctive of revelation. The assumption is that the internalist stance of purism will protect against the introduction of error in interpretation. This idea is misguided, for Barr recalls that danger can come just as much from within the tradition as from the exterior; independence from philosophy is no guarantee of theological correctness. If the linguistic or theological arguments are incorrect, no amount of presuppositionalism will make them right. Barr adduces a purist argument against purism: Opposition against the underlying philosophy of life of a people such as in the BTM is uncharacteristic of the Bible.[251]

The fundamental perspective of purism involves greater dangers for the understanding of Scripture than externalism. It implies the threat of complacency associated with exclusivism. Purism for many theologians has a strong pull of inner consistency. If a view of theology as dependent on revelation is proposed, it is attractive to think

---

248. *ONI*, pp. 171ff.; *IDB*(S), p. 108. A way of avoiding the dilemma of purism and externalism is the distinction between what Scripture meant and what it means, made by K. Stendahl. See section 3.4.3.
249. *Biblica* 49:384-85.
250. *ONI*, p. 172.
251. Ibid., p. 58; cf. p. 173 and *BWT*, p. 206.

of this theology not only as putting the Bible at the centre but also as finding a way of interpretation in the Bible. So it is that presuppositions are thought of as controlling the quality of interpretation of the Bible. This is particularly so in purism, where to identify an alien assumption is to throw discredit on the proposed exegesis. Evaluation takes place not on the level of what the work is saying but in terms of its presuppositions. Barr thinks this sort of attitude has been prevalent as an answer to the ideal of objectivity. It has therefore been thought that, since the Bible is theological, it is necessary to have certain presuppositions conform to the nature of the object of exegesis in order to avoid misunderstanding. The claim of objectivity is impossible as it ignores the nature of Scripture itself. Pushed to extremes, anti-objectivism can itself imply a claim of rightness in interpretation.

Barr thinks it essential to criticise the purist position since it seems difficult to maintain an externalist position with consistency. Such theologies tend to be philosophical theologies in which the basic externalist presuppositional position is hard to hold together with the biblical content. Barr says Bultmann illustrates the case well. In adopting an existentialist philosophy of pre-understanding in the line of Heidegger, his position seems to involve an externalist presupposition. However, his equation of the philosophy of Heidegger and the NT view of life involves him in a purist type of argument. Barr sees two levels of criticism. The historical parallelism involves an exegetical backlash as the identity of the philosophical and the theological positions must be demonstrated exegetically; hence the demythologising process. Philosophically, it is doubtful to take a system of thought and regard it as the right one. This assumption of philosophical correctness is an authoritarian imposition of a philosophical position on the NT, and is similar to the authoritarianism of the traditional dogmatics. This illustrates the difficulty of doing justice to the interpretation of Scripture on an externalist presupposition. The difficulty is one of establishing the contact between the accepted assumption and the content of Scripture.[252]

---

252. Ibid., pp. 174ff. See also *BMW*, pp. 41, 50, 105. In these passages Barr proposes that Bultmann's position about biblical authority is quite traditional in that he assumes that a demythologized NT will provide content for the Christian faith today. Rightly interpreted the NT is still the locus through

The problem Barr is concerned with here is that of the amount of objectivity which might be achieved in the exegetical process. Given the current reaction against neutrality in exegesis and the emphasis on involvement in interpretation, what is the possibility of understanding what the text really means? The danger is particularly great in the purist approach of the BTM, where the method is held to be constituted in the light of the character of the Scripture itself, and where the results can consequently be claimed to tally with the true teaching of Scripture. In other terms, the objectivity in exegesis is achieved by the abandonment of the objectivity of the interpreter in favour of biblical presuppositions. To claim another form of objectivity than that constituted by the scriptural presupposition is to fall prey to a subjectivity influenced by conditions other than the biblical ones.

Barr advances a number of arguments relative to the usefulness of talking about presuppositions in interpretation. As well as the fact that there is a lack of clarity about what the term "presupposition" means, as a model for evaluating the processes of exegesis the presuppositional one is a bad one. The reason for this is simply that within biblical study exegetical argument works inductively with the evidence involved and not on deduction from presuppositions. It is the sense the argument makes of the evidence that furnishes the criteria for evaluating it, not the presuppositions of the exegete. Added to this, where certain presuppositions have been criticised as "external" by purist definition, there have simply been no alternative "Christian" presuppositions to replace the ones criticised. The purist principle argues, regarding "Christian" presuppositions, in a way that overlooks the revolution of historical criticism. Biblical studies no longer share the same methods as theology. The criteria used

---

which revelation is mediated, and can be normative for theology today. On the OT see *Int* 25:30ff., where Barr points out certain elements in Bultmann's thought which make the OT similarly indispensable. These remarks of Barr's seem to me to be to a certain extent *formally* correct. However, as far as material content is concerned this traditionalism is a lot less apparent. Even if there are presuppositions at play in a similar way in Bultmann and in the traditional dogmatics, the nature of these assumptions will in fact influence the content of what is interpreted in different ways. The question is whether preunderstanding in the Bultmannian sense does not narrow the text in a way the traditional dogmatics never did. See also Braaten, op. cit., chap. 6; Berkouwer, *Holy Scripture* (Grand Rapids, 1975), p. 118.

are not theological ones; rather (as we saw in the introduction to our first section) Barr contends that the meta-language of biblical studies is in contact with a number of other disciplines and not merely theology. So it would be a mistake to think that a theology could be evaluated on the biblical nature of its presuppositions. If we accept that there is no biblical view of language or of time as such, there are no specifically biblical presuppositions to cover these fields.

Thus purism has tended to minimise both the effects of the rise of historical criticism, and the fact that it has placed exegesis and theology in a different relation. Purist theologies have problems making room for historical criticism, and many of the presuppositional concerns of such theologies are no longer relevant. Barr seeks to clinch his point with the line that if purism rejects philosophy and external influences in one sense, in another it relies on them in the refutation of externalism. Here it plunders the treasure trove of historical deviations to find labels for opposing opposite tendencies. Barr sees this as an abuse of the power of knowledge which is made to support an accepted view.[253]

Barr must be given a great deal of credit for this lucid discussion of the presupposition question. It is, in modern theology, quite a unique presentation, and one which is stated in terms of great simplicity because of its rejection of a good deal of high-flown but often impenetrable verbiage.[254] Whether Barr's rejection of theological presuppositions as related to exegesis in the way he describes is acceptable, is quite another matter. Barr himself would seem to assume here that the meta-language of biblical studies is not theology alone but is formed by contact with other disciplines. How would it be possible to prove the validity of this justification? Has Barr actually attempted such a demonstration? This does not appear to be the case. Barr seems to accept as a matter of course that this is so. But the question is whether theology, even when it uses methods in exegesis borrowed from extra-theological disciplines, simply appropriates

---

253. These arguments against presuppositions are found in *ONI*, pp. 178-84.

254. Barr criticises the "esoteric language and frenetic air of the hermeneutical discussion" and the "dreadful incoherence" in English of the philosophical bases borrowed from Heidegger. *IDB*(S), p. 107. Such plain speaking is obviously in accord with the ethics of theological discussion praised by Barr in *ONI*, loc. cit.

these without reflexion on their own theological significance. Can theology assume that these methods have their sense in themselves, or should it not seek the theological meaning of such procedures?

If Barr's analysis of purism is correct in a great measure, the question remains here as to whether this presupposition of Barr's about the separation of theology and biblical studies can be theologically justified. Can it just be accepted as a matter of *common sense?* To this question we will have to return later. For the present, in the context of our on-going reflexion on the christological analogy, the matter can be formulated in another way. Where the correlation of the human and divine were accepted with respect to Scripture, exegesis invariably followed a theological model. The human element was thought to be in service to the divine. The methods of exegesis served in this perspective. The goal was one of stating the normative content of revelation, and the methods of exegesis had little independence from this goal. Historical criticism, as Barr says, may have changed this. The text is no longer interpreted in terms of a human analogy with the divine mind. However, when the analogy of revelation is replaced, what does it mean for theology to interpret the Bible in terms of the analogy of modern consciousness?[255]

The question raised in this paragraph has also cropped up in another context, in the debate with fundamentalism. Here Barr uses many hard words about this position of extreme purism and the way it accuses non-conservative positions of being governed by presuppositions. The fundamentalists, on the other side, accept only the facts of the Bible. Barr calls this "irresponsible carping" and a lot more:

> . . . the argument about presuppositions, as used by conservatives, is mere hypocrisy: they will accept any presuppositions, so long as they seem to lead to a conservative result.[256]

Barr argues back at length against fundamentalism's accusations about criticism being influenced by evolutionism and Hegelianism. Barr states that fundamentalism is against academic freedom. This makes an awful lot of remonstrance, and accusations such as these

---

255. The expression is borrowed from E. P. Clowney, *Preaching and Biblical Theology* (London, 1962), p. 13.
256. *F,* pp. 145ff., 152.

are difficult to handle. Perhaps two things could be noted here. Firstly, even if the examples Barr quotes from fundamentalist argument are doubtful ones, this does not remove the exactness of the fundamentalist criticism that nonconservative interpretation is governed by presuppositions. Leaving aside this word—Barr comments on its ambiguity—what the conservatives seem to be rejecting is the way non-biblical assumptions enter into interpretation. It is difficult to see how Barr can argue against this, as he expressly states that present methods of interpretation are formed non-theologically. Barr still can argue that the fundamentalist position is wrong, but he can hardly reject totally their opinion that critical interpretation is governed by presuppositions.

In the second place, it might be doubted that there is the large measure of hypocrisy which Barr claims in fundamentalism. Can Barr show a conservative scholar who says he accepts only facts, but then takes any presupposition to get a conservative result? Barr may be straining our credibility beyond its reasonable limits by asking us to accept this. I tend to think that the problem fundamentalists have with critical biblical studies is related to what seems to them to be an *uncritical* acceptance of modern hypotheses in interpretation. These are thought to distort the biblical "facts." Once again here we may register some disappointment at the way Barr passes over the question of the supposed immediate legitimacy of methods from other disciplines being used in exegesis.

Some remarks about Barr's own view of presuppositions may adequately conclude this discussion. Barr steers clear of the idea that the interpreter can approach the text with an empty mind; there is no neutrality on this level. This does not mean that exegesis need be governed by theological presuppositions. Barr thinks he can fruitfully speak of what the exegete knows before his work of interpretation. This prior knowledge is not a logically coercive element which guides exegesis. It is temporally prior, a fact which exists already at the point where the work of exegesis begins. In interpretation, what is accomplished is the reassessment of the meaning we have previously accepted. The breaking of the logically coercive character of presuppositions in interpretation opens the process of understanding to new insights and favours new theological constructions. Interpretation avoids being traditional by recognising the temporal priority of a tradition of interpretation and reappraising this meaning. Here there is a need for what Barr calls a "relative objectivity," in the discrimination between various possible interpretations. For interpretation does not work *from* text *to* one interpretation, but *with* the text to discriminate *between* a number of interpretations. This relative objectivity does not measure the interpretation by the canon of a presupposition to evaluate correctness. The interpretation is lined up with the evidence of the text. Traditional interpretations of the text are therefore held to have a hypothetical status until they are confirmed afresh. Interpretation is then a reappropriation of the meaning of the text which is open to a new depth of understanding.

Through these suggestions Barr seeks to move the evaluation of interpretation out of the domain of presuppositional analysis into the context of a relation between an old and a new understanding within a tradition. A relative objectivity is secured by the fact that within this tradition the text of Scripture constitutes the reference point by which the validity of the interpretation proposed is measured. It is clear that in this proposition the fundamental approach to exegesis is seen as being implied in the relation which Scripture sustains to the on-going tradition. The way in which this relation is construed is formative of the conception of the function of exegesis. As the acceptability of Barr's reflexions on interpretation depend basically on his understanding of this relation, we shall return to this question after having described Barr's view of Scripture in general. This is to say that even with his formulation of relative objectivity Barr does not escape in questions of exegetical method certain "presuppositions" about the relation of Scripture and tradition.[257]

Barr's rejection of purism and its stress on the use of theological presuppositions in interpretation is typical of his general critique of interpretative methods in the BTM. Purism claims to have the "right" presuppositions, these being theological ones. Interpretation is thus confined in this narrow orthodox circle of right interpretations based on right presuppositions: ". . . learning is a movement within a conceptual area already defined and so controlled."[258]   It

---

257. See section 4.2.4. Barr's position discussed in this paragraph is developed in *ONI*, pp. 184ff.
258. Ibid., p. 196.

is difficult to make a real place for historical criticism, and it is para-
doxical that purism does not, like fundamentalism, reject this. Traditional beliefs become an obstacle to the accurate evaluation of
linguistic phenomena. The assumptions of the unity and distinctiveness of Scripture are regulative for exegesis, which becomes a way
of getting the required answers from the Bible. Thus the interests
of dogmatics come to dominate exegesis. Barr's critique is in its
essence a rejection of the imposition of certain presuppositions on
the text of Scripture as regulative of what the text might teach. The
refusal of such authoritarian procedure is the constant element in the
various criticisms Barr makes of interpretation.

2.5. *Fundamentalism: Tradition-conditioned interpretation*

Barr's work on fundamentalism must be considered as an application of some of these criticisms to this particular case of conservatism.
Fundamentalism, like the BTM, though in a more extreme way, presupposes the traditional view it holds to be true of Scripture, and
proceeds to back up this position with arguments from the text itself.
Fundamentalism is typical of interpretation being dominated by the
needs of confirming traditional views. Barr seeks an understanding of
the way fundamentalism works, not for intellectual reasons alone, but
because of the broader church problem it poses and also because
theologically it bedevils other alternatives by its very presence and influence in the theological situation.[259] Barr develops two lines of
argument by which he seeks to show how fundamentalist interpretation works. Firstly, he indicates that the intellectual structure of
fundamentalism, and in particular its methods of interpretation, are
conditioned by its religious attitudes. Fundamentalists:

> . . . do not believe in the inspiration of scripture purely and solely
> on the grounds that such inspiration is asserted within the Bible.
> . . . they believe in it because of a multitude of reasons: because
> it fits in with their experience as evangelicals. . . .

> . . . the doctrinal pattern of Warfield's doctrine of inspiration
> . . . is quite in agreement with the normal social pattern of per-
> sonal experience within fundamentalism.

The conservative apologist sees all the evidence as showing that

---

259. *F*, pp. 8f., 343; *BMW*, pp. 11f.

the Bible is "right." He sees it this way, quite sincerely, and for one simple reason: that he has been a fundamentalist all along.

The fundamentalist believes all these things in any case, because believing in them fits into the total character of his religion.[260]

The second theme is the other side of the coin: The doctrines of inerrancy and infallibility of the Scripture are used as bulwarks for the traditional opinion. "The fundamentalist position about infallibility and inerrancy of the Bible is an attempt to prevent this tradition from being damaged through modes of interpretation that might make the Bible mean something else."[261] Thus a perfect circularity closes off a hermetic system of doctrines from distortion. We shall now discuss these themes in a little more detail.

2.5.1.   Scripture in the fundamentalist tradition

Barr's presentation of fundamentalism as tradition-dominated religion seems far from what is generally thought about it and from the picture the fundamentalists present of themselves. For it is thought that fundamentalism relies on the authority of Scripture alone and excludes other authorities. It affirms a distaste for tradition, which is opposed to Scripture. Barr denies that this is the reality of the case. It is not because of the Scripture that the fundamentalist believes in the *sola Scripture,* nor can his views regarding the attributes of Scripture be confirmed from it. These views are canons of the fundamentalist tradition.[262]   Barr argues then that not the *sola Scrip-*

---

260. These quotations are from *F,* pp. 260f., 266f., 341, 75.
261. Ibid., p. 37.
262. Barr's basic thesis about fundamentalism seems to owe a little to E. R. Sandeen's *The Roots of Fundamentalism* (Chicago, 1970). Fundamentalism, which Sandeen associates with millenarianism in America, took over a view of inspiration tied to an inerrant Scripture as source of divine truth. This idea was maintained, not because this was the intention of the writers, but because of the climate of the day. This belief in a divine document could not be abandoned without the faith being denied as well. Cf. pp. 108-112. Questions may be raised as to the accuracy of this as an historical judgment, but also as to the way Barr seems to generalise this as a theological criticism of fundamentalism as such. Even Barr's use of the term "fundamentalist" is suspect on this level, as it runs the risk of generalising judgments about restricted views to a larger body of opinion. See on this, Packer, op. cit., pp. 30ff.; D. F. Wells and J. D. Woodbridge, *The Evangelicals: What They Believe, Who They Are, Where They Are Changing* (Grand Rapids, 1975), pp. 148ff., 160 n. 10, 196ff. W. Hordern, in *New Di-*

tura but the very extreme character of *tradition* is the most common characteristic of fundamentalism. Between the Bible and the religious tradition of this conservatism there exists a reciprocal relation. Tradition is not verified by the Bible but taken as the true interpretation of the Bible. This is the paradox of fundamentalism, for this is not recognised to be a form of traditionalism at all. Just as in the BTM the implicit idealism of the interpretational approach is not seen, so in this more extreme conservatism its adepts are oblivious to their rank traditionalism.[263] As far as Barr is concerned this traditionalism is plain to see. The dogmatic positions of the fundamentalists are never placed in parenthesis for the purpose of exegetical study. This eliminates give and take between the text and the doctrines of fundamentalism, which are merely confirmed from the text. All methods are good for getting the text to support the traditional "doctrines" of fundamentalism. The appeal to the authority of Scripture is only deceptive; the real authority here is that of the tradition itself. This pretention of the authority of Scripture which really hides another authority is a blank cheque to unlimited distortion of the sense of the text. This explains the harshness of Barr's polemic and the hostility which surfaces at many places in his book.[264]

Barr compares this traditionalism with other like religious forms. The fundamentalist attitude to the Bible is therefore compared with that of some Roman Catholics to the Virgin. As a traditional symbol, attributes of perfection are referred to the Bible. In the tradition it occupies the place of a venerated symbol which transcends human imperfections and scrutiny. It is the tangible sacred reality.[265] In this setting the use of the Bible becomes ritualistic. Scripture becomes a kind of Christian myth which supports a certain form of culture

rections in *Theology Today* (London, 1968), vol. I, *The New Face of Conservatism.*

263. *ONI*, pp. 202ff.; *F*, pp. 36ff. Barr is not the first to take this line. C. H. Dodd has insisted on the traditional character of fundamentalist belief in *The Authority of the Bible* (London, 1960), pp. 21ff.; R. Prenter, in *Biblical Authority for Today,* ed. A. Richardson and W. Schweitzer (London, 1951), says that fundamentalism deriving from traditionalism makes the Scripture a tradition.

264. See the review in *ET* 88:353-55. This hostility is surely not conducive to the understanding Barr speaks of.

265. *ONI*, p. 204; *F*, p. 36.

which is fundamentalistic. Thus the form rather than the reality of the Bible authority is used to support the tradition.[266] It is for reasons of form that the fundamentalist believes about Scripture what he does. He does not believe in inspiration or any other doctrine because the Bible materially teaches this, but because such a belief fits in with the religious experience of his tradition. The doctrines of Scripture and doctrines about Scripture undergo, in this conservative matrix, a severe formalisation. Thus the doctrines inherited from previous orthodoxy are conserved formally in the tradition as tests of orthodoxy.[267] Their status is that of presuppositions in the tradition.

In fundamentalism, thinks Barr, external and objective authority for religion is sought in the authority of the Bible as the supreme religious symbol. Faith in Christ cannot be considered as well grounded unless the principle of biblical authority is conceded. Objectivity for fundamentalism, according to Barr, comes from the Bible as inspired and inerrant. The Bible becomes the criterion standing outside human processes which lends objectivity to the religious beliefs of the tradition. But this is not real objectivity as pretended. All these affirmations about the Bible do is give sanction to the collective ego by supporting the evangelical view and creating a world where there is no room for the possibility of other ideas. So fundamentalism as a religion separates itself from other forms of Christianity.[268]

2.5.2. Tradition and interpretation

Fundamentalist interpretation uses Scripture in a purely formal way to authorise its tradition. In this tradition Scripture is considered to be the infallible word of God, and this point is called on to defend the fundamentalist doctrines, which supposedly are established in recognition of this fact. Thus to maintain his system the fundamentalist depends on showing that the Scripture is inerrant. In this way he can protect the tradition from interpretations which seem to make

---

266. *F*, p. 11.
267. Ibid., pp. 175-79.
268. Ibid., pp. 312ff. Following P. Berger and T. Luckmann, Barr speaks of the reification of the Bible as the element which lends objectivity to the fundamentalist outlook.

the Bible say something other than the view of fundamentalism. For this reason Barr argues that the specificity of fundamentalist interpretation is not that it is *literal,* but that it seeks to avoid the idea that there might be an error in the Scripture. Fundamentalists twist from literal to symbolic ways of interpretation in order to maintain inerrancy.[269] Barr calls the idea of inerrancy the "architechtonic control" of fundamentalist exegesis which exists at the start of the interpretative process as a control on the result. Inerrancy is the dominant feature of fundamentalist exegesis, acting as guide in the search for understanding the text. Barr thinks that what is important is that a correspondence between the biblical materials and external reality should be established, as then the truth of the Bible can be claimed. Moreover, in this way the truth of fundamentalist religion is corroborated in unimpeachable fashion. Barr concludes that there is really no principle at play in fundamentalist interpretation other than that of following the dictates of its tradition.[270] This consideration reveals that in one sense fundamentalism is essentially recent in its approach to truth. For it cannot see beyond the possibility of truth as factual correspondence to external reality. The idea that the Bible can be "proved true" corresponds well with secular credulity; it satisfies the modern appetite, which demands a true book. The claim to the exactitude of Bible truth is really not a religious claim at all. It is one which corresponds to a secular view of truth which is "scientific and materialistic."[271]

Therefore, although fundamentalism claims that its view of the inerrancy of Scripture is in conformity with the tradition of the

---

269. *BMW,* pp. 168ff.; *F,* pp. 40ff., 248f. Barr contends that it is the critical exegesis of modern scholarship that takes the Bible text literally. He parts company on this point with a good many other critics of fundamentalism who seem to have followed each other in insisting on literal interpretation. See M. Barth, *Conversation with the Bible* (New York, 1964), pp. 113ff.; J. K. S. Reid, *The Authority of Scripture* (London, 1957), pp. 27, 160; A. G. Hebert, *The Authority of the Old Testament* (London, 1947), pp. 98f., and *Fundamentalism and the Church of God* (London, 1957), pp. 95ff. D. Patte, op. cit., pp. 7f., and D. E. Nineham, *The Use and Abuse of the Bible* (London, 1976), chap. 2; cf. p. 58 (on traditional interpretation in general).

270. *F,* pp. 49ff.

271. *F,* p. 139. This argument is frequently made against the doctrine of inerrancy in fundamentalism. See Reid, op. cit., pp. 160f.; A. Richardson, in *The Cambridge History of the Bible,* ed. S. L. Greenslade (1963), III:306ff.; Hebert, *Fundamentalism and the Church of God,* p. 98.

church, and that it is the true successor of the fathers and the Reformers, it is really a modern view originating in the last century. By the time its view of inerrancy was worked out, historical critical methods were already widely accepted. For a fundamentalist to claim the inerrancy of Scripture against these methods and their results is to take quite a different stance from that of one claiming inerrancy prior to their existence. Fundamentalism, in setting inerrancy in the face of the revolution of historical understanding, is deliberately regressive, in a way that its predecessors were not in making similar claims. Theology in "the pre-critical period was not animated by the anti-critical animus and passion of modern conservative theology."[272] Alan Richardson claims that the doctrines of fundamentalism are "new" in the twentieth century, as to hold them has a different meaning today. He sees the fundamentalist lineage in reformed scholasticism and modern science. Others have made the same claim. D. Patte claims that fundamentalism is essentially modern in its consideration of history. The Bible must be historical to be true, and if it is true the nature of this truth is historical. A. Hebert put it with a little more pungency: "Fundamentalism may claim the Bible for its mother, but it has Hobbes for its father."[273] These and similar views tend to play on the supposed irony of the situation of fundamentalism in which the claim to the authority of the Bible is woven together with a view of truth which is modern.

In line with these judgments, Barr thinks that fundamentalism, with its emphasis on the inerrancy of Scripture, differs from orthodoxies of the past. It is fossilised, fragmented, and essentially apologetic. In its interpretation of Scripture it seeks essentially to defend certain "doctrines" as true. These are emptied of their content and function as test-cases in the polemic relations fundamentalism sustains with other theological options. Two procedures in particular are characteristic of the way the claim to inerrancy works in conservative theology. Harmonisation seeks to sustain inerrancy in showing how two or more accounts of a single event can correspond with what happened without contradiction. If this correspondence cannot be established, then the principle of inerrancy is destroyed. Harmonisation is thus essential for inerrancy. Barr thinks that the

272. *F.*, p. 174.
273. Patte, op. cit., p. 7; Hebert, *The Authority of the Old Testament,* p. 95.

conservative interpreters tie themselves in knots in seeking such harmonies. Behind such an attempt is the thought that ultimately the Bible has God as its real author and must within the variety of the human authors reveal the unity of the divine mind. This is very much the case with dispensationalism, which is interested in deciphering the future divine plan in the Bible.[274] Barr considers the same sort of procedure to be operative where miracles are discussed. Just as fundamentalism juggles with different accounts of the same event to produce a harmony and avoid contradiction, so, in the case of miracle, it switches back and forth in interpretation in order to assure correspondence. It resists reducing the miracle to a non-event of literary character, but is quite prepared to explain miracles by natural causes when this can be done. When it is not possible to explain the event by merely natural causes, so establishing correspondence and inerrancy, inerrancy is sought in a switch to the supernatural. If inerrancy can be maintained in a naturalistic way, so much the better; otherwise the supernatural will do what the natural cannot achieve.[275]

The second characteristic of the way the claim to inerrancy works in conservative scholarship is through what Barr names "maximal conservatism."[276] This indicates the approach by which fundamentalist biblical scholarship abandons a simply dogmatic affirmation of the dogmas of its tradition and seeks to affirm these by using the historical methods of modern biblical scholarship. To validate the dogmatic positions of conservatism it selects in the field of modern historical scholarship the most conservative solutions. The results are valued for the support they lend to the tradition. Barr thinks this to be typical of the neglect of methods of interpretation in fundamentalism, which do not really matter as long as the results are right ones. Thus Barr thinks that J. A. T. Robinson is incorrect in thinking his work on *Redating the New Testament* will bring no comfort to conservatives as its results are achieved with the use of the historical method. Barr rejoins: ". . . the position of fundamentalists . . . is not that critical tools must not be used, but that when they are used they will produce conservative and traditional results; so long

---

274. *F*, pp. 55ff. On dispensationalism, pp. 190ff.
275. *F*, chap. 8.
276. *F*, pp. 85ff., 124ff., 232ff.

as conservative results are produced, they do not care what sort of tools are used, indeed the more critical the better so far as that goes."[277] Barr is basically affirming that for conservatism the end justifies the means, even if as far as means go, the fundamentalist shares in the same thought-world as the liberal scholar. As far as methods go, many fundamentalist "maximal conservatives" share the same critical methodology as their liberal counterparts, but because of their dogmatic suppositions, manoeuvre to achieve the most conservative results possible from the evidence. So even where a dogmatic argument for inerrancy is avoided, this still influences the solutions that are sought in interpretation. In this case also interpretation is still controlled by considerations of the inerrancy of Scripture and the need to protect the fundamentalist tradition by maintaining this doctrine.

One final point must be made here concerning the fundamentalist tradition and interpretation. Fundamentalism sees a reciprocity between inerrancy in interpretation and inerrancy in Scripture. If it aims at interpreting the Scripture as inerrant, this is because the Scripture declares itself to be inerrant.[278] This is the fundamentalist's version of the Reformers' *sacra Scriptura sui ipsius interpres*. Once again on this question Barr contends there is a great formalisation of the former theological approach. The narrowness of fundamentalism is seen in that it founds the inerrancy of the Bible on one factor: The Scripture affirms itself to be inerrant. Barr contrasts this stance with that of the Westminster Confession, which speaks of "many reasons" for which we believe in the authority of Scripture, the most effective being the "inward work of the Holy Spirit."[279] Barr attributes this difference to the hardening of the doctrine of Scripture under the influence of the Princeton theology in its reaction to the development of criticism in the last century. The difference is particularly notable in the work of C. Hodge and B. B. Warfield, the forerunners of today's fundamentalists, who take their notion of the inspiration and inerrancy of the Bible from the Bible itself and raise it to the level of a presupposition. Scripture is inerrant because divinely inspired, and this must be accepted for the reason that this is the witness of

277. *F*, p. 158.
278. Barr formulates this in two passages in *F*, pp. 72-84, 260-99.
279. *F*, p. 261; cf. The Westminster Confession of Faith, I. V.

Scripture. To claim there is an error in Scripture is to deny inspiration and refuse the witness of the Scripture to its own identity. So
in contrast with the "many reasons" that Barr sees in the Westminster
Confession this constitutes a narrowing to one reason for believing
the Scripture. This reference to the self-witness of Scripture functions in fundamentalism as another way of defending the tradition
and assuring that interpretation will not produce other meanings.

Perhaps it is worth pausing at this point to ask the question whether
Barr's contrast between Princeton theologians and the Confession
is correct. His distinction seems to rely on the description given by
E. R. Sandeen, although this is not specifically acknowledged. Sandeen sees a difference between Princeton and the Confession, but
also between the Princeton men themselves which signifies a hardening of the position over inerrancy and inspiration.[280] J. H. Gerstner
has severely criticised Sandeen's argument at just this point. Gerstner
thinks that Sandeen confuses the proof or evidence that the Bible is
the Word of God and the persuasion of acceptance of this evidence.
This shows inability "to understand the positions involved."[281] In
the same place Gerstner claims there to be no essential difference
between Hodge and the Confession:

> The Confession recognizes the necessity of evidence prior to
> persuasion and so states; Hodge recognizes the necessity of evi-
> dence prior to persuasion and so states. Sandeen fixes on the
> persuasion element in the Confession and the evidence element in
> Hodge and, of course, notes a difference.

It would seem to me that Barr's section on this makes the confusion
even worse, if that is possible, for he seems to put the "multiple
reasons" the "incomparable excellencies" of the Confession on the
same level as the inward work of the Spirit in actual conviction. Barr
does not seem to observe the difference between "excellencies" and
the inward work of the Spirit, yet the construction of the article would
seem to make this quite plain.[282] Through this confusion of the

---

280. E. R. Sandeen, op. cit., pp. 118ff.; cf. *F*, pp. 261ff.
281. J. H. Gerstner, in *God's Inerrant Word,* ed. J. W. Montgomery (Minneapolis, 1974), pp. 117f.
282. Westminster Confession, I. V.; cf. *F*, p. 262, second paragraph. The
article is constructed around the relative apposition between the objective
evidences of the divinity of Scripture and our subjective conviction concerning
them, which is the work of the Spirit. "We may be moved and induced . . . ;

"entire perfection" of Scripture as evidence of its nature, and the witness of the Spirit, Barr overlooks the fact that the "multiple reasons" of the Confession are in fact founded on the "one reason" Barr rejects in the fundamentalists. These reasons are related to the fact that God is said to be author of Scripture, which is therefore inspired and to be received as his Word (I.IV and I.II of the Confession). Because the Scripture has this character, the Spirit witnesses "by and with the Word." The Spirit witnesses in conformity with what the Scripture really is in an objective way as inspired Word of salvation. Barr does not seem to have caught a view of the distinction between the perfections of Scripture as evidence of the conviction of the Spirit's witness, or of their interrelatedness. The Spirit convinces us "by and with" these evidences which are really in the Scriptures. Included in these is not only the message of salvation, but also the fact that Scripture witnesses to its own inspiration. It is little wonder, in the light of this confusion, that Barr cannot understand why Warfield should want to demonstrate historically that Scripture is inspired and inerrant and concludes that Warfield's argument has "an air of almost deliberate fantasy about it."[283]

Barr thinks that fundamentalism formalises away the multiple reasons for believing in Scripture which *include* the witness of the Spirit and replaces these with one reason, namely, the explicit declaration of the text. This can also be related to what he considers to be the search for objectivity in this tradition. This self-witness is considered to be the objective absolute standard of truth outside the reach of human subjectivity.[284] Barr contrasts other Christian groups who find objectivity in Christ and not in the Bible. For fundamentalists, "Faith in Christ cannot be considered grounded in objectivity unless the principle of biblical authority is fully conceded."[285] It is not

---

yet notwithstanding . . . " (italics mine). Warfield had no difficulty seeing this. Commenting on this passage, he refers what the Confession says about the inner witness of the Spirit here to the way it speaks of faith (XIV.I). See his "The Westminster Doctrine of Holy Scripture," *Presbyterian and Reformed Review* (1893):582-655, reprinted in B. B. Warfield, *The Westminster Assembly and Its Work* (Cherry Hill, N. J., 1972), pp. 210ff. See also J. Rogers, *Scripture in the Westminster Confession* (Grand Rapids, 1967), pp. 314ff.

283. *F*, p. 265.
284. *F*, pp. 311f.
285. *F*, p. 312.

really possible to rely on Christ as a person except where this faith is objectively grounded in inspiration and inerrancy. What this amounts to is that unless we accept the witness of the Scripture as to its inspiration and inerrancy, we cannot interpret it in such a way as to ground our faith in Christ objectively. For the fundamentalist, Barr thinks, faith in Christ relies on the discernment of what the nature of Scripture is. Right interpretation is determined by one's attitude to the self-witness of Scripture.

Yet it may well be doubted if Barr has gotten this quite straight. Perhaps the formalism does not come from the fundamentalist, but from the interpretation Barr makes of his position. For Barr speaks as though in fundamentalism the two sorts of witness are isolated and the Bible itself is "reified" as an authority beyond human subjectivity. However, it is doubtful whether in fundamentalism there has been this separation of the witness of Scripture to itself and the inner witness of the Spirit. No one could find a better "fundamentalist" than John Murray. Yet he says:

> The internal testimony of the Spirit is the necessary complement to the witness Scripture inherently bears to its plenary inspiration. The two pillars of true faith in Scripture as God's Word are the objective witness and the internal testimony.

Or, to quote one of Barr's old fundamentalist friends, J. I. Packer:

> The ground of faith, then, is the recognition of man's word as God's word. How does this come about? Through the work of the Holy Spirit . . . so that man "sees" and knows the divine source and spiritual meaning of the message that confronts him.[286]

---

286. J. Murray, in *The Infallible Word,* ed. N. B. Stonehouse and P. Woolley (Philadelphia, 1946), p. 53, and Packer, op. cit., p. 118. When Barr contrasts faith in Christ and faith in the Bible in fundamentalism and other forms of Christianity, he is ignoring the basic methodology of a book such as J. W. Wenham's *Christ and the Bible* (London, 1972), which argues that belief in the Bible comes from faith in Christ, pp. 9f. Barr knows this argument well and criticises it at length (*F,* pp. 74ff.). Yet if he wants to make this criticism of the way fundamentalists appeal to faith in Scripture on the basis of faith in Christ, he must accept that they do recognize a faith in Christ apart from a complete understanding of Scripture and abandon his insistence on the "one reason" for which they accept the Bible. Elsewhere Barr seeks to explain the difference between the "one reason" and the fact that inspiration fits in with tradition as a whole and is accepted for broader reasons, as a difference be-

What has in fact happened in Barr's analysis is that he has separated the two witnesses which in fundamentalist theology are thought of as being continuous. Because of the formalisation he introduces in his evaluation, he regards the fundamentalist theologian's belief that Scripture is inspired "because it says so" as an effort to found the truth of Scripture in something objective which can be demonstrated to be so. Such a demonstration of the inerrancy of Scripture supports the tradition of fundamentalism as being the right one. In interpretation the appeal to letting the Scripture speak for itself is an artifice in the defence of the tradition.

Is Barr's evaluation of fundamentalist interpretation correct? It is difficult to give a simple reply to such a question owing to the multiplicity of criticisms Barr makes in his discussion. Nevertheless something can be said in conclusion about his two main lines of approach. Firstly, it may be asked whether Barr's view of the function of Scripture in fundamentalist tradition is a correct analysis. The opinion he emits that the Scripture is used in the tradition to uphold its accepted views is no doubt correct of certain quarters. But whether it is more widespread in fundamentalism as opposed to any other form of Christianity, as Barr would seem to indicate, is another matter. This problem is rather a general one for any religious text taken as authority. Our temptation is always to read it in the context of certain accepted ideas. As far as this is concerned, the performance of the liberal tradition would be at least as susceptible on this score as the fundamentalist one. If it is healthy to relativise Barr's criticism on this point, this does not altogether answer our question about fundamentalism. What is more disquieting about Barr's criticism is that he is essentially accusing the fundamentalists of a form of blindness; they appeal to Scripture as authority but really it is the tradition which is the authority and the Bible is used to support the doctrines of fundamentalism. Yet in their writings certain fundamentalists affirm the contrary. J. I. Packer, for example, speaks of the over-simplification which forgets that our theological construction of biblical authority must be open for challenge from the biblical texts: ". . . theological theories have to be tested by seeing whether

---

tween the instructed hierarchy and the general laity (p. 261). This distinction is tenuous, as Barr himself recognizes the importance of the "Bible-teacher" in fundamentalism.

they fit all the relevant biblical data."[287] Is Packer just pulling the
wool over our eyes with this? Has not the evangelical thought tried
to define the character of Scripture not only with reference to its
self-identification, but also in consideration of the phenomena of the
Bible? It is true that because of their particular conception of the
organic nature of inspiration evangelical theologians have often
affirmed that the phenomena of Scripture should be seen in continuity with the witness of Scripture to its own identity. However,
this is very different from making a simply formal statement about
Scripture to fit in with the requirements of a tradition.[288] We may well
wonder whether the relation between Scripture and the fundamentalist
tradition is as Barr presents it, or if a certain analysis has not been
too widely generalised as a key for the interpretation of fundamentalism.

The second point which might be raised is as to whether Barr's
analysis of inerrancy, as an attempt in fundamentalist interpretation
to protect the tradition, is well founded. Are the procedures such
as the search for correspondence in the case of events, the attempted
"rationalisation" of miracles, harmonisation, and the appeal to the
self-witness of Scripture really efforts to protect the tradition? Perhaps Barr's analysis of this matter is over-facile and he assumes the
case in his polemic. The matter may be approached in another way.
Karl Popper has spoken of two attitudes towards tradition.[289] One
is an uncritical attitude, of which Popper says that not knowing we
are acting under the influence of tradition, we cannot help accepting
the tradition uncritically. The other possibility is a critical attitude
toward tradition in which it is accepted, rejected, or a compromise
is sought. A critical acceptance of tradition frees us from the taboo
of the tradition. Now if Barr thinks that fundamentalists accept their

287. J. I. Packer, in *Themelios* 1:7. See also R. Nicole, "Induction and
Deduction with Reference to Inspiration," in *Soli Deo Gloria*, Festschrift for
J. H. Gerstner, ed. R. C. Sproul (Nutley, N. J., 1976).
288. See C. Van Til, *The Doctrine of Scripture* (Philadelphia, 1967), pp.
26f. Van Til claims that it is the specific character of orthodoxy in the Reformed sense that it interprets the phenomena of Scripture in the light of the
Scripture's self-witness. This is not to impose a tradition on Scripture, but
is the academic attitude required with respect to the nature of the object
studied.
289. K. R. Popper, *Conjectures and Refutations* (London, 1963), p. 122.

religion uncritically, then there would be no need at all for them to speak of inerrancy. The tradition would be right anyway, and there would be no need to demonstrate it. Such protection as could be afforded by inerrancy would be unnecessary. However, if the acceptance of his religious tradition by the fundamentalist is of a critical nature, then this is a critical decision and in this case, even though inerrancy may function in the tradition, it will not *necessarily* do so to protect the tradition. This seems to me to be the equivalent of what Packer is saying when he affirms that theological constructions are open to questions from the text. The relation is one of mutual interrogation.

The assumption that inerrancy functions in a particular way is a possible source of weakness in Barr's discussion of fundamentalist interpretation. It is as though he cannot get beyond the idea that inerrancy must back up the tradition and ask the question of the nature of the relation between the two or what sort of tradition is involved. So, for instance, when Barr refers to the interpretation of Genesis 1 by fundamentalists, he notes a change from literal to non-literal interpretation. Barr seems to assume that this change has taken place in order to maintain an error-free Bible in the face of modern science. However, there is no discussion of the criteria which might be used to demonstrate that the change of interpretation was for this reason, nor any consideration of the possibility that the change might be for reasons other than those assumed by Barr.[290] Does M. G. Kline interpret Genesis in such a way as to avoid clashing with science; or may it be for literary reasons?

Whether this criticism of Barr is correct or not is not the main point of this discussion. This has been to show how things are in fundamentalism for Barr. It is obvious that he is concerned here with what he considers severe distortion of the text of Scripture in the context of an authoritarian religious tradition. The pressure to interpret the Scripture in accord with certain presuppositions is stronger here than in the BTM. In the case of fundamentalism it is no longer a case of distinctive biblical concepts or the *Heilsgeschichte* which are used to point to the unity and authority of the Bible. The distinctiveness is found in the inerrancy of Scripture. The use of this doctrine

---

290. *F*, pp. 40ff.

as a principle of interpretation, according to Barr, creates a multiple sclerosis of the text in a tradition-bound setting.

In all the criticisms about interpretation in this section, Barr sees the problems as arising in the context of the association between the human word of the Bible and revelation. Patterns taken to be revelatory are imposed on the text with too great facility. Barr's critique is an argument in favour of the liberty of the exegete, who stands before the text as before a totally human word.

3

Analysis of the Present Status of the Bible

The earlier theological work of James Barr on the interpretation of the Bible has stigmatised certain fundamental inadequacies of modern practice. The exegetical distortions which Barr seeks to underline in his analyses cannot be kept for long within the confines of methodological considerations. The exegetical problem leads on quite naturally to the theological question. Faced with what is discerned to be faulty interpretation, the question of what kind of theology sponsors this exegesis soon surfaces.

Without drawing hard and fast distinctions, it can be said that chronologically the discussion concerning interpretative method occupies Barr in the earlier part of his work, while in the more recent stage there is a deeper discussion of questions concerning the present status of the Bible. The questions concerning interpretation are related to a criticism of the christological analogy as a model for understanding Scripture. The criticisms of Barr are consequent upon his desire to find the meaning of Scripture as a human document, expressive of the faith of Israel and the church. Just as his interpretative critique reveals the breakdown of correct interpretation on the basis of a revelational analogy, so his later works, dealing more directly with the status of the Scripture itself, point to the same crisis in the doctrine of the Bible. From this follows Barr's own attempt to reformulate the doctrine in a way which will correspond to the requirements of a "free" interpretation. In his interpretative critique Barr argues against the imposition of authoritarian notions on the exegesis of the text; here we shall examine his evaluation of authority-centred notions of Scripture itself. Both the interpretation and the notion of Scripture itself must be revised. What is no longer useful must be removed, but elements in the traditional approaches can also be transformed in the new setting of a more acceptable view of the status of Scripture.

Part of the problem with the BTM can be located, as we have seen, in the ambiguities of its evaluation of language in the sphere of a concept of revelation. Tension exists between its use of orthodox biblical language and its cosmology and ontology which are modern.[1] To say that God speaks and acts does not signify for the modern man the signs and wonders of the "old time religion." To put it another way, the theology of revelation in the BTM was not adequate to sustain this use of language. It was never really clear where revelation in fact lay: in the story as related in the texts, in the history itself, or in the traditions which culminated in the texts.[2] Various forms of criticism had made the relation between revelation and the inspiration of the text very tenuous indeed. In any case, Biblical theology had tended to steer well clear of theories which would identify the text too closely with revelation. The problem of relating the linguistic units of the text with the doctrine of revelation held cannot be glossed over by the use of christocentric slogans. Rather than being helpful, Barr maintains that these are a source of embarrassment.[3]

Barr's linguistic critique touches this whole delicate area of the relation of language and the revelation which it is thought to indicate. "A valid Biblical theology," says Barr, "can be built only upon the *statements* of the Bible and not on the *words* of the Bible."[4] The special revelatory content that the BTM saw in units of language cannot be reconciled with normal linguistic usage. Since Biblical theology lacked a doctrine of inspiration in a verbal sense, coherence was sought in a revelatory structure based on the relation of concept and event.[5] The question is, then, if the distortions of linguistic evidence are not indicative of a problem in the formulation of the doctrine of revelation itself.

The theological critique of Barr, examined in this chapter, would

---

1. L. B. Gilkey, "Cosmology, Ontology and the Travail of Biblical Language," *JR* 41:194ff., 204.
2. Barr, "Story and History in Biblical Theology," *JR* 56:16.
3. *ONI*, pp. 99f.
4. *BWT*, p. 154.
5. *SBL*, p. 271, n. 2.

suggest that the central place assigned to revelation in neo-orthodoxy both in interpretation and in the doctrine of Scripture was not matched by an equal clarity in the formulation of what revelation was. The authority of Scripture as revelation was assumed in theological statement. Barr thinks this to be well illustrated in the leader of the neo-orthodox revival of biblical authority, Karl Barth. Barr states that in his thought the Bible and revelation are linked on the basis of a presupposition. "Yet," remarks Barr, "Barth does not provide a preliminary exegetical establishment of what might, on grounds of biblical evidence, form the contours of the concept of revelation."[6]

Revelation dogmatically presupposed, in this or similar senses, gave an impetus in the BTM to attain and sustain in theological statement the unity and authority of the Bible. Barr's criticism of these two notions as stated in his analysis of the interpretation of biblical language and *Heilsgeschichte* contains an implicit criticism of the current notion of revelation. This criticism becomes explicit when Barr surveys the various notions used to describe the status of the Bible.

3.1. *The crisis of the notion of the authority of Scripture*

3.1.1. The impossibility of assuming the authority of the Bible

Traditionally, the authority of the Bible has been a leading concept used to indicate the special status of the Bible. Very often this authority has been related formally to the inspiration of the Scriptures, or alternately to the message of Scripture in a material sense. In contrast with such views, which seek to locate the authority of the Bible in its origin or its content, Barr contends that this authority cannot be taken for granted, but has to be shown on sufficient grounds. The major works in OT theology, and perhaps those in NT theology, have been too optimistic about the normative status of their formulations; they generally assumed that the Bible had authority and took it for granted that in making the sense of the Bible plain, the authority inherent in Scripture would appear in the process. Barr adds: ". . . our present situation, however, makes it impossible to proceed very

---

6. *ONI,* pp. 90f.

far on these assumptions."[7] There are two levels on which this authority can no longer be taken for granted—that of the authority belonging to Scripture itself, and that of the way Scripture functions to authorise theological formulations.[8]

Barr thinks that the authority of the Bible in neo-orthodoxy was axiomatic. Efforts were made to explain this authority, "but there was no room for discussion of whether or not it was so."[9] Of Barr's own particular field, the OT, he states that theology provided a framework within which the OT could be seen as "an entirety which was deeply impressive and authoritative."[10] Concentric with this notion of the authority of the Bible was the understanding that the Bible was normative as a unity. The authority of Scripture in neo-orthodoxy was localised in the redemptive events or perhaps more frequently in the theology of the Bible, which was thought to be normative for later times. However, not only is the construal of biblical authority in terms of event tenuous, but to point to the theology of the Bible also has its problems. Two weaknesses in this respect lie in the diversities of the theology of Scripture itself, but also in that the continuities between Scripture and postscriptural theology make it difficult to maintain a clear distinction between the theology of Scripture and other theologies.[11]

Beyond neo-orthodoxy is the claim of evangelical conservatism to the authority of Scripture, which is the mainstay of fundamentalist theology. By contrast with other theologies, in fundamentalism this authority is tied to the infallibility and inerrancy of the Bible. This formulation is the "one question" of theology for fundamentalism and its narrow definition of authority in these terms places it in polemical relations with other sorts of theology, even those which are also glad to make some sort of reference to the authority of Scripture.[12]

---

7. "Trends and Prospects in Biblical Theology," *JTS* 25:282.
8. "Scripture, Authority of," *IDB*(S), p. 795.
9. "The Old Testament and the New Crisis of Biblical Authority," *Int* 25:25.
10. Ibid., p. 26.
11. *IDB*(S), p. 796. Barr is probably thinking in this context of the intertestamental literature. See in particular his lecture, "Judaism—Its Continuity with the Bible" (Montefiore Memorial Lecture, Southampton University, 1968) and "Le judaisme postbiblique," *Revue de Theologie et de Philosophie* (1968): 209-17.
12. *F,* p. 163.

Between these two positions, the neo-orthodox BTM and the fundamentalist conservatism there has not been much love lost. Barr thinks that the polemical relations should not hide a certain similarity concerning the question of authority. Even if neo-orthodox Biblical theology was critical of fundamentalism's propositionalism, in this rejection it only fell back on something comparable in its formulation of authoritative biblical concepts or authoritative propositions about events. On the other hand, if fundamentalism stressed revealed truths, in practice it remained a very event-centred religion with a strong adherence to personal encounter with Jesus Christ. Both options have the same sort of authority problem, and for this reason the criticisms of fundamentalism from within the BTM were confused and ambiguous.[13]

Before continuing to describe Barr's statement of the nature of the crisis of biblical authority, perhaps a word of reflexion could be interjected at this point. Barr's criticism of the BTM and of fundamentalism in their approach to authority is that they accept the authority of the Bible in an unreflecting way as a *sine qua non* for theology. This will not do, thinks Barr, in today's climate. His statement is rather misleading on this point, I think, as theologians working within a conservative position, such as that of fundamentalism or the BTM, probably do not assume the authority of Scripture *de facto,* but do so on grounds they deem sufficient as warrant for their theological position. In so far as the facticity of the situation is concerned, Barr is probably quite right in saying that the authority of Scripture can no longer be taken for granted. However, this does not mean necessarily that where authority is still spoken of, this represents an assumption that it fits the situation. One might be very aware of the anti-authoritarian spirit of the age and yet still find within a theological system sufficient warrant for talking of the authority of the Bible. Even if this authority is "axiomatic," surely it cannot be reduced to a simple assumption; the nature of the authority would refer to a certain theological structure which would indicate that Scripture's authority could justifiably be considered in axiomatic fashion. Certain of Barr's statements seem to tend to oversimplification on this subject, and it may be that the question of

---

13. Ibid., p. 226.

authority is more complicated with respect to Scripture than meets the eye. Even if there is widespread doubt as to the authority of the Bible, this does not mean that where the Bible is still thought to be authority this view (to use the expression of J. D. Smart) "is usually dependent upon a naïveté that perpetuates a childish, unquestioning attitude."[14]

3.1.2. The *present* crisis of authority

Over against the traditional views of the authority of Scripture which tend to accept that authority is inherent in Scripture on the basis of its properties, Barr points to the present crisis of the concept of authority in recent years. This crisis is one which is *new,* and theology simply cannot continue as before, but must face this situation. The traditional formulations of biblical authority which connect it with revelation or inspiration do not really get us very far in seeing how this authority applies to the present situation.[15] Early on in his theological activity Barr shows a consciousness of these problems:

> . . . the authority of Scripture is interlocked with our conceptions of other realities—the true method of exegesis, the best way to test doctrine against a criterion, the nature of the Church, the problem of the Canon, the submission of life ethically to the Bible . . . Biblical authority . . . is definable not only by relation to the ultimate Word of God but by reference to other instances which claim some kind of authority.[16]

This means that the authority of Scripture does not exist as an extrinsic principle which is independent of the normed objects and is brought to bear on them as standard, but that it is rather of intrinsic nature. The Bible exists as part of the living organism of God's people and its authority cannot be experienced in a formal way apart from the faith and life of the church.[17] Its authority is *relational* and is perceived in continuity with other co-existing factors. Thus at a later date Barr develops the same point as in his earlier article and insists on authority as a relational and hierarchical concept which

---

14. J. D. Smart, *The Strange Silence of the Bible in the Church* (London, 1970), p. 90.

15. Cf. D. Kelsey, *JR* 48:1ff.

16. Barr, review of Reid, *SJT* 11:93.

17. H. H. Farmer proposes this distinction between intrinsic and extrinsic authority in his article on the subject in *The Interpreter's Bible,* ed. G. A. Buttrick (New York/Nashville, 1952–1957), I:4.

relates the various sources of authority to each other and orders them in their relation to us. The concepts of authority and norm indicate relations between the Bible and ourselves and between the Bible and other sources which influence us.[18] As D. E. Nineham states: ". . . the problem of biblical authority cannot be cleared up in isolation. . . . [It] is inextricably connected with other authorities. . . ."[19]

The implications of such a relational formulation of the authority of the Bible cannot be avoided for long. It would appear first of all that Scripture is not thought of as the sole authority for Christian faith and practice in the sense of being an ultimate authority placed over against other factors to judge their value. The relational character of biblical authority means that even if the authority of Scripture is granted a more preponderant place than other authorities, the difference is only a relative one. There is no absolute qualitative distinction between Scripture and other factors based, as in the traditional theology of Protestantism, on the character of Scripture as revelation. This relational approach to authority fits in, then, with Barr's criticism of conceiving of the Bible in the context of a God-to-man movement of revelation. To say the authority of Scripture is to be considered relationally is already to have adopted an implicit stance as to the nature of revelation. In the case of Barr's view of the authority of Scripture, the criticism of the traditional view of authority as a property of Scripture is a correlate of his vision of the Scripture as the expression of the relation of the people and the Spirit of God crystallised in the tradition. Many factors enter into the development of the tradition beside the element of divine communication. Similarly, in considering the authority of Scripture, this cannot be merely stated as a consequence of revelation, but in an hierarchical way. Thus it is not a case of opposing the authority of Scripture as revelation and other authorities as being merely human, the one being above criticism and the other being subject to it. It is a question, to use Barr's terminology, of *how far* the recognition of biblical authority is "relative to the nature of other kinds of authority which may also be recognized in the Church."[20]

---

18. Barr, *BMW*, p. 23. Cf. "The Authority of the Bible," *ER* 21:148.
19. D. E. Nineham, "Wherein Lies the Authority of the Bible?," in L. Hodgson, *On the Authority of the Bible* (London, 1960), pp. 95, 96.
20. *ER*, loc. cit.

This view of the authority of Scripture as relationally defined in continuity with other instances of authority means that it is also possible to consider Scripture as not being an authority at all. Barr has touched upon this in various places in his work, and has indicated two aspects of this problem. The authority of the Scripture can be questioned on the basis of a reflexion concerning the difficulty of applying the biblical authority of the past to the much-altered situation of the present. Alternatively the authority of Scripture as relational becomes susceptible in a situation where the notion of authority itself is no longer accepted without question.

Concerning the first of these questionings with regard to authority, it is obviously Barr's subject, the OT, which is the most open to doubt. If there is an unease with regard to the idea of the authority of the OT today, Barr thinks that this is not a modern Marcionite reaction.[21] Doubts about the authority of the OT today belong to an intellectual setting other than one which is characterised by world-denying philosophies. The present doubt about the OT stems rather, thinks Barr, from a world-affirmation of a modern kind. The OT seems remote from the kind of decisions which the man of today is required to make. The problem is that of seeing why the OT should be in any necessary way authoritative for the situations in which the church finds itself today. As Barr puts it: ". . . the critical question is no longer 'What was said back then?' but 'What should we say now?' "[22] Nor is it a question of denying the authority of the OT in order to affirm the NT. If the OT is more remote, the difference with the NT is only quantitative. The NT is also very often remote from issues of present concern, and its authority is only apparently more real than that of the OT. The crisis of authority is one which touches the whole Bible: Its roots lie in the present. Today our situation seems remote from the biblical ethos in general. This temporal distance raises not only the problem of concepts of the Bible which are foreign to modern worldviews outside the *kerygma,* but also creates difficulties in connection with the central message itself and our understanding of it in the present situation.[23] Barr discerns

---

21. See on this J. Bright, *The Authority of the Old Testament* (London, 1967), pp. 60-79. Bright thinks a Marcionite strain has existed in Christian theology down to the present. Barr's discussion is in *Int* 25:32ff.
22. *Int* 25:36.
23. *ER* 21:147.

a loss of authority-centredness and a greater accent on relevance, especially in certain quarters:

> In Bultmann the question is between Old and New Testaments; in America, it may well be . . . between the Bible and no Bible in the actual life of the churches, whatever the confessions and creeds may say.[24]

When the question of relevance becomes central in the reflexion on the authority of Scripture, the traditional arguments for the authority of the OT cease to be convincing. To say that the OT is necessary for understanding the NT carries little weight when the NT itself is considered remote. Even if this is so, it does not constitute the OT as an authority, particularly if the authority of the NT is doubted. The authority of the OT was accepted in the context of a structure in which authority defined the nature of the general framework of the religion. When this central understanding of authority recedes, the authority of a part such as the OT, which depended on the general framework, is no longer self-evident.

Beyond the difficulty of bridge-building between the remote past and the need for present relevance, the second, more radical, problem for the authority of the Bible lies in the dispensing with the notion of authority itself. There is a movement in Barr's thought in this respect. In 1965 Barr shows himself concerned with the situation in which the self-assertion of the church in search of relevance tends to obscure biblical guidance.[25] In *ONI* he is quite critical of those who see the answer to the problem of church proclamation in terms of relevant communication. The quest for relevance can even be a disobedient self-assertion on the part of the church.[26] In the post-1968 era the tone of Barr's remarks changes as the consequences of a general questioning concerning authority filter into theological discussion. In 1971 Barr reflects that the problem for the Bible does not lie in an antipathy for the Bible *per se,* but derives from the crisis of authority itself. Our notion of authority is changing; authority is no longer accorded *a priori,* but is conceded where it actually "proves itself as such." This changed attitude makes it

---

24. "Taking the Cue from Bultmann," *Int* 19:219.
25. Ibid., p. 220.
26. *ONI,* pp. 192ff.

difficult to "assert biblical authority in a general way."[27] The passing away of the framework of authority leads Barr to wonder whether the idea of authority can continue to be "the central concept with which we should operate" or whether theology should not seek a structure which is not authority-centred, of which faith, rather than *a* faith is the outcome.[28]

This is very different from the views of the authority of Scripture held traditionally in the church or even from those sponsored by the BTM, which admitted that to speak of authority was contrary to the spirit of the age, yet necessary as ultimately only the Bible can indicate whether a theology is Christian or not.[29] In his critique Barr swings from a view of the authority of Scripture in a relational context to a position which questions the notion of authority itself. He is quite aware of a certain irony in this situation, as the notion of the authority of Scripture itself is a lot more flexible than other ways of speaking of the Bible which demand an affirmation of its infallibility. To speak of the authority of Scripture in no way implied perfection but allowed elbow-room as to the nature of the origin of Scripture. As affirmed in the recent protestant neo-orthodoxy the ground of authority was ultimately in God himself, and the authority of Scripture is derivative by reason of its special standing in relation to God's manifestations.[30] The vagueness the concept implied was in fact not authoritarian but liberating.[31]

Perhaps this vagueness was also something of a burden. Anyone who has tried to reconcile the following two statements by Alan Richardson on biblical authority, found within a quarter of a page,

---

27. *ER* 21:138; *Int* 25:38f.; *BMW*, pp. 23f.

28. *Int*, loc. cit.; *BMW*, p. 129.

29. J. Bright, op. cit., pp. 20, 30.

30. A standard affirmation of neo-orthodoxy was to the effect that the authority of Scripture was grounded in the authority of God. See, for example, H. H. Rowley, *From Moses to Qumran* (London, 1963), pp. 9ff.; J. W. C. Wand, *The Authority of the Scriptures* (London, 1949), pp. 107ff.; H. Cunliffe-Jones, *The Authority of the Biblical Revelation* (London, 1945), pp. 18ff.; J. K. S. Reid, *The Authority of Scripture* (London, 1957), p. 28; A. Richardson, *Christian Apologetics* (London, 1947), pp. 220f.; R. Abba, *The Nature and Authority of the Bible* (London, 1958). See also the commentary of H. D. McDonald, in *Theories of Revelation* (London, 1963), pp. 320ff.

31. On the advantages of "authority" see *BMW*, pp. 23ff., and *IDB(S)*, p. 795.

in his *Christian Apologetics* might realise the problem with neo-orthodoxy:

> Thus, for Christians the authority of the Bible is the authority of God Himself. . . . Today the belief of Christians concerning the inspiration and authority of the Bible is based upon an induction from the empirical facts both historical and contemporary.[32]

The problem with this and such statements seems to lie in the disparity between the ground of authority and the method proposed to establish belief in this authority. Surely Richardson is not proposing that we establish the authority of God by a human induction! If the authority of the Bible is that of God, it is inherent in the Bible, the case of an *a priori*. On the other hand, if it is founded inductively by historical and contemporary considerations, it is a relational concept. How the two positions can be held together is not clear. What does seem clear is that this relational concept of authority in neo-orthodoxy was only possible in a context which supposed that the induction from the continuity of Scripture and other factors of authority would yield a view of the authority of Scripture.

Barr's critique of this supposed authority, which is concretised in his doubt about the notion of authority itself, is carried over from his reflexions on interpretation, where he has sought with some consistency to demonstrate the authoritarian character of certain procedures. Now, as far as the doctrine of Scripture is concerned, Barr debunks the supposition of authority inherent in itself the nature of the Bible. Just as there are no special "revelational" concepts or *Heilsgeschichte* which can be established behind the text as controlling notions in interpretations, so also there is no "revelational" authority of the Bible which can confer on it an absolute status. Scripture does not escape, as a human document, from the relativities of history, and in any case not from the relativising of authorities in our day.

3.1.3. Authority or relativism?

The problems associated with the notion of authority itself raise the alternative of considering the Bible in a status-less way. Why should the Bible be considered normative at all? The present se-

---

32. A. Richardson, op. cit., ad. loc.

ductiveness of this possibility, which Barr calls "cultural relativism," leads him to devote a chapter in *BMW* to this theme. He discerns its basic appeal as lying in an apprehension of the fundamental absurdity of an authority concept as such. In recent theology it has been largely D. E. Nineham who has pointed to this fact.[33] Some passages of the Bible have no meaning for today; to pretend otherwise leads to absurd debates. We must see, insists Nineham, that a good deal of the Bible is a result of non-theological factors. It is dependent on cultural factors, and in our time it may have another meaning, or none at all. The biblical materials cannot be divorced from the cultural assumptions of their writers. Today, however, our assumptions are different ones, and although this does not mean our culture is necessarily superior in all ways, this does mean it is different. Such considerations motivate a less dogmatic attitude about the authority of the Bible. Would it not in fact be better to jettison the dogma of normativity altogether?[34]

This gives the lie to the theological problem of the status of Scripture not in terms of divine and human, but in terms of ancient and modern. Instead of pretending that Scripture is always contemporary, as authority-centred theologies have often done on the grounds of the changelessness of divine and human nature, or that the chasm is overcome in the eternal present of existential encounter,[35] cultural relativism proposes a Christianity in the present. The weight of decision lies in the present; we can no longer rely on past authorities but must say what it means now to be a Christian or a Christian church. Whether this present affirmation centres on the individual or on the church, it must be made on the basis of present cultural considerations. This, Barr comments, is more radical than a hermeneutical discussion which tries to translate the authority into present terms, but supposes there to be something normative about it all along.[36]

---

33. See D. E. Nineham, "The Use of the Bible in Modern Theology," *BJRL* 52:178-99, and *The Use and Abuse of the Bible* (London, 1976), chap. 5.

34. Nineham, art. cit., pp. 180ff., 192ff. Cf. *BMW*, pp. 38ff.

35. Cf. J. D. Smart, op cit., chap. 9.

36. *BMW*, pp. 41-43. Another work offering a similar perspective on cultural relativism is that of C. D. Batson, J. C. Beker, and W. M. Clark, *Commitment without Ideology* (London, 1973), which illustrates the thesis that ideology is not determinative of religious life, but derivative from it. In this case experience relativises the Bible.

In the case of cultural relativism, the distinctions between past and present relativise the message of the Bible which is no longer thought of as having a universal application. The meaning of the writing is not to be distilled from its cultural context to give an eternal truth, as was attempted in past orthodoxies; these assumed that what the text meant and what it means are equivalent. This put exegetes in the position not only of saying what the Bible said in terms of its own culture, but also of showing in some way how what it said was right. To suppose thus that the Bible must give a message having authority for today not only ignores that its message is relative to a certain cultural form which is not ours, but also passes over the accidental nature of the formation of the Bible. Arguments à la Cullmann about apostolicity which confer an order and an authority such as that of salvation history on the Bible are responsible for "one would not say dishonesty . . . but for fantasy."[37]

Cultural relativism proposes a more relaxed attitude toward the Bible rather than one which makes appeals to its authority as founded on salvation history, apostolicity, or inspiration. In the words of C. Evans, it suggests that the church might be better off saying, "Here are these books; we believe them to be profitable books from experience; they have come out of the lives of some of us, and they express something of our faith; they are all we have, let us get on with it."[38]

Even though Barr is critical of theologies which are tightly authoritarian in their structure and see the authority of the Bible in terms of the deduction of a unified message from Scripture, he distances himself from the position of cultural relativism. While recognising the attraction of its arguments, he is not convinced by the totality. Some of its perspectives are proper, such as its protest against nonsensical authority, but its overall usefulness is to be doubted.[39] Barr raises several points of objection. If the insistence on the church saying what it believes in the present is correct, this does not by-pass the question of how the church does this; it just moves the issue back

---

37. C. Evans, *Is 'Holy Scripture' Christian?* (London, 1971), p. 30; for his attack on the apostolic reason for the acceptance of the NT see pp. 24ff.

38. *Ibid.*, p. 17. Cf. Nineham, op. cit., pp. 193, 196, on accepting the "pastness" of the Bible without immediately asking what it says.

39. *BMW,* pp. 44f. In spite of his doubt, Barr does not feel he can formulate adequate counter-arguments against the position.

one stage. In addition, is Christianity as passive as cultural relativism would suggest in relation to the prevailing culture? Would its view of incapsulation in a culture not tend to ignore continuities and the memory of cultural traditions? Finally, cultural relativism's arguments about the character of human nature seem to be assumptions. Such considerations dissuade Barr from a wider acceptance of these arguments. He believes this radicalism tends ultimately to self-damaging irrationalism, since the elements important to the church in stating her present belief are subject to the same relativising as the traditional view of the Bible.[40] When cultural relativism does away with the authority of the Bible, it is caught in the net of its own relativism and therefore can hardly command the ultimate commitment of those it addresses. H. E. W. Turner has brought this point out with incisiveness in his criticism of the position of Nineham:

> The argument that the quest for norms is a false trail in principle ignores the vital importance of the givenness of God. An unmitigated theological pluralism leads at once to a theological relativism which would make all theological statements possible with an equal chance of success or failure. This would mean the end of Christianity as we or anybody else have understood it.[41]

Profiting from this critique of normativity Barr returns to the question of how the Scripture may be said to relate to present belief. This raises the question of hermeneutics and the function of Scripture.

3.1.4. Authority and the function of Scripture

In the post-neo-orthodox era, discussions have tended to relate the authority of the Bible and the search for the correct way of understanding the Bible. It seemed to be assumed that if the right hermeneutic key were applied, the authoritative element of the Scripture message would appear. This in its turn would provide a way for the understanding the text as a whole and give an indication for the structuring of theology. So Barr remarks that "the authority of Scripture has been associated with the search for one over-arching principle which might justify and support that authority in all the

---

40. *BMW*, pp. 51f.
41. H. E. W. Turner in *The Churchman* 86:166-73, quoted by R. Nixon in *New Testament Interpretation*, ed. I. H. Marshall (Exeter, 1977), p. 341.

diverse applications of Scripture."[42] In this setting, the authority of Scripture is linked with the discernment of the right principle of interpretation. It is somewhat inevitable that in a discussion about such a principle there should arise a greater consciousness of the diversity of the Bible rather than its unity. As the diversity and even the possibility of disagreement in Scripture appear in the hermeneutic discussion, it becomes clear that to name a principle of interpretation implies a choice in the Bible. Such a choice raises the question of whether there can be a unitary authority of Scripture which constitutes a ground for the idea of right interpretation. So the circle is closed; when the authority of Scripture is delimited in terms of a methodological choice within the totality of Scripture, such a procedure can only raise afresh the question of the authority of the Scripture. Barr traces this development in the context of the ecumenical discussions of hermeneutics and authority.[43] The hermeneutical debate necessitates a new formulation of biblical authority which will fit in with the needs of modern interpretation and its consciousness of the diversity of Scripture.

Arising from this context and together with the questions about the notion of authority in recent years, a different approach to the authority of the Bible has appeared. As Barr says: ". . . some recent thought has tried to distinguish between the various functions of Scripture, suggesting that the Bible had no single form of authority but that its influence and importance varied from one to another of its functions."[44] In this sense "authority" is used of Scripture in a variety of ways, and there is no one concept of authority. The authority of the Bible is construed in different ways by reference to the way the text functions, and the way in which this is discerned by the theologian.[45] In this respect Barr has made his own proposition for viewing the authority of Scripture in functional fashion. He discusses the possibilities of speaking of *hard* and *soft* views of authority as describing our expectation of the way Scripture might be expected to make its authority felt. A hard view of biblical au-

---

42. *IDB*(S), p. 795.
43. *ER* 21:135f., 138.
44. *IDB*(S), loc. cit.
45. See Kelsey, *The Uses of Scripture in Recent Theology* (London, 1975), chaps. 6, 7.

thority is one which sees authority as being prior to interpretation and having general application. It would be expected that the Bible would be authoritative before the message of Scripture has been discerned. A soft view, on the other hand, would leave the question of authority open until the interpretation had been carried out and found to have an authoritative effect. In this sense the authority of the Bible can be spoken of consequent upon its having been experienced as authority.[46] Barr recognises that the problem with this view of authority as more personal lies in applying it to the Bible in particular as such authority may be found outside the Bible.[47]

Nevertheless, even in such a limited formulation of authority as Barr's soft authority, the critique of the principle is never far from the surface. It cannot be forgotten that authority is a *legal* notion, and traditionally carries with it connotations of hardness. The idea of soft authority itself cannot be generalised, for if it is "given the *logical* status of the *ground* for belief in biblical authority, it is manifestly wrong."[48] Barr contends that it can be asked whether the authority concept is properly part of the Christian tradition; it is not itself a biblical term when used of a book like the Bible. Perhaps it is used in Christianity as a result of the influence of Roman law and government.

However, the greatest problem for the notion of the authority of the Bible is not even to be found here. It lies in the fact that an authority concept is out of joint with the practice and shape of theology today. This is characteristically pluralist, and within this newer context the idea of the "authority" of the Bible has become anachronistic. An authority concept no longer fits the intellectual structure in which theological activity is carried out. The Bible is no longer the final court of appeal in which a theology is evaluated. There are many factors for evaluating a theology, and the account that

---

46. *BMW*, pp. 27f., 113, 180. Barr says he finds the *Faith and Order* report of Louvain (1971) to oscillate between hard and soft views of authority.

47. R. Nixon in op. cit., ed. Marshall, p. 336, criticises Barr's view of soft authority as not making sufficient allowance for sinful blindness to the truth and the fact that we have to wrestle with Scripture before it comes to mean something in our experience. It may indeed be wondered whether soft authority is any authority at all, or whether it simply opens the door to arbitrary preferences with respect to Scripture.

48. *BMW*. p. 29.

theology gives of its relation with Scripture is only one of these. The old status of the Bible as authority does not fit the present theological pluralism. In this climate theologians have the opportunity of living with other theologies which are also considered legitimate, without the compulsion to confute them by exposing their errors. "In the future," says Barr, "we shall judge theologies not by their antecedent criterion but by their output, their results."[49] In this new context we have passed from an authority structure to pluralism; the Bible must function in this new context.

* * * * *

Before proceeding further with Barr's critique of the status of the Bible, it is as well to draw together certain of these elements which have been discussed in this section. Perhaps the most striking point of all is Barr's inveterate dislike for the notion of authority. The main points of his argument against the authority of the Bible are that this does not fit either with the climate of our day or with the present shape of theology. Because of this, authority can no longer be assumed for the Bible. More generally this questions whether Christianity is an authoritative religion at all and suggests that perhaps authority should not be considered central.[50] Barr's critique of the authority of Scripture applies, then, in two areas. Firstly against the notion of authority of the Bible as it is used to strengthen acceptance of the Bible itself as Word of God. Secondly against the hard application of such an authority as a necessary condition for accounting for Christian experience. In both of these areas Barr militates against a view of the Bible as having authority in an *a prioristic* sense. This critique is but a consequent application of Barr's refusal in his earlier theological work of the christological analogy with respect to Scripture. When the Bible is considered in a context other than that of revelation from God to man, that is, as a human word of the people of God "in the Spirit," the former ground of the authority of Scripture is removed. One possibility which lies open when the past-oriented view of the Bible as revelational authority is abandoned is to posit that the conversation between God and his people established in the past will continue in the present and future. Authority would not

---

49. Ibid., p. 51; cf. pp. 28f.
50. Cf. C. Evans, op. cit., p. 36.

then lie in transferring the meaning of the past to the present but in a "similar conversation" today.[51]

The problem inherent in this suggestion is that it seems to move the criterion of authority out of the past to the present. It appears to be not an abolition of authority but a relocation of it. Even when Barr criticises the authority principle as such, if this criticism is to have any weight, it must be grounded in something other than conjecture to be considered sufficient to justify the argument. To put this another way, when the authority of revelation is abolished in the destruction of the christological analogy, is this anything other than the relocation of an authority in human judgment? And if, as must be the case, the locus of this authority in human judgment is subject to similar relativisation, does not the relativity process, the "vertigo of relativity," to use the expression of P. Berger and T. Luckmann, itself acquire a strange sort of normativity? If on the other hand we wish to relocate authority in "similar conversation," "in the Spirit," can anything be said to help establish criteria for measuring the normativity of this, more than could be said for the authority of Scripture as revelation?

Such considerations may lead us to the conclusion that Barr's rejection of the authority of Scripture is a little inconclusive, and certainly not as innocent as first would meet the eye. Such questioning might have seemed in order when there were students occupying the Sorbonne or pressing the railings of the White House, but 10 years later they seem rather dated; there is a certain boredom in the continual challenge of authority. Perhaps the authority of Scripture must not be swept away with too much facility. In any case, if Barr wants a theological pluralism, the possibility of an authority-structured theology must be granted as a valid option, in order for him to remain pluralist in anything other than word.

3.2. *The ambiguity of the concept of revelation*

The association of the concept of the authority of the Bible and that of revelation has been so close that the one has virtually implied the other. To locate revelation is to find the seat of authority of the Christian religion. The maxim of F. W. Camfield is typical in this

---

51. Barr formulates this possibility admirably in *ER* 21:147f.

respect: "We must find authority in Revelation, for authority is its hall-mark."[52]

Does the revelational model offer a suitable way for stating the nature of the Bible? In recent theology it is above all the concept of revelation which has been used in discussions of the status of Scripture. Carl Braaten remarks that "every modern Protestant theology . . . has felt obliged to establish itself as a theology of revelation, as if thereby it has achieved all that matters or what matters most."[53] This would be comprehensible if there had been any concensus as to what revelation meant, but this does not seem to have always been the case. Perhaps it was a case of revelation becoming a fashionable linguistic container capable of receiving the desired contents, and Braaten is right in speaking of the compulsion attached to the concept.

This twentieth-century way of speaking of revelation was in any case much different from the classical formulations of the doctrine, even though the similarity of vocabulary might make it seem otherwise. Neo-orthodox views of revelation distanced themselves from "propositionalism," which associated the text of Scripture and revelation too closely. This older theology considered Scripture not as a witness to revelation, but as itself a redemptive act of God by which he reveals his salvation. Scripture in this context is revelation and the special inspiration is upheld by a concept of divine providence as being "that which controls all of history and each man as a particular contribution to history."[54] In this scheme the need for word-revelation is implied in the nature of the salvation accomplished and in the nature of the recipient of redemption. The witness of Scripture is not merely *to* revelation, but a witness *of* revelation and a part of it: ". . . any approach to the witness of the New Testament which is truly scientific must accept this witness as the witness of the Holy Spirit."[55]

---

52. F. W. Camfield, quoted in H. McDonald, op. cit., p. 347.

53. C. Braaten, *History and Hermeneutics* (Philadelphia, 1966), p. 12.

54. C. Van Til, speaking of Warfield's view of Scripture in *In Defense of the Faith* (Philadelphia, 1967), I:25; cf. Kelsey's discussion of Warfield in op. cit., pp. 18ff., and B. B. Warfield, *Inspiration and Authority of the Bible* (Philadelphia, 1948), pp. 79ff., J. Orr, *Revelation and Inspiration* (Grand Rapids, 1969), chap. 8.

55. H. Ridderbos, *The Authority of the New Testament Scriptures* (Philadelphia, 1963), p. 67.

W. Pannenberg has commented on these two ways of approaching the question of revelation and sees a common point in them in spite of their differences. Until the Enlightenment, he says, theology appealed to supernatural revelation:

> The authoritative revelation was found in the "Word of God," i.e., in the inspired word of the Bible. In the twentieth century the neo-orthodox theology of the Word no longer sought the "Word of God" primarily in the Bible. It was found rather in the event of Christian proclamation . . . or else in Jesus' history also interpreted as "Word" of God. In both cases the authoritarian character of the appeal to revelation remains untouched.[56]

For Pannenberg, neo-orthodoxy's theology of the Word is simply a modern expression of an authoritarian theology of revelation, which is defenceless against the charge of interchanging the divine and the human. Barr's criticism of the concept of revelation as a central category for describing the status of the Bible is taken from a different angle than that of Pannenberg. The conclusion is nevertheless similar, as we shall see.

3.2.1.   The critique of revelation as a central concept

In section 2.3 we examined Barr's analysis of the notion of history as connected with revelation, and the ambiguities he discerns when the idea of *Heilsgeschichte* is made a controlling notion in interpretation. When he comes to discuss the idea of revelation itself as a central concept for describing the status of the Bible in recent theology, he makes it clear that in his view we cannot hope to question the notion "history" in a revelation-in-history formula and leave that of "revelation" intact. Barr wonders also whether revelation itself is necessarily a useful way of describing the status of the Bible. If this cannot be demonstrated on the basis of the biblical texts themselves, "the breaking down of the idea that it is a mandatory concept is necessary if we are to attain freedom to discuss the exegetical questions."[57] This illustrates once again Barr's concern for the freedom of exegesis untrammelled by dogmatic considerations. The weakness

---

56. W. Pannenberg, in *Theology as History,* ed. J. M. Robinson and J. B. Cobb (New York, 1967), p. 226. Cf. C. Geffré in *La Révélation,* P. Ricoeur et al. (Bruxelles, 1977), p. 172, and P. Berger, *A Rumour of Angels* (London, 1971), p. 104.

57. *ONI,* p. 83.

of the blanket-use of a category such as revelation is that it groups together a number of biblical concepts in such a way as to distort them.[58] When revelation is taken to be descriptive of the Bible, this results in ambiguous classification of the biblical material. Thus the interest in circumscribing the nature of biblical authority in connection with revelation endangers the freedom of exegetical construction.

It is therefore essential to evaluate whether revelation is a central category in the Bible in the same way as in modern theology. Here, as in his observations on the authority of Scripture, Barr decides that it is not the case. In his article on "Revelation" in Hastings *Dictionary,* Barr states that "it is doubtful whether we can identify any 'Biblical concept of revelation' with which all cases would fit. In particular it is doubtful whether the common theological use of 'revelation' for the Divine self-communication is appropriate in the light of Biblical usage."[59] In the Bible the use of terms corresponding to revelation is limited and specialised. There is little justification for using the term to apply exclusively to the source of man's knowledge of God.[60] However, not only is revelation lexically peripheral in Scripture; Barr affirms also a conceptual limitation. This conceptual marginality goes together with the lexical aspect and results from the fact that nowhere in Scripture is God totally unknown. Referring to the infrequent references of God revealing himself in the OT, Barr states that "These are . . . sufficient to indicate that God is covered or hidden from normal human access but hardly to show how far this hiddenness is complete or absolute."[61] In this exposition, Barr is not denying that it is possible to use the word revelation. He allows for a loose usage and the legitimacy of speaking of "communication" or revelation as "uncovering" in a broad sense.[62] What Barr is calling into question is the assumption that the word is a central biblical one and that its usage as "self-communication of God" is the equiva-

---

58. Ibid., p. 86.
59. "Revelation," in Hastings *Dictionary of the Bible,* ed. F. C. Grant and H. H. Rowley (Edinburgh, 1963), para. 14. See also W. Pannenberg, in *Revelation as History* (London, 1968), p. 8 (". . . at first glance there is no terminological usage concerning the self-revelation of God in the biblical writings"), and the detailed analysis of F. G. Downing, *Has Christianity a Revelation?* (London, 1964), passim.
60. *ONI,* p. 88; also Downing, op. cit., pp. 206ff.
61. "Revelation," para. 6.
62. Ibid., para. 14; *ONI,* p. 86.

lent of the biblical concept of revelation. Where it occupies such a central place this involves the introduction of an element which is foreign to the development of the biblical tradition itself. In recent theology this tendency to make revelation mandatory probably reflects an effort to confront two modern problems—that involving a doubt about the existence of God and that of demarcating the knowledge obtained from revelation from the knowledge of modern sciences. In the milieu of the Bible neither of these problems was compelling.[63]

Barr indicates four problems, among others, which become pressing when revelation is made a central notion for describing the status of Scripture. One of the most important difficulties which arises in a revelational theology is the way of indicating the relation between what is considered revelatory and the Bible itself. The possibilities are legion, but Barr concentrates mostly on the Barthian tradition in his critique.[64] The difficulty in this case is indicating in what way there is continuity and discontinuity between the Bible and revelation. God reveals himself in his revelation, not chapters and verses. The Word of God's revelation is the person of Christ himself. All the same, a continuity does exist, as the Bible is witness to revelation, and in its human character is a necessary and appropriate witness to revelation. Barr resumes this identity and distinctness: ". . . though the Word of God is not identical with the Bible, the Bible is an essential and appropriate access to the Word of God, and one cannot hope to hear the Word of God except through the mediation of the Bible."[65] Thus the Bible can be called Word of God in the sense that it functions as witness to God in his self-revelation.[66] Scripture is "holy" in a rhetorical sense because of its witness to revelation. Scrip-

---

63. *ONI*, pp. 89ff.

64. For a general survey of different views of revelation see D. Evans, "Protestant View of Revelation," in *Canadian Journal of Theology* 10:258-65; McDonald, op. cit., pp. 161ff.; A. Richardson in *Cambridge History of the Bible*, ed. S. L. Greenslade (1963), III:299; J. K. S. Reid, op. cit., chap. 6; Pannenberg, op. cit., pp. 3ff., and J. Hick, *Philosophy of Religion* (1973), chap. 4.

65. *BMW*, p. 19.

66. K. Barth, *Church Dogmatics* (Edinburgh, 1956), I.2, 512ff., 527ff.; and on Scripture as witness, I.1, 99ff. See on this T. F. Torrance, *Karl Barth: An Introduction to His Early Theology, 1910–1931* (London, 1962), pp. 95-105; K. Runia, *Karl Barth's Doctrine of Holy Scripture* (Grand Rapids, 1962), chap. 2; Reid, op. cit., pp. 194ff.

ture as witness to the Word of God is one with the Word not in terms of *being* but of *becoming*.[67] In this position there is a unity of revelation with the Bible, without this passing into an identity. This is too well known to make a long description useful here, and we shall pass directly to Barr's points of criticism.

Barr affirms that the expression "Word of God" has not solved uncertainties existing over the status of the Bible. The arguments he gives to back up this assertion are deceptively simple, when one considers the superstructure of reflexion of which they are critical. Barr is not concerned, for example, to discuss the subject-object problem that the doctrine of revelation poses in the theology of Barth. His remarks are those of an exegete and centre rather on the practical difficulties in terms of exegesis raised by this idea of revelation. The problem Barr points to in particular is that of the necessity of distinguishing revelation from the Bible while identifying them. If God has to be distinguished from the Bible, the difficulty is in stating how what is said in the text relates to the revelation behind it. Also, if the revelation is distinct from the text, and if in the interpretation of the Bible revelation is thought to be the controlling factor, that which is said in the interpretation is just not what is said in the linguistic form of the text. If the Bible is thought of as "witness to," the danger is that what the Bible says be interpreted in terms of that reality to which the Bible is witness rather than in terms of what is verifiable in the Bible as such. Barr therefore states that the exegete must work with the text as it is, rather than according a controlling place to a revelation distinct from the text.[68] Where revelation controls, this procedure is typical of dogmatics, which has little contact with the world of biblical scholarship. It is an embarrassment for the exegete working with precise texts to know how to apply a revelational superstructure to the results of his work. In neo-orthodoxy, and especially in the theology of Barth, revelation gives the key to exegesis and preaching in such a way that it functions as a presupposi-

---

67. J. Wirsching, *Was ist Schriftgemäss?* (Gütersloh, 1971), pp. 39ff.

68. *ONI*, pp. 93ff. What Barr is doing in this passage is affirming in theological terms the structuralist's theory of the independence of the text from the author's intention and also from a function of direct referential nature. The text carries in the autonomy of the written word its own references within itself. See P. Ricoeur in *Exégèse et Herméneutique,* R. Barthes et al. (Paris, 1971), pp. 47ff.

tion regarding the conditions on which exegesis is possible. Barr
thinks that this reliance on revelation is "by no means certain to
assist or sustain good biblical interpretation." On the contrary, when
revelation is made central to the understanding of the Bible, it may
well "form an obstructing and distorting influence to the more empirical analysis of biblical evidence."[69]

Barr's second reason for reserve as to the usefulness of revelational
concepts for describing the status of the Bible is the ambiguity which
enters into the role of historical criticism in this context. It does
not matter that revelational theologies claim the legitimacy of historical criticism; Barr thinks that in practice the desire to get at the
revelation behind the text is a virtual annulment of the aims of
biblical criticism. The authority of the text lies in the revelational
connection, and the aim in interpretation is to locate and elaborate
the content of the revelation. In the relation of the divine and the
human, the human aspects of the witness are inevitably considered
as having a secondary place. If the revelation lies beyond the empirical realm of historical enquiry, the critic can go as far as he likes
on that level, but he is not likely to do so, as his heart is elsewhere.[70]

A third ambiguity of a revelational model centres upon the distinction it makes between revelation and religion. Barr considers such
a division unprofitable in biblical studies, particularly with respect
to the OT. The materials of the OT cannot be fitted into a scheme
dominated by revelation. On the other hand, revelation as a notion
does not fit in with the examination of the religious traditions on the
historico-cultural level as in biblical studies. The traditions which
go into the forming of the OT must be regarded in the context of a
religious development, and appeals to revelation are not relevant in
this historical study.

Finally, this point can be developed in the sense that revelation
as distinct from normal conditions of human cultural production has
to rely on itself for its own validation. It cannot be demonstrated by
recourse to arguments of a historical-cultural nature. Revelation
which is distinct from the text is also distinct in a similar way from
the empirical realities of history. It can be neither proved nor dis-

---

69. *ONI*, pp. 91, 92; *BMW*, p. 21.
70. *ONI*, pp. 92, 93; *BMW*, loc. cit.

proved, only believed. As Barr puts it: ". . . this leaves revelational theology naked and out of touch."[71]

The fundamental enigma with which Barr is struggling in all these remarks lies in the fact that this-worldly phenomena are interpreted in terms of a revelation which is distinct from conditions governing this world. The human elements involved in Scripture are validated in connection with the central reality of revelation, which itself is distinct from them. In each of the four cases cited, the human aspect seems to be preliminary only to the main issue. Barr as an exegete is doubtful of the continuity created when the human is seen in the context of the divine in this fashion and thinks this creates ambiguities in the interpretation of the empirical evidence.

The tendency in Barr's critique is to detach the human elements of the religious tradition from the continuity with revelation and seek to explain their significance apart from a revelational model. Barr's suggestion runs something like this. The acts of divine self-disclosure in the Bible are not properly "revelations" of God; they are further acts of God who is already known rather than new first self-manifestations.[72] Revelation is not then *in* the Bible or in the event interpreted by it, but is presupposed by it. The Bible is a locus of revelation in so far as it is the expression of the tradition formed in consequence of what Israel has heard and learned.[73] In this way Barr seeks to formulate a view of revelation which does not eliminate the religious tradition but which generates it and depends on it for its reception. The following statement is typical:

> Revelation not only produces but depends on religion. Whatever was the action of God in the early days of Israel, one of the ways in which it works for our salvation is through the religion which it eventually produced. . . . This religion was factually the way which led to Jesus' understanding of himself as Christ and also to the reaction against him . . . which in turn brought men to their salvation.[74]

---

71. *ONI*, p. 96. Barr thinks that Barth is very frank about this alienation from biblical scholarship. In the Barthian tradition, however, he notes that there has been a good deal of effort to back up the revelational approach on the historico-cultural level, as the BTM shows.

72. Ibid., p. 82.

73. "Story and History in Biblical Theology," *JR* 56:16.

74. *ONI*, pp. 29f. The statement that revelation depends on religion allows for the directness of revelation in a "charismatic" way in the early Christian communities. Cf. Hastings *Dictionary*, para. 12. With this dual emphasis on

Perhaps it is possible to see the main element in this statement through formulating more precisely the difference between it and the preceding neo-orthodox formulation. It is clear that Barr's conception is removed not only from the old orthodoxy with its emphasis on the text as revelation, but also from the revelational-centred approach of neo-orthodoxy. This is evident with reference to the overall structure of the neo-orthodox theology of the Word. For the Barthian, having affirmed the discontinuity of Scripture and revelation and thus guarding against the idolising of the text, the problem is to affirm positively what is the attachment between the two. This is done with reference to the appropriate and necessary character of the human witness in terms of its *becoming* revelation. Two problems arise in seeking to establish the continuity between this witness and revelation. The first concerns the cognitive status of such "becoming"; the second the relation between this form of revelation and the unique revelation of Christ in the Word. In this second sense, when the comprehensive view of the Bible as revelation of the traditional orthodoxy is reduced to the idea that revelation is the self-revelation of God, what remains of revelation is a notion which sees it as the unique act of God in the person of the incarnate Word.[75] Yet how is this act of revelation, the unique Christ-event, to be related to other "revelatory" situations? W. Pannenberg has exposed this problem in a concise way: ". . . a multiplicity of revelation implies a discrediting of any particular revelation, for then the form of the divine manifestation is no longer the singularly adequate expression of the revealer."[76] If, therefore, the self-revelation of God is unique, other situations cannot be revelatory, or cannot be revelatory in a sense other than that they are indirect instances of the one revelation. Yet in such multiplicity of indirect revelation, the absence of particular revelation is as significant as the continuity affirmed with the unique revelation. If self-disclosure is not concretised in the multiple situations by the communication by God of truth about himself, the element of discontinuity remains at least as significant as that of continuity. The problem of such indirect

tradition and direct revelation one might imagine that Barr's ideas could have had a good deal of impact on, say, Catholic charismatics, had they been in more popular form.

75. The reductionism of neo-orthodoxy has been underlined by C. Henry in *God, Revelation and Authority* (Waco, 1976), II:88.

76. Pannenberg, op. cit., pp. 6f.

revelatory action is that it never seems to get into the forum of history; it is visible only to faith and falls outside empirical reality.[77]

It is at this point that Barr's criticisms operate and force apart the Barthian synthesis by attacking the dialectic of continuity and discontinuity with regard to revelation. In a practical sense, Barr affirms the discontinuity between revelation and the text of Scripture and radicalises this element. The problem for revelation-centred theology is to affirm that attachment between Scripture and revelation, and this cannot be done, thinks Barr, without distorting the sense of the text. For this reason Barr rejects a christocentric interpretation of the OT in rather unequivocal terms.[78] Barr radicalises the idea of the discontinuity between Scripture and revelation and uses this to criticise the attachment of Scripture and revelation in terms of christocentric interpretation. There is just no way of seeing in the variety of OT materials a multiple indirect manifestation of the one unique Christ-event. Barr is affirming on the exegetical level Pannenberg's dogmatic affirmation.

The other point is that of the cognitive status of the revelation involved in the Scripture "becoming" revelation. In neo-orthodoxy, that Scripture becomes revelation in spite of its discontinuity with it, is a presupposition of faith. Barr criticises this presupposition in the way it applies to the interpretation of Scripture. Having criticised the continuity element, there remains in his thought the discontinuity, which becomes a more radical detachment. Barr presupposes revelation, but in a different sense. God is presupposed as known *before* this consciousness comes to expression in the tradition. Scripture is not, then, a God-to-man movement, but a human reflexion which ponders the fact that God is known. The ongoing knowledge depends on the religious tradition generated on the supposition that God is known; God uses this to make himself further known. Biblical studies are no longer embarrassed in this context by the question of establishing the continuity of revelation. They can undertake their

---

77. Criticisms of this aspect of Barth's thought are found in R. Prenter, "Dietrich Bonhoeffer and K. Barth's Positivism of Revelation," in *World Come of Age,* ed. R. G. Smith (London, 1967), pp. 93-130; J. Brown, *Subject and Object in Modern Theology* (London, 1955), pp. 140-67; J. Moltmann, *Theology of Hope* (London, 1967), pp. 50ff.; D. Emmet, *The Nature of Metaphysical Thinking* (London, 1966), pp. 121ff.; C. Van Til, *Christianity and Barthianism* (Philadelphia, 1962), pp. 120ff.

78. *ONI,* p. 100.

study of the historical development of the religious consciousness which presupposes the knowledge of God. Revelation itself lies beyond the bounds which are circumscribed to biblical studies in the historical-cultural interpretation of the religious traditions.

However, it can and must be noted that Barr has not avoided the problem of the cognitive value of the human religious statements about God. That God is known is presupposed, but this can tell us nothing really about the truth value of what is said about God. God is presupposed, but if there is no revelation of God to man by God, the problem remains very troublesome. Is it *God* who is known? In a sense, in attacking the Barthian dialectic at the point of continuity between revelation and Scripture, Barr makes the problem of discontinuity even more pronounced in his work than it is in neo-orthodoxy. The question this leaves open is as to the reality of human knowledge of God.

3.2.2. Propositional revelation

When revelation has been taken as central in theology, this has given rise to a debate as to whether it is to be interpreted in terms of a personal or a propositional revelation. Neo-orthodoxy, with its emphasis on the personal aspect of revelation, has sustained polemical relations with fundamentalism, which has insisted in its theological formulations on the words of Scripture as revelation. This interpretation of revelation as personal self-disclosure sees the Scripture as a commentary on a non-conceptual experience. The main aspect of this revelation is not in the literary content of the propositions but in the historic act or encounter with God, the personal character of which cannot be reduced to propositional form.[79] Barr thinks that the entire debate—personal vs. propositional—has been a circuitous evasion of the point; he considers the opposition to be not very important when revelation is not taken as a central category. Barr's view of revelation as presupposed by the literary tradition of Scripture and following on from it would make way for a consideration of both the literary-propositional character of the tradition and the personal directness of revelation. Thus the opposition propositional-

---

79. *F,* pp. 214ff. See the comments of C. Pinnock in *Biblical Revelation* (Chicago, 1971), pp. 21f.; J. Hick, loc. cit.

personal is transcended. Barr's argument on this point is along two different lines: He indicates the weaknesses inherent in the rejection of the propositional material in the Bible in neo-orthodoxy and criticises the fundamentalists' over-emphasis on revelation as propositional.[80]

Barr thinks that the opposition to propositional revelation by neo-orthodoxy has been founded on several misunderstandings. Firstly, it shows a confusion between the way God reveals himself and the logical status of sentences in the Bible. To deny revelation as propositional need not imply a denial of the propositional material in the Bible. This can be recognised without inferring that it is revealed or that revelation itself is propositional. Barr observes also that the sharp distinction made between truth as personal or as propositional, which neo-orthodoxy has often made in indicating where the core of the discussion lies, does not seem to have been consistently applicable to theological formulation. The insistence on personal revelation has relied on a good deal of propositional material to fill out the content of such revelation.[81] In addition to this, when propositions have been attacked by those adhering to personal revelation, some meaning has often been introduced so that "proposition" becomes equivalent to "timeless truth" or "impersonal statement."[82] However, on this understanding, the discussion is no longer one concerning propositions themselves but about the function of propositions which might be acceptable in the context of revelation. Barr thinks that the issue has been confused when it has not been seen that the distinction is to be made between the use of propositions in itself and the right function of such propositions. P. Helm has also made this point in a different way, after examining different philosophical uses of the term

---

80. *BMW*, pp. 122ff.; *ONI*, pp. 201f.; *F*, pp. 225ff.

81. *BMW*, p. 123. At several points in this argument Barr follows P. Helm's article, "Revealed Propositions and Timeless Truths," *Religious Studies* 8: 127-36. Helm argues against a dichotomy between personal and propositional truth. F. Ferré makes a similar point as that of Barr by affirming that a non-propositional view cannot get by without the use of propositions that would be formulated on the basis of the experience. *Basic Modern Philosophy of Religion* (London, 1968), pp. 98f. G. Downing also holds this to be untenable, op. cit., pp. 222f. Downing thinks, like Barr (*F*, pp. 218ff), that this approach based on a distinction between the form and content of revelation breaks down into more conservative views.

82. Helm, art. cit., pp. 132ff.

"proposition." The theologians who refuse propositional revelation are in fact denying that the Bible contains any revealed truths. "What is objected to is the idea that the Bible *expresses* propositions, not that it consists in them. . . . What seems to be objectionable to some in the notion of propositional revelation is the idea of revealed *assertions,* i.e., true propositions revealed by God."[83]

Even though Barr rejects the neo-orthodox approach to the question of propositional revelation and thinks that this represents a confusion, he himself would share its objection by denying that the Bible is revelation as "true propositions revealed by God." Therefore he criticises those fundamentalists who regard the Bible as propositional revelation. Barr thinks that the neo-orthodox "attack on conservatism for its propositional view of truth, though in many ways justified, was also very confused and ambiguous."[84] Nevertheless, it was correct to criticise fundamentalist doctrine; he himself wishes to make an attack on the same idea, unimpeded by a commitment to a revelational-centred theology. It is largely against the arguments of J. I. Packer that Barr has reacted. These Barr labels the "automatic regressivism of the conservative apologist."[85] Packer argues that God's revelation consists of his exercising power and his speaking of truth. There is a complementary character in revelation between God's mighty acts and his revealing of truth. Thus the word of God consists of revealed truths which interpret God's acts, embodied in a system of truths conveying to man information about God himself. Barr replies principally in two ways. The first difficulty Barr indicates is that Packer proposes a system of truths which calls for assent as true information from God. Barr objects to the correlation of faith with such a system as assent to propositions. Barr does not think that Packer is representative of evangelicals on this point.

Although it is not immediately apparent to the reader where the difficulty lies in this, and Barr makes no effort to refute the idea, a second point is brought out. This "greater difficulty" is that to speak of propositional revelation as Packer does in no way justifies the inspiration of *the Bible.* At most, thinks Barr, it covers the texts

---

83. Ibid., p. 132.
84. *F,* p. 226.
85. Ibid., p. 227; the passage referred to is in J. I. Packer, *Fundamentalism and the Word of God* (London, 1958), pp. 91ff.

which interpret the acts of God, or those which speak directly of God. Packer's argument can lead to the view that the theological assertions of the Bible are inspired; it cannot prove that the whole Bible is inspired, which is what Packer wants to do. Barr thinks that to prove his point Packer would have to show that because some propositions are revelational, all the propositions of the Bible are revelational. He maintains that Packer has ruined his argument by making the mighty acts of God the basis for defining revelation as propositional. In doing this he has already conceded too much to neo-orthodoxy by admitting that different propositions have different functions. The older orthodoxy of men like C. Hodge was more consistent, adds Barr, as it maintained the truth of the Bible on the grounds of the inspiration of its writers, independent of whether there were prior revelatory events. This tacit admission by Packer that different propositions have different functions makes it impossible for him to secure his argument concerning revealed propositions for the *whole* of Scripture. It also gives the non-fundamentalist a way of handling the argument. Paying attention to the difference of literary function of propositions, it is possible to reply that the propositions taken in the function proposed by fundamentalist opinion are false ones. This is so, if I have understood Barr's argument, because fundamentalism is constantly making literary category mistakes and attaching the wrong kind of truth-value to biblical propositions.

Concerning the biblical material, the question is not really between propositional and nonpropositional views of revelation, as has often been supposed, but between a correct interpretation of the function of the biblical propositions and an incorrect one. The incorrect truth value attached to biblical propositions in fundamentalism, based on the inability to discern the function of the material, leads it into severe straits through contradictions with modern knowledge.[86]

Barr's argument on this point is very compelling, and the reason for his rejection is plain. Propositional revelation is no way to describe the status of the Bible as a whole, as not all the propositions of the Bible can be shown to be revelatory. The form of many of the books is man-to-man communication; the letters of Paul are letters of the apostle to the churches, not from God to St. Paul. However,

---

86. *BMW,* p. 125; *ONI,* p. 202.

if there is one thing in Barr's argument about propositional revelation which might cause the reader to hesitate, it is the seeming facility with which Barr refutes the propositionalist approach. This alone, perhaps, may raise the question of whether Barr has in fact represented Packer's argument correctly. Barr tells us that Packer has, in reaction to Barthianism, "rushed cheerfully into the net" of propositionalism and lets himself be trapped into saying "that revelation was indeed propositional and nothing else."[87] Later we are told that Packer bases his view on the fact that certain revelatory propositions interpret God's acts, but that this cannot explain all the biblical propositions. If this is Packer's argument, there is certainly something very strange about it. Barr's analysis seems to contain two opposing views when he affirms of Packer that for him revelation is "propositional and *nothing else*" and then tells us it is also based on God's acts. In fact, neither of these statements seems to convey the sense of Packer's argument.

What Barr overlooks in his analysis is the all-important point that for Packer the propositional revelation is *itself* an act of God. It is a necessary part of redemptive activity. Thus the inspiring of the Bible is seen itself as one of God's redemptive acts, complementary to his acts of salvation. Barr may not agree with Packer's argument here, but he must at least recognise that in so far as Packer maintains that Scripture is itself a revelatory act of God and a necessary part of redemptive activity, it is not limited and dependent on the act-basis which Barr describes. Nor is Barr correct in saying that propositional revelation cannot be extended to the whole of Scripture. If it is itself an act of God, on Packer's view it evidently can.[88] When, therefore, Barr says that Packer has conceded too much to neo-orthodoxy by separating out redemptive events as basis for propositional revelation,

---

87. *F,* loc. cit.

88. Barr is therefore not correct in making the contrast he makes between Packer and the view of C. Hodge (*F,* p. 228). It is simply an artifice Barr uses several times in his book to infer that older conservatism was more consistent than recent fundamentalism, so strengthening his rejection of present views (cf. p. 290). This consistent ridicule thrown on contemporary fundamentalism is one of the most objectionable features of Barr's book. The view Packer proposes regarding revelation as propositional is hardly new, however. B. B. Warfield makes just the same point in *Inspiration and Authority of the Bible* (Philadelphia, 1948), pp. 79ff.; see also H. D. McDonald, op. cit., pp. 168ff., and N. B. Stonehouse in *Revelation and the Bible,* ed. C. Henry (Grand Rapids, 1959), pp. 75ff.

this is a piece of imagination on Barr's part. For Packer we are not likely to know of the acts of God apart from the final act of verbal revelation in Scripture.

Nor does Barr's other point concerning the function of propositions carry weight in the case of Packer. Packer seems quite aware that not all the propositions of the Bible are interpretations of acts of God or direct affirmations of God. If Packer speaks of Scripture as consisting of a system of truths which conveys information from God, there is no reason, according to him, why this must exclude the outworking of such truth (or the rejecting of it) in human lives. Formal statement is not the only way God could reveal himself, or his salvation, to us; God can reveal himself and his salvation in human reactions and situations. Such covenantal example naturally falls within the scope of inspired Scripture.[89] If this is the case, propositional revelation need not involve the literary category mistakes Barr considers endemic in it. Packer makes special mention of this fact: When it is said that Scripture is a body of truths containing matters of fact and principles about God and man and that these form God's inspired Word, this does not prejudice literary interpretation.[90] If it is true, as Barr says, that fundamentalism has been led into contradiction with modern science because of its view of propositional revelation, this may be because its interpretation of Scripture has not always been correct; it may also be conceivable that modern science has not always been correct as well. Such divergences would not in themselves prove a propositional view of revelation wrong.

In conclusion to this section, it may be remarked that if there are

---

89. Packer, op. cit., p. 94. Cf. K. Hamilton, *Words and the Word* (Grand Rapids, 1971), pp. 74ff., and C. Van Til's Introduction in Warfield, op. cit., pp. 29ff.

90. Packer, loc. cit. P. Helm has pointed to the fact that while the Bible contains few sentences in the revelation regarded as assertions and many more which are commands, prayers, promises, etc., this is not itself a problem for speaking of propositional revelation. For a prayer to be valid it must contain a propositional element. Thus the prayer, "Save your people," can be construed, "Your saving your people, please," art. cit., p. 135. Taken in this sense, Packer's distinction between the theological statements and their practical outworking can be worked out in the context of a scheme of propositional revelation. The prayers, etc., in the inspired word, which are evidently not words from God, nevertheless contain propositions relative to him. As such they are used by God in his inspired word as propositions revelatory of his disposition toward man.

inadequacies in Barr's evaluation of propositional revelation in fundamentalism as we have sought to show, it may well be because of the lack of sympathy for a position which is diametrically opposed to the direction in which his thought is moving. The certainty of faith for Barr cannot be bound up with the authority of the Bible as a propositional revelation. Faith must find its resting place other than in the authoritarian security structure of a God-to-man movement. Revelation and authority are no longer adequate concepts for describing the status of Scripture.

3.3. *Problems of traditional inspiration and inerrancy*

3.3.1. The reconstruction of inspiration

It has been widely held since the second half of the last century that the rise of historical criticism has invalidated the traditional view of verbal inspiration handed down from pre-critical times. As A. Richardson said: "The rise of Biblical scholarship made necessary a new doctrine of the inspiration of Holy Scripture."[91] The old doctrine has disappeared forever with the rise of criticism.[92] So, since the time of W. Sanday and before, there have been many efforts to reconstruct the doctrine of inspiration.[93] The most attractive early solution was the rather obvious one of claiming the inspiration of the writers rather than the texts. This construes the Bible as the record of men who were inspired and has the advantage of preserving something of the older view in a way which would allow criticism to do its work. Thus the reality of an inspiration was maintained without the fateful consequence of inerrancy, as implied in views which held to the inspiration of the texts. Different degrees of inspiration can account for fluctuations in the text; as such it is not free from "other growths."[94] There were, however, problems in this solution; not among the least of these was the fact that the theory did not found the authority of Scripture firmly enough in inspiration. There is something

---

91. A. Richardson, *A Preface to Bible Study* (London, 1943), p. 33.

92. See R. P. C. Hanson, "The Inspiration of Holy Scripture," *Anglican Theological Review* 43:146; C. Pinnock, *A Defense of Biblical Infallibility* (Philadelphia, 1967), pp. 2, 3, 7; K. Koch, *The Growth of the Biblical Tradition* (London, 1969), pp. 11ff.

93. H. D. McDonald, op. cit., pp. 218ff., and J. K. S. Reid, op. cit., pp. 156ff.

94. W. Sanday, *Inspiration* (London, 1901), pp. 349f., 398f.

lacking in the authority of a Bible which is a by-product of inspiration in the writers; the uniqueness of the Bible is diminished. Its inspiration comes to mean that it inspires us in a similar fashion as the early writers. This, as J. K. S. Reid comments, "is hardly adequate to explain how the Bible is inspired."[95]

The other way to go at the problem is to reconstruct a doctrine of inspiration in which the focus is not on the inspired experience of the writers of Scripture or on our being inspired, but on an inspiration which expresses an act of God with regard to the Scripture. This view can also handle the presence of errors in Scripture, as Karl Barth does in a robust way in his *Dogmatics*.[96] The inspiration of Scripture is not an inspiredness which inheres the text. If this is an authorised witness, it is nonetheless a fallible one; inspiration resides in the present in the event of God's grace, which permits us to recognise Scripture as God's Word. This view obviously seeks a closer relation between the text of Scripture and the event of inspiration, but the question still remains as to the closeness of this association. J. Hamer, in particular, has suggested that in Barth's system there is no real continuity between the text itself and the act of inspiration. He affirms, "inspiration for Barth is the momentary and mysterious intervention of the Word, that gives itself and withdraws without human consciousness becoming aware of it." Inspiration is elusive: everywhere and nowhere. Another critic, W. Young, affirms likewise: "Barth, however he may assert even a verbal inspiration for all parts of Scripture, does not allow a strictly objective inspiration for any part." Both these writers think Barth confuses inspiration and the internal witness of the Spirit in the gift of faith.[97] It is true, moreover, that in the deutero-Barthian tradition much was made of the contrast between the dead letter of Scripture and the living Word of God.[98]

---

95. J. K. S. Reid, op. cit., p. 170; R. P. C. Hanson, art. cit., pp. 147ff.; A. Richardson in op. cit., ed. S. L. Greenslade, pp. 313ff., and *The Bible in the Age of Science* (London, 1961), pp. 67ff.; B. B. Warfield, op. cit., pp. 115ff. These all refer to the inadequacy of Sanday's view.

96. K. Barth, op. cit., I.2, 503ff., 507, 509. Commentary in Reid, op. cit., pp. 214ff., and N. Smith in *SJT* 2:156-62.

97. J. Hamer, *Karl Barth* (London and Glasgow, 1962), pp. 93f.; W. Young in *WTJ* 8:14.

98. An excellent page to illustrate this is in Reid, op. cit., p. 101; cf. pp. 127f.

These considerations reveal something of the importance of the attempts made to reconstruct the doctrine of inspiration in a way concordant with the results of the inductive study of the Bible. Such reconstruction is necessary to the modern theologian, as in discussions of the status of the Bible inspiration can rightly lay claim to some kind of authority. The nature of the authority of Scripture is determined by the locus and the nature of the inspiration attributed to Scripture. This being the case, it is quite expected that Barr in his evaluation of the present status of the Bible should discuss inspiration.

One problem as far as the notion of inspiration is concerned is that it has been very often associated with Roman Catholic discussion of the status of Scripture, for in Protestantism, because of fundamentalist extremism, theologians have tended to shy away from the term.[99] If the term is used, it indicates the origin of the Bible as coming from God; it is here that questions enter, thinks Barr, as to the way this can be so. Even where the emphasis on the origin of the Bible is maintained, the discussion of the *mode* of the inspiration is vague. If the fundamentalist extremes are avoided and we manage to steer clear of inspiration correlated with inerrancy, the problem remains. In what way did God inspire Scripture? The average reply of the laity that God "in some way inspired the Bible" is quite characteristic of what Barr calls "a field of blank ignorance" for the majority of modern Christians.[100] Barr adds: "We do not have any idea of ways in which God might straightforwardly communicate articulate thoughts or sentences to men; it just doesn't happen." In the light of this modern dilemma, of which we are now totally conscious, if the notion of inspiration is going to remain useful in describing the status of the Bible, it must be separated from the traditional ideas about it. In particular it would have to be redefined without appeal to a special mode of communication between God and the biblical writers which ceased at the end of the biblical period. Inspiration would have to

---

99. Barr in *Religious Studies* 6:192f.; J. T. Burtchaell in *Catholic Theories of Biblical Inspiration Since 1810* (Cambridge, 1969), p. 164, remarks that in Catholicism inspiration and inerrancy have been considered in some quarters as protective of Catholic biblical interpretation and customary doctrines. This is similar to Barr's analysis of these in fundamentalism. Cf. section 2.5.

100. *BMW,* p. 17.

be spoken of in a way which is equivalent to the mode of communica-cation between God and his people today. In other words, to be valid today, inspiration would have to be pried away from a view which welds inspiration to a special revelation.

This perspective is an application to the problem of inspiration of the critique of the christological analogy in Barr's earlier work. If the divine and human scheme for considering the nature of Scripture has broken down, and the human word is considered as the bearer of revelation, then if we use the notion of inspiration we must do so in terms of a human character. That is, one which would be explicable in terms of human activity at present. In this respect one conceivable way in which inspiration might be spoken of is in a literary or poetic sense. This would by-pass the problems of the accuracy of the text and bring out a "softer" meaning of inspiration, in terms of power and insight in expression. Barr's openness to such an approach, to-gether with his reticence about the "two-word" formulations of Barthianism, indicates a breakdown of the Barthian synthesis regard-ing inspiration and a return to a view similar to that which insists on the inspiration of the writer. However, it is now time to consider Barr's objections to the traditional view of inspiration in greater detail.[101]

3.3.2. Verbal inspiration

Barr has written some of his most virulent polemic against the idea of verbal inspiration as stated in fundamentalism. It comes as some-thing of a surprise, then, when Barr tells us that he does not "regard it as a very important issue."[102] The issue is not as peripheral as it would seem, since a couple of pages after this declaration we also read that it is necessary that the fundamentalist idea of verbal inspiration be totally dismantled. Only then is it possible to hold a correct view of inspiration without any of the connotations of inerrancy, infalli-bility, or perfection which are incompatible with modern historical critical scholarship. When these false notions are removed, it is

---

101. It is somewhat remarkable that in this section in *BMW*, pp. 13ff., Barr does not refer to the fact that our word "inspiration" does not have the same precise sense as the *theopneustos* of the NT. Cf. Warfield, op. cit., pp. 132ff., and G. C. Berkouwer, *Holy Scripture* (Grand Rapids, 1975), pp. 139ff.

102. *F,* p. 287.

evident that verbal inspiration can be reconciled with a conception
of the Bible as a fallible human document. Verbal inspiration in this
sense would indicate that the fallible thoughts of the human authors
are expressed in the linguistic form appropriate to their meaning.
A thorough critique of the fundamentalist idea of inspiration will
liberate us, thinks Barr, from seeing the Scripture in terms of a God-
to-man movement in which authoritative teaching is conveyed. It
also debunks the idea of the dual authorship of Scripture, which is
used to "explain" the mode of inspiration, but which has been introduced to get away from dictation. Finally, it would detach inspiration
from the point of writing. Such notions are irrelevant in terms of
modern biblical studies.[103] Barr's dismantling of these theses of fundamentalism is not by direct attack, although he does point to what
he considers their inner inconsistencies. However, his main points
against inspiration in fundamentalism seek to undermine the doctrine
that Scripture is to be believed to be inspired because it bears its own
witness to its inspiration. Three arguments can be considered by
which Barr attempts to disprove this case.

The first argument concerns the fundamentalist's attachment to the
witness of Jesus to the Scriptures. He believes the Bible to be inspired
and inerrant because Jesus taught it to be so. On the basis of the
self-interpretation of Scripture the argument runs: Jesus teaches in
the Scripture that Scripture is inspired; to reject this witness is not only
to reject the witness of Scripture, but also that of Jesus; since Jesus
is divine, this rejection is disobedience to God.[104] This kind of argument, summarised far too brutally here, which ties the inspiration of
Scripture in with the witness of Jesus, really provokes Barr to anger.
A "grotesque argument," it is not worthy of refutation; it should inspire our distaste.[105] The problem for Barr does not lie in the fact

---

103. Ibid., pp. 289ff.

104. On Christ's view of the Bible see McDonald, op. cit., pp. 139ff., for a
general survey of views. Examples of views which correlate the authority of
Christ and the status of the Bible are found in A. Kuyper, *Principles of Sacred
Theology* (Grand Rapids, n.d.), pp. 429ff., 438ff., 550; W. Shedd, *Dogmatic
Theology* (1888), I:103; Warfield, op. cit., pp. 116ff., 128; E. P. Clowney,
in *Scripture and Confession,* ed. J. H. Skilton (Nutley, N.J., 1973), pp. 178ff.;
J. I. Packer, op. cit., pp. 54ff.; C. Pinnock, *Biblical Revelation* (Chicago, 1971),
pp. 59ff.; J. W. Wenham, *Christ and the Bible* (London, 1972), chap. 4, and
P. Marcel, in *La Revue Réformée* IX, 4:14ff.

105. *F,* p. 74.

that we might speak of the value of the OT by referring to the view of Jesus or Paul. What Barr dislikes rather vehemently is that such an argument should be used to prove the inspiration and inerrancy of the Bible. It is highly objectionable that the status of Jesus or the apostles be used to constrain acceptance of fundamentalist ideas on the authorship, date, or historical accuracy of the Bible. The implication is that if one does not follow the fundamentalist argument, the credibility of Jesus is put to the test. Barr thinks this approach is used to play on the loyalty of Christians to Jesus to get them to accept fundamentalist dogmas.

However, the argument just does not demonstrate what the fundamentalist apologetes hope to achieve. For Barr these manoevres are simple cases of a literary function-mistake. No distinction is drawn between the message Jesus seeks to convey in his utterances and the elements of which these are composed. Barr considers this is another example of the objectivist mentality of fundamentalism. It handles the Scripture like this because it produces results that fit in with the total character of fundamentalist religion. This didactic attitude deals with the question of the inspiration of the OT, its usefulness, and the inspiration of the NT at one fell swoop, for if the OT can be accepted thus, how would it be possible to withhold judgment concerning the NT, which touches the central act of revelation?

Another argument concerning the self-witness of Scripture and inspiration in fundamentalism seeks to root the inspiration of the Bible in the teaching of the texts which speak explicitly of this. Reference is made particularly to the texts in II Timothy 3:16 and II Peter 1:20. However, it is not possible to show that these texts refer unambiguously to the books in our accepted NT canon or in the biblical corpus as a whole. It is an "open question" as to which books the writer included and excluded in speaking of inspiration.[106] The fundamentalist takes it that these passages can be interpreted as the witness of the Bible to itself. According to Barr, all this is nonsense. There is no "Bible" which makes claims about itself. There is only a source which makes statements about other writings, which are themselves unspecified in instances such as that of II Timothy 3:16. Even if it could be shown that this passage does refer to the books we accept

---

106. Ibid., pp. 78f.; *BMW*, p. 14.

as canonical, this would make little difference, as it would hardly constitute the view of the Bible about itself. At most we could consider this as the reference of a late and marginal document which expressed an opinion of limited value about the NT writings at a stage when these were almost complete. There is in addition no indication as to what the nature of this inspiration could be for the author of this text. Barr seems at this point to have made short work of the fundamentalist argument which presses for the inspiration of all of Scripture on the basis of the witness of certain precise texts.[107]

A third and final argument of Barr to which we can point is that which he advances about the inspiration of the autographs.[108] He considers this hypothesis as an attempt to make the demonstration of errors in Scripture impossible. The appeal to the inspiration of the autographs is an apologetic one, establishing the inerrancy of Scripture at the point of inspiration. Errors may be found in the present text of Scripture, having crept in during the course of transmission. However, a real error would have to be proven in the inspired autograph for it to be accepted as such. The inspired text is the original one, the "infallible Bible-X," to use the scornful expression of E. Brunner.[109] Barr thinks there is little point in arguing this position on the inspired authographs on the basis of superficial considerations such as: What is the use of an inspired Bible if no one knows what is in it? The fundamentalist point can appear quite sensible in that if an inspiration is maintained, it is necessary to specify in which set of words the inspiration is found. Even if the original is not recoverable, this is not a totally useless suggestion, particularly if it is thought that the copies approach the original and are thus reliable. The apparent justification of this Barr concedes, as an adept polemicist, in order to press home his refutation.

Barr thinks that the fundamentalist mentality is again laid bare if the argument about the autographs in the nineteenth-century funda-

---

107. B. B. Warfield, for example, argued that the passage in II Tim. 3:15f. refers not only to the OT but also to the NT Scriptures, op. cit., pp. 133ff., 163; a different point of view is found in conservatism represented by James Orr, op. cit., pp. 181-82, who argues that no text in the Bible claims inspiration for all the Bible, not even II Tim. 3:16. However, Orr does argue that the principle which such texts establish for the OT has bearing on the NT; cf. p. 192.

108. *F*, pp. 268, 279, 293ff.

109. E. Brunner, *Revelation and Reason* (London, 1947), p. 274.

mentalists A. A. Hodge and B. B. Warfield is contrasted with that of the Westminster Confession. In article I.8 of the Confession, we read that not only were the OT in Hebrew and the NT in Greek immediately inspired by God, but "by his singular care and providence" were "kept pure in all ages [and] are therefore authentical." Warfield and Hodge, on the other hand, speak of the inspiration of the texts, but appeal to discrepancies to get rid of problems in the actual copies. This shift of attitude can be attributed, according to Barr, to the fact that in the nineteenth century the advance of criticism had made it impossible simply to affirm the Westminster doctrine about the providential preservation of the text.[110] At the end of the century it was no longer viable to dismiss the problems of the text, as Charles Hodge did in his *Systematic Theology,* as flecks of sandstone in the Parthenon marble. Some way had to be found to reconcile the number of variants with the affirmation of the inspiration of the Bible. Barr considers that the admission of textual corruptions on the part of Warfield and others was not an acceptance of criticism, but a way to back up the inerrancy of the inspired originals. Where instances of textual corruption are found, the argument about such discrepancies in transmission was used to support the notion that no such imperfections were present in the original autograph. Inspiration for Warfield is a precise and quantitative notion and extends only to the words of the original autograph. These words are the inspired ones, and textual variations are human intrusions in the chain of divine communication.[111] For this reason, textual criticism assumes a great im-

---

110. Barr's argument at this point again uses the work of E. R. Sandeen, *The Roots of Fundamentalism* (Chicago, 1970), pp. 127ff., as far as I can see, without acknowledgment. Sandeen sees the doctrine of A. A. Hodge and Warfield as a hardening in the face of the rise of criticism. This is so particularly in their appeal to the inspiration of the autographs. He also remarks, as does Barr following him, that the lay fundamentalists still treated their Bibles as though they were original autographs. The contrast Princeton/Westminster Confession is articulated in Sandeen. J. H. Gerstner in *God's Inerrant Word,* ed. J. W. Montgomery (Minneapolis, 1974), pp. 136ff., roundly denies the validity of Sandeen's argument here and affirms that the appeal to the authographa is a standard feature of the Reformed tradition and not an innovation of Warfield's. On the contrast between Westminster and Princeton regarding the autographs see J. Rogers, *Scripture in the Westminster Confession* (Grand Rapids, 1967), pp. 391ff., and B. B. Warfield, *The Westminster Assembly and Its Work* (Cherry Hill, N. J., 1972), pp. 236ff.

111. *F,* p. 295.

portance in discerning the inspired set of words now present in many texts.[112] This is complete in the autographs themselves, and we do not have these in our possession. On these grounds the perfection of the original divine inspiration is placed beyond the vicissitudes of the history of transmission; it is impossible to demonstrate the existence of an error in the original text.[113]

However, what can be said of the present corrupt text we possess? Strange though it may seem, the presence of these human intrusions in the inspired autograph serve to illustrate the great reliability of the Bible in the multiplicity of noninspired copies. If the fundamentalist, following Warfield, asserts that only the autographs are inspired texts and admits the presence of some corruptions in the actual texts, he is proposing that these copies are to a great extent reliable. So the fundamentalist has it both ways: It is impossible to prove an error because we do not have the autographs, and since there are some discrepancies in the present texts we can affirm that these are minor and that the corrupted text is reliable.[114] By this argument, the fundamentalist affirms in a positive and negative way the inspiration of the Scripture in the autographs. So the witness of the Scripture to its inspiration and inerrancy is maintained in fundamentalism in opposition to criticism.

Barr's criticism is that this theory about the inspiration of the autographs breaks down into absurdities once one looks at it closely. It is incompatible with our present understanding about the way biblical texts actually came into being. Barr's rejection of the argument about the inspiration of the autographs is an application of his refusal to accept inspiration as being at the point of writing of the text when God in his act of revelation inspired the sacred authors. His position is taken on critical grounds. A modern doctrine of inspira-

---

112. *F,* p. 296.

113. *F,* pp. 268, 281.

114. Barr seems to push the argument too far in the propositions he uses to represent it in *F,* p. 284. As he sets this down, they constitute a contradiction. It may well be that there is a paradox in Warfield's argument, but this does not mean that it sets the fundamentalists marching in two directions at once. It is in a way profoundly logical. Barr would have better represented this logic if he had formulated his proposition (a) "The Bible is reliable because its text has been to a great extent preserved free from corruptions." If Barr had not exaggerated this point, he may have been able to see more similarity than he does between Warfield and the Westminster Confession.

tion could not limit this to a precise moment of revelation in which the Scripture is produced by dual authorship. Today, if we could admit that inspiration extended to the words of the texts, this inspiration could not be limited to the autograph, but would have to extend to the various sources of the texts and the subsequent transmission of the text in tradition. It is not possible, on the grounds of our knowledge of the formation of the texts, to locate inspiration at any specific place. Inspiration, if we are to speak of it, thinks Barr, must be ascribed in a fallible way to the textual tradition as a whole.[115] Fundamentalists with their rigid stand on inspiration want to avoid making the connection between the text of Scripture and the development of tradition in Israel and the church. Barr considers that it is impossible not to see in the Scripture "one total complex of tradition"; this makes the fundamentalist view of inspiration simply "irrelevant."[116]

The point at issue between Barr and the fundamentalist as far as these three cases are concerned seems to lie in the fact that the fundamentalist authorises his theological proposals by a direct appeal to the Scripture. The biblical texts function as bearing directly on theological statements. Thus the witness of Jesus is seen as authorising present theological statements about the divine origin of the OT and passages such as II Timothy 3:16 directly attest the inspiration of the Scriptures. Likewise, the witness of the Scripture to itself bears only on the autograph, as there could have been no error in this owing to its divine origin. In each instance the Scripture authorises directly the theological statements enunciated by the fundamentalist.[117] In order to refute this claim it appears that Barr would have to demonstrate that the fundamentalist's conclusion is not warranted because exegesis of the passages referred to cannot support the argument in the way he supposes. This is what Barr in fact seems to attempt

---

115. A broader view of inspiration which is not limited to the text at the point of writing, but which includes the milieu of the tradition is also current in recent Catholicism. Cf. P. Grelot in *Recherches de Science Religieuse* 51: 346, and in *Concilium* 20:13-29; also R. A. F. McKenzie in *CBQ* 20:2ff., and D. J. McCarthy in *ThS* 24:553ff. The most important single study is perhaps that of K. Rahner, *Inspiration in the Bible* (Frieburg and London, 1961); also his article, "Inspiration," in *Encyclopaedie de la foi* (Paris, 1967), vol. II.

116. *F*, p. 297.

117. See D. H. Kelsey for an analysis of Warfield's argument, in op. cit., p. 141.

throughout his *Fundamentalism;* the witness of Scripture to itself cannot bring us to the conclusion that the Bible is inspired by a special divine act at the point of the writing of the autograph. The limited view of inspiration held by Warfield just does not hold good on the correct interpretation of the text. No argument from the special knowledge of Jesus can support the doctrine the fundamentalist wants it to. Nor is it possible from our actual knowledge of the text's formation to infer the existence of an original perfect autograph free from present corruptions.

However, it is doubtful that the issue can be left just there. If Barr wishes to refute the fundamentalist arguments by an appeal to exegesis, this inevitably raises the question of the methods of exegesis. It is at this point that Barr's direct refutation of the fundamentalist position by exegetical arguments would seem to flounder in its effectiveness. For Barr seems to think that if he can illustrate in an objective way that the text does not show this, the fundamentalist position will be refuted. However, what exegesis shows for the follower of Warfield and what it shows for the modern critic are two different things. For Barr supposes that a proper interpretation of the text can be attained only on grounds of the application of a modern critical method of exegesis. A proper exegesis for the fundamentalist is one which accounts for the fact that Scripture is the Word of God; the warrant for the way he moves from Scripture to doctrine is analytic in his consideration of what Scripture is. As Word of God, Scripture must not be tested by critical hypotheses, but it must test them. In other words, an understanding of the nature of Scripture is incorporated into the method of exegesis. The same is true, however, of Barr. If he considers that the fundamentalist way is an outmoded piece of uncritical antiquaria, such an opinion does not deliver him from the fact that there is an understanding of Scripture built in his method of exegesis as well.

Our intention here is not to discuss the relative justifications of these approaches, but to point out that a refutation of the fundamentalist position on the basis of arguments valid in a critical system has a limited value. It will be convincing for him who accepts already that critical position, but it will not be generally valid unless it has been shown that there are ultimately binding reasons in that position which constrain acceptance. To put this another way, it would seem to me that if Barr wishes to refute the fundamentalist position, it is not sufficient to show on his own critical ground that it is wrong. This would simply constitute a refutation on Barr's own suppositions, not a refutation of fundamentalism as such. A refutation of a fundamentalist argument would have to show it to be inconsistent on its own conditions of argument or establish some principle generally accepted as true with which the argument would be incompatible.

We may now proceed to apply these reflexions to the analysis of fundamentalism's view of inspiration as discussed by Barr. In the case of Barr's examination of the fundamentalist appeal that Scripture can be considered inspired and inerrant on the basis of Jesus' witness, Barr broadly tries to show that this is to mistake the function of certain elements in the teaching of Jesus and their relation to his whole saving purpose. Jesus, however, is not an expert in literary matters, but the promised Saviour. In Barr's argument, the idea that the fundamentalists are making a literary function-mistake seems to be appealed to as a general principle which renders the fundamentalist argument invalid. Barr provides some backing for his analysis by pointing to two characteristics in fundamentalism which account for this literary negligence on the part of fundamentalists. Firstly, they think in this way because it fits the character of their religion in general and also because fundamentalism is highly didactic. The Scriptures are considered as "teaching."[118] However, the general principle to which Barr appeals at this point cannot function as a refutation of the fundamentalist position unless it can be shown that Jesus as Son of God had no intention of making statements concerning the inspiration and inerrancy of the OT, even indirectly. As far as this is concerned, the evidence for the fundamentalist case may not be as tenuous as Barr infers. Even the moderate Abraham Kuyper affirmed, "If it be true that in no given instance Jesus utters an express declaration concerning inspiration, it appears sufficiently clearly that he considered the Scriptures of the Old Covenant to be the result of a Divine act of revelation, the original and real subject of which was God." Elsewhere Kuyper affirms that Christ gave no theory of graphic inspiration, but that the authority he attributed to Scripture admits of no other solution.[119]

---

118. *F*, pp. 75f.
119. A. Kuyper, op. cit., pp. 438f., 550.

In fact, the fundamentalist may have a very strong point when he refuses to distinguish between the message of Christ *in toto* as to himself as Saviour and the parts of the message. He can point to the fact that in the teaching of Jesus the source of authority Christ attributes to the OT Scriptures and to himself as Messiah is in God the Father in each case. As E. P. Clowney says: ". . . if Jesus so identified Scripture with the authority of his Father, we cannot accept his authority without accepting his view of Scripture's authority."[120] Barr's appeal to literary category-mistakes studiously by-passes these arguments.

In another place, it is true, he makes reference to the question of Christology and the knowledge of Jesus.[121] Barr thinks that the problem of the traditional discussion regarding accommodation is that it has been framed in terms of the divine and human natures of Christ. Thus accommodation theories have been associated with a kenotic Christology, while more conservative views have attributed a preponderance to considerations of Christ's divinity with respect to his teaching.[122] Barr thinks that when the question is put in this way, the issue is wrongly framed from the start. Rather than the categories of divinity or humanity, we must approach Scripture in a *functional* way. Jesus does not teach eternal truths, but he addresses his own situations. This functional approach to the sayings of Jesus may well, for all I know, command general assent among theologians. However, to use it as an argument against the possibility of determining the status of the OT by reference to the teaching of Christ it would have to be shown that this is the proper view or the "true" view of Christology. It may be doubted whether this could be achieved on the basis of the witness of Scripture.

In conclusion to these remarks, it may be asked whether Barr has in fact fulfilled the conditions necessary for his argument regarding Christ and the Bible to constitute a rebuttal of the fundamentalist claim. It has not been shown that fundamentalism is inconsistent in its own argument. On the contrary, there is a consistency in the way the fundamentalist aligns the authority of Christ and that of the Bible

---

120. E. P. Clowney, in op. cit., ed. J. H Skilton, p 179.

121. *F,* pp. 171f.

122. Cf. Warfield's remarks about Sanday in *The Inspiration and Authority of the Bible,* pp. 116ff.

in the context of the revelation of the Father. Nor has Barr established a principle which of itself is conclusive in demonstrating the
error in the argument of fundamentalists about Christ and the Bible.
The argument about literary category-mistakes does not show that
Christ did not want to teach things relative to the OT in his individual
declarations, or that he intended merely to point to his saving role.
The argument concerning functional Christology would have to be
accepted as "true" Christology to refute the fundamentalist view of
inspiration based on Christ's witness. However, no demonstration of
this is made. It may well be doubted on the grounds of Barr's own
acceptance of theological pluralism whether one such christological
option is possible.

The inspiration of the Scripture in the second case is grounded
in the appeal made by fundamentalism to certain texts. Barr seems
to oppose the fundamentalist argument in this appeal on the basis of
its inconsistency. Such particular Scriptures do not validate the conclusion regarding Scripture itself; the opinion represented in these
passages is a limited one. This seems to be a strong point. Yet its
usefulness to Barr is limited when it is compared with what has actually been claimed by fundamentalist appeals to such passages. Warfield himself spoke of the "gross misconception," the "inexplicably
odd misapprehension" of thinking that the witness of Scripture is
contained in a few outstanding passages which speak of inspiration
and that the witness can be discarded by refuting these passages. The
witness of Scripture to its inspiration cannot be avoided by discount-
ing individual passages; to attempt this is like trying to dodge the individual stones in an avalanche.[123] Likewise, Barr's thrust against
fundamentalism that passages such as II Timothy 3:16 cannot prove
the inspiration of the biblical canon flounders on the explicit statements of Warfield. Referring to the *pasa graphē*, Warfield states:

> . . . the apostle does not stop here to tell us either what particular
> books enter into the collection which he calls Sacred Scriptures, or
> by what precise operations God has produced them. . . . It was
> the value of the Scriptures, and the source of that value in their
> divine origin, which he required at the moment to assert.

---

123. Ibid., pp. 119ff. Cf. pp. 179, 208. A. Kuyper also discounts in similar
fashion a naive appeal to proof texts for establishing the doctrine of inspiration. Kuyper speaks of the "conscious life" which comes to expression in all
the Scriptures, op. cit., pp. 428ff.

However, if it is not possible for us to assert which books are in the reference to "all Scripture," it may be possible to propose that the *pasa graphē* does affirm that there is an organic scriptural unity. In this respect Abraham Kuyper says that the apostles did not look on the OT as a collection of literary documents, but as one codex, organically constructed and clothed with "Divine authority."[124] Barr has not taken such arguments current in fundamentalist circles into account. For this reason his remarks fall short of meeting the fundamentalist positions on their own ground.[125] To affirm that there is no "Bible view of itself," Barr would at least have to meet Warfield's argument that Scripture thinks of itself in terms of the "oracles of God," as the voice of God speaking in all parts to the reader. In addition, to the claim that the *pasa graphē* has no definite reference for the apostle to a body of writings, it would seem to be necessary to deny that this can be referred to as a codex of writings, organically united because of a common origin. However, Barr's remarks on this subject do not seem to get to the heart of the matter. His argument might gain some credence on his own theological basis, but for those who see Scripture as the historic revelation of a God who disposes everything according to his providence, Barr's argument falls far short of the mark.

It is equally doubtful, in the case of the reference to the question of the inspiration of the autographs, whether Barr's argument has been effective.[126] The position of Warfield, as already stated, seems to be quite a logical one. The distinction between the inspired autograph and the relative corruption of the apographs is one which is neither illogical in itself nor incompatible with the Reformed tradition

---

124. Warfield, op. cit., pp. 134ff.; Kuyper, op. cit., pp. 444f.

125. A significant fact concerning Barr's book on fundamentalism which points up Barr's failure to meet the fundamentalist arguments can be seen from a brief analysis of the index. Warfield is the most often cited writer (27 times). Yet in 344 pages the footnotes refer only *twice* to the principal book of Warfield, one of these being a quotation. In addition, there are three references to an article Warfield produced with A. A. Hodge. The disparity between Warfield's presence in the index and his absence in the footnotes is disquieting. This is even more so because Barr refers to Warfield as the father of fundamentalism, *F,* pp. 262, 270.

126. I must admit that I have had some difficulty in describing what seems to be Barr's position. His critique of the argument of the autographs is stated in three different places (see note 108 above). Some difficulty has been experienced in synthesising these three arguments.

of the Westminster Confession. It is an open question whether the distinction between autograph and apograph made by Warfield was in fact an apologetic device, as Barr seems to think. Warfield tended to stress the continuity between the two:

> The autographic text of the New Testament is distinctly in reach of criticism. . . . we cannot despair of restoring . . . His book, word for word, as he gave it by inspiration to men.[127]

I may misunderstand Barr's rather dispersed argument at this point, but it seems to me that Barr has missed Warfield's main emphasis in his distinction between autograph and apograph. This was that the autograph is preserved in the copies and is accessible in these. The genuine text is kept safe "in a multitude of copies."[128] To refute this argument, Barr appeals to the fact that our present understanding of the nature of inspiration is incompatible with the autographic inspiration of Warfield. The general principle which invalidates the fundamentalist approach is that of the understanding of historical criticism. This, however, is not likely to hold much water unless we wish to ignore the hypothetical nature of critical constructions and set them up as absolute norms of judgment. Some critical scholars might implicitly do this, of course, but their preferences are not ultimately binding, unless they can prove that their constructions are in fact correct beyond any shadow of doubt. Until this can be done, Barr's refutation of the argument of Warfield about the autographs remains hypothetical. For the fundamentalist it will always be accepted that it is necessary to define the role of criticism in the context of the doctrine of inspiration and not *vice versa*.

3.3.3. The logic of inerrancy

Barr concedes that the fundamentalist makes some sort of a case for the inspiration of Scripture, although he thinks this to be a lot weaker than the one made by liberal scholars. However, regarding the question of the inerrancy of Scripture, Barr thinks that there is no case at all made. This is because it is exegetically impossible from the texts used about inspiration to conclude that these teach the his-

---

127. Warfield, *An Introduction to the Textual Criticism of the New Testament* (Toronto, 1887), p. 15, quoted by J. Gerstner in op. cit., ed. J. W. Montgomery, p. 137, n. 80.

128. Warfield, *The Westminster Assembly and Its Work*, pp. 238f.

torical accuracy of the Bible. "The link between authority or inspiration on the one side and inerrancy on the other rests on one basis
only: supposition."[129] Barr attacks this supposition in two different
ways.

First of all, Barr advances in *Fundamentalism* a criticism of the
logic of inerrancy. There is no biblical way of proving inerrancy, so
fundamentalists resort to a philosophical form of reasoning. God is
perfect, and having inspired the Scriptures it is not conceivable that
these should not partake in his perfection. This perfection is at once
historical and theological.[130] Barr's main criticism of this is that it is
tributary of an idea which envisages the perfection of God in a static
way. God is not thought of in a living historical manner but in terms
of a perfection which does not touch the ambiguities of the historical
process. When the supernatural comes into contact with this-worldly
realities, the fundamentalist is not much interested in articulating the
relationship between natural and supernatural; what concerns him is
only the fact that God has intervened in a supernatural fashion. In
the case of Scripture such supernatural intervention guarantees the
perfection of the text in terms of inerrancy of fact and teaching.[131]
This attitude constitutes the rejection of the possibility of an historical
approach to Scripture and reality in general and leads fundamentalism
into incoherent appeals to the supernatural.

The second consideration Barr advances in respect to the claim
of an inspired, inerrant text of Scripture concerns the relevance of
this idea in the light of modern semantics. Words on paper are not,
says Barr, true or false. "They have meaning only through their
nexus with the semantics of the language in which they are written."[132]
To interpret the text, what needs to be known is the structure of
meaning in the natural language. It is in continuity with this structure
that the meaning of the biblical text is known. The doctrine of the
inerrancy of Scripture is a piece of "useless information"; it does not
help with interpretation. In the context of fundamentalism, the meaning of the text is not constituted in relation with the natural language,
but by means of the key of the religious tradition of fundamentalism.
This forms the context in which the inerrancy doctrine is validated,

---

129. *F*, p. 84. Cf. p. 267.
130. *BMW*, p. 14; *F*, p. 72.

131. *F*, pp. 277f.
132. *F*, p. 301.

apart from any consideration of the extra- or post-biblical areas of meaning.

Considering the weight which the notion of inerrancy carries in Barr's *Fundamentalism,* through his oft-repeated thesis that inerrancy protects the fundamentalist tradition, it is surprising how little consideration Barr has given to what fundamentalists actually say about it. No real reflexion is offered as to what the meaning of the notion of inerrancy could be when it is attributed to Scripture, nor as to the motivation of such an attribution. Barr's contention that there can be no exegetical demonstration of inerrancy, but that this relies on a kind of philosophical logic, is plausible in its way, but hardly meets up to the fundamentalists' own explicit declarations concerning the subject. For the fundamentalist, belief in inerrancy is far from being the fruit of a piece of apologetic logic, born out of necessity. Rather, it is implicit in his belief in inspiration itself. As a concomitant consequence of inspiration no philosophical argumentation is necessary to sustain it; it is implied in the nature of God's speaking in Scripture.[133] To confess inerrancy of Scripture, according to Packer, is simply to state our confidence in the divine origin of the Scriptures and their trustworthiness as the word of God.[134]

Paul Helm, writing about the infallibility of Scripture, states that this "has to do not with the truth as such, but with the guaranteed status of the proposition in question, and so its utter credibility"[135] Inerrancy might be said to function in much this way in fundamentalism; the truth of Scripture is secured in its inspiration by God's speaking. To affirm the inerrancy of this word is simply to indicate the guarantee implicit in the speaking of God. As a recent fundamentalist declaration states: ". . . *inerrant* signifies the quality of neither misleading nor being misled and so safeguards the truth that Holy Scripture is entirely free and trustworthy in all its assertions."[136] Barr does see that the fundamentalist believes the Scripture to be inerrant "because it itself says so,"[137] but does not seem to articulate the re-

---

133. See the remarks of R. Preus on the Lutheran scholastics' view of the relation of inspiration and inerrancy, *The Inspiration of Scripture* (Edinburgh, 1955), pp. 86f.

134. Packer, op. cit., pp. 94f.

135. P. Helm, "The Concept of Infallibility," p. 5 (unpublished paper).

136. *The Chicago Statement on Biblical Inerrancy* (1978), p. 9.

137. *F*, p. 72.

lation between inspiration and inerrancy in an explicit way and for this reason accords too much importance to the philosophical approach he discerns. Likewise, he does not seem to grasp the motivation behind the way the appeal to inerrancy functions in fundamentalism. This he puts down to a static view of God's perfection, combined with a material view of the nature of truth. This involves a denial of the full humanity of the biblical traditionists and an abandonment of an understanding of the Bible based on a consideration of the nature of the historical process.[138]

However, rather than these factors, what would seem to motivate a good deal of fundamentalist conviction about inerrancy is a consideration of the nature of sin and salvation. When he speaks about inerrancy the fundamentalist is not so much concerned with protecting the Scripture from accusations of human fallibility, but rather with setting it in the context of a redemptive act of God which also enters into the realm of linguistic communication. The desire is to recognise the new creation rather than avoid the old. The real motive of the claim of inerrancy lies in the understanding that Scripture is redemptive revelation and does not partake of the fallibility of *fallen* human nature. The fundamentalist will be likely to refuse correlating erring and humanness and to consider such correlations as a sort of formalisation which overlooks the present fallen state of humanity. When considering redemptive revelation he will probably refuse that this can be formally connected with a view of human nature which *a priori* supposes its fallibility. Fallen man must recognise his limitations in judging what claims to be the redemptive revelation of God. Such considerations, quite common in fundamentalist works, take us a long way from the static perfection which liberals have tended to see in fundamentalist teaching on inerrancy. Against this interpretation, J. I. Packer, to name one example, has stated with vigour that inerrancy does not express an irreligious concern with scientific accuracy, but it provides a bulwark *against* rationalism in preserving the mystery of the truthfulness of the sacred text.[139] Such affirmations from the fundamentalist side deserve some consideration if any-

---

138. On this point see the remarks of H. H. Farmer in *The Interpreter's Bible,* I:16; H. McDonald, op. cit., pp. 208ff.; A. G. Hebert, *Int* 11:197ff., and *The Authority of the Old Testament,* p. 98; Reid, op. cit., pp. 25ff.

139. J. I. Packer, *Themelios* 1:11.

thing is to be made of their theological position.

As far as the second opinion regarding inerrancy and semantics is concerned, some problems are present in the interpretation of Barr's point, and I am not entirely sure that I have grasped his argument. It is not clear to me whether Barr is merely affirming that the idea of inerrancy is of no use practically in interpretation, or whether he is saying that there is no such thing as a set of inerrant words separate from other words in a natural language. Possibly both are implied, as to affirm that the truth value of words must be measured in the context of the natural language means that the Scripture cannot be interpreted in terms of "comparing Scripture with Scripture." If this is so, inerrancy is not much use for interpretation since, as Barr says, it does not "decide anything" about the meaning of the text. If this is Barr's argument, and I reserve judgment here, it will hardly impress the fundamentalist who, following Warfield, Kuyper, or Bavinck, has adopted an organic view of inspiration, in which the language of Scripture is seen in continuity with the linguistic context. Inerrancy will in this case be discerned with reference to the author's intention in respect to that context and will not be devoid of consequences in the practice of interpretation.[140]

3.4. *Criticism of the unity of Scripture and theology*

When the notions of revelation, inspiration, and the authority of the Bible are challenged, it is not long before the question of the usefulness of speaking of the unity of the Bible appears. In the traditional approach to Scripture in the context of a theology of revelation, the unity of Scripture is an important concept, as it indicates the unity of the divine revelation and, indirectly, of the divine mind. The authoritative nature of Scripture appears in the oneness of the biblical message rooted in revelation. Theology finds its own unity by articulating the unity of the biblical message and thus itself participates in the authority of revelation in so far as it represents the message faithfully.

The problem for the unity of the Bible as a unity of revelation surfaced in contact with the development of the historical method. Whereas in pre-critical times the unity of the revelation had been

---

140. See *The Chicago Statement,* ad. loc., and Packer, ibid.

brought out by means of harmonising the diversities of Scripture on
the basis of the analogy of faith, historical critical research concentrating on the literal sense of the text produced results other than
those of the harmonising method. No longer did it appear possible
to speak of a self-evident unity of the Scriptures. W. Pannenberg
thinks this left two possible approaches to the question of unity: the
way of finding unity through a hermeneutical principle chosen by the
interpreter, or that of the Christ-event attested by various witnesses.[141]
There are problems implicit in each of these efforts which replace the
old idea of the unity of Scripture being in a doctrinal entity free from
contradiction. Where a hermeneutical principle is sought to express
the unity of Scripture, this unity is no longer objective and self-
evident. In the second instance, if the Christ-event cannot be separated
from the witnesses to it, it is difficult to see how it can be effective as
a standard for judging the different forms of proclamation.[142]

Whichever line of solution is sought, the problem remains the
same, namely, that of articulating wherein lies the principle of the
unity of Scripture, once the Bible is no longer considered as revealed
text, and secondly that of applying the chosen principle of unity to the
question of the relation of the testaments. In this section we shall
briefly examine Barr's critique of the way the issue was handled in the
neo-orthodox tradition and the implications of this for the relation of
Scripture and theology.

3.4.1. The unity of Scripture and Biblical theology

Barr notes the change of climate in recent years from the attitude
which considered the Scripture as a whole to the greater acceptance
of diversity. The biblical unity of the previous generation, which was
an essential factor in theological prolegomena, has given way to
diversity. Commenting on this in 1969, Barr says that "theology today

---

141. W. Pannenberg, *Basic Questions of Theology* (London, 1970), I:192ff.
Also on the unity of Scripture and criticism, G. Ebeling, *Word and Faith*
(London, 1963), pp. 91f., and "The Meaning of Biblical Theology," *JTS*
6:220.; G. Maier, *The End of the Historical Critical Method* (St. Louis, 1977),
pp. 55f.

142. Pannenberg, op. cit., p. 196. Pannenberg opts for this second solution,
i.e., seeking to understand the unity of Scripture in terms of the inherent
meaning of the Christ-event unfolded in various forms of the kerygma. Barr
tends to go the other way and locate the unity of the Bible in the unfolding
of the living tradition of the church.

looks more openly at the way in which the Bible hangs together because it is free from the former pressure to *insist* upon its unity."[143] In this period, rather than an attempt to redefine the unity of the Bible, we are faced by the prospect of a theology which tacitly condones the demise of the neo-orthodox principle. If we are to speak of the unity of Scripture, this must emerge from theological research, rather than being presupposed at the outset.[144]

The insistence on the unity of the Bible in the BTM was essentially a reaction against the earlier liberalism. It rejected the purely analytic approach to Scripture and sought a synthesis, a unity in the diversity of the biblical materials. The Bible's diversities were recognised, but these were thought to form the different voices of a "harmonious choir."[145] In this context also the testaments were seen together as one distinctive corpus.[146] The neo-orthodox emphasis on the unity of the Bible was therefore a studious attempt at synthesis over above the diversities of the historical method.[147] It sought the message of the Bible in a global sense and thought that the "parts" could be properly seen only in relation to the authoritative message of the whole.[148] The task of Biblical theology was to seek the unity of Scripture in terms of a single redemptive process.[149] This process very often was analysed after a christocentric model, which reinforced the unity of Scripture in terms of a single interpretative principle.

The weakness of this view of the unity of Scripture probably lay in the fact that it was a high-level unity, which defined the unity in terms of God and his action in the world as over against human processes. It is not "objective" in the Bible, but depended more on a will to believe that this is the way things are. Biblical unity is not the theological unity of the Bible itself, but depends on the unity of God's plan and act. As such, unity lies beyond the Bible.[150] It is not necessarily evident on the level of concrete theological demonstration.

---

143. *BWT,* p. 170.

144. Barr, *ER* 21:146; *BMW,* p. 99.

145. *BMW,* pp. 3f.; *IDB*(S), p. 108.

146. *Int* 25:26; *BMW,* pp. 97f.

147. *BMW,* p. 63.

148. Ibid., p. 99.

149. J. Bright, *The Authority of the Old Testament* (London, 1967), pp. 110f.

150. See the remarks of G. E. Wright in *SJT* 8:341ff. Also the various articles in *Int* 5:2, and summary by Wright in *Int* 5:3:304ff.

Comparing the unity proposed in the BTM and that of older orthodoxy, S. V. McCasland remarked that "it appears unlikely, however,
that in tangible, demonstrable, generally accepted results in terms of
unified concepts of theology, the new theologies can be more successful than were their predecessors."[151]

In previous sections we have examined Barr's criticisms of the
methods used on the BTM to articulate the unity of Scripture by
means of typology, salvation history, or distinctive biblical concepts.
At present, we wish to point to what was a central concern of neo-
orthodoxy, that is, the unity of the two testaments secured on the
basis of a Christ-centred model. In the BTM the unity of Scripture
was seen in terms of witness, the OT pointing forward to Christ and
the NT pointing back, with Christ at the centre of the whole. The
two testaments were considered one in their witness to revelation in
Christ.[152] Barr thinks that this approach to unity, which won widespread acceptance, carries with it a particular problem.[153] A Christ-
centred model of biblical unity imposes a theological unity on the
Bible which is other than that of the perspective of the writers themselves. For them, the problem was not to understand the OT, but to
understand Christ. We speak of Christ as the key to the OT and we
take too much for granted when we assume that Christ is a known
quantity for evaluating the OT. This heuristic key is of little use in
particular cases of exegesis and can foster a bad christologising interpretation. Furthermore, when a Christ-centred approach is applied
to the OT with a view to the unity of Scripture, the connections made
between the testaments are random ones. The question immediately
raised is as to the degree of arbitrariness which can be permitted
in stating the connections, in the light of the nature of the biblical
material itself. Barr proposes that two factors must be kept in mind.
We cannot suppose that Christ was a known quantity for the writers
of the OT and apply a Christ-centred interpretation as a key for
understanding the OT. On the other hand, this does not mean that

---

151. S. V. McCasland in *JBL* 73:5. Cf. also J. Branton in *Religion in Life*
26:17.

152. See D. L. Baker's account of christological solutions to the problem of
the unity of the Bible in *Two Testaments, One Bible* (London, 1976), chap. 5.

153. Barr's criticism of the Christ-centred interpretation as a model for the
unity of the Bible in *ONI*, pp. 139ff.

the OT does not help us to know what it means to be the Christ. Israel provides the religious matrix into which Christ is born and in which his understanding of his mission is formed.[154]

Without going any further in the description of the problem, these remarks can help us to pin-point the reason for Barr's criticism of the unity of the Bible articulated in terms of a Christ-centred principle. It is, in a word, a critique of a theological search for unity as lacking sufficient historical perspective. Or, to put it differently, the normative theological search has occupied a place of centrality without always having sufficient support in the materials dealt with.[155] Thus Barr criticises christocentric views of the unity of Scripture as failing to take into account the multiplex nature of the OT tradition, the diversity of which makes this model difficult to apply. For the exegete, the way in which the unity of the testaments was established by Biblical theology was "strangely abstract, unreal and unhistorical."[156] Direct theological links were sought rather than historical links through Jewish interpretation. This approach, which neglected the historical-descriptive links between the testaments, has its roots, Barr thinks, in the opposition of revelation and religion. Theological links in the unity of Scripture are sought as indicative of the revelation lying behind the canonical books. In his criticism of the search for the unity of Scripture in neo-orthodoxy, Barr is protesting about the selection of normative-theological concepts which tend to ignore the historical realities of the text and its extra-biblical context. His critique amounts to the assertion of the need of freedom from theological dogmas in the historical interpretation of the materials. The unhistorical character of the theological attempts to describe the unity of the Bible in recent Biblical theology is an expression of a conceptual approach dominated by considerations of authority.

Perhaps the problem of the unity of Scripture in the context of this tension between history and theology can be described in the following way. In pre-critical days and in the present fundamentalism the Bible account of revelation in history was authentic on the grounds of the inspiration of Scripture. History was as the Bible presented it

---

154. Barr's own approach to the relation of the testaments is described in 4.1.2.

155. *ONI,* pp. 24ff.

156. Barr, *BJRL* 58:28.

in the inspired records, which themselves are revelation. No conflict is felt between history and theology and both are revealed in complementary fashion in the inspired Writ. With the rise of criticism, however, there was a greater consciousness of the difference between the history in the text and the critical reconstructions. Historical research freed itself from the influence of theology and developed its own methods. In liberalism, it established its own principle of unity in terms of an evolutionary historical process. Theological statement came to depend for its validity on the historical reconstruction of the text and the events spoken of in the text. Biblical theology in this sense is a descriptive discipline and the unity of Scripture, if it is proper to speak of this, is seen in terms of the unity of the historical process uncovered by historical investigation.

The problem in this analytic approacn is to find a synthesis in theological terms which is justified by the diversity of the historical analysis. From the other end, there remains the possibility of seeking a unity in terms of theology by means of the selection of a theological theme and seeing the Scripture in terms of this. This tends, however, to concentrate on the theologically relevant sections of the text and runs the risk of synthesis which does not accord full weight to the historical constructions. The tension remains between history and theology. In his critique of the unity of Scripture in neo-orthodoxy, Barr points out the loss of contact between the theological affirmation based on revelation and the reality of the historical process. This tension between the theological normative approach and the historical descriptive discipline is a fundamental one for modern theology and raises the problem of the relation of biblical studies and dogmatics which seem deeply alienated because of it.

3.4.2. The method of Old Testament theology

This problem of the relation of history and theology, which surfaces in relation to the unity of Scripture, is also discussed by Barr in his scattered reflexions on the nature of Old Testament theology. One of Barr's early articles (1957) deals directly with the question and he also touches on it again in *ONI*.

Old Testament theology must grapple with the question of how far it goes beyond a merely descriptive study of religion and the relations it bears with theology as a systematic science. The issue is therefore one which concerns the extent to which OT theology can be a merely historical description and in what sense it could achieve normativity.[157] In recent years, states Barr in his article, the tendency has been to an emphasis on OT studies as a descriptive science which elaborates from the OT material a critical account of Israelite religious history. Many of the works that appear entitled "Theology" are in fact nothing other than systematic exegesis and do not form a radical break with the historical approach.[158] Their concerns are primarily philological, literary, and historical. Barr cites Eichrodt's work as an example of this descriptive approach; even works such as Vriezen's which adopt a specifically Christian starting-point seem to work with a descriptive method.[159] However, the issue is still open as to whether OT theology should go beyond the descriptive confines of systematic exegesis. It may even be asked whether systematic exegesis itself does not represent something more than a mere description. There is some suspicion as to whether the "theologies" based on systematic exegesis are descriptive or whether the project of a "theology" does not involve some normativity. Thus the clarification of the relation between the descriptive science and normative theology is necessary.

In so far as OT theology involves a search for meaning, it goes beyond the simply descriptive. When OT study seeks the sense of the belief of Israel that God acted in history, or asks whether God has indeed acted, it leaves behind the realm of the purely descriptive. The approach of the history of religion can inform us that Israel believed that God had acted in some way. However, the further implication of this historical affirmation and whether or not it has any substance cannot be avoided. As Barr says: "To point to the 'spiritual values' of a faith centred in acts done in history, while obscuring the question of the reality of such acts, is at this point to pull the wool over our eyes."[160] Rather the historical method should leave itself open to the possibility of the action of God. If it is not possible from the historical enquiry itself to answer the question of whether God did in-

---

157. See Barr's criticisms of the lack of clarity of L. Koehler's method in his *Old Testament Theology,* in *JSS* 4:173.

158. Barr, "The Problem of Old Testament Theology and the History of Religion," *Canadian Journal of Theology* 3:141ff.

159. Ibid., p. 143; *ONI,* p. 168.

160. Ibid., p. 145.

deed act, it cannot have a preconceived notion of the impossibility of this. The historical method presents its material in such a way as to leave the possibility of such a case open, and in doing so it also avoids introducing dogmatic conceptions into its own research. OT theology considered as an historical enterprise has no direct answer to the question of normativity. In the light of this, there is no special method of OT theology as such in terms of theological procedure. It should remain a largely exegetical science which would take "seriously but not accept dogmatically the claim [of the texts] to know of divine acts or divine revelation."[161] Such an approach would not be dominated by dogmatic considerations of normativity, and would avoid engaging in the vindication of biblical authority.

Barr's position is quite clear at this point. Exegetical work must be kept free from the imposition of dogmatic normativity; the historical descriptive and the theological are separated out. Their subsequent relationship is defined in terms of a possibility left open by the historico-exegetical scholar in his work. The historical domain is not the realm of faith/truth affirmations of the scholar; such attitudes lie in another, albeit "possible," domain. At this point Barr seems to be quite willing to divide the historical and the theological, the historical reason and the faith commitment areas, and leave their relation quite unarticulated. This explains Barr's attitude concerning the unity of the Bible, which lies in the realm of the dogmatico-normative, but cannot be demonstrated successfully in the realm of historical realities of the text.

A similar statement appears in Barr's later remarks in *ONI*. Here Barr proposes that no final answer can be given to the question of the method of OT theology. In so far as we are concerned with a theology of the OT, this is incomplete and partial, as the OT itself does not permit us to reach any definite conclusions. Questions which have theological ultimacy are asked within Christianity, but the way of answering them must be related to a total Christian theological insight, which cannot be confined to the OT. Such insight is reached after taking stock of the OT, but this is totally different from defining a Christian criterion and then understanding the OT in terms of it. This is another way of stating that historical work must be free from

---

161. Ibid., p. 146.

obstructions of normativity, but cannot rule out the possibility of these questions. The specific function of the OT scholar in the light of this is not to produce books entitled "theologies," but to test critically the use made by theology in general of the OT material.[162] Barr doubts the validity of producing theologies *per se*. In his review of Von Rad's *Theology*, he states that it is a great book, which may also indicate that no more books of this kind may be written.[163] The most immediate need is further detailed exegesis and more thought about the logic of the subject. The task of the OT theologian is to see that justice is done to the OT text. If this is his prime concern, the pitfall of submitting to prevailing dogmatic trends, which has not always been avoided in the attempts to develop theologies of the OT, will be less of a threat.[164]

From this point of view, it is not difficult to see why Barr is reticent about theologies of the OT which articulate the unity of the material on the grounds of a principle of selection. This has been used to state the difference between the history of religions approach, which includes all that is relevant, and theology, which seeks a statement of the normative by means of selecting in this material. This method may well seem to throw the doors open to arbitrary subjectivity.[165] Barr recognises that any treatment of a subject involves a certain limitation on the part of the writer, but this is quite different from limiting the subject by means of a presupposition which selects only a part of the data as relevant. This is harmful to the scientific character of the work. For this reason, Barr suggests that selectivity in this sense should be abandoned. Where it has been used, it illustrates the pressure towards synthesis in OT theology; the search for the normative can enter in at this point to influence the treatment of the material. In Barr's view, OT theology is "primarily an exegetical science and its reference is no narrower than the totality of the texts to be interpreted."[166] Where synthesis is sought, this cannot be legiti-

162. *ONI*, p. 169.
163. *ET* 73:146. Cf. "Old Testament Scholarship in the 1960s," *Church Quarterly* 2:201.
164. *ONI*, p. 170.
165. "The Problem of Old Testament Theology," p. 147. Here Barr criticises the way Koehler and Dentan have applied a principle of selection. See also his review of H. H. Rowley's *The Faith of Israel* in *JSS* 2:398.
166. Ibid., p. 149.

mately done by eliminating a part of the material, but with a view to bringing us afresh to the exegesis of individual passages.

An OT theology, then, when it seeks a synthesis of the data, does not do so in order to get a normative view out of the material. If this were the case, exegesis would just be a preliminary task. The relationship Barr sees is not a linear one running from text to normative theology abetted by a principle of selection in the material; rather he proposes a circular movement from the texts as a whole to a synthesis which returns to the texts. Under these conditions theology will remain open to correction from exegesis and avoid imposing dogmatic norms on the text. It is for this reason that Barr criticises the pretension of Von Rad to have found the method for OT theology which corresponds to the biblical materials and the exclusiveness implied in this claim.[167] This indicates also why Barr affirms that there is no one method for OT theology, but that several methods may well be equally legitimate in the pursuit of theological synthesis.

These remarks are also of relevance in the discussion of the possibility of finding the "centre" of the OT. In the BTM it was widely held that in spite of the diversities revealed by criticism it was possible to state a core of the OT or the Bible which would express the unity of the whole. Now, states Barr, there is less occasion to speak of one theology of the Bible, but the diversity of theologies in the Bible can be recognised.[168] However, even where it is held that Scripture contains a diversity of theologies, this does not necessarily mean that the search for a "centre" must be abandoned. The point which needs clarification is that of whether such a centre must be found in the biblical material itself or whether it is simply an organising principle chosen by us in the light of present needs. The plurality of theologies in the Bible aids us to see that ultimately there is no one centre on the basis of which a unitive theology of the Bible can be articulated. This diversity in the biblical corpus denies exclusive rights to any one theological formulation but opens the possibility to a number of different ways of organising a theology. A theology which is organised in relation to one centre of biblical interest must be able to justify itself with reference to that centre by showing its importance in

---

167. Cf. 2.3.3 and *ET,* loc. cit.

168. "Trends and Prospects in Biblical Theology," *JTS* 25:270ff.; *IDB*(S) p. 108; *ONI,* pp. 130f.

the biblical materials. Nevertheless, as there is a diversity of theologies in the Bible itself, the choice of the centre for the construction of theology is a personal one: ". . . biblical theology, at least at some levels, partakes of the nature of an art, rather than of that of a science."[169] What Barr seems to be telling us is that Biblical theology, and theology in general, in articulating a theology does not scientifically indicate *the* centre in the biblical data. As there exist a diversity of theologies in Scripture, the choice of a centre of organisation is a matter of the intuitive creativity of the theologian. It is a personal matter, and does not, or should not, pretend to ultimate objective correctness.

It is perhaps time to draw together some of the remarks made in this section. Barr's thought on the nature of OT theology is an expression of his criticism of the notion of the unity of the Bible. When unity has been spoken of and sought, this has often been detrimental to the liberty of the exegete with regard to the text. The scope of the material has been restricted to fit in with the conception of unity proposed in the context of a normative theology. The compulsion to state the biblical view in a normative way has foreshortened the exegetical task. Barr refuses this impingement of dogmatic concerns on the freedom of exegesis. His solution is a critique of the idea that the unity of Scripture is an *a priori* upon which exegesis proceeds. Exegesis must be undertaken in complete liberty, and perhaps a unity will appear at the end of the theological process. Then a certain kind of unity may be creatively experienced in the same way as we might expect the authority of Scripture or its inspiration to make itself felt. This critique of Barr represents a return to the concerns of analysis for its own sake, which had been neglected during the period of the revival of biblical authority.

One question which remains is that of the function of the "centres" of theology. Does the recognition of the diversity of the biblical materials imply that we must abandon all talk of the unity of Scripture itself? What is the relation between the various "centres" and the plural theologies they represent? Such questions will retain our attention in examining Barr's own suggestions on this topic.[170]

---

169. Ibid.; *JTS,* p. 272.
170. See 4.1.2. Barr's refusal of the unity of Scripture seen in our discussion hitherto has been a critique of the methods of neo-orthodox Biblical theol-

3.4.3. The unity of Scripture and the hermeneutical debate

Another factor which Barr points to as illustrative of the impossibility of speaking blithely of the unity of Scripture is seen in the debate about hermeneutics. As we have seen above, Barr contends that the diversity of theologies in the Bible prevents us from pretending that there might be one correct theological method. There is not one theology in the Bible; there are theologies. No one theological method can claim an exclusive right on the grounds that it corresponds to the shape of the biblical materials; there are different methods which may correspond to the different elements in the biblical data. This is to say also that there is no theological method indicated by the Bible itself which provides the key through which a theological system analogical to that of Scripture can be elaborated. However, if there is no explicit biblical principle of authorisation given, this opens the question as to what other hermeneutic considerations may presently permit us to justify the appeal to the biblical materials made by a theology.

Barr is far from giving a blank cheque to the various hermeneutical approaches that have been elaborated.[171] In fact these run the risk of smuggling in various dogmatic presuppositions which will then condition the interpretation of Scripture. Nevertheless, the recent discussion of hermeneutics has shown rather strikingly a change of attitude concerning the authority and the unity of the Bible. Ultimately, it is the method itself which becomes decisive in determining the unity of meaning of the text.[172] In the end, it appears there are two authorities, the Bible and the interpretative method.[173] The hermeneutic debate also points up that it is no longer possible to treat the Bible as a doctrinal textbook, as the traditional dogmatics did.[174] The relation-

ogy. It is not entirely foreign to the concerns Karl Barth himself expressed on this subject. Biblical theology, for Barth, cannot systematise the biblical witness. There is no Biblical theology in terms of a conceptualised unity, neither of one of the testaments, nor of the whole. Biblical theology is never more than "a collection of individual exegeses." The unity of revelation lies not in a system, but in Jesus Christ. This unity is never behind us, always ahead of us. "We cannot think it . . . assert and prove it; we can only believe it. . . ." Barth, op. cit., I.2, 483f. Barr's exposition of the problem can be considered a radicalisation of these remarks from the exegete's perspective.

171. See 3.1.4 on hermeneutics and authority.
172. *IDB*(S), p. 107.
173. *BMW,* p. 96.
174. Ibid., p. 89.

ship between Bible and theology cannot be simply treated as though the Bible texts referred directly to overt theological entities. The emphasis has changed in theological studies from a referential approach which related the text to explicit doctrinal formulation to one which takes account of the mind of the writer.

In the traditional approach the unity of theology was founded on a unity of the divine mind expressed in Scripture. The concentration on the author's intention, on the other hand, was bound to shift the emphasis away from the referential view which saw Scripture as a codified textbook of doctrine. Also the unity of Scripture was relocated in "thought categories" or biblical concepts; it is not defined in a direct referential way, but by reference to the mind of the writers.[175] The relation of Scripture and theology becomes indirect, passing as it does through the mind of the biblical authors. This movement from a referential view of the relation of theology and Scripture to one of intentionality corresponds according to Barr with the rise of historical criticism, which points to the difference between the actual historical realities and the purposes of the writers.

Another consequence of this shift is that when the Scripture is no longer held to refer to objective truth of universal validity coming from the divine mind through human instrumentality, the normativity of the expression of the mind of the biblical writers can be doubted. K. Stendahl has insisted on the need to distinguish between the descriptive and normative tasks of Biblical theology. To say what Paul meant is not to say what he means; the first is descriptive and must be kept separate from the normative question of what it means. The question of what Paul means implies contextualisation within the community, and this involves a translation of the meaning of Paul into the modern situation.[176] This is to say that even if a unity of the biblical mind can be observed, it is not necessarily normative for a unity of theological expression today.

This, as B. S. Childs says, "struck a blow at the very heart of the

---

175. Ibid., p. 92.
176. K. Stendahl, in *The Bible in Modern Scholarship,* ed. J. P. Hyatt (Nashville/New York, 1965), pp. 199ff., and *IDB,* I.420. Cf. D. E. Nineham, *The Use and Abuse of the Bible,* pp. 12f., 27. See Barr's comments on Stendahl in *IDB*(S), p. 106. Stendahl's distinction is close to Barr's appeal for the separation of the historical and normative aspects of theology.

[Biblical theology] movement, as it was originally conceived."[177] For the BTM had worked on the supposition, it would seem, that if the difficult problem of finding the unity of the biblical thought could be achieved, this would be immediately normative for theology. The hermeneutic problem indicated by Stendahl has it otherwise. It indicates that the unity of Scripture through the intention of the writers, even if it can be stated, is not directly constitutive of the unity or authority of present theology. Barr's criticism follows somewhat different lines, but the conclusion is similar. The notion of the unity of Scripture has lost its savour and no longer salts present theological discussion. It is not suitable to define the status of Scripture, which is characterised by a diversity of theologies and authorises a similar diversity today.

3.5   *Uncertainty about the status of the Bible*

The critique of Barr presented in this chapter concerning the status of Scripture is fairly representative of an uncertainty that grew through the 1960s and '70s. In the particular case of Barr this questioning is motivated by a consciousness that in the movement of the revival of biblical authority the quest for normativity fostered enigmas in the interpretation of the text. Inconsistencies take hold of exegesis when the interpreter's desire is to formulate the sense of the text out of consideration for some normative structure to which it is thought to refer. Explanation gets something out of the text which apparently is not immediately there in terms of normal grammatico-literary procedures. These difficulties arise because it is expected that the biblical material ought in some way to have a special character. Chosen and blessed among books, the Bible is looked upon as the church's hope for receiving the Word of God. Barr's critique of the present status of the Bible, following on from his examination of interpretative procedure, constitutes a rejection of the idea that a special character can be attributed to the Bible as normative divine revelation. We must liberate ourselves from a way of looking at the Bible which imputes to it attributes belonging to God himself.

In this perspective, Barr's critique calls into question the validity of attaching an authority based on divine act or word to the human text of Scripture. This is the problem with fundamentalism, which

---

177. B. S. Childs, *Biblical Theology in Crisis* (Philadelphia, 1970), p. 79.

sees the Bible as the transcript of God's will, but also of neo-orthodox Biblical theology, which expected to find the authority of God attested in an indirect way in Scripture. The weakness of Biblical theology in recent years, according to Barr, is that it has been too concerned with a claim to authority which it could not substantiate. It was assumed that the Bible had some unarguable normative status, that Biblical theology makes this authority intelligible, and when this is achieved, the message must be accepted.[178] However, Biblical theology was not really able to demonstrate with its arguments, perhaps valid in themselves, that *this* book is the supreme authority. More radical opinion felt that between the arguments advanced and the conclusion as to the absolute authority of the Bible there lay a gap that could be bridged by only a presupposition, if not a prejudice.[179] Such a prejudice has been determined by some critics to be a "failure of nerve."[180] The reaction against liberalism in the movement of the revival of biblical authority was relatively right, thinks Barr; the problem is that this reaction was absolutised and its assumptions concerning Scripture and theology were taken as absolutely correct.[181] Now the situation has changed and there is an awareness of the failures of Biblical theology.[182] After this period of reliance on biblical authority, Barr thinks we may be able to accept that the questioning of the status of the Bible in the church is permanent and normal. It is no longer clear why we "should affirm at all anything as strange as 'biblical authority.' "[183] There is a recrudescence of doubt about authority, which is very different from the attitude existing previously and is characterised by misgivings about speaking of the authority of the Bible.[184]

Why this doubt about the Scripture, it may well be asked? Speaking about the OT in particular, Barr affirms that there is no one source or theologian responsible for the doubts about the status of this section

---

178. Barr, *JTS* 25:282; *IDB*(S), p. 111.
179. *BMW,* p. 36.
180. See the remarks of D. E. Nineham on this subject. Biblical theology is a "good servant," but a "bad master" when it wants to monopolise the field, in L. Hodgson, *On the Authority of the Bible* (London, 1960), p. 94.
181. Barr, *JR* 56:2.
182. On the reasons for the decline of the BTM see Barr, *BWT,* p. 173; *BMW,* pp. 5ff.; *JTS* 25:266f. Also B. S. Childs, op. cit., chap. 4.
183. *BMW,* pp. 8f.
184. *Church Quarterly* 2:205.

of Scripture: ". . . they are part rather of the popular ethos within theological study."[185] If, as we have stated in our account, the question of authority is closely related to that of revelation, so that the nature of the authority attributed to Scripture depends on the nature of the revelation involved, the present doubt about the authority in the church may well express an alienation from former views of revelation. In this respect Barr remarks that in the neo-orthodox period dogmatics contributed to the general acceptance of the authority of Scripture. The centrality of dogmatics lent support to the authority of the OT.[186] In this period also dogmatics was above all revelational in its orientations. Revelation which was dogmatically presupposed by exegetes gave an impetus to the BTM in its search for theological formulations which would sustain the unity and the authority of the Bible. Inspiration too was linked closely with revelation and was itself defined in terms of an act of God with respect to the Scripture.

However, the ambiguity of this approach can be noted. The rejection of the traditional doctrine of inspiration with its implication that God inspired revealed propositions left neo-orthodoxy with the task of defining the unity and authority of Scripture in a location beyond the statements of Scripture itself.[187] This notion of revelation was cut off from its biblical foundation in the doctrine of inspiration. Thus the biblical language of revelation used in the BTM and in neo-orthodoxy was grafted onto a secular view of the nature of the Scriptures themselves. The tension of using the revelational vocabulary of Scripture apart from its epistemological basis in the doctrine of inspiration could not be borne for too long. In a way, it was inevitable that the revelational categories should themselves be seen in their isolation as lacking in real support, and that their validity be called into question.[188] C. Pinnock states this point quite abruptly when he says that neo-orthodoxy, which wedded the secular worldview of liberalism and the supernatural outlook of the Bible, relegated the acts of

185. Ibid.

186. *Int* 25:27f. B. S. Childs in *Int* 26:27f. remarks that whereas biblical scholars have prided themselves on their independence from systematic theology, their greatest achievements have been in times when it was virile.

187. B. S. Childs remarks that the BTM failed to get to grips with the doctrine of inspiration but concentrated on revelation, *Biblical Theology in Crisis*, pp. 103f.

188. This point is stated with great intensity by L. Gilkey in his well-known article in *JR* 41:194ff.

God to an existential never-never land.[189] As Packer remarks, Biblical theology wanted to present itself to the world as scientific and to the church as Christian, and so have it both ways.[190] While speaking of the revelation in terms of *magnalia Dei* and refusing the interpretation of these acts in terms of Near Eastern mythological patterns, the BTM was in fact busy applying an interpretation germane to modern theories of history.[191]

Barr is very conscious of this ambiguity. His criticism of the status of Scripture is that the former revelation-centred approach is unsatisfactory in the light of modern thought. The dogmatic *a priori* which places interpretation or discussion of the doctrine of Scripture in the context of a God-to-man movement must be thoroughly unmasked in order that these questions be approached comprehensibly in categories more acceptable to the modern knowledge which is ours. This critique is, in the light of his earlier work, an application of his doubts about the possibility of holding the divine and human characters of Scripture together in interpretation or in the formulation of a doctrine of Scripture. The Bible must be understood in a thoroughgoing human way.

This factor is at the heart of his critique of describing the Bible as revelation, authority, inspired or unitive word in the sense that the adjective "divine" might be attached to these terms in a God-to-man movement. As modern men we have no way of knowing what an act of revelation attested in Scripture might be, of accepting an external authority on blind faith, of imagining how a text might be inspired by God, or how such a text might have a divine unity founded on inspiration. We have no real answers to the questions when they are asked under these conditions. All that may be done is to point to the ambiguity of pretending that we can imagine an intersection of the divine and human factors and get on with trying to recuperate the evocative possibilities of these notions in a human context. How Barr proposes that such a reconstruction could be accomplished we shall subsequently see.

As far as fundamentalism is concerned, it is perhaps less ambiguous

189. C. Pinnock, *Biblical Revelation,* p. 10.
190. J. I. Packer, op. cit., p. 156; cf. pp. 152ff.
191. B. S. Childs, *Myth and Reality in the Old Testament* (London, 1960), p. 76.

than neo-orthodoxy. However, this does not make the situation any better, only worse in a sense, as fundamentalism is totally alienated from the present and also from contact with other theological options. Fundamentalism's arguments are exclusive, thinks Barr, because it is socially exclusive. It is all or nothing, and one is in or out of the fundamentalist milieu.[192] Perhaps Barr could even agree formally with J. G. Machen that between fundamentalism and "liberalism" it is a question of two different religions, although it is difficult to say whether Barr would think fundamentalism to be really non-Christian.[193] Perhaps just one point can be made here in conclusion concerning fundamentalism. Between Barr and Warfield, it is not simply a question of a divergence over one doctrine, that of Scripture. The issue is deeper than this, as Warfield's doctrine of the Bible is simply an aspect of his views about God. His view of Scripture is impossible without his view of providence and history in general, as being directed by the divine will. For Warfield, God is personal and infinite and works all things for his glory. The real point at issue is not simply the doctrine of Scripture; it is nothing less than the doctrine of God which is to be held in Christianity.

Barr does not seem to get around to examining this relationship in the fundamentalism of Warfield and his spiritual heirs. Nor is it made clear in Barr's *Fundamentalism* what his view of God might be and how this might be related to a more proper view of Scripture which he supposes in his criticism of the fundamentalist viewpoint. This may constitute a great weakness of Barr's critique of fundamentalism; it may be the root of some of the problems we have sought to indicate in the evaluation Barr proposes. It seems to me to boil down to this: If Barr's view of God is not that of the Warfieldian fundamentalist, he cannot simply suppose that a critique of fundamentalism's doctrine of Scripture on the logic of his own view will apply to the fundamentalist view as a refutation. Two approaches are possible for Barr: Either he could demonstrate fundamentalism to be inconsistent with itself, or by claiming his view of the relation of God and Scripture to be the correct one he could point to the misunderstandings of fundamentalism's view of that relation. Readers may well doubt that Barr has done either in *Fundamentalism*.

192. *F*, p. 266.
193. J. G. Machen, *Christianity and Liberalism* (1923), chap. 1.

4

Reconstruction: James Barr's "Rational" View of the Status of the Bible

In the previous chapters some attempt has been made to describe what Barr finds unacceptable in recent biblical interpretation and in the views of the status of Scripture it supposed. Once this critique is carried through, as far as interpretation is concerned the question can be raised as to whether "anything recognizably like our recent biblical theology can survive." The need for modifications is pressing, and Barr adds that good theology requires that "where an interpretative method is found to be systematically faulty no pains should be spared to make the necessary adjustments."[1]

In the other field of reflexion about the status of Scripture, Barr finds G. D. Kaufman's analysis of the present situation of the Bible to be thought-provoking. The fundamental orientation of Western man has altered and the worldview traditionally accepted has broken down. When man's fundamental orientation is no longer directed by a biblical framework of life in which the world is seen in its aspects as illuminated by the biblical message, then it is tenuous to speak of the Bible as a source-book for guidance on questions of truth and ethics or as an authority for theology. The question which Barr raises is as to whether anything "rational" can be said now about the status of the Bible in the church.[2] The alternative, as Barr sees it, lies between continuing to affirm that the Bible has a "special" status without really being able to explain why this should be so, or abandoning the idea of a special status and seeking a description of the nature of Scripture which makes sense in the world-framework in which we live.

---

1. *BWT*, p. 167.
2. *BMW*, p. 111.

Biblical theology in recent years sought to restate the authority of the Bible and the normativity of its contents in a world in which the framework for the acceptance of such a view has passed away. The Bible no longer has unique authority for Western man, as Kaufman states:

> It has become a great but archaic monument in our midst. . . . It is one of the great sources of the very form of our life, but its norms no longer bind us.[3]

When Barr raises the question of the possibility of the formulation of the status of the Bible in a rational way, he seems to be asking whether a doctrine of Scripture can be advanced which makes sense of the biblical materials in the world in which we are living as theologians. What can be properly said about the nature of Scripture in the light of the present knowledge and orientation of our culture?

In this chapter we shall seek to develop the approach which Barr proposes in a positive way, following upon his critique of views of the Bible and the interpretation he finds insufficient in the present situation. Perhaps it is a little too explicit to speak of a theological "reconstruction" in this respect, as Barr's propositions reveal some uncertainties concerning the way forward. From the end of the phase in which Barr criticised Biblical theology there cannot be said to be a uniform development of his thought. It is characterised by the search of a theological direction rather than by the pursuit of a theological programme. The suggestions are of a partial nature, often being proposed in a tentative way, and systematic formulation is rare. Although this makes the description of Barr's theological vision as a totality difficult, several lines of stress can be observed which might indicate the shape of a developing theology.

4.1. *The biblical tradition—the formation of a "classic model"*

Barr's criticism of the centrality of the notion of revelation in neo-orthodoxy has as its correlate a re-valorisation of the approach which sees the Bible materials as expressing the development of a religious tradition. Tradition becomes a central category for describing the status of the Bible; several aspects of this idea can be developed here.

---

3. G. D. Kaufman, "What Shall We Do with the Bible?," *Int* 25:96.

4.1.1. The tradition process

It is largely in *ONI* that Barr presents his view of Scripture as a developing tradition.[4] The tradition of Israel which is crystallised in the OT is multiplex in character. Different factors enter into this multiplicity, and there is no central motif which provides the key to the interpretation of the tradition. The diversity of the tradition must be recognised; we cannot reduce it to the expression of a single formative element such as the acts of God or a direct verbal revelation. Such features as the acts and words of God cannot be separated from the tradition process for the purpose of providing a key for explaining the process as generative factors. It is rather within the framework of the tradition that these notions have their own meaning.

In this perspective, which proposes that we see the OT as a progressive tradition rather than a progressive revelation, there is a cumulative expression of the dealings of God with man in the tradition.[5] The OT materials can be considered as being a progressive story, which has a starting point from which it proceeds, incorporating new elements into the material through the interpretation of the new situations in the light of what is already known about God in the ongoing tradition. For Barr such a starting point of the biblical tradition process can be seen in the creation story. This is not to say that the creation is a vantage point for the interpretation of the biblical material in general, but that it has a kind of logical priority in the tradition which precedes the other aspects present. "It is from the creation story onwards that the progression and the cumulation of the story is built up."[6] Thus it is not sufficient to say that the production of tradition was initiated by an act of God. The formation of the creation theme illustrates the way the process of thought and worship reconstructed ideas already present by relating itself to them. Barr says that the "movement of tradition is a movement of thought relating itself to what was there before."[7]

It may well be asked at this point, since there is no reference to a special act or revelation of God as generating the tradition, where in fact the idea of creation came from. Barr tells us here that the formation of the creation story as the starting point for a cumulative tradition

---

4. *ONI*, pp. 15ff.
5. *BMW*, p 146.

6. *ONI*, p. 19.
7. Ibid.

lies in "a series of facts and thoughts which emerge from impenetrable antiquity." This means that the starting point in the formation of the biblical tradition is not necessarily the event of the creation itself, but the coming together of certain elements which coalesce to provide a framework or a model with which later events are understood.[8]

It is certainly possible on this basis to consider the OT material as illustrating how the framework provided by the creation story comes to give meaning to events as the tradition develops. What is less clear is why these elements come together in the way they do, to form the starting point of the tradition process. We can only, says Barr, speak in a general way of the "situation" at the point of generation of the tradition. There is no attempt on Barr's part to introduce into the historical description a factor which might because of its appeal to normative divine intervention be considered the starting point of the tradition. Barr's description limits itself to the historical, and this itself is limited in its scope. "Impenetrable antiquity" may in fact strike some as approaching the primeval speculations of the evolutionists of a former generation, but Barr makes specific denial of this. His view of cumulative tradition does not involve the implication of a movement from a lower form to a higher one, as was sometimes the case in notions of progressive revelation.[9] Barr's concern is to leave the mode of the divine influence in the tradition process rather vague. When the tradition process advances, perhaps the most we can say is what the NT writers expressed rather vaguely when they spoke of holy men being moved by the Holy Ghost. If this is so for the progress of tradition, it must be the case also for the formation of the tradition in the "situation" in antiquity.

Historically speaking, then, as far as the origin of the biblical tradition is concerned, no affirmations about divine origination of the tradition through direct intervention can be advanced. Nevertheless, there remains the possibility of the leading of the Holy Spirit in the coming together of the elements which originate the tradition. The vagueness about which Barr speaks would seem to imply this divine influence to be imperceptible; God works behind the tradition process, which is itself a human one. Thus Barr speaks of situations in which

---

8. *IDB*(S), p. 796; *ONI*, p. 20.
9. *BMW*, loc. cit.

God "moves to call for a response," moving the tradition in a new direction. Only in the speaking of God in the Son is there a unitary and final presence of God.[10] In this perspective, Barr speaks of "an openness of the Old Testament not only at its beginning and its end but also during its central period. . . ."[11] Barr adds that OT theology has not displayed great assurance in dealing with the pre-history of the biblical tradition.

In characterising the literature of the OT in terms of the expression of a developing process of tradition, Barr is able to avoid some of the ambiguities related to the idea of revelation in history. Barr thinks that Biblical theology was right in pointing to the presence of narrative material as predominant in the biblical corpus. The mistake which was made was to assume that this could be described as history. It would have been more correct to call it *story*.[12] As story, it has certain features which belong to history. Among these Barr includes the unitary and cumulative character and the chronological framework against which the stories are set. Some of the stories are useful for historical reconstruction, although the reliability is variable. Finally, in some cases, the writer comes close to history writing.

Notwithstanding, these similarities of the OT stories and history should not cause us to overlook the fact that they have features which do not belong to history. There are large sections of Scripture which are not regarded as history, but contain myths, legends, sagas, and so on. The biblical story is tangential with history, but is different from it, spiraling back and forth across history. This movement backwards and forwards across history is characterised by the alternating use of divine intervention and human causation as originating events. The stories of the biblical tradition are also devoid of that essential factor which constitutes the value of the history, namely, the critical evaluation of the sources. These considerations should make us hesitate before speaking of the biblical texts in terms of history. "History means," says Barr, "only what we mean by our use of the word 'history.' "[13] The great difference is that we do not resort to divine intervention as a factor in historical explanation.

---

10. *ONI*, pp. 26, 15.
11. "Old Testament Scholarship in the 1960s," *Church Quarterly* 2:204.
12. "Story and History in Biblical Theology," *JR* 56:5ff.
13. Ibid., p. 8.

The category of history can apply to the OT tradition in only a very partial way. Its narratives would be better termed, in the expression of H. W. Frei, as "historylike." This does not, however, imply a devaluation of the biblical narratives. A story has its own integrity and consistency in its literary character. The literary form of the tradition expresses a sequence which has the character of an ongoing story; it builds cumulatively from the beginning and incorporates various elements into the chronological sequence. The character of the story also belongs to a literary form which becomes complete in the course of Israel's development. Barr states his agreement with the point of an OT scholar who declared: "Salvation history did not happen; it is a literary form which has its own historical context."[14] In addition, this story is not generated out of the religious tradition of Israel in isolation; some of the elements have been incorporated from other ancient Near Eastern sources.

The import of these reflexions on the relation of story and history in the tradition process is that to speak of the tradition crystallised in the OT in terms of history violates the variety of the literary materials present. It is more in conformity with the nature of the texts to speak of stories in which God is represented as speaking and acting.[15] The faith of Israel expressed in the tradition is not reducible to a belief in saving events; it is a faith which exists in the womb of history and which generates its own self-understanding of faith in God. Thus when Barr concludes his study on words for *time* in Scripture, he states his doubt that it is possible to arrive at a biblical view of time. Barr appreciates Eichrodt's "moderate and sensible" treatment: ". . . the important thing for the Bible lies not in the idea of time itself but elsewhere, in the use made of the historical sequence for the presentation of an encounter with God."[16] Israel has an ex-

---

14. T. L. Thompson, *The Historicity of the Patriarchal Narrative* (Berlin, 1974), p. 328, quoted by Barr, art. cit., p. 11. Cf. *ONI*, p. 20.

15. "Revelation through History in the Old Testament and in Modern Theology," in *New Theology no. 1,* ed. M. E. Marty and D. G. Peerman (New York, 1964), p. 66. See also an earlier article which speaks of the Exodus as being not *precise history:* "What is important for us is that the central expression of the religious mind took place . . . in what was understood to be history" ("Tradition and Expectation in Ancient Israel," *SJT* 10:32).

16. W. Eichrodt, *ThZ* 12:125, referred to by Barr, *BWT,* p. 150. See the similar conclusions of J. R. Wilch, *Time and Event* (Leiden, 1969), p. 171.

perience of the presence of God in history and expresses this in the
tradition, which develops through the reinterpretation of this insight
in different situations. What is suggestive here is that it is not a view
of history as the forum of God's acts which explains the existence of
the OT witness; rather Israel forms in her traditions a response expressive of the life of communion of the people of God in which the
faith in God is seen in the historical context.

The tradition process, then, is characterised by the continuation of
the story which has as its starting point the creation, and progressively
builds up from there. In it the relation of God and his people is expressed. The acts of God and the speaking of God take their place
as elements in the literary form of the tradition. The progression of
the story is not through these interventions of God, but is found in
the combination of these with the deeds and sayings of men.[17] The
literary form of the tradition shows a process of restatement in the
transmission. This involves the compilation of sources, reworking
of the material, and the reinterpretation of older elements in the new
context. The development of the tradition is therefore characterised
by the continuing reinterpretation of older traditions in terms of re-
editing or the formation of new materials added to the existing ones.
Barr says that the "continuous stream of production of tradition and
literature . . . really runs on to the present day, since there is no
valid historical cut in it."[18]

Even where tradition forms into Scripture, the tradition process
continues in much the same way subsequently. If it has a new character owing to the existence of Scripture and functions as interpretative tradition, the "dynamics by which it operates are not essentially
different from those of tradition before scripture."[19] This vision of tradition forming into Scripture and flowing from it, has the effect of dissolving the distinction between revelation and religion which was widely
accepted in neo-orthodoxy. Tradition, proposes Barr, is not itself
the same as religion, but is that which is handed down through successive stages of religion. Religion "clusters around tradition," but does
not itself become tradition.[20] However, the religious situation in which

17. *ONI*, p. 21.
18. *BMW*, p. 151. See also B. J. Oosterhoff, "Hereinterpretatie in het Oude
Testament," *Random het Woord* 15:95-117.
19. *ONI*, p. 29.
20. Ibid.

tradition is formed does have a bearing as a whole on religion as it develops in later times.

These remarks concerning the nature of tradition in relation to religion and Scripture obviously raise a question of burning interest in recent discussion, as to the priority of tradition. An ecumenical document of not too long ago affirmed:

> . . . the Reformers could speak as though traditions were always consequent upon Scripture, both logically and chronologically and as though it were possible to preclude the development of traditions by firm adherence to the Scriptures as both the source and the norm of Christian teaching. Such defiance makes less and less sense.[21]

Barr does not make any bones about the view which it is necessary to adopt on this question. If we cannot ignore that tradition changes in the course of history and that often a value-judgment is attached to these changes, the problem cannot be glossed over by affirming the authority of Scripture over tradition. It is now acknowledged "universally," says Barr, that the Bible itself grew out of tradition. The Bible is made up of traditions. As J. D. Smart remarks, ". . . the Scriptures themselves are a palimpsest of tradition, old traditions overlaid by new traditions and then the new by yet newer."[22] The living tradition of Israel, which is an ongoing human formulation incorporating many elements, is a process of transmission which issues in the recognition of a Scripture. In this sense it is not possible to simply state the priority of biblical authority as God-given as over against the deformations of human tradition.[23] The Protestant view of *sola Scriptura* breaks down in face of the progress of our knowledge of the formation of Scripture, which itself is a precipitate of a traditional history of transmission and not the result of a direct divine intervention.[24]

---

21. "Tradition and Traditions" (Faith and Order Paper no. 40) in *Faith and Order Findings 1963* (Genève), p. 20.

22. J. D. Smart in *Int* 30:21.

23. *BMW*, pp. 126f., 115.

24. On this see the remarks of W. Pannenberg, *Basic Questions in Theology* (London, 1970), I:186; the writings of K. E. Skydsgaard cited in the Bibliography, particularly *SJT* 9:337ff.; D. Ritschl in *Int* 25:113; J. R. Geiselmann in *Christianity Divided*, ed. D. J. Callahan et al. (New York, 1964), pp. 35ff., 58; D. Jenkins, *Tradition and the Spirit* (London, 1951), chap. 2.

This recognition of the priority of tradition represents quite a reversal of the view held in Protestant confessions. In neo-orthodoxy too, where tradition was spoken of, it was usually made clear that two senses of tradition were not to be confused; the doctrinal tradition of the church, the gospel given to the church, and the traditions the church itself creates as it proclaims the gospel.[25] The traditions the church creates demand consideration as the "church in dialogue with itself," but they lack the objective authority of Holy Scripture.[26]

This opposition between Scripture and tradition has resulted, according to some commentators, in the idealisation of the Bible, whereas it should really be seen as part of tradition.[27] When the Bible is idealised in this way, what happens in fact is that an infallible book is substituted for Roman Catholicism's infallible Church.[28] Between infallible book and infallible Church there is a sameness of principle in that both locate authority in an external factor believed to be infallible. Yet J. K. S. Reid seems to think that in the case of the two streams that illustrate this principle, namely the Roman Catholic Church and fundamentalism, the greater offender would be fundamentalism, as at least Rome does recognise the importance of a living tradition in the life of the church.[29] J. D. Smart calls this the treacherousness of tradition which is manifest where the interpretations of an infallible book take on themselves the infallibility of the book. In this case, Scripture spawns a tradition so absolute that it shuts men's ears to Scripture.[30] Against views such as fundamentalism's, D. Jenkins says: ". . . it is wrong to think of a revelation given independently of tradition or to be sharply distinguished from tradition, in the sense of the living stream of the Church's life. It is always in, with and under the tradition."[31]

Barr adds his pinch of salt to these reflexions on the relation of Scripture and tradition. When we recognise that Scripture is itself not

---

25. See J. K. S. Reid, *The Authority of Scripture* (London, 1957), p. 141.
26. Ibid., p. 199.
27. D. Jenkins, op. cit., p. 24; cf. Skydsgaard, art. cit., p. 346.
28. Ibid., p. 21; cf. the remarks of C. J. Cadoux in Reid, op. cit., p. 131.
29. Reid, op. cit., p. 132.
30. Smart, art. cit., pp. 22f.
31. D. Jenkins, op. cit., p. 32; G. Ebeling, *The Word of God and Tradition* (London, 1968), pp. 102ff., 144ff.

errorless, but that it is the result of a tradition process containing positive and negative elements, the distinction no longer lies between unerring Scripture and erring tradition. In both Scripture and tradition, on this understanding, we are dealing with members of the people of God, sinful and yet justified, serving God yet strongly influenced by their own convictions.[32] If such is the case, and the tradition process is not in essence different in biblical and post-biblical times, but continues down to the present, several pressing questions force themselves upon the theologian. Some of these will be considered in the following sections, as discussed by Barr: What could be the unity of this tradition process, how might it be connected with revelation, what are its implications for the normativeness of theological activity?

4.1.2. The unity of the biblical tradition

In the light of Barr's proposal that the biblical materials express a developing tradition in the life of the people of God, it is evident that if we are to speak of the unity of the tradition this cannot be done on the basis of the selection of some theological elements. Nor would it be possible to develop a view of the unity in the tradition starting from the perspective of the NT. Interpretation of the OT is not automatically dependent on the NT interpretation of the OT.[33] If the biblical tradition bears the character of a cumulative story into which various differing sorts of material are worked, it follows that if we are to speak of a unity of the tradition this must be done in an historical way. Therefore, with respect to the problem of the relation of the OT and NT, Barr affirms that we must seek to relate these historically. It is not sufficient to find theological links which might exist between the two and then proceed to relate the testaments in a direct way. The historical linkage must be established in the continuing tradition, and on this ground the theological nature of the connections can be considered. "A theological statement of the connection of the Testaments must include, and not pass by, an interpretation of the historical connection.[34]

Two consequences, among others, can be pointed to here. Firstly,

---

32. *BMW*, p. 127.
33. *ONI*, pp. 154f.
34. Ibid., p. 130.

because the relationship between OT and NT is articulated in an historical way, and by historical we must recall that Barr means what is historical for us, the unity we may discern in the tradition is different from the picture presented by the NT writers themselves. Barr is quite explicit about this: ". . . a restatement of the 'unity of the Bible' will, just *because* it seems to justify this unity for us, fail to explain the way in which this unity was *then* seen."[35] Therefore the historical unity we construct in the tradition may offer no explanation in theological terms of the way the NT writers use the OT. When they used the OT, they did not recover it in a way which matches modern historical understanding. There is no homogeneous use of the OT by the apostolic writers. This would seem to imply that there is no NT key to the unity of the Scripture in terms of our being able to reconstruct the apostolic view of that unity as being normative for us today. Further, in discussions of the unity of the testaments there is no priority of the NT over the OT. In a formulation which takes the historical as primordial, if we are to speak of priority, this must be done in an historical sense.

A second consideration arising from Barr's approach to the unity of the tradition in terms of historical reconstruction is that such a method cannot exclude from its account anything which is relevant to the historical enquiry. This means that the unity is not stated in a way which is limited to the material contained in the present biblical canon. The unity of the tradition cannot be historically recovered unless the inter-testamental Jewish tradition is included. The Jewish tradition has not only historical significance for the NT, but theological importance as well. To state the unity of the testaments in the context of the movement of tradition, it is necessary to go beyond the testaments themselves. The development of Jewish tradition is relevant for the linking of the testaments.[36] This emphasis corresponds to a trend in recent years to recognise the importance of materials which have no home in the biblical canon. Barr suggests that this could mean a breaking down of the distinction between revelation

---

35. Ibid.
36. "Le Judaisme Postbiblique," *Revue de Théologie et de Philosophie* (1968), pp. 209ff. See also "Judaism—Its Continuity with the Bible" (Montefiore Memorial Lecture, Southampton University, 1968), and "Jewish Apocalyptic in Recent Scholarly Study," *BJRL* 58:8-36.

and religion as applying to the OT and NT books on the one side and the inter-testamental literature and the Jewish interpretative tradition on the other.[37]

The theological unity of the biblical tradition can be described in the light of its historical character. This means that the priority of the OT must be respected, for on this basis the Jewish tradition of interpretation and the NT develop. However, this is not to say that this basis is to be approached in terms of a naive attempt to let the OT speak for itself.[38] The issue is more complex than this. Barr indicates several different levels at which the OT operates in relation to the NT.[39] The religion of late Judaism, which develops from the OT, provides the framework in which the story of Christ is meaningful. It gives the context for the ministry of Christ. Moreover, between the OT and the NT there is in Judaism a real substantial community of faith between the two testaments. At this point of intersection in Judaism a substantial part of the OT and the NT message is present. Barr states as examples the common conception of God, or of holiness. This, however, is very difficult to define because of the developments taking place in the inter-testamental period. A second way in which the OT functions in respect to the NT is as a text which is read and meditated upon. Barr insists that the text is not simply a transcript of the religion, but it exercises a critical function with respect to the religion. The existence of an OT text provided a means by which the men of the NT could appeal to earlier sources against the later religious tradition and so produce out of this critical movement a new turn in religion. The existence of a text is not something which stifles but which leaves the door open to new approaches; the apostles, in their appeal to the text of the OT, can be considered as religious reformers.

Another way the OT may relate to the development of the religious tradition expressed in the NT is through its operation upon the mind of Jesus and the apostles. The self-understanding of Jesus was formed with reference to the patterns of the OT, which Jesus interprets as one speaking with authority.[40] On a similar level the apostolic comprehension of the work of Jesus is formed in terms of the OT, which

37. *BJRL* 58:29.
38. *ONI,* p. 170.
39. Ibid., pp. 134ff.
40. Ibid., pp. 137f., 157ff.

is used to interpret the meaning of how Jesus was the Christ. Finally, the OT constitutes a point of reference for understanding the existence of a community of Jews and Gentiles as the body of Christ.[41]

These considerations are important for understanding the function of the tradition in salvation. The Christian salvation is not founded on the NT alone, so that the OT comes to be understood in the light of the NT. Barr states that the Christian salvation is situated at the juncture of the OT and the NT, which can be called "the hinge of fate in the drama of salvation."[42] The tradition of the OT is soteriologically functional as in its growth it provides the matrix for the accomplishment of the divine acts and an impulse which leads to them. Salvation grows out of the development of the OT tradition. It is for this reason that the OT has a priority over the NT and that it is not possible to read back a NT version of salvation into the OT in a christocentric model of interpretation. The flow of traffic moves the other way. Barr states that our approach to the OT must be trinitarian, not christological. "The direction of thought is from God to Christ, from Father to Son and not from Christ to God."[43] Fundamental in the Christian view of salvation is the belief that the God of Israel is the Father of Jesus Christ. God is already known in Israel, and it is through the soteriological outworking of the OT tradition that the known God is revealed in his relation to the Son.

In this outworking of salvation, the tradition functions in a positive and negative fashion. It is through the OT that Jesus sees his way of obedience to the Father, as, in interpreting his messianic role, elements of the OT are brought together in the situation of post-biblical Judaism. Negatively, the same process of the exegesis of the OT leads his enemies to put him to death. The opposition between Jesus' understanding of himself and the Jewish interpretation can be referred to the fact that there is a difference between both what Jesus

---

41. Ibid., pp. 164ff. D. L. Baker in *Two Testaments One Bible* (London, 1976), pp. 147ff., compares the position of Barr with that of A. A. van Ruler and K. H. Miskotte with regard to the priority of the OT, but states that Barr's position is not so extreme in that for him the relation is mutual and neither is more important than the other (p. 149). Baker's choice of the word "mutual" is not entirely appropriate, as it refers to a situation in which elements co-exist, whereas Barr's development of the relation is primarily in terms of an historical relation.

42. Ibid., p. 155.

43. Ibid., pp. 153f.

says and what his opponents say, and the original Scriptures. Neither party simply says what the original Scriptures say; Jesus does not oppose them but in his applications goes far beyond their sense, by heightening a meaning or striking out in a new direction. He uses the Scriptures to oppose the Jewish traditions; for the opponents of Jesus the relation between the Scripture and the Jewish tradition is different. The opposition is the outcome of two different interpretations of the text in the post-biblical Jewish context. This situation represents a crisis in the religion of the post-biblical period, in which two interpretations are opposed. The crisis in the interpretation of Scripture in Jewish tradition is an integral factor leading up to the atonement in a positive and negative sense.[44]

To say that the God of Israel is the Father of Jesus and that the tradition works in a positive and negative way in the accomplishment of salvation is to go beyond the domain of purely historical affirmation. These statements are not the object of historical demonstration and are therefore open to question; they lie in the domain of faith. Barr admonishes us to preach it, not prove it.[45] However, if these are faith assertions, that is not to say that their relation to historical research is an arbitrary one. Even if scholarly historical study can proceed in ignorance or denial of faith interests, assertions of faith do not play fast and loose with historical realities. They seek rather to maintain conformity with what is historical. Faith can learn and grow from the study of history. As far as the unity of the biblical tradition is concerned, historically speaking, this unity would seem to not be liable to historical demonstration. Historical research does not make normative statements about the God of Israel working through the tradition process to grant salvation through the Son. These remarks echo Barr's former affirmations about historical study leaving open the possibility of a normative statement beyond the realm of the purely descriptive (cf. 3.4.2).

The unity of the tradition is therefore in the realm of faith which discerns the unity of the one God working in the diversities of the historical process. Although the OT has priority in terms of the historical development, for the Christian faith, which discerns the

---

44. Ibid., pp. 157ff., 28ff.; "Le Judaisme Postbiblique," pp. 209ff.
45. Ibid., p. 150.

unity of God in the movement of tradition, there is an equality of status in the OT and NT which is an aspect of the unity of God.:

> The Christian faith stands equally upon the basis of the Old Testament and of the New or, more correctly, upon the basis of the God of Israel and of Jesus of Nazareth. In this sense the importance of Old and New Testaments is in principle more or less equal. . . . In my view the status of the two Testaments is independent for Christian faith, which rests upon the God of Israel and Jesus of Nazareth; and if for Christians Jesus is the finality . . . which might place the New Testament in the higher position, Jesus himself stands under the God of Israel, which might place the Old Testament in the higher.[46]

The biblical tradition as an ongoing development is multiplex. Its unity lies in the unity of God, who is known differently in OT and NT. The status of the testaments is thus independent but equal, as the one God is known in different ways.

This formulation of the unity of the tradition which is discerned in faith, calls forth several questions which will be left open at this point. First of all, Barr would seem to have criticised neo-orthodox formulations of the unity of the Bible as relying on an authority structure in which this unity was assumed and lay ultimately in God. While removing the shackles of the authority structure Barr continues to relate the unity of the tradition to the unity of God. In his theology the problem of the historical validation of this unity remains unresolved, or so it would appear. If for the Barthian the problem was that the divine act was tangential with history, for Barr the contact between the divine unity and the historical process is even more vague. In spite of Barr's affirmations, the foundation he proposes for faith affirmations would seem to leave this faith out of contact with the forum of history. The question remains whether Barr, in denying the continuity and discontinuity in the revelational theology of neo-orthodoxy, is not left with a greater discontinuity on his hands. A second problem which might be raised in this presentation of the unity

---

46. *BMW*, pp. 166f. See the comments on Barr's view of the unity of God by J. A. Sanders in *Int* 28:322f. It is difficult to agree with the judgment of J. D. Smart in *The Strange Silence of the Bible in the Church* (London, 1970), p. 107: "Barr . . . because of his failure to identify the substance of the revelation as a unique life sustained in the community by its relation with God, . . . leaves the problem [of the unity of the elements of the OT tradition] still in confusion."

of tradition might lie in the fact that, if it does in some way illustrate that unity, it does not do the same for the unity of the *Bible*.[47] If it wished to do so, some justification would have to be made of the principle of using an ex-organic factor (i.e., the inter-testamental literature) in establishing the unity of the organism.

4.1.3. Tradition and revelation

When the Scripture is seen as the crystallisation of the tradition of the people of God in a cumulative story, the problem is how to describe the character of this knowledge of God in the tradition. Once man's way of relating himself to God in this developing tradition has been described, some statement must be attempted to relate God to the tradition. If faith could not discern some way in which God could be related to the progressing tradition, then the reality of the relationship with God described in the tradition would be in jeopardy. Barr considers both of these aspects in formulating his view of the Scripture as tradition of the people of God. The formulation Barr presents grows out of his early reflexions on the relation of the Spirit of God and the people of God (sec. 1.4) and his critique of the revelational models in which knowledge of God is part of a God-to-man movement (sec. 3.2).

It is immediately apparent that the previous models of revelation accepted in theology which conceive of the knowledge of God as the result of a divine act revealing God himself or inspired words which convey truths about him, cannot fit in with the approach to the Scripture as a cumulative tradition. "The term 'revelation' as it has come to function within theology, does not fit with the structure of communication through cumulative tradition within the Bible."[48] Revelation in this sense is a concept foreign to the biblical material as the development of a tradition. This tradition flows out from the fact that God is already in communion with man; it is the passing on of the knowledge of God resulting from this communion in a stream where it is recognised that the true God is known. It emerges from the mythical milieu at a point where the concept of God which

---

47. On the unity of the biblical tradition see H. Gese, "Erwägungen zur Einheit der biblischen Theologie," *Zeitschrift für Theologie und Kirche* 67:417-36. Also F. Mildenberger's remarks on this in *Int* 29:391ff.

48. *IDB*(S), pp. 748f.

was later recognised in Israel came to be accepted.[49]

Barr's criticism of the centrality of revelation and his affirmation that knowledge of God is presupposed in the biblical tradition are therefore in correlation with the idea that Scripture is a progressing human tradition. Thus when Barr, using the accepted vocabulary of the former Biblical theology, puts the question as to where revelation might lie in his formulation, the reply comes back that "there is no single or simple answer." Revelation is not in the Bible or narrated by it; the tradition brings new information about God. The locus of revelation could then be said to be seen in the growth of the tradition which shows the dynamics of revelation. It is, says Barr, a justifiable approach to regard revelation as being not in the OT, the book, but in the dynamic growth of the tradition as God is further known. In this sense the locus of revelation would be in Israel, the people, set against a certain period. No doubt Barr thinks that historical critical study would then be an aid to the recovery of the dynamic of revelation.

However, this is not all. It is possible to adopt an approach in which the Bible is the locus of revelation, in so far as the Bible story as a whole expresses what Israel has learned about God. On these grounds the reading of the story would be the means of meeting the God whom the Israelites claim to know in the tradition. These two possibilities represent divergent ways of approaching the question of revelation in connection with the tradition. Barr concludes there is no single locus of revelation, and theology will do best to adopt a multiplicity of approaches in dealing with the knowledge of God expressed in the tradition.[50]

What is common to these two possibilities as described here is that in neither case does God reveal in the sense of making himself known to man in a direct fashion. Revelation on Barr's definition of the term would seem rather to be God's becoming known of man and his continuing to be known by him. Revelation in the tradition of the people of God takes place in the consciousness which men have of God through communion with him. Whether this is viewed from the angle of the dynamics of the growth of tradition or as located in the

---

49. *ONI*, p. 89; see also B. S. Childs, *Myth and Reality in the Old Testament* (London, 1960), pp. 71ff.

50. "Story and History in Biblical Theology," *JR* 56:16f.

stories into which the tradition crystallises, the knowledge of God originates in a quite human way.

Some account of the human character of the tradition can now be given. In describing the status of the Bible in relation to the knowledge of God which might be gained from it, Barr frames his account in human terms, without reference to supernatural interventions in revelation or inspiration. The decisions made about the tradition, its formation and canonisation by the people of God are decisions which can be accounted for by human factors. These are made by mental processes which are analogical to our way of acting in the church today. They can be described by means of historical analyses, without any special pleading.[51] This implies that the Bible makes no claim to distinctiveness through the correctness of its information or ideas. It is fallible in this respect in the same way as other books. Barr's thought is well expressed here:

> Scripture does not come into existence by direct action of God, but by a human action which is a reflex of contact with God. Should we doubt that this human action shares in the distortion and inadequacy which applies to other human acts? . . . May we dare to assert that scripture meets the needs of sinful men just because it is itself not free from its sinful element?[52]

Two features of this statement can be commented upon here. Firstly, the revelation which comes through human tradition is above all indirect, arising out of a human "reflex." This notion might be said to take the neo-orthodox idea of "witness" out of the revelational context which was attached to it in relation to a God-to-man communication. In *BMW* we see that Barr has stated this thought even more explicitly by saying that the Bible is not communication from God to man, but is characterised by a man-to-man disclosure. The Bible is man's "statement of his beliefs,"[53] the word of Israel or the church. Revelation follows on from the tradition in the framework of reference provided by it. Barr does not consider revelation in terms of verticality, but as the result of a disclosure on the level of a hori-

---

51. *BMW*, pp. 118ff.
52. *ONI*, p. 163.
53. *BMW*, p. 120. Certain affinities could be pointed out between the idea of tradition and indirect revelation in Barr's work and some emphases in W. Pannenberg's idea of indirect revelation and history as the transmission of tradition, in *Revelation as History* (London, 1968), pp. 125ff.

zontal witness from man to man.

A second consideration about the position of Barr concerns the existence of errors in the tradition. The Scripture is imperfect not only in the sense of historical inexactitude but also theologically. Barr does not mean this as a particularisation of the general fact that all human language about God could be thought inadequate: ". . . we can go further and accept that theological statements about God which are more precise and correct than those of the Bible can be made and perhaps even have been made."[54] Maybe it is even possible to say that the men of the Bible were not concerned with perfect theological conciseness; their work reflects a struggle with God, a personal conflict with other men about God. So it must be recognised that tradition is at once faithful and sinful. We can speak of how "God, in working through the tradition-production of the Bible, is . . . using sin to conquer sin."[55] Tradition is ambiguous, at once faithful and sinful. Following a suggestion by Karl Barth that we can speak of "true" religion only in the sense in which we can speak of a "justified sinner," Barr proposes that it might not be incongruous to say that the Bible is an expression of justified-sinful religion which has produced it.[56] This would certainly align the Bible with the common life of the people of God then and now, allow Barr room to manoeuvre concerning errors in the Bible, and avoid a view of the status of Scripture which identifies it as a perfect document.

Having emphasised the human character of the religious tradition which gives birth to the biblical story, the question remains as to how it might be possible to relate this human tradition and God. This question might be said to have two aspects: It could firstly be enquired as to how God relates to the tradition process as it developed *then* and secondly how the relation could be construed with respect to the Scripture *now*. Barr states that an essential continuity exists in the past and present relations sustained by God with regard to the tradition of his people in which he is known. God was in contact with his people in ancient times in the formation of the tradition;

---

54. Ibid., p. 119. In this section we find echoes of the statements of Karl Barth concerning the imperfections of the Bible in *Church Dogmatics,* (Edinburgh, 1956), I.2, 506ff.

55. *ONI,* loc. cit.

56. *ONI,* pp. 94f.

God worked in the life of Israel in the tradition which turned into Scripture. This presence is not different from the presence of God today as God continues to make himself known through a similar relation which is operative when we read Scripture. To say the Scripture is inspired is to say two things: that God was at work in Israel, and the same relation with the Spirit is at work today. "Inspiration may well mean that the formation of scripture, and our use of scripture, are both part of that larger relationship with the Spirit which applies to all our experiences of God."[57] Inspiration is from below, not from above. God is present in the life of his people as men produce their human testimony that he is with them. This movement is paralleled by a similar one as we read the Bible today. This God is present as our God, as He was in ancient times.[58]

This is patently an inspiration with fallibility. Inspiration is redefined without the content of a divine-human communication or the idea of the cessation of revelation at the end of the apostolic period. Nor is Barr embarrassed by linking God's presence with a process which is typified by human erring: ". . . why should God not have inspired a scripture with errors in it, through which he might nevertheless truly communicate with men?"[59] The Scriptures are inspired as the fallible documents they are, and God, who inspires them by his presence with his people, makes them into the vehicle used in subsequent generations to express his word to man.[60]

The way in which God takes up the word of the tradition of his people and makes it his own word for future generations, suggests

---

57. "2 Timothy 3:16," unpublished sermon preached in Keble College chapel (Oxford, 1977), p. 1.

58. Ibid., p. 3. It is interesting to compare this presentation of Barr's with views prevalent in pre-Barthian times. For example, H. D. McDonald presents the view of G. P. Mains (*Divine Inspiration*, 1915), in which the Bible is said to "lead up" to God. The Bible "finds us" and the reality of its inspiration lies in its spiritual appeal, in *Theories of Revelation* (London, 1963), p. 239.

59. *BMW*, p. 16.

60. This idea expressed in *BMW*, pp. 179f., was presented also in 1958 in Barr's review of Reid's book. *SJT* 11:92. Barr states that this review contains some ideas since abandoned, p. 180, n. 12. As far as this idea is concerned, Barr does not seem to have deepened it much in further clarification over the years. It remains close to Pannenberg's statement about the way God uses human speech to reveal himself: "God makes our metaphorical speech his own through his revelation, and thereby for the first time gives our words of praise their ultimately valid content" (*Basic Questions in Theology*, I:237).

another relation of tradition and revelation. The tradition is generated on the understanding that God is known and is present with his people. This tradition is not response to revelation but revelation follows on from the existent tradition. The Scripture-tradition provides the framework in which new events are interpreted. The tradition is therefore directed to a future revelation of God in the expected fulfilment of God's promises. This future-directed view of revelation in reference to the existing tradition is a more proper use of the word than the definition which insists on past revelation.[61] With this statement, perhaps the structure of the relation between revelation and tradition in Barr's thought becomes more apparent. God is known by his people, and this is the presupposition for the formation of tradition, which takes place because of the presence of God through his Spirit. This is not itself revelation, although God is known and continues to make himself known through the tradition once it has formed into a Scripture. Revelation, properly speaking, might be considered to be the future confirmation of God's promises expected in the tradition.

Barr's formulation of this delicate relation has three things going for it. Firstly, it gives a very positive sense to the presence of God among his people, which is real but not overbearing. God is known by his people who are in communion with him in the Spirit. Secondly, this view of the presence of God is also one which fully allows for man to be what he is as man and even as a fallen man. Barr's approach makes a positive statement of man's freedom for obedience or disobedience in the historical context. There is no playing down of history in the evaluation of the tradition. Thirdly, Barr's view may be thought to be positive as it is open ended, particularly with respect to the future revelation of God. These three factors taken together can be seen as an encouragement to a freedom in the faith, in God as Creator, Saviour, and future Revealer of himself.

One problem, however, does arise in the formulation of Barr. It concerns the *mode* of the presence of the Spirit of God with his people. Barr does not attempt to camouflage the difficulty. The mode of the presence *then* was not different from the way God continues to make himself known *now*. "I do not see, he says, how else we can

<hr>

61. *ONI*, p. 101. Barr refers here to Pannenberg's future-looking idea of revelation. Cf. *BMW*, pp. 121ff., 143f.

think in the present day."[62] Even this vagueness is preferable to the traditional ways of seeing revelation as antecedent to the Scripture. These simply explain the obscure by the unknown.[63] Barr admits that he is "at a loss" when it comes to describing the mode in which God was with his people. We might say it was "in the Spirit." To say that the traditions were formed in the Spirit would not mean that the Spirit was responsible for them, but that "they were accompanied by a mode of presence of the one of whom they speak."[64] The Spirit accompanies human actions and thought, which themselves can be described without reference to supernatural interventions.

The problem remains in this vague formulation that the Spirit's presence is so imperceptible that it may be impossible to say anything concrete about it at all. If nothing tangible can be said about this being "in the Spirit," does the Spirit's presence make any difference to human situations? Would its absence amount to the same thing? Such a tacit presence may demand more faith than it is able to give. This difficulty cannot be avoided with reference to the fallibility of Scripture. Barr has told us that God might have inspired a Scripture with errors to communicate truly with man. How might errors truly communicate something of God to us? Such inspiration might lead us to doubt the efficacy of the presence of the Spirit.

4.1.4. The fixing of the tradition: canonisation

Barr's emphasis on the development of tradition plus his accent on the Spirit's work being essentially the same today as it was in the time of the biblical writers might seem at first to imply that the canon is not closed. It could be said of Scripture that "fundamentally it does not lie on another level than all the teaching of the Spirit throughout the history of the Church. Therefore the canon is still open."[65] Again, it would be possible to say that because tradition continues there is no canon of the NT and precisely for this reason it is necessary for the survival of Christianity to take the tradition itself

---

62. *BMW*, p. 18.
63. Ibid., p. 121.
64. Ibid., p. 132.
65. E. Schweizer, "Scripture, Church Tradition and Interpretation," in *New Theology no. 1,* ed. M. E. Marty and D. G. Peerman (New York, 1964), p. 57. The writer maintains this to be a purely theoretical thesis.

seriously.[66] Whether these positions are adopted or not, it is certain that when Scripture is considered as formed out of the developing traditions of the church, it is no longer evident that inspiration can be limited to the canonical documents in a scheme which sets Scripture as revelation over against church tradition. Since tradition became Scripture, it is tenuous to distinguish it from continuing tradition in a qualitative sense.[67] Therefore Barr rejects the canonical model proposed by fundamentalism which sees the reason for canonisation as lying ultimately in inspiration, so constituting the Scripture different from traditions which are of human origin.[68] A distinction between canonical and non-canonical writings on the grounds of inspiration lacks historical verification.[69]

Barr's approach to tradition is one which is largely historical, and he proposes to treat the question of canon in an historical way. Canonisation must be regarded as a historical process rather than as a question of theological decisions. "Formation of scripture, and canonization of scripture, are processes which were characteristic of a certain time, a certain stage in the life of the people of God."[70] This can also be expressed by saying that at a certain time in the life of the people of God the story becomes complete, falls into the past, and tradition takes a new form.[71] Thus Barr speaks of the *facticity* of the canonisation of Scripture. The issue does not really lie in whether or not we can give reasons for the justification of the canon in a theological sense. The theological reasons for the constituting of the canon may or may not be proper ones. In many cases scholars would agree that the canonical literature rises above the non-canonical even though there may be marginal cases. Barr does not himself consider that if the Apocrypha of the English Bible were considered as canonical it would make any difference to doctrine as held by Chris-

---

66. See R. Scroggs, "Tradition, Freedom and the Abyss," *New Theology no. 8* (New York, 1971), pp. 84ff.

67. C. Evans, *Is Holy Scripture Christian?* (London, 1971), pp. 7ff.

68. *F,* pp. 79, 180ff.

69. Inspiration was also identified with the canonical writings in the neo-orthodox period. See, for example, A. G. Hebert, *The Authority of the Old Testament* (London, 1947), pp. 104ff.

70. *BMW,* p. 154.

71. Art. cit., *JR* 56:14f. See H. Gese's view that the OT "comes into being as a result of the NT; the NT forms the end of a process of tradition which is essentially a unity" (art. cit., p. 420).

tians today.[72] The church today could undoubtedly alter the canon
and might be entitled to do so. This is, however, a hypothetical question, and no such action is likely to be taken, as the decision for the
recognition of a canon is an historical one which lies in the past of
the church. We are no longer in this period; the canon is a matter
of historical fact to us. Even if the historical decision of the church
is "full of contingency and relativity,"[73] it is a past fact for us and we
are no longer at that stage.[74]

The historical fact of the canonisation of Scripture must be, in
Barr's way of thinking, distinguished from the formation of a Scripture which precedes it. The formation of a Scripture is more important than the act of canonisation which comes relatively late and
does not mean that the books of Scripture attain their status only then.
To speak of canonisation is to recognise in principle the existence of
a Scripture. Such recognition is built into Christianity through its
historical roots. A Scripture has been formed in the origins of the
Christian faith and recognised as canonical. This fact is fundamental
to that faith and so there is no possibility of removing the principle
of a Scripture today without denying the historic fact built into Christian faith on the foundational level. To speak of modifying the canon
by changing the list of books does not then imply a questioning of the
principle of a Scripture.[75]

If the motives and the circumstances in which the Christian canon
came into being are uncertain, the effect of the formation of the free
complex of tradition into a Scripture, a more closed body of writing,
produces several results. The tradition, previously more fluid, becomes fixed in a distinct form. The recognition of a fixed Scripture

---

72. *BMW*, loc. cit.

73. Ibid., p. 156.

74. Barr's emphasis on the facticity of the canon may be traced to the
thought of Karl Barth, who points to the facticity of the canon in the sense that
the Bible constitutes itself as canon; we cannot say why this should be so. This
facticity is of divine origin. The church does not give the canon to itself. In
Barr's thought the facticity remains, but in a totally immanent sense as the
historical decision of the church. Cf. Barth, op. cit., I.1, 107; I.2, 473ff.

75. BMW, p. 155. Barr does not seem to discuss in this context the implications of his distinction between formation and canonisation of Scripture for
the modern search for a canon within the canon and whether this could be
considered as an implicit denial of the Scripture principle in the historic roots of
Christianity.

tended to consign excluded texts to a relative obscurity. Furthermore, when a written tradition attains scriptural status, the problem of relating such fixed tradition to further productions of tradition is raised. The existence of a Scripture modifies the sense of tradition, which takes the form of an interpretation of the Scripture. Rather than developing in a free manner, the tradition, because of the presence of a Scripture, tends to "curve back on itself."[76] Finally, the according of scriptural status to some books opens the question of the status of other books and whether they should find inclusion within the body of scriptural materials. This is the question of the canon of Scripture as such.[77]

The relation between tradition and canon in the thought of Barr would seem to be describable in terms of a movement: tradition-Scripture-canon-tradition. Tradition formed in the life of the people of God is fixed in texts recognised to be Scripture. Canonisation is a recognition of tradition as Scripture and further tradition is of a different character. As D. H. Kelsey has said: ". . . although 'canon' is not necessarily part of the concept 'scripture,' 'scripture' is necessarily part of the meaning of 'canon.' When a community of Christians calls a set of writings the 'Christian canon,' she affirms that it is her 'scripture.' "[78] Barr's description of the status of Scripture in terms of canonicity accounts for this status in a purely human way without appeal to the inspiration of the canonical writings by a special divine act. Thus he sees the formation of Scripture in terms of a decision which was made for us in a generation not our own.

If we talk of inspiration as applying to the canonical books, this is something we attribute to them to express the belief that God led his people in times past and continues to work among us today.[79] The canon is not of divine origin; the Scripture is the church's book, formed out of her traditions and recognised by her decision as Scripture. To use another expression of Kelsey's: ". . . to say, 'These writings are the Christian canon,' is analytic in 'This community is

76. Ibid., p. 117.

77. Ibid., p. 116.

78. D. H. Kelsey, *The Uses of Scripture in Recent Theology* (London, 1975), pp. 104f.

79. See on the subject of canon and inspiration R. P. C. Hanson, *Tradition in the Early Church* (London, 1962), pp. 235ff.; K. Stendahl in *IDB*, I:428f; A. C. Sundberg, *Int* 29:352-71.

a Christian Church.' "[80] Barr and many others think that it is unavoidable that it was the church which determined the canon of the
NT.[81] Relating the formation of the Scriptures to a process of human
tradition and canonisation to a decision of the church, there is on
Barr's understanding no ultimate difference of value between the
books inside and outside the canon. "It is certainly not possible,"
says Barr, "to draw absolute distinctions of value between books that
have become canonical and others which have not."[82] If such distinctions are made between a canonical and a non-canonical book,
the same distinction can apply to two books within the canon. The
variety is such that if the canonisation of the Scriptures as the
church's book implies a sort of wholeness, the multiplicity of elements
cannot be overlooked. The diversity and contradiction which we find
in the church today, might well be expected in the earlier stages of the
life of the people of God.

Our description shows that Barr can explain the status of the biblical tradition as canon of the church in a "rational" way. His account
proposes a view of canon which rests on an analysis of the processes
involved on a human level without any appeal to the origin of the
canon in revelation. In a religion, origins explain little.[83] Formation,
ordering, and selection of tradition is a matter of historical contingency. The Bible is not perfect, nor is other religious literature totally perverse. To receive it as canon is to recognise that it
precedes us in the church as a sufficient model for Christian understanding.

The problem which may be thought to arise in this formulation
centres around the question of the facticity of the existence of the
canon. It may well be wondered whether the fact that the canon is
prior to us can constitute a sufficient reason for us to accept it today. The priority of a Scripture in its facticity need not necessarily
constitute a justification for the accepting of this in the church today.
The fact that it provides a framework for Christian understanding
because of its presence at the origin of the Christian faith would not

---

80. Kelsey, loc. cit.
81. See R. P. C. Hanson, op. cit., p. 234; H. von Campenhausen, *The Formation of the Christian Bible* (London, 1972), pp. 253-62.
82. *IDB*(S), p. 797.
83. "Tradition and Expectation in Ancient Israel," *SJT* 10:29.

seem to be an argument that it should or could be considered as the exclusive framework by reference to which this understanding is developed, nor an argument as to why its continuing validity should be recognised. For there to be any sense in this fact of the canon, some kind of normativity constitutive of canonicity would have to be demonstrated.[84]

These questions lead us to look a little closer now at what Barr means when he calls the Scripture a model for Christian understanding.

4.1.5. Scripture as a "classic model"

Barr's account of the development of the tradition of the people of God as a human process which can be examined in terms of historical study, has certain precise implications as to the way we may consider the status of Scripture. If the Bible is no longer to be thought of as representative of a revelation from God to man, how can its function in the church be described?

Rather than being thought of as the norm of Christian faith and conduct in giving access to the way in which God wishes the Christian to believe and behave, Barr suggests that the Bible may be considered as an exemplar set before the church of how the people of God relate to their God in faith. Thus Barr affirms that "Christian faith is not whatever a modern Christian may happen to believe, on any grounds at all, but faith related to Jesus and to the God of Israel."[85] It is the Bible which gives us the model of how faith may thus be related to God. This is different from seeing the Bible as a source of right doctrine. The Bible is not a textbook of refined Christian doctrine. "I have based my position on its status as the classic model for the understanding of God, not on the idea that the model is a perfect one."[86]

Perhaps the implication of this approach is seen in contrast with the

---

84. Barr is critical of B. S. Childs's suggestion that the Christian canon should be taken as the context for interpretation. Barr doubts that the canon can be used as normative exegetical context. The final form of the text may never have been meant to function in this way in the church's tradition. We can take the canon more lightly than this. "Trends and Prospects in Biblical Theology," *JTS* 25:273ff.

85. *BMW*, p. 118.

86. Ibid., p. 119.

more traditional views of our preceding chapter. In these the Bible as authority functioned as the basis for theological assertions and also as the judge of sound doctrine. Theology stood or fell with its conformity to what the Bible said as the fundamental norm. Barr's propositions would seem to change this, in suggesting that the Bible ought to be considered as a model for Christian faith rather than a source. The Bible gives us a paradigm of how God's people in history express their faith in God. Christian faith in the present implies a similar relation as the faith expressed in the Bible; our way of belief in God today is like the way portrayed in the biblical model. Reference to this model is implied in Christian faith. Barr puts it like this:

> . . . the status of the Bible is something implied in the structure of Christian (and of Jewish) faith. . . . it is a corollary of the faith, something implied by the basic constituents of faith.[87]

The model of Christian faith has been worked out in Scripture, in the OT in the faith of Israel in God and in the NT by restating this faith in terms of God being the Father of Jesus Christ. The God in whom Christians believe is the God known and believed in the biblical traditions and this model of faith is thus built into the nature of faith.

This view of the Bible as a classic model is congruous with Barr's approach to the questions of revelation and inspiration. That God is known is the departure point of the tradition process which states the life of faith of God's people with the known God. God makes the word of man which witnesses this faith his own word to subsequent generations. This is basically the same as saying that the Bible gives us a classic model of Christian understanding. In so far as revelation might be said to follow on from the tradition, it may be also that this means that in the continuation of the life of the people of God faith is similarly open to the future. As a classic model the Bible is sufficient, not perfect. Its inspiration lies in the fact that as a classic model of God's people it expresses faith in a human way as the relation with God develops in the life of his people. Scripture is inspired as the book of the people of God which provides a model of human faith.

So it might be said that the Bible is at once the objectification of the people of God's faith and the model of faith for subsequent times.

---

87. Ibid., p. 115.

Thus God speaks to us through the erring and fallible faith of his people to our faith. There is no direct revelation from God to man expressed in the Bible. There is a model of faith for our faith, which is fallible just as our faith is.[88] This is well resumed by Barr in these terms:

> The relation of the biblical writers and traditionists to God through the Spirit is thus not basically other than that of the church today in its listening to God. There is, however, a difference in the *stage*. . . . the biblical men had a pioneering role in the formation of our classic model, and this may make it fitting for them to be called "inspired" in a special sense.[89]

The Scripture is not a "closed revelation" in this formulation; on the contrary, it is the crystallisation of a tradition which opens out a continuing history. The Bible has been "opened" here as the first step of many continuing ones. This means, of course, that it may continue to function as model, but is no longer to be thought of as the final authority for church or theology. In its function as model it has the advantage of presenting the outlines of the model in the day in which it was first worked out and incorporating the historical references of the period. Had no classic model been formed, the outlines of the model would have been lost in the development of tradition and the historical rootings would have become obscure.[90] Faith is "Christian" when related to this model of understanding and "historical" since the model is formulated in terms of historical circumstantiality.[91]

By proposing to consider the Scripture as classic fixed model of God's people for Christian faith, Barr seems able to affirm at once the continuity and discontinuity present in the development of the tradition. The discontinuity is centred in the consideration that the beliefs developing in the present traditions of the church cannot immediately be taken as legitimate developments of Christian faith because they are stated in ecclesial context. They must be related to the classic model of the faith. The fact that such a model exists

---

88. In a similar vein, see C. Geffré, in *La Révélation,* P. Ricoeur et al. (Bruxelles, 1977), pp. 187ff.. Cf. *BMW,* p. 128.

89. *BMW,* p. 132; cf. p. 120.

90. Ibid., p. 128.

91. Ibid., pp. 118, 128.

creates a discontinuity between the recognised model and the development of the faith today. Since the classic model of faith is now
there before us, the character of tradition changes. It is no longer
the total life of the people of God; tradition is limited in terms of the
objectified classic model which is appropriated by faith. This discontinuity in tradition created by the existence of a classic model
may represent a deterioration in the character of tradition.[92] This
price is worth paying, thinks Barr, as the classic model is an historical
one. However, discontinuity in tradition resulting from the fixing of
the model implies also the possibility of a certain continuity, in that
faith is related to this model: "It seems to me normal," states Barr,
"that the biblical material bears on the whole man, his total faith and
life, and that out of that total faith and life *he* takes his decisions as a
free agent."[93]

G. F. Downing, whose thought on the traditional formulations of
the doctrine of revelation is quite close to Barr's, says that "the Christian has a myth that enables him to make certain decisions, express
certain attitudes."[94] Therefore in the discontinuity created in the
tradition's development because of the existence of a classic model,
there remains an essential continuity of faith, which relates itself to
a common understanding of God. This continuity of faith might well
be seen in Barr's thought to be constituted by the work of the Holy
Spirit. "In the Spirit" the people of God relate their understanding
of faith to the classic model provided by the church in the Scriptures.
When the words of Scripture are heard in faith, this is the mode of
the abiding presence of the Spirit. The classic model is constituted
by a dynamic analogy between the people of God and the Spirit of
God. The Spirit is present in the formation of a model which is expressed in a totally human way. There is an analogy between the
work of the Spirit and the striving of the people of God to express
faith. The basis of this analogy is the "presence" of the Spirit. Likewise there is a continuing analogy between the understanding of the

---

92. Ibid., p. 128.
93. Ibid., p. 142.
94. G. F. Downing, *Has Christianity a Revelation?* (London, 1964), p. 290.
On the "normativity" of the Scripture tradition see D. Jenkins, *Tradition and
the Spirit* (London, 1951), p. 35; R. P. C. Hanson, op. cit., pp. 244ff., 256;
E. Flesseman-van Leer in *Holy Book and Holy Tradition,* ed. F. F. Bruce and
E. G. Rupp (Manchester, 1968), pp. 164ff.

church and the leading of the Spirit when the church today seeks to state its faith in relation to the scriptural paradigm.

This would seem to mean that we seek in reading Scripture to gain understanding of how the Spirit dynamically led the people of God to express their faith in response to the total situation of their time; this can be paradigmatic for the leading of the church by the Spirit in the situation which is ours. Because these situations, then and now, are human ones, this understanding in relation to faith is aided by the proper use of historical analysis in exegesis. So the Bible is not read for an answer to today's problems, but as a model which might encourage us with similar discernment to find the leading of the Spirit in terms of the present. J. A. Sanders, commenting on Barr's view of this relation, writes: "The Bible should be looked upon as a paradigm on how one may conjugate the verbs of God's past and present activity and presence."[95]

Barr's statement regarding the Bible as classical model for the faith of the church tells us a little about how Barr now envisages the relation between God and historical reality. In the traditional models, the analogy of the divine and human in Christ served as an indicator of how to approach the Scripture. In the parallel, there was a unity of the divine and human elements which was the organic result of the work of the Spirit. Incarnation and inscripturation bespoke a conjunction of the two natures, in a way which accorded with the special nature of the union involved. Such unity of the divine and human could be possibly conceived as the assimilation of the human to the divine in an act initiated by the divine decision. Barr has developed a consequent criticism of the ramifications of this view and the authority structures it erects in theology. His own propositions may be seen as a model for theology which avoids the unity of the divine and human on the level of this-worldly realities, at least in the case of Scripture. The Scripture is a human word and can be understood as such. There is an analogy between the life of the people of God and the action of the Spirit which is expressed in the Scripture-model. However, this presence of the Spirit does not enter the realm of observable realities in a way which would provide authentification of the Spirit's influence. The work of the Spirit seems to be imper-

---

95. J. A. Sanders in *Int* 28:329.

ceptible to intellectual rational scrutiny in its application to the life
of God's people. However, it may be discernible to the eye of faith
and a stimulus to a life in faith, even if there is no validation of Christianity as a revealed truth. God works with man in a way that leaves
him a free agent. Faith in this respect is not grounded in the revealed
truth of the Bible ascertained by a correspondence between the text
and factual realities. Faith may rather be expected to express itself
as a consciousness of the value of human freedom that the life in the
Spirit assures for man.

If there is no divine self-revelation in Scripture in terms of a God-
to-man movement and no christological analogy, but only a relation
between God's Spirit and his people, what might constitute a more
precise definition of the contact between God and the historical milieu
in Barr's thought? This question is difficult to answer, as Barr's references to it are fleeting, oblique, and unsystematic in his published
works. However, some tentative remarks can be made on the basis of
suggestions which are made here and there by Barr. It is largely at the
end of *BMW* that Barr makes some revealing remarks. Concerning
the unity of the Bible, we read:

> . . . the profoundest unity is not *within* the Bible on the level of
> its common patterns of thought. . . . it is rather the unity of the
> one God, which also is a unity within a variety, and—dare we
> say?— a unity with a history. The use within the church of a
> book so diverse as the Bible must imply a conviction that ulti-
> mately all this diversity will not lead off into totally irreconcil-
> able opposites. Such a conviction, however, does not necessarily
> have to be comprehended now by us, or to be expressed . . . as
> something we now perceive; its realization belongs rather to faith
> and to hope.[96]

Barr rejects a static view of God based on the perfection of the divine attributes and works. The breakdown of this view of God which
sees God as existing in static perfection would not be a bad thing for
Christianity. This view conflicts with the biblical view of the living
God, undermines the theological significance of what happens in the
world, and puts the study of the Bible out of the range of any modern
categories. Barr states tentatively that "God has a history—though,
naturally, not identical with human history."[97] God operates in nar-

---

96. *BMW*, p. 181.
97. Ibid., p 179, n. 11; cf. *F*, p. 277.

rative sequences, not out of a static perfection.

The temptation must be avoided to read too much into these passing remarks. Barr cannot be made a process theologian as a result of a couple of asides! Two things may be said. God is one and in God alone is there an ultimate unity of truth. This unity cannot be stated by man in any comprehensive way; it is non-objective. Nor can it be seen in its entirety in the present; it lies in the realm of faith and hope, not in that of knowledge. On another level, there is a diversity within this divine unity which might be related to the historical process. If God is a unity and as such the object of faith, this unity is known in only a very partial and fractional way in the course of history. God's contacts with history, the narrative sequences, show him to be the living God, but we know him only in this diversity. The diversity of this knowledge seems to prevent us from identifying our history with God's in too strict a way; God's history is therefore different from human history.

To resume: God alone is whole as truth in unity; we behold this unity of truth only in a fractional sense in the diversity of our knowledge of God in history.[98] This means that truth concerning God transcends human knowledge. Our statements of truth are of limited significance and cannot claim any ultimacy, since there is no revelation of truth. The classic model of faith in God we have in the Bible is itself not a unity of truth but reveals the diversity of the actions of the living God. It is, however, sufficient to foster faith and hope in God. In spite of this, no human formulation can capture the object of this faith and hope. Within the classic model itself there is therefore a diversity of theological expressions which in its turn validates a diversity in the theological construction. The transcendence of the truth in God justifies a pluralistic situation as no one theology can claim to attain the unity of truth in its formulation.[99]

It has often been pointed out that the theology of neo-orthodoxy, divine revelation is tangential with human history. In Barr's view, it may be even less than this. An inevitable consequence of Barr's proposition that the Bible is not part of a God-to-man movement

<hr>

98. Cf. the remarks of Sanders,. art. cit., p. 323.
99. Barr might have done well at this point to interact with the more systematised thought of W. Pannenberg on this subject, particularly with respect to the formulation of the doctrine of God in relation to the future. Cf. *Theology and the Kingdom of God* (Philadelphia, 1969), pp. 62ff., 70f., 127ff.

is the raising of the question of the validity of man's knowledge of God and the reality of the faith which it expresses.

4.2. *Theology and the interpretation of the tradition*

To say that Scripture is a model of faith for the church has certain precise consequences for the way the interpretation of the text is to be carried through and for what is aimed at in the process. As a classic model is being interpreted, interpretation cannot be simply an application of what was said in the past to a present situation. A present theology cannot be just a repetition of the biblical material. The model of what faith meant in certain situations cannot be immediately extrapolated to other situations as a transcript of the Bible in modernised form. The Bible can be interpreted in a purely historical or literary way, but in order to interpret it as a document of faith it is necessary to venture beyond description to theological formulation. The Bible as a model of faith is therefore related to the faith of the church today expressed in theological assertions. Theology in its basic form affirms what is now believed by the church, and as such it is constructive, not just determinative. Interpretation in this context would seem to have the task of relating what is believed now by the church in her present situation and stated in her theological affirmations to the model of faith which is found in the foundational documents of Christianity. It concerns the decisions as to how the earlier thoughts of faith can be related to theology today. In this way the theological patterns which are implied in the biblical material are disengaged from it and incorporated into the statement of the Church's belief. The process is at once critical in that the theological elements of the Bible are drawn together and evaluated, and constructive in that these elements are integrated into a present theological statement.[100]

In this section some important points about interpretation in Barr's work will be described. Firstly the critical evaluation of the biblical material to be integrated into theological statement can be approached in terms of an assessment of the function of the materials in Scripture. Secondly the question of the shape of theologies which might emerge in relation to the Bible can be considered. Thirdly

---

100. *BMW*, pp. 133ff.

something can be said about the relevance of the biblical texts in an approach which is centred on the formation of a tradition and the fixing of that tradition as a model of faith. Finally, a word on pluralism will be added.

4.2.1. The function of Scripture and theology

The theme of the function of Scripture is well developed in two sections in *BMW*.[101] It represents an effort on Barr's part to relate the interpretation of Scripture to an analysis of the functions of the biblical text rather than to an attempt to apply the text on the assumption of its authority. Such an assumption, as Barr has maintained in his critique of interpretative methods, can have a bad effect on the stating of the message of Scripture and also on people.[102] Therefore when Barr proposes that the contents of Scripture might be considered with respect to the different functions of the biblical materials, this is an aspect of seeking a structure for theology which is not centred on authority. It can be taken to imply that there is no unitary view of biblical authority which might be discovered in the Scripture, and different types of texts must be recognised as having different functions in the authorisation of theological statements in the church today.[103] Interpretation must include an account of the processes involved in the interpretation of the biblical text itself, but also of the processes by which the text relates to questions of the present. These processes are functions of various persons working in the different theological disciplines on the text of the Bible. The diversity of function between the exegete and the apologist, for example, can lead to animosities, but this does not mean that the various functions are contradictory, and some understanding of the processes of thought which function in the interpretation of Scripture and the way these relate to theology as a whole must be sought.

This emphasis is rather typical of the swing away from interest in questions of authority in the post neo-orthodox era. Authority to be stated required the search for a unitive biblical view; to speak of interpretation in terms of the function of the texts encourages a diversity which corresponds to the different methods of the various

---

101. Ibid., pp. 30ff., 61ff.
102. Ibid., pp. 128ff.
103. See *Int* 25:39f.; *ER* 21:149.

disciplines. The great advantage of speaking of the functions of
the Bible is that it permits different answers according to the various
functions of the biblical material and different processes in interpretation, unhampered by an antecedent view of authority related to one
doctrinal system. The diversity of processes will give a legitimate
expression to the different types of literature in the tradition.[104]

Barr points to three possible processes of the study of the Bible.
One traditional approach to the study of the Bible seeks to understand the entities, theological or historical, referred to in the text.
The text is a vehicle which refers to a set of realities beyond the text
itself. A second approach centres on the intentions of the writers, the
motivations which moved them to express themselves in a certain
way, theological or other. Thirdly, Barr is interested in the literary
approach to the text of the Bible which concentrates on its surface
form and evaluates its qualities as a literary work.[105] In the older
theology, all of these approaches functioned in concert. The mythopoeic literary aspect of the text was referred to external realities in
a direct sense and not seen as functioning in a literary way; the ideas
of the writers were understood as revelatory of the one divine mind.
From the Bible lines could be drawn out directly to real events and
theological doctrines which both had the sanction of divine authority.
In this context the three approaches were aspects of one hermeneutical *démarche*. It is only in modern times, with the development of
the human sciences and more detailed reflection on methodology
that the unity of these three processes has become problematic.

Of these three aspects of study of the Bible, Barr has developed
that which concentrates on the literary character of the text in his
discussion. This is doubtless because it has been somewhat neglected
by theologians in favour of an accent on the intention of the writer
discerned through the application of historical criticism.[106] Today
such an approach can be particularly valuable, as through it the dichotomy between the man of today, who does not read the Bible as
authority, and the Christian can be broken down. To read the Bible
as literature is a good corrective against a reading of the Bible which

---

104. *BMW*, pp. 180, 31f. Cf. D. E. Nineham, *BJRL* 52:178ff., and D. Kelsey, op. cit., chap. 9.
105. *BMW*, pp. 61ff.
106. See Barr's remarks in *BJRL* 56:12ff.

simply seeks its truth-value. This opens the Bible to wider audiences.[107] In the church's use of the Bible in liturgy the man of today and the man of the Bible become one in the continuity of the church by sharing a common model of understanding.[108]

This approach to the Bible as literature which comes to occupy a place in Barr's hermeneutics is made possible on the grounds of his previous critique of the idea that Christianity models language in a particular way requiring a special theological interpretation. Christianity does have a peculiar vitality, Barr admits, but there is no necessity to assume that this can be applied "univocally to semantic change in a language."[109] Barr's understanding of the nature of biblical language which is influenced by structural thinking is related to this possibility of considering the Bible as literature. The narrative structures of the Bible can be analysed in a similar way to the patterns of other literature. No special hermeneutic is required; by using interpretative procedures normally accepted in literary study, the Bible can be understood as literature. Thus the Bible is read as the "foundation myth" of Christianity. By this Barr means that the Bible constitutes the basic story or document which provides the community with "pictures, types and categories" which structure its experience.[110] As a literary myth the place the Bible occupies for Christians is comparable with that of Homer among the Greeks. The use of "myth" must not be equated with the idea of "fabricated story." In the literary sense which Barr intends, it indicates that meaning and value do not lie primarily in the informational content of the story, but in "the structure and shape of the story, and in the images used within it."[111] These stories and images pattern our lives independent of whether they really happened or not. Christian experience is therefore experience in the tradition which has the Bible as its foundational paradigm.[112] This literary approach fits in well with the tradition process

---

107. *BMW*, p. 60. Barr thinks the book of Job lends itself best to this approach. See "The Book of Job and Its Interpreters," *BJRL* 54:39, 46.

108. *BMW*, pp. 58f., 66. See A. Hanson, "Alan Richardson and His Critics in Hermeneutics," in *Theology and Change*, ed. R. H. Preston (London, 1975), p. 31, for a brief note on the views of Nineham and Barr on this subject.

109. *SBL*, p. 248.

110. *BMW*, p. 53.

111. Ibid., p. 55.

112. *IDB*(S), p. 795.

expressed in the Bible and the fixing of Scripture as a classic model of faith.

In line with Barr's contention that the concept "history" cannot be applied in univocal fashion to the biblical narratives is his proposition that when we consider the Bible as literature, it is possible to evaluate the fiction-character of the Bible stories: ". . . what if we were to think of the Bible as a supremely profound work of fiction?"[113] Barr thinks several factors could justify this approach. Some sections of the Bible demand this kind of interpretation, such as Job, Jonah, or Genesis. To adopt it more generally would not be a sign of scepticism; it is simply a recognition of the fact that the impact of the Bible is antecedent upon the reader to questions of whether the event actually happened or not. However these questions are answered, the impact of the biblical stories remains the same. Rather than encouraging scepticism, to accept that the material has the direct impact of an evocative foundational myth seems to direct faith to its real object by detaching it from questions concerning obscure events. On the contrary, real scepticism may lie in the refusal to let the Bible function in this way on the understanding by dragging in the doctrinal and referential questions which damage the effectiveness of the myth.[114] Barr thinks that this literary function is the way in which the Bible actually has impact on the average church-goer and is close to the use of the Bible in devotional and liturgical practice.

Barr seems willing to go quite a way along this road, although when it comes to the central core of Christianity he hesitates a little:

> The Genesis story of creation is no longer read as if it told us how the universe came into existence; it conveys to us something about God and his nature, something about ourselves, . . . something different from the surface meaning of the text as it lies before us. And, if this can be said of the story of creation, why not the same of the story of Jesus' birth, or his resurrection? . . . I do not say I want to go so far; I only assert that some steps in this direction are already accepted as normal.[115]

---

113. *BMW*, loc. cit.
114. Ibid., pp. 57f.
115. *BJRL* 56:16. See as an example of an approach to the creation and incarnation as stories which represent a "dimension of human experience," M. F. Wiles, "Does Christology Rest on a Mistake?," *Religious Studies* 6:

This points to a problem with reading the Bible as literature. Literary study has the advantage of studying the myths and images of the text as it is, and so it can recapture the sense of the text as a unit in its present state.[116] However, the difficulty remains in that literary approaches, and in particular structuralist ones, tend to leave in suspense the status of the Bible as "holy writ"; as soon as the question of the status of the Bible is asked, the interpreter may well be back in the arms of the historical critical approach again. Barr affirms therefore that various insights are necessary: To read the Bible as literature is enlightening, but theology goes beyond this.[117] In itself a literary approach is not sufficient, and in isolation it could produce a reactionary effect unfavourable to historical criticism.[118] Its major limitation is the low level of theological articulation which could be achieved if practised exclusively. Precisely because it places the theological status of the Bible in parentheses, it would leave the theologian enlightened but unsatisfied if used in isolation from other methods.

Quite apart from these limitations, it might well be thought that in Barr's discussion of the Bible as literature the whole question of what it means to speak of the mythical or fictional character of the text has not been really adequately explored. For when we speak of the Bible or another text as fiction, this has implications not only for the consideration of the text itself, but also for the situation of the reader of the text. This has been pointed out quite recently by

---

69-76. The function of Scripture as fiction expressing such a human experience and understood as foundation myth could also put biblical interpretation in line with psychoanalysis. See for a Freudian interpretation F. Dolto, *L'Evangile au Risque de la Psychanalyse* (Paris, 1977), pp. 10ff., 79ff.

116. Art. cit., pp. 25ff. An important present trend in this direction is in structuralist interpretation which concentrates on the synchronic unity of the text over against the atomism of historical criticism. See D. Patte, *What Is Structural Exegesis?* (Philadelphia, 1976), pp. 36f.; also the remarks of R. M. Frye in E. Krentz, *The Historical Critical Method* (Philadelphia, 1975), who has criticised theologians' ignorance of the canons of literary study in their critical reconstructions, pp. 80f.

117. See the remarks of C. H. Dodd, *The Authority of the Bible* (London, 1960), p. 19.

118. Barr envisages an unholy alliance between the literary approach and authoritarian reactionary theology. *BMW*, pp. 65, 73. See also Barr's criticism of L. Alonso Schökel's book on the inspired word, where he thinks that literary analysis is used to make the traditional theological terms of inspiration and inerrancy more subtle (*Religious Studies* 6:194).

Paul Ricoeur in two articles.[119] Ricoeur maintains that literature, while abolishing the ostensive character of reference to the world, creates a new form of reference which is separated from it. Poetry, fiction, myth, story, etc., abolish this first kind of reference but create another level of reference at a distance from the world. This second level of reference is a *mimesis* of the reality of the world on a fictional level. It is real only in so far as it is fictitious:

> . . . just as the world of the text is real only to the extent that it is fictitious, it must be said that the reader's subjectivity is accomplished only in being held in suspense as potentially unrealised, in the same way as the world projected in the text.[120]

Appropriation of the text is therefore linked with distancing of the reader from the real world. Fiction is a fundamental dimension of the subjectivity of the reader. "Reader, I find myself by losing myself in the imaginative variations of the *ego*. In this game, the metamorphosis of the world is also the ludic metamorphosis of the *ego*."[121] This metamorphosis of the ego implies a distancing from one's own self in the subjectivity of the appropriation of the text (distanciation dans le rapport soi à soi). The text thus speaks to our *imagination* in proposing the images of our liberation.[122] Understanding the fiction is not merely a work of appropriating the meaning of the text; in Ricoeur's analysis, it is also a disappropriation of the self in the ludic imagination before the text. As such, hermeneutics must, according to Ricoeur, make the detour necessary via the Freudian and Marxian critique of the illusions of the subject.[123]

Whatever one might think of Ricoeur's analysis or the reservations which might be entertained as to the philosophical roots of his thought,[124] his analysis shows that if we want to talk of the Bible as literature, the implications of this are a good deal more far-reaching

---

119. P. Ricoeur in *Exegesis,* G. Antoine et al. (Neuchâtel-Paris, 1975), pp. 201-28.

120. Ibid., p. 214.

121. Ibid., p. 215.

122. Ibid., p. 228.

123. Ibid., p. 215. See Ricoeur's *Le Conflit des Interprétations* (Paris, 1969). F. Dolto in her Freudian approach to the Gospel text says, "si nous voulons nous abstraire de l'imaginaire, c'est qu'alors nous voulons abstraire notre corps et notre coeur du message que les évangiles apportent" (op. cit., p. 79).

124. See the article by H. Blocher, "L'herméneutique selon Paul Ricoeur," *Hokhma* (Lausanne), 3:11-58.

than would first meet the eye. Many theologians might well be inclined to agree with Markus Barth, who says concerning the appreciation of the aesthetic qualities of the Bible that "lyricism leaves man alone with himself, in a 'hell' from which there is no exit."[125] Thus we are back again at the question raised concerning calling the Bible the classic myth of the Christian faith, as to the reality of our knowledge of God. Can the approach to the Bible as literature give us anything more than a human faith, or at best a faith in the "New Being as revealing" in the whole of the sphere of reality, including our individual existences and histories?[126]

Barr would seem to come rather close to these ideas out of a different philosophical context, when he says, for example, that "we should consider the possibility that great literature possesses a kind of theological dimension of its own."[127] All great literature possesses a "spirituality." In this respect Barr raises the proper question when he asks what the relation is "between the spirituality implied in such reading of the Bible . . . and the religious and theological belief of those who read it as the sacred text of Jewish and Christian faith."[128] If the Bible were read consistently as literature, could any specificity be claimed for it by contrast with the other great literature, religious or secular, produced by man? Or, to put it another way, if the Christian faith is an expression of human spirituality, is there anything special about the Christian religion as such which distinguishes it from other forms of spirituality? However, more than this is at stake, for if the understanding of the biblical texts is carried into an imaginative domain which contains its own fictional system of reference, it may well be that Christian faith cannot escape the critiques of Feuerbach, Marx, or Freud, as to the illusory nature of religious belief.

It must not be thought that Barr puts all his eggs in one basket. If he shows more interest in the study of the Bible in a literary sense than a good many exegetes, the emphasis he maintains is that it is one possible process which is useful for understanding some parts of the Bible. These parts, moreover, are those which do not constitute

125. M. Barth, *Conversation with the Bible* (New York, 1964), p. 141.
126. Ricoeur in *Exegesis,* p. 223.
127. *BMW*, p. 60, n. 5.
128. *BJRL* 56:33.

the central structure of the faith, which is constructed on the basis
of special events or specific doctrinal articulations which formulate
the theological aspects of the faith. The Bible functions in other ways
as well as the literary, which are regarded as far more important for
the faith.[129] The most common way has been to consider that the
Bible gives information focused on the external entities about which
the text speaks. The Bible provides in some cases the only information about the entities referred to. As a document of faith it points
beyond itself to the realities on which faith is based; the heart of
Christian faith lies in a set of historical facts, as interpreted in the
biblical faith-representation.

This second process of study would seek then to press behind the
text to the reality about which the text speaks, which may in some
cases be an historical event or an "eternal" reality as God himself.[130]
Barr's criticism of the localisation of the authority of the Bible in
saving event and his suggestion that the Bible narratives can be approached as stories which have a variable relation to history[131] have
already been discussed (secs. 2.3 and 4.1.1). The implications
of this work are that the referential function of the text is by no means
as straightforward as formerly thought. There is a wide range of
disagreement as to how the reference might function; the entities referred to are "vague and equivocal."[132] For this reason Barr suggests
that talk of saving events referred to in the Bible comes a lot closer
than is apparent to the literary function of myth. It is more the form
of the story than the events referred to which determines the status
of the Bible. In addition to this, when the Bible is valued for information, theological indications retain the attention more than details
relative to the events in themselves. Theological significance is what
is envisaged, as this can be related to theology today. However, Barr
maintains that a process of interpretation which seeks to relate events
described in the text to theology does not demonstrate the normativity
of the theology of the Bible. The interest of concentrating on the

129. *BMW*, pp. 74f.

130. See on this H. W. Frei, *The Eclipse of Biblical Narrative* (New Haven,
1974), chap. 1, pp. 16, 323.

131. Ibid., pp. 280f. See also A. N. Wilder, "The Word as Address and the
Word as Meaning," in *The New Hermeneutic,* ed. Robinson and Cobb, (New
York, 1964).

132. *BMW*, pp. 78, 83.

function of the Bible in terms of its information as event or theology is therefore a concern of secondary nature. Large sections of the Bible cannot be read in a referential way; this cannot therefore be applied globally as *the* method of biblical interpretation. Its scope is limited.

The third process of interpretation to which Barr addresses himself is the one which interprets the text with reference to what the writer wished to say through the form of words selected. In contrast with the referential approach, the concentration on intention works with the supposition that the texts do not signify directly, but the reality referred to can be approached only indirectly via the mind of the writer. This means that theology is not to be read directly off the face of the text: ". . . we no longer move in theology from biblical texts directly to external realities, but from biblical texts to the theological intentions of the writers and only from there, and thus indirectly, to external realities."[133] This perspective corresponds to Barr's critique of a referential view of language in which words are taken to refer directly to objects, and to his proposition that a biblical theology must be built up from the longer units of sense in the Bible.[134]

It is in this perspective that Barr seeks to relate theology and historical study, since an understanding of the mind of the writer based on a correlation of the textual material is the domain of historical reconstruction. This is to say that what appears on the surface of the text in terms of historical or theological information is not necessarily the same as the event which happened or the thought the writer is trying to express. In this respect critical reconstruction is a *sine qua non* for the formulation of the theology which the author sought to express.[135] In interpretation, when the attempt is made to relate theology to the intention of the writer, the literal or verbal form of the text assumes a great importance. "The detailed verbal evidence is the route to the mind of the writer."[136] Barr insists on the importance of a particularised approach to exegesis in which the *differences* on the verbal level between writers, stages of tradition, different traditions are sounded as indicators of theological mean-

---

133. *BJRL* 56:17f.
134. Cf. chap. 3, n. 4, and *BMW*, pp. 91f.
135. *BMW*, p. 93; *BJRL* art. cit., 19ff.
136. Ibid., p. 174.

ing.[137] By the use of this method respecting literary features which aims at a critical reconstruction, distinctions of status, function and application are made which theology can use.[138] The search for the meaning of the writer in interpretation in terms of intentionality reveals a diversity of historical and theological senses which must be accounted for in theological construction.

The overall effect of the way Barr develops these various processes of interpretation is to foster a great diversity in theology. The fact that the Scripture functions in many ways makes legitimate various expressions of the biblical message. It is no longer possible to assume the authority of the Scripture and the unity of its message, and on the basis of this to draw theology which would be "true" directly from the Bible statements. Such an approach would be possible only where the Bible was accorded some special status as divine revelation. However, Barr holds that the theory of the dual authorship of Scripture has broken down and the text must be considered as a human document. As such, a diversity of human thoughts and ways of expression is found in it and can be accounted for in terms of normal interpretative procedures both literary and historical. In these processes Scripture functions in different ways and therefore no one view of its authority can be held.

It can be commented that there is a certain complementarity between Barr's view of Scripture as the crystallisation of tradition and the role of interpretation. Within the biblical tradition there is a reworking of certain elements in relation to new situations which arise in the life of the people of God. Now that the tradition is fixed as a model for faith, tradition has an interpretative aspect; in interpretation the diverse elements in the fixed tradition are rendered functional in new theological contexts. It may even be remarked that Barr's view of Scripture as a fixed tradition and his view of interpretation are involved together in a certain circularity. The diverse human traditions we see developing in Scripture require different processes of interpretation, which in turn indicate the stresses and tensions present in the classic model. Thus we can move round a kind of hermeneutical circle in Barr's thought, from the diversity of present theologies to the diversity of interpretative processes which

137. Ibid., pp. 176f.
138. Ibid., p. 110.

express the functions of the biblical texts to the diversity in the biblical material itself. The present theological pluralism is the correlate of the pluralism of biblical theologies. In a certain sense, theological pluralism is a sign of conformity with the classic model. Although Barr does not say as much, it may be a test of the authenticity of the faith. This may explain in part Barr's attitude to fundamentalism: For the churches today the question is as to "how far they can recognize fundamentalist attitudes, doctrines and interpretations as coming within the range that is acceptable in the church."[139]

One final feature of this discussion of the processes for interpretation can be noted. Scripture is the classic model of *faith*. What is important is not primarily its cognitive function but the faith it expresses. The function of the Bible is a pistic one; it bears witness to man's faith in God. For this reason in interpretation the cognitive value of the text is secondary to the significance it has through the value of its faith assertions. To read the Bible as literature is not to read it for factual knowledge; the "saving events" of Scripture themselves have an uncertain reference in historical terms; concentration on the intention of the author means that the referential sense of Scripture can be pointed to only indirectly. These considerations constitute a strong argument against locating the authority of Scripture in the surface theology thought to be overt in the text or in the proximity to the real event to which it refers. The function of the Scripture is thus not to provide true information, but to encourage dynamic trust in God, similar to that which it expresses as a model of faith.

This observation can be correlated with our evaluation of Barr's thought as a move away from the christological analogy to an analogy between God's Spirit and God's people. It would seem that the abandoning of the christological analogy as a way of approaching the status of Scripture is reflected on the hermeneutical level in the eclipse of the reading of Scripture with a view to information which will found faith. When the model of the divine and the human for Scripture is rejected and the Bible is classed as human word, its informational value becomes relative and contingent. On this level truth is ultimately unattainable; all knowledge in terms of information is sub-

---

139. *F,* pp. 343f.

ject to the vicissitudes of the historical process and must be relativised. The truth of God is a non-objective truth, belonging to the domain of faith. As we have seen, it is known only fractionally in the course of history. If the Bible cannot give an objective knowledge of God's truth, it does give sufficient grounds for faith in the sense of dynamic trust. This trust is established in the analogy between the people of God and the Spirit of God. The life of faith, of which the Bible gives a model, is the life "in the Spirit."

Once again, this brings us back to a fundamental problem in the doctrine of Scripture and interpretation as Barr develops it, namely, the relation between faith and knowledge and the question of the reality of faith which in terms of cognitive content travels relatively light.

4.2.2. "Centres" in theological construction

In a previous section (3.4.2), we saw how Barr was critical of the arbitrary selection of material within the OT with a view to stating the unity of the biblical writings. Such selection was seen to run the risk of imposing a dogmatic unity on the diversity of the materials in the text. The choice of a centre in the biblical materials is a question of personal creativity and need not claim to be the only choice possible.

The present question refers to the role of such centres of reflexion in interpretation and their function in theology. This becomes a matter for concern in the context of the theological diversity now recognised in the human traditions of the Bible. What method can be used for operating a selection within the historical and theological material of the biblical corpus and what is the justification for this?[140] Barr raises the crucial question in this respect, namely, whether it is possible to look for a centre within the Scripture itself, or whether it is simply a questiton of establishing a functional centre for the sake of our theological reflexion. If Scripture is an accumulation of sediments of tradition, can a centre be located in the biblical materials themselves?[141] In addition, redaction criticism has made

---

140. *ER* 21:146.

141. K. Koch raises the problem of the unity of the biblical materials in the context of a tradition history approach and suggests that the various literary types of the traditional material could be linked with the history of concepts, *The Growth of the Biblical Tradition* (London, 1969), pp. 102ff.

us more aware of the differences in Scripture, which uncover in some cases polemical relations between the biblical writers.[142]   In this context, if centres of theological reflection are spoken about in interpretation, it must be in recognition of the fact that there is not necessarily *a* centre in Scripture itself, but that such a selection is made as an aid to organising our account of the material.[143]

In his later discussion of this problem in *BMW*, Barr shows less scepticism about the choice of a centre around which theological construction can be organised. This is perhaps because now such centres are not in the situation of an authority-centred theological structure but are related to a recognition that Scripture is characterised by a diversity typical of human productions. A centre for theology selected in the Scripture is justified by the diversity we find in the biblical material. Priorities and preferences of theologians are to a certain extent legitimate because the "biblical material itself invites and requires" the need of selection.[144]   To this reason for a certain selection inherent in the nature of the biblical material can be added the factor that in interpretation the theologian works within a precise ecclesiastical and academic tradition. Already he has certain priorities in view as he approaches the biblical texts. These theological priorities act as an interpretative structure which is used as a framework for organising the biblical material. Two factors, then—the diversity in the biblical material and the diversity of theological frameworks in the tradition of the church—would seem to lead us to posit the plurality of centres of theological discussion which can be related to elements in the Scripture in interpretation. No one such centre could claim exclusively to be the centre of interest for correct interpretation of the Bible, or to be the core of the biblical message around which a unitary view of the Bible teaching could be articulated.

Consideration of these factors leads Barr to reject the idea that the "material centre" or a canon within the canon of the Bible can be found. He sees a danger in elevating certain elements in Scripture to a status which would be superior to the rest of the text. This would

---

142. *IDB*(S), p. 108.
143. *JTS* 25:272.
144. *BMW*, p. 157. Cf. D. Evans, *The Logic of Self-Improvement* (London, 1963), pp. 19f., who says that the work of the biblical theologian is not only descriptive but selective, interpretative, and prescriptive.

mean that a portion of the Bible, one aspect of its teaching, or some events related would acquire a kind of normative status that could place them beyond critical weighing. Thus the inner canon would be exempt from theological criticism.[145]

If Barr rejects the idea of a canon within the canon, he does not deny that it is possible to centre theological reflexion round an element in Scripture. It is possible to speak of certain nodal points or relational centres in the biblical corpus, such as the love of God or the resurrection of Christ, upon which other teaching depends.[146] Nodal points such as these would not involve us in a great deal of controversy, as their importance in Scripture is self-evident. However, other centres could be chosen which have a much lower representation in the Bible; some may not be immediately obvious in the biblical materials at all. These centres in interpretation are not necessarily of more than temporary and personal significance. The multiplex nature of the tradition makes the identification of centres in the Bible a tentative process; to state that the centre of the OT lies in the acts done by God is a "simplistic approach to a theological understanding" of the OT.[147] The variety of possibilities in the biblical material opens up the theological vista to a diversity of biblico-theological landscapes.[148] In selecting a relational centre and ordering the material by it in interpretation, there is a great deal of decision. Barr's thought is well resumed here:

> In the modern theological scene, these matters come not under the control of an authority which prescribes what is to be done . . . but under the criticism of a discussion which looks at what comes out of it.[149]

It is not the case of stating the unity of Scripture in an authoritative way but of indicating certain patterns which might be fruitful for the work of interpretation in the dialogue with other theological positions. The usefulness of selecting one element of Scripture as a relational

---

145. Ibid., p. 161; G. Maier in his book, *The End of the Historical Critical Method* (St. Louis, 1977), attacks the idea of a canon within the canon in a detailed way, with particular reference to the work edited by E. Käsemann, *Das Neue Testament als Kanon* (Göttingen, 1970). See also the study by I. Lonning, *Kanon im Kanon* (Müchen, 1972).
146. Ibid., p. 162. Cf. *Louvain 1971* (Faith and Order Paper no. 59), p. 17.
147. *ONI*, pp. 19, 23.
148. *BMW*, pp. 157, 162.
149. Ibid., p. 162.

centre is tested by what it produces. No doubt centres which fail to integrate biblical material successfully in interpretation, which are not fruitful in terms of theological productivity, or which gel into authority structures should be discarded.

An example of Barr's own approach in terms of exegesis is in an article on salvation in the OT.[150] In his conclusion, after having examined the use of words for salvation and found this to be concentrated in the poetic tradition of the OT in prayers and confessions of assurance of salvation, Barr raises the question whether the religion of the OT can be regarded as a religion of salvation. Barr appears to be enquiring here as to whether the notion of salvation could be a nodal point around which OT religion could be interpreted.[151] His reply to this question is that it can be answered only ambiguously: ". . . it depends on how you read the Old Testament, and what authority and what importance you attach to one element against another." The implication of this would seem to be that Barr does not expect to find any central unity in the OT which might be referred to in interpretation as the unifying factor of a theology in an objective sense. The weight we attach to various elements of the text depends on certain factors of personal choice. There is no one way of reading the Bible or connecting its elements in interpretation; nor is there necessarily a self-stabilising of elements from within the Scripture itself.

All this fits in with the pattern we have sought to develop with respect to Barr's approach to the Bible as a document of faith. As the real dynamic of Scripture is in its expression of the faith of the people of God rather than in an objective formulation of truth, so also in interpretation the selection of central elements is a matter of personal decisions. Just as the meaning of Scripture is not treated in a referential fashion which indicates realities which are intellectually known, so also a centre of Scripture cannot be referred to which would remain a fixed entity in the construction of a theology. The truth of Scripture is not stable in a fixed objective form having a universal application. In this way Barr preserves the liberty of the interpreter, both with respect to the text he is using, but also with regard to his own

---

150. "An Aspect of Salvation in the Old Testament," in *Man and His Salvation,* ed. E. J. Sharpe and J. R. Hinnels (Manchester, 1973), pp. 39-52.

151. Ibid., pp. 48, 51.

theological construction. Interpretations come and go, Barr is telling us, and we must be aware of the relativity of our intellectual absolutes. Faith transcends these.

However, it may be wondered whether Barr has been radical enough in his formulations concerning the use of nodal points in interpretation. In the factuality of a non-authoritarian situation which Barr recognises, surely the use of such centres must either receive a justification or be posited as useful in *a priori* fashion. Barr has not really offered a justification for searching for such centres in the diversity of the biblical traditions and seems rather to presuppose that such centres can be discerned and profitably used. It may well be the case that no Christian would doubt the centrality of the love of God in Scripture, but this may be only half the matter. In a non-authority-centred situation it may be doubted that this is a nodal centre for theological reflexion today. Barr's weakness at this point appears to lie in the fact that he has not shown that there are centres which exist in the Bible *as* centres, nor should this be demonstrable, that they can be taken as theological centres in interpretation today. The problem would seem to be that when the authority of Scripture is relativised, it is difficult to argue for the use of nodal points which structure theology even on a temporary basis, if there is no external backing for such structuring principles. Such centres are no way of mitigating the problems created by non-normed diversity, to say nothing of their usefulness in the search for a theological unity.

4.2.3. The function of Biblical theology

Barr's approach to Scripture in terms of diverse functions and his affirmation that the "centres" of theological reflexion are of temporary and personal nature raises the question as to the function that Biblical theology might have as a discipline.

Barr articulates his suggestions in this connection with respect to what he discerns to be the shift of interest in theological studies in modern times. This is characterised by a move from OT study as a study of the history of religion to a concentration on OT theology demarcated from the history of Hebrew religion and based on structures of revelation. More recently a further shift is noted from OT theology to the hermeneutical question which results in a corresponding interest in methodological issues and a certain loss of contact with the text itself. In this latter situation Barr advocates that Biblical theology must incorporate a positive attitude to the history of religions. When interpretation moves towards an interest in formal hermeneutical questions, the emphasis on the history of religion becomes necessary to offer valid criticism of theology. If this is not achieved, theology can fall foul of a structure which is derived from the modern situation. The study of the history of religion will permit the checking of the interpretations current. Barr basically considers that the history of religions approach is a theological balance which encourages proper consideration of the text in the situation.[152]

This conception proposes that a Biblical theology is not just an account of biblical concepts set in the context of a notion of revelation as over against religion (see sect. 3.4.2). Biblical theology must incorporate a comprehension of the development of religion in Israel.[153] Barr's outlook is well summarised in this quotation:

> All that [Biblical theology] does differs only in level from various kinds of historical, linguistic, and religious study; and on the other hand, insofar as it seeks to exercise a truly theological function, its work is linked with logical, philosophical, and systematic-theological judgments also. It will do its best service and understand its own function best if it is aware that it is only one part in the total functioning unity of religious and theological study.[154]

The function of Biblical theology is to stand between an approach which is purely historical and the more systematic disciplines of theological reflexion. It looks, as it were, in two directions and must understand itself in these relations. Biblical theology, therefore, cannot claim an authority independent of these connections. In fact, it relies to a great extent on them for its usefulness. It will be helpful to clarify how Barr envisages this.

The effort made in certain cases in the BTM to develop a theological approach distinct from the study of religion is both a failure and misguided, thinks Barr.[155] Future study will have to amalgamate

---

152. *ONI,* pp. 97f.
153. "Le Judaisme Postbiblique," *Revue de Theologie et de Philosophie* (1968):215; *ONI,* p. 29; "Some Old Testament Aspects of Berkhof's 'Christelijk Geloof,'" in *Weerword* (Nykerk, 1974), p. 9.
154. *IDB*(S), p. 111.
155. Ibid., p. 110.

these two approaches. This is to say that a theology of the OT or
NT cannot be a history of the relevant religion à la Wrede; nor can
it be a theology strictly limited to the canon seen from "within." For
Biblical theology the choice is not either history or theology. It must
justify itself by relation to the two.[156] Barr claims that the approach
of Biblical theology has much in common with the history of religions approach. The two disciplines tend to coalesce, and it is
probably only when a synthesis of the materials studied is attempted,
in the writing of a theology of the OT, for example, that the need for
differentiation in principle is evident.[157] In terms of specific study,
Biblical theology uses a method which moves back and forth across
the boundary of the canon. Because it cannot be divorced from the
history of religions in the method of its study, it does not work on the
basis of a distinction between the biblical and the non-biblical material.

One of the aspects of Barr's attitude to Biblical theology is thus his
emphasis in several articles on the importance of extra-biblical culture and texts. The OT as a canonical document grew out of the
religious tradition of the Jews, and understanding of it cannot be cut
off from the religious tradition in general. One of the problems in
recent years is that the approach to the non-biblical materials has
tended to be a negative one. The Jewish traditions outside the biblical corpus have been considered as a deterioration or a distortion
of the biblical religion. Such an absolute distinction lacks in historical justification and breaks down when Biblical theology is seen as
related to the study of the history of religions. The same may be said
for the broader religious context of the Jewish traditions, which cannot be divorced from the surrounding religious cultures of the Near
East. Here again, the Jewish religion emerged from this culture.[158]
These overlaps prohibit the writing of a theology of the canonical
books without the inclusion of the non-canonical and inter-testamental
materials.

Barr's view of the inter-relation between history and theology in
the method of Biblical theology fits in well with his general consideration of the Bible materials as expressing a developing religious
tradition. The study of this traditional material cannot ignore the

---

156. See J. C. Beker in *Int* 24:304ff.
157. *JTS* 25:276f.
158. *IDB*(S), p. 110; *JTS* 25:279ff; *BJRL* 58:29ff.

historical processes in human terms which furnish the input in the development of the tradition. However, nor can the religious aspect of this historical process of development be neglected. This means to say that there is no "biblical" method for the discipline of Biblical theology. It is not a distinct discipline possessing a methodology of its own which operates separately from other disciplines, such as the historical. This is true of Biblical theology, but also of other theological disciplines. About this Barr says, "There is indeed no pure theological method."[159] In fact, the methods of Biblical theology are not determined by it, but are elaborated independently by other disciplines having no direct relation with Biblical theology, such as history, linguistics, psychology, social studies, etc.[160]

What Barr seems to be telling us here is that there is no unique theological method which can be deemed to govern the work of the theologian. Theology touches several different fields of enquiry, and for this reason no one theological method can be stated. This basic perspective is obviously a fundamental one for the understanding of Barr's whole criticism of the BTM, his linguistic outlook, his view of the character of the historical material in the Bible, or his attitude to the Bible as the crystallisation of a religious tradition. This approach, which is not exclusively theological, can help us today in evaluating the Scripture to have a deeper insight into its nature than the Jews or the early Christians were able to. Thus Barr says:

> The comparative religionist of today, tied by no view of canonical authority, and reading the text against a wide background of extra-canonical texts, may perhaps be able to see values which the ancient religions in their developed forms were not able to discern.[161]

In maintaining the complementarity of the history of religions approach and Biblical theology as far as their method is concerned, Barr is also careful to point out differences which exist between them. In most cases, the construction of works in the field of Biblical theology does not have a simply historical motivation. The motivation involved is very often beyond the scope of the simply descriptive. It will very often seek to relate the biblical faith to the theology of

---

159. *JTS* 25:282.
160. "Does Biblical Study Still Belong to Theology," p. 4.
161. Art. cit., in Sharpe and Hinnells, eds., p. 52.

later times; an application of the truth for the present is attempted. Again, if Biblical theology takes into account extra-biblical materials, its prime effort is geared to throwing light on the biblical texts. The focus too is different: It will seek the accredited theology in the biblical writings, rather than a global descriptive account of all the factors in the religious situation.

This constitutes a substantial difference between Biblical theology and a history of religions approach. Yet this difference is not an absolute one. It is rather a question in Biblical theology of a multiplicity of levels of study. On one level, Biblical theology shares a common method with an historical approach; on another level it overlaps with concerns of normativity characteristic of systematic study.[162] In terms of actual study this must mean that a certain awareness of the level of work is necessary on the part of the theologian, so as not to confuse the varying levels, for example, in introducing normative considerations into the study on the historical level and thus operating a selection of the material which would be unjustified on that particular level. On the other hand, accuracy of historical reporting or an abundance of information is not a guarantee of theological significance.

The advantage of this formulation of Barr's seems to lie in the fact that it avoids severing the links either between Biblical theology and historical study or between Biblical theology and disciplines which seek normative statement beyond the descriptive. It seeks to relate both to Biblical theology without the one dominating the other or becoming fused into the other, as the levels involved are different. It may be wondered whether on this showing there is really *a* discipline called Biblical theology, or whether there could really be any unity which might justify speaking of Biblical theology. It seems that Barr regards Biblical theology as a somewhat loose relation of processes of theological study which need not seek any specific unity of method. This looseness is accepted rather factually, just as Barr accepts a certain looseness in speaking of the various ways in which the Scripture functions in the processes of interpretation. This comes through quite clearly, when Barr asks whether a biblical theology or a theology of the OT/NT is possible. Barr's answer is that this is not a question

---

162. *JTS* 25:278.

of principle, but of convenience. It may be helpful to bring together the theological insights of the Bible as a whole in order to relate these to the final theological decisions which apply to a given situation. Yet one may also be not unjustified in thinking that the material of the Bible is too diverse for this to be accomplished.[163]

If it is accepted that there is no one method of Biblical theology and that a unitive theological statement of the biblical materials is not a pressing question, there still remains the difficulty of the relation between the different levels of study. Biblical theology incorporates in its study on one level the historical approach; on another level it is linked with theological judgments. In Biblical theology there is an overlap between the historical and theological in terms of methods, but on the theological level there is a difference of motivation, scope, and focus from that of purely historical study. In spite of the affirmation that there is overlap, it seems at least legitimate to ask what common ground might exist between a judgment which is historical and claims neutrality and one which is theological and therefore claims some form of normativity as the theology of the Bible or the theology for today. In relating these two different levels which enter into Biblical theology, it might be possible to say that the theology is founded on the historical description. However, as K. Stendahl has pointed out, the ideal of the History of Religions School was one of non-modernisation which sought to study the historical materials at a distance.[164] It may be doubted that theological assertions can be based on this historical approach in such a way as to give a Biblical theology without extensive selection. In this case, the principle of selection would have to be established, but since the critical historical study is descriptive, the means of selection would not be likely to be by historical considerations. Thus the selection would be a theological one and to that extent would be separate from the purely descriptive considerations. The normative theological formulations would then be divorced from the level of critical study.[165] Another possibility would be to begin with the theological principle and integrate certain

---

163. *BMW*, pp. 135f.
164. K. Stendahl, in *IDB*, I:419ff.
165. On the relation of historical study and theological affirmation see P. Wernberg-Moller, "Is There an Old Testament Theology?," *The Hibbert Journal* 59:21-9, where it is argued that there is no comprehensive theology of

historical considerations.[166] In this case it might be objected that the historical elements cannot be legitimately used if the global historical perspective is not adopted.

In speaking of the differences between the historical approach and the theological statement in Biblical theology, Barr recognises that such a difference is inevitable once the Bible is no longer considered as revelation. By placing historical research and theological statement on different levels in Biblical theology, he domesticates the problem, but it may be wondered what real complementarity there is between these two aspects of Biblical theology. This brings us to look at the role of historical criticism in Barr's thought.

4.2.4. The relevance of tradition

In Barr's approach to Biblical theology in which the historical level of study is recognised as an integral part of its work, historical criticism is not merely a preliminary. It is of the essence of biblical theological study. As K. Grobel says, ". . . it is not always recognised that Biblical theology is itself a part of biblical criticism . . . the constructive and positive phase of biblical criticism, which, when it is responsible, justifies the descriptions of it as 'discriminating appreciation.' "[167] Barr's rejection of the view that criticism is negative if necessary prolegomena is one of the ways in which his criticism of the BTM leads to a more detailed reflexion on the function of biblical criticism in his own thought. In the context of his view of Scripture which seeks to do full justice to the human aspect of the text, it is evident that historical and literary criticism are essential for the understanding of the human processes of the formation of the text we now possess. There can therefore now be no opposition between Biblical theology and the historical critical method when it functions in a proper way.[168]

---

the OT as there is no literary unity or uniform theology governing all writings. To deny this is to deny the historical perspective.

166. Such a position would seem to be adopted by R. de Vaux, who distinguishes an historical, a history of religions, and a theological approach to the OT. Theology judges the results of the history of religions approach in conformity with the truths of faith in the context of revelation—"Method in the Study of Early Hebrew History," in *The Bible in Modern Scholarship,* ed. J. P. Hyatt (Nashville/New York, 1965).

167. K. Grobel in *IDB,* I:413.

168. For some description of the opposition between criticism and Biblical

Barr associates the rise of the historical critical method with the shift away from a study of the Bible axed on a referential understanding of Scripture. The rise of criticism and the move from a referential approach to theology involve one another. The redirecting of interest to the intention of the writer apart from entities referred to in an overt sense, either theologically or evenementally implies the development of the historical method of study. It is not, then, a case of theology accepting or becoming subject to the historical method, but rather of a common intellectual standpoint. Historical criticism has "essential links with the mode of working of the theological process itself."[169]

There is therefore a coincidence between the theological approach and the development of critical methods, which corresponds on both levels to a doubt that theology is contained in the Bible as *theologia revelata*.[170] This means, as we have already seen, that theology does not lie on the face of Scripture but is constructed with the evidence contained in the biblical documents. In practical terms, this also implies that faith is no longer rooted in revealed theology or facts considered objective because found in the Bible. The shift Barr talks about implies a conception of faith related to significance on the level of personal understanding. For its reality, faith depends not on objective factuality but on the personal conviction of the significance of faith for the individual, although this may also imply a certain relation with external realities.

This double shift which Barr describes provides the basis for an intellectual standpoint which can relate itself at once to the material of the Bible and also to the modern advances in scientific study. It is necessary to an approach which seeks to do justice at once to the biblical material and to the state of our modern knowledge. When the two are related in terms of critical historical study, the relevance of the Christian faith for our modern situation becomes a possibility. The politics of fundamentalism is thus typical of a regressive and fixed mentality which absolutises a certain theological viewpoint, shuts itself off from modern discussion and in doing so shuts the Bible up in

---

theology, see Frei, op. cit., pp. 8ff; J. K. S. Reid, *The Authority of Scripture* (London, 1957), pp. 17ff.; G. Ebeling in *JTS* 6:218ff.
169. *BMW*, p. 93.
170. G. Ebeling, *Word and Faith* (London, 1963), p. 93.

a ghetto mentality. Thus when fundamentalists point to the divergence of critical positions as a sign that historical criticism is on the wane, they are simply confusing the wide acceptance of the method in its many diverse forms with their own wishful thinking. If criticism does make reading the Bible a more complicated business, this is not an argument against it. It is a question of honesty before the material.[171]

If it is possible to see the rise of historical criticism in relation to the needs of academic scholarship today, Barr insists on the fact that it is not simply a matter of theology giving itself up to a problematic which is essentially foreign to itself. Modern theology and modern historical criticism grow up together, and it is difficult to say which influences the other. Barr considers that it is possible to see the adoption of the historical method in relation to the problems contained in the older orthodoxies. The inner contradictions of these systems motivated the need to change. Such contradictions produced theological conflicts but also underlined the fact that the biblical basis appealed to no longer seemed to fit the theological conclusions which were based on it.

Barr thinks that it was therefore within the bosom of necessary theological change that the critical approach was adopted. Although the method was originally attached to certain philosophical positions, he claims that it is not dependent on these and can stand independently of them in relation to other presuppositions. The use of critical methods in literary analysis does not mean that it is necessary to hold the positions on the basis of which the analysis was worked out. The analyses practised by historical criticism do not depend logically on one set of philosophical assumptions; they are adopted by scholars holding a wide variety of theological and philosophical assumptions. Thus Barr states that even if it were true that Pentateuchal criticism was worked out on the basis of Hegelian and evolutionary thinking, this would not particularly matter[172]

This basic description of the development of the historical method offered by Barr would seem to claim a certain neutrality for the actual

---

171. *F*, pp. 132ff.

172. *F*, p. 184. Barr refers here to the thesis of L. Perlitt's work, *Vatke und Wellhausen* (Berlin, 1965), that Wellhausen's thought was not developed in a philosophical straitjacket but in concern for historical detail. Cf. *F*, p. 149. C. Braaten makes the same point as Barr in *History and Hermeneutics* (Philadelphia, 1966), pp. 33ff.

mechanics of historical critical study, although Barr himself does not frame the issue in these terms. However, this appears when Barr contrasts the fundamentalist view of criticism with these positions. The critical position is an *open* one in that the critical methods are shared by people having different philosophical or theological positions. The position of the fundamentalists is *closed* in that it is held and works only for those who have their lifestyle and view of Scripture. This contrast would seem to indicate that Barr considers the methods of criticism to have some sort of objectivity or grounding in fact that constitutes their neutrality with respect to varying theological formulations.[173] This openness to which Barr refers would seem to be a condition for the proper exegesis of the text and the free speaking of the Scripture in new situations. It makes it possible to modify theological formulations.

The meta-theological character of historical criticism, as we have seen in the previous section of this chapter, is the factor which comes into play when Barr speaks of Biblical theology sharing its methods of work with nontheological disciplines. The idea that the Bible is to be studied as other literary documents has been the subject of controversy for over a century, but is almost universally held, as recent ecumenical documents serve to illustrate: "The Bible contains a group of literary documents and it has to be studied by the same methods as are used in the study of other literary documents."[174] Barr insists on this point. The meta-language of biblical studies is no longer found in theology, but in disciplines over which theology no longer has any control. This means that the relationship between exegesis and theology is no longer the same.[175] The theological problems are encountered only when the exegetical groundwork has been gone over, which can be and is done without reference to questions of theological normativity. The basic exegetical method is held in common with non-Christian scholarship.[176] It is not controlled by the logical struc-

---

173. *F*, p. 185.
174. *New Directions in Faith and Order: Bristol, 1967* (Faith and Order Paper no. 50), p. 33. W. Sanday said that it would be futile to try and stop this approach to the Bible at the turn of the century, *Inspiration* (London, 1901). p. 1; E. Krentz, op. cit., pp. 61ff., resumes the approach; Maier has been a rather lone if strident voice against this in recent years, op. cit. pp. 53ff.
175. *ONI*, pp. 180f.
176. *ER* 21:136.

tures of Christian theology.[177] In this frame, when discussing the distinctiveness of Christianity, Barr says that although we may not like the idea that Christianity is a syncretistic religion, we cannot rule this out theologically; it is a matter for historical research to find out whether this is so or not.[178]

Barr draws together several of these ideas and his views on biblical studies in his inaugural lecture of 1977 at Oxford. This is a most useful contribution, as Barr's thoughts on method in biblical studies, which are scattered widely in his works, are set out in detail. Here Barr points to the difference between theology which emphasises current problems and biblical studies which are historico-technical in their bias, as illustrative of the drawing apart of the two disciplines in academic study. This factor is important for the independence of biblical studies.[179] In biblical studies beliefs are not structurally essential for the study. Does this necessarily mean that the exclusion of theological beliefs means objectivity of study? Barr rejects the idea that objectivity in biblical studies is achieved by the exclusion of theological concerns. It is more, according to him, a question of the *quality* of the theological attitude which will encourage the biblical material to speak with liberty, even when this means going against theological fashions. On the other side, Barr thinks that it reveals also the quality of the non-theological biblical studies when these permit theological questions to be asked. Objectivity in biblical studies is not attained by the exclusion of theology. If this is attempted, either certain questions remain unasked, or other metaphysical assumptions are smuggled in.[180] In addition to this, Barr rejects the other face of the coin, which supposes that a non-theological study of the Bible is not possible. What is important to biblical study is not theological opinion, but the use made of the materials available for study. True objectivity is gained neither through the exclusion of theological questions nor by allowing them to dominate our understanding of the biblical materials. It is more a question of the quality of approach which relates the different fields of study to each other.

---

177. *ONI*, p. 198.
178. *BMW*, p. 98.
179. "Does Biblical Study Still Belong to Theology," pp. 5f. Also on the relation of exegesis and dogmatics see B. J. Oosterhoff, *De vrijheid van de exegese* (Kampen, 1976), particularly pp. 20ff.
180. Ibid., p. 11.

Thus the viability of a theology is seen in its ability to take up the findings of non-theological work into its structure.

These remarks on objectivity are important for understanding Barr's view of the role of historical criticism in theology. If no ultimate objectivity is obtainable, the historical method used on the level of biblical studies can attain a *high level* of objectivity. This is possible if theological concerns are those which, instead of dominating the lower level of biblical study, seek to preserve its independence of enquiry and show a willingness to relate to its findings. What is important is not objectivity itself, but the openness of our theological constructions. Theology must, by nature, encourage this free speaking of the biblical material to be proper theology. In this sort of theology the historical method has an integral place in the total scope of theology.

In Barr's view therefore the method of historical study is formed meta-theologically and shared with other disciplines beyond theology. It is necessary for theology that this should be so in order that the material be studied with a high degree of objectivity on the basis of modern insights. In this way theology can benefit from the openness of the exegesis. In recognising this factor, theology encourages this openness by not seeking to impose on the material ideas which are foreign to it. Here once again we may discern a kind of circularity in Barr's thinking. The historical method of biblical research is open in that it takes up methods used by other non-theological disciplines and studies the Bible like other literary texts. Theology is open to the insights of the historical research and must give account of itself to the biblical material. This in turn aids theology to be valid and relevant in being a theology which opens out onto a given situation. So it may be that the Scripture speaks in a relevant way.

Many of Barr's perspectives on historical criticism are no doubt held by many scholars in slightly modified form. His discussion of the methods of historical criticism would be unlikely to raise much controversy, although his propositions on the nature of objectivity in theological research are quite original. What is more particular to Barr's own approach to historical criticism is the way he links this study to his general approach to the Scripture as the formulation of a religious tradition and also the way in which this tradition becomes relevant in the present.

Barr maintains on this issue as elsewhere that questions of the origin of Scripture are irrelevant as far as the exegesis of the text is concerned:

> The historical-critical exegete explains the Bible through its derivation from the thought of the writers and the tradition behind them. . . . he does not find any element which in principle is not so explicable. Thus even if the Bible is thought of as "coming from" God, it does not seem to make any decisive difference to exegesis.[181]

The inspiration extends to the different parts of the tradition which reflects the life of the people of God in the Spirit, and is not limited quantitatively to the text. As K. Koch says: ". . . inspiration does not appear to have been a unique quality held by a few, but the development over centuries of moulding and remoulding of linguistic traditions into established literary types and sharply defined settings in life."[182] This being supposed, historical criticism in its work of uncovering the historical process of the development of the traditions of the people of God, may be seen to be recovering the various stages of the way in which the people were led in the Spirit. K. Koch does not appear to be troubled at drawing this conclusion: ". . . not only the biblical text as it stands but also the earlier stages in the history of its transmission are imbued with the spirit of God. . . ."[183]

A similar perspective is found in Barr's discussion, which is not unexpected and may be attributed to the wide influence of the tradition-historical method developed by Von Rad.[184] Barr states that three elements go into evaluating the biblical story. The story is evaluated in the literary form of the text as it stands, it is related to "external" data, but also to the reconstruction of the internal history of the text not found at surface level which is achieved by historical methods. Thus historical criticism discerns the various stages of the tradition as it develops. No one stage is theologically

---

181. *IDB*(S), p. 794.

182. K. Koch, op. cit., pp. 100f.

183. Ibid., p. 101. Koch adduces from this that these earlier stages are also canonical.

184. See W. E. Rast, *Tradition History and the Old Testament* (Philadelphia, 1972), pp. 72ff. The recent work edited by D. A. Knight, *Tradition and Theology in the Old Testament* (London, 1977), was not available to me at the time of writing.

decisive for the interpreter, who can concentrate on one of the stages uncovered or take them as a whole. However, Barr maintains that even though no one stage of the tradition is final, the text in its present form is, in practical terms, most objectively available. The other stages are the objects of historical reconstruction and have only a hypothetical status. Barr notes that in redaction criticism and structuralism, as over against the form critical approach, which tends to concentrate on the pre-history of the text, there is a move to emphasise the fundamental character of the final form of the text.[185]

To say that the Scripture is the crystallisation of the tradition of the people of God and that this can be uncovered by critical study, even though this recovery may be hypothetical, ascribes an almost religious function to historical research. Through it the living past of the people of God is uncovered, as it is made apparent in what ways God has guided his people in their history. To put this in more traditional language, this would seem to mean that the historical method points to the inspiration of the tradition which is discerned when the step of relating the historical process to the presence of God is made. The question may now be raised as to the way in which this past tradition, whether in its final form as fixed Scripture or in its stages of development, becomes relevant to the present life of the church.[186] In a strict sense Barr would seem to refuse the idea that the Bible becomes relevant in the present by an application of its message to the situation. "The task of interpretation," says Barr, "is not to drag the texts out of their original situation and 'apply' them to the modern world."[187] The Bible is essentially an ancient book, and nothing we can do can make it otherwise. The more we can understand it as an ancient work in its particular situation, the more we can appreciate its effect for us. This means, of course, that the Bible will

185. *BMW*, pp. 162ff. See also the comments on H-J. Kraus's *Die Biblische Theologie* by B. S. Childs in *Int* 26:26. Whereas Childs has pointed to the concentration on the pre-history of the text as the essential data for Biblical theology in Von Rad, P. Ricoeur has by contrast indicated what he considers to be the structural approach to the organisation of the narratives in Von Rad (*Exégèse et Herméneutique*, pp. 44f.).

186. The question was already raised in direct fashion in C. H. Dodd's *The Authority of the Bible* (London, [1929] 1960), which bears certain points in common with Barr's positions. Dodd says that through history we accede to the "living past," which is a factor of importance for the present (137ff.).

187. *IDB*(S), p. 797. Cf. Stendahl, art. cit., *IDB*, p. 422.

not be "appreciated without study and without guidance from competent persons—which guidance today is amply available."[188]

In this respect historical study becomes essential to the present relevance of the Bible by giving us understanding of the text as an expression of a human situation which is totally in the past. So Scripture, "as a work of the past and so understood, feeds and illuminates the understanding of modern men and women in their situation."[189] In a way, Barr emphasises as markedly as possible the two polarities of interpretation: the pastness of the text interpreted and the situation in the present of the interpreter. The goal of interpretation cannot be achieved either by transposing the biblical meaning from past to present, or by reading our modern questions back into the text in a search for answers.[190]

How, it may well be wondered, can these two elements of the pastness of the Bible and the presentness of the interpreter be fused together? In his discussion of cultural relativism, Barr points out that where a culture has a memory of the past, that memory is part of the culture.[191] However, this does not constitute a main argument of Barr's regarding the relation between past and present in the understanding of the text. Two factors, for Barr, provide the continuity: the context of the ongoing people of God and the relation of faith to the biblical model of understanding. In the context of this continuity, the Bible of the past moulds faith in the present according to the insights it brings as model of faith.[192] What Barr seems to say here is that if we cannot apply the Bible to the modern situation, what we can do is to see in the Bible a model of the way in which faith functioned and in which God was present in past situations. This il-

---

188. *BMW*, pp. 140f.

189. *IDB*(S), loc. cit.; *BMW*, p. 141.

190. See the comments in Barr's review of H. H. Rowley's *The Faith of Israel*, in *JSS* 2:397f.; also in *ER* 21:136f.

191. *BMW*, p. 46. Dodd affirms this point in a much larger sense in speaking of religious thinking as an experience of the historic society of mankind, op. cit., pp. 135ff. The function of tradition in interpretation has been discussed by H-G. Gadamer in *Warheit und Methode* (Tübingen, 1965), which has influenced the biblico-theological discussion in recent years, particularly in connection with the Pannenberg school. But see the comments of F. E. Tupper, *The Theology of Wolfhart Pannenberg* (London, 1974), pp. 116ff., for Pannenberg's criticism. Barr, to my knowledge, makes little reference, if at all, to Gadamer.

192. *BMW*, p. 141.

luminates us in the present by enriching our faith in God. D. Ritschl puts this same thought very clearly in a passage to which Barr refers in *BMW:*

> It is not the ancient words which are artificially transported into the present in order to become relevant, but it is the present occasion, the situation, which becomes transparent and relevant both to the ancient message and to the hope which permits the interest and concern for ancient texts.[193]

It is then in the church in the present that enlightenment for the situation is sought with reference to the model of understanding provided by biblical texts. In contact with these models of faith we come to see our own situation clearly and how we should act in it. When we stand in the continuity of the people of God, we behold Scripture as the start of the ongoing process in which Yahweh's promises are fulfilled.[194] Scripture is clearly here not a source for constituting a theology by translation, but it has its authority as a pattern for faith. The Christian constructs his theology and his faith in terms of the present on the basis of the understanding he gains from the model.

This way of formulating the relevance of the tradition to the present incorporates several of the important elements of Barr's perspective. It allows theology to be a statement of what the church believes in the present and avoids the problem of translating the content of the Scripture into the present from the past. This procedure is connected with the idea that Scripture carries a normative revelation. It maintains the centrality of historical research, as the Scripture must be understood as an ancient book which requires study. In addition, it points to the leading of the people of God by the Spirit of God in the fulfilment of the promises. All this means that Scripture is kept open to new insights and theology is not a completed thing in any one moment of the church. It also allows for a wide liberty of theological formulation as Scripture itself contains a diversity of theologies and as model encourages faith to express itself in a variety of ways today. D. H. Kelsey has expressed in similar fashion how the notion of tradition functions in the continuity of the church: "Used as a theological concept, 'tradition' names a process. It is the process which embraces both the church's use of Scripture and the presence of God

193. D. Ritschl in *Int* 25:126, *BMW,* loc. cit.
194. Ibid., p. 128.

which, in dialectical inter-relationship, are together essential to the church's self-identity."[195] For Barr it would appear that it is in the continuing tradition of the church that the presence of the Spirit of God with his people is known through the church's self-understanding constituted by reference to the Bible as the classic model of faith.

This general perspective is well illustrated in the section on the Bible in preaching in *BMW*.[196] If the Bible contains errors, if the church in theology seeks to say what she believes today, and if the Bible is not the source which provides an application of its content to the present situation, why bother preaching on biblical texts? In answer to such problems, Barr reminds us of the many-sidedness of the Bible as the foundational myth of Christianity. The various qualities implied in the notion of a foundational myth make the Bible a provocative tool for the reflexion of the church. Apart from this factor which may encourage us to use the Bible in preaching, Barr is prepared to allow that there may be a multiplicity of ways in preaching, just as there is a multiplicity of theological formulations having reference to the Bible:

> I find it very hard to lay down a definite rule about the use of the Bible as a basis for preaching. It would seem to me strange that I should predicate this book on the multiplicity of possible theologies and at the same time take it upon me to lay down the correct form and content for the task of preaching.[197]

In conclusion, we have tried to point out that, in Barr's understanding of interpretation, the historical method is an essential factor for the relevance of the biblical model to the Christian faith today. It aids us to an understanding of the way God led his people in the past and helps to develop a suitable view of the status of the Bible as the foundational myth of the Christian faith. This does not mean that Barr is never critical of the methods of historical criticism. In several places he is quite severe about some of the exaggerations in which it has resulted. Sometimes the accepted theories are not useful in dealing with some sections of the biblical material and are unproductive.[198] It alienates the layman, involves an immense amount

---

195. D. H. Kelsey, op. cit., p. 95.
196. *BMW*, pp. 136ff.
197. Ibid., pp. 138f.
198. See Barr's comments relative to the way criticism has approached

In the present theological situation, it may well be that doubts about revelation are the cause, or at least the correlate, of theological pluralism. Barr's criticism of the christological analogy in his early work, carried through on various levels in his later thought, is significative of a move in modern theology in general from structures of authority to a pluralistic situation. The present pluralism of the Christian tradition is a good thing, thinks Barr. Not only does it allow a greater freedom of the biblical materials in the church, but in a certain sense it mirrors the multiplicity of the biblical tradition. The conflicts in the biblical materials have their corresponding conflicts today. As Barr says, the tradition is soteriologically functional in a positive and negative sense. It leads Jesus to obedience and his enemies to put him to death.[201]

So in the church today, although Barr does not always develop these points as much as one would like,[202] pluralism which implies theological confrontation can be soteriologically functional as it leads us to a faith, not in one theology, but in the one God who stands beyond theological formulations. As men struggle with each other and with their God, the Spirit leads the people of God in the living-out of the paradigm for Christian faith which is given in the classic myth of the faith. In this respect Barr remarks: ". . . if we are wise we shall build into our thinking an elasticity which will be able to accept, if need be, evidence of a much more positive part played by religions, opinions, and groups which later came to be regarded as idolatries, heresies and perpetual antagonists of the biblical faith."[203]

The major problem for Barr as far as putting this project into practice is concerned, obviously lies in the existence of such a confrontational group in the present situation as the separated brethren of fundamentalism, who do not show much intention of loosening their view of biblical authority and accepting theological pluralism. Fundamentalism is a thorn in the side of pluralism and quite a sharp one at that. Yet if the Bible contains a multiplicity of theologies, fundamentalism can hardly be labelled heretical and banished. Nor can the Bible be appealed to as a criterion for distinguishing between ortho-

---

201. *ONI*, p. 27.
202. J. A. Sanders says for this reason that chap. 8 of *BMW* is disappointing, and no advance over *ONI*. See *Int* 28:323.
203. *BMW,* p. 149.

doxy and heresy, for within the Bible itself there is no fixed standard of orthodoxy to which its writers conformed. The Bible is not "the document of one religion, clearly demarcated against all others."[204] It is anachronistic to think that the Bible can be used to discriminate between orthodoxy and heterodoxy. In our theological situation the idea of heresy has ceased to function in a meaningful way today, even if it did so in the past.[205] Yet if fundamentalism is not called a heresy, it does remain a rather objectionable manifestation of a pathological sort of Christianity. Fundamentalists are not willing to admit that it might be good to have the other view. They do not see the church as a mixed body with opposites of theology welded together in a society of faith and trust.[206]

Well, what's to be done with the fundamentalists? Barr thinks of fundamentalism as an intellectual sect which creates a problem by its alienation from mainstream theology. For modern Christianity this does not pose an intellectual problem, as fundamentalist theology is not really very coherent. The problem is an ecumenical one; but here Barr is at a bit of a loss. Once the category of heresy has been abandoned, it becomes in the present situation almost impossible to say whether fundamentalists are working positively or negatively within the context of the church as a whole.[207] The church seems curiously hamstrung by the paralysis of the loss of normativity. If a major operation is needed to deal with the wart of fundamentalism, this is perhaps indicative of the ability of present Christianity as it is developing to deal with other, more serious, problems.

The problem may be localised in stating the obvious. In a pluralistic situation where a multiplicity of theologies is predicated, if there can be no heresy, there can really be no orthodoxy either. Not even Barr can claim that his thought is orthodox, although he might wish to claim that it does give a reasonable account of the materials of the Bible on the basis of the information available. Theologies

---

204. Ibid., p. 148.
205. *F*, p. 197. A. Hanson considers that Barr's claim that orthodoxy and heresy were not in the Bible or not there as fixed entities is disputable: ". . . we do find the biblical writers on their guard against what they considered to be false teaching" (art. cit., in *Theology and Change*, ed. R. H. Preston, p. 46).
206. *F*, pp. 316f.
207. *F*, p. 344.

can justify themselves in a relative way in the use they make of the Bible:

> My own view is that no criterion is prescribed to a theology at its starting point; rather any theology has to provide within itself . . . an account of the criteria it accepts, including its relation to the Bible; but it is only at the end of the process, as the final output of a theology is discernible, that it can be judged, and not by its relation to an antecedent criterion.[208]

Barr is not, it is evident, opting for a theology of chaos, even though it may no longer be possible to make a dogmatic stand as to the ultimacy of one's own hold on the truth. Theologies must justify their criteria; no doubt this can be done with the aid of the checks and balances of careful exegesis on the grounds Barr has discussed. What is more intricate is the kind of grounds upon which the output of a theology can be judged. If output is not judged as orthodox or heretical in terms of the Scripture principle of Protestant orthodoxy, how can it be judged? I may be very much mistaken, but there is perhaps no clear answer to this question in *BMW*. Barr affirms that he wishes to leave open the structure and the principle of what a theology may be. The indications he gives are formulated in terms of two "restrictions" which must be borne in mind if a theology is to be Christian: (a) it must give some central place to Jesus of Nazareth, and (b) its God must be the God already known in Israel.[209] Perhaps it could be said then that the value of a theology might be seen to lie in its output in terms of the way it presently states the faith of the church in the Son and the Father, that is, in its ability to illuminate the meaning of the classic model of Christian faith in the situation of today. There may indeed be a multiplicity of ways of doing this.

---

208. *BMW*, p. 113.
209. Ibid., p. 114.

5

Comments on Some Basic Issues of Barr's Work

Many features in the corpus of Barr's work make it one of the most interesting and original contributions to the recent discussions of the interpretation and authority of the Bible. Its interest lies above all in the fact that the questions are approached from the perspective of the present positions of exegetical enquiry concerning the text of Scripture. The way in which Barr seeks to place these positions in contact with the methods of work of non-theological disciplines and use the insights obtained in theological discussion constitutes a significant contribution to biblical study. This is most evident, for example, in the use Barr has made of modern semantics in his linguistic discussions of the sense of the biblical text, or in the effort to incorporate in exegesis aspects of literary criticism which offer possibilities for analysing the character of the biblical stories. In addition to the depth of exegetical insight which Barr seeks to open up in his work, there is a noteworthy effort on his part to think through the implications of the progress in exegetical research for the doctrine of Scripture itself. This concern leads Barr to a much broader discussion than one might expect from a biblical scholar, in which he confronts dogmatic questions about the nature of Scripture and its authority. This is particularly the case in Barr's two more recent books. The breadth of Barr's corpus is accompanied by a depth of insight which is the hallmark of a very able scholar, whose work has not been hitherto fully appreciated.

In our discussion we have sought to point out the continuities in this developing contribution to recent theology. Barr's work, which has its starting point in a critical appraisal of the Barthian tradition, begins by asking several questions about the accepted ways of indicating the status of Scripture as Word of God. Barr's interest in the text as a human document leads him to reflect upon the problems of exegesis in theologies which approach interpretation with a presupposition about revelation. The exegetical incongruities discerned by Barr necessitate not only a critique of the linguistic methods quite widely practised, but also of the theology which such methods imply. The development of Barr's work in this sense can be seen as a search for a way of handling the biblical data which does justice to the nature of the texts. However, Barr's concern to "encourage the Scripture to speak freely" implies the need of a theology of Scripture which will encourage this. Both in criticism and constructive suggestion, interpretation and theology are correlated in Barr's work.

Indeed, the effort to relate exegetical questions and theological structures is a most positive point in the development of Barr's thought. It is to some extent exemplary of the greater efforts which must be made by exegetes and dogmaticians alike at a time when their disciplines seem like continental blocks moving away from each other. This desire to relate interpretation and theology, together with the understanding of the humanity of Scripture and a concern to explain it as man's word encourages a theological attitude which seeks a new understanding of the status of Scripture. In this respect Barr is in the forefront of the present debate in his attempt to relate the understanding of the development of the biblical tradition in the Scripture and the evaluation of this traditional material in the context of present theologies. By suggesting that Scripture be considered as the classic model of the Christian faith, Barr integrates in a thought-provoking fashion the present understanding of the tradition-historical development of the biblical material with the possibility of relating this as a model of faith to Christian theology and practice in the present. This integration of the historical considerations and the relevance of the Scripture as model is an original contribution which Barr seeks to develop. It makes some steps to overcoming the polarity which is felt rather acutely either when Scripture is taken as a special past revelation which is normative but difficult to apply in the present, or when the present situation is emphasised and distances the Bible-world from it in an insuperable way. By taking into account the past-ness of the biblical materials as ancient documents and the presentness of theological affirmation in the church, Barr accounts for the historical discontinuity which is unavoidable in the relm of reflexion. At the same time he affirms the continuity of the tradition and the paradigmatic nature of the biblical tradition for Christian faith today.

Thus, in the midst of historical relativities, there is a continuity of the Christian faith as it relates itself to the foundational model by the expression of similar faith in the God of Israel and Jesus as the Son of the Father. This perspective has the advantage for Barr of integrating the historical criticism into the foundation of theological reflexion as an instrument which uncovers data relevant to the leading of the people of God in the past. It also makes way for the affirmation of faith in God as a central element in the present statement of the church together with the possibility that God can lead his people in new ways today. When faith is related to Scripture as classic *model*, not as revealed truth, the search for a rooting for faith in objective revealed truth which causes clashes with modern knowledge is avoided; faith is liberated to find its value in terms of confidence in God, who transcends the limits of human formulations. Thus faith seeks its foundation not in the factual significance of certain past actions revelatory of God and communicated truthfully in Scripture, but in the leading of the Spirit in the church today. This leading is illuminated by the reference to the way in which God has led his people in the past through the understanding we can gain from the classic model of the faith.

These features might all be considered in a positive way by representatives of a wide range of theological opinion today. In particular, the openness of the theology which Barr constructs would no doubt win widespread approval. Barr shows a willingness to place theology in contact with other nontheological branches of learning and to use these methods to deepen theological insight into the meaning of Scripture. In his study of Biblical theology he breaks down the division between the canonical and the noncanonical materials and thus opens a possibility of understanding the Jewish tradition in a more fully historical sense; the tradition is open in the milieu of its development. In present interpretation too, Barr predicates the validity of a multiplicity of theologies, which in some measure corresponds to the diversity of the biblical tradition. This openness constitutes the possibility of a dialogical character for theology, in which constructions are evaluated not in terms of an *a priori* standard of truth, but according to their ability to be concrete in the way they can relate the biblical materials to the present theological situation. The quality of a theology is measured in terms of its openness to the historical information furnished by biblical studies and the way it can enter into fruitful discussion with other theological positions, accepted as possibilities worthy of equal consideration. Barr recognises the temporary nature of theological formulations, which themselves must be passed under the review of critical evaluation. This does not necessarily mean that they will be discarded, but it can mean that current interpretations can be retained or that the understanding of the tradition deepened by new insights. The contact between the various interpretative possibilities and the text will serve to promote a certain "freshness" in the reappropriation of the tradition.[1]

5.1. *Exegesis, tradition and Scripture*

It is above all in the field of exegesis that Barr's work has its importance, and many of the points he makes can help the interpreter in his approach to the text and its milieu. Barr's consideration of the Scripture as human document encourages a close look at the processes involved in the production of the text and also those necessary for well-balanced interpretation. These two aspects of Barr's work have been referred to at various points; our intention is here to say a little on how Barr's *fundamental* approach may afford practical help to the exegete.

In so far as Barr's propositions concerning method of interpretation are concerned, Barr shows admirable balance in picking his way through the ideological minefields of modern hermeneutics. Fundamental to Barr's contribution to the tool-box of the exegete is his valorisation of the insights of the structural approach for exegesis. Thus, as we have seen, Barr indicates the primary importance of the synchronic examination of the text. Yet this is done without adopting the anti-historical ideology of much modern (French) structuralism. So Barr manages to avoid the extreme positions of structuralists who seek meaning in the "universal human mind" considered in abstraction from the historical realm.[2] While he relativises the importance of the

---

1. *ONI*, p. 190.
2. R. A. Spivey, *Int* 28:143.

historical method and its claim to hold the key to meaning through diachronic examination, Barr is far from wishing to eliminate the positive contributions of historical research. The value of the discoveries of historical research must not be overlooked.

The interpretation of the text must therefore include analysis which is synchronic-structural and diachronic-historical. The balance of Barr's position is that on the one hand he is not willing to reduce exegesis to the examination of textual structures as giving the key to meaning, and on the other he refuses a unilateral historical quest for meaning apart from literary research. Both the literary structure and the historical milieu supply information relative to the meaning of the text. In Barr's "eclectic structuralism" applied to exegesis a fundamental insight of F. de Saussure finds expression: Synchrony and diachrony are not mutually exclusive but indicate different methods of approach to meaning.[3] If the synchronic approach is primary, the two are complementary: Succeeding historical states of the text must be studied in synchronic fashion. As is frequently indicated and also in Barr, "a synchronic description is pre-requisite for a proper approach to diachronic study."[4]

How exactly do the criticisms and methods of analysis developed in Barr's works, and particularly his distinction of synchronic and diachronic forms of study, aid the exegete in his approach to the meaning of the text?

The distinction between synchronic and diachronic approaches to meaning which Barr utilises constitutes a means to avoid certain confusions which arise with respect to the sense of biblical texts as well as opening up a deeper understanding of their message. In particular, synchronic analysis seen as primary is a great aid to seeing the specificity of a text. It avoids the danger of projecting onto the text meanings prior to its production, or the accepted meanings of subsequent interpretation. In taking a cross-section of the use of language in a given social situation at a given time, the individuality of the text can come into focus. The temptation to seek meaning in the place of origin of a word or an idea is avoided. The text means primarily what it meant to the people using that particular language, in

---

3. F. de Saussure, *Course in General Linguistics* (London, 1960), p. 81.
4. D. Crystal, *Linguistics, Language and Religion* (London, 1965), p. 58, cited by A. C. Thiselton in *New Testament Interpretation* (Exeter, 1977), p. 82.

that particular culture at a given time-point. Included in this synchronic approach to the text is the linguistic and cultural memory of the group in which the text is generated. A mistake of biblical studies to which Barr continually points is that of thinking that once the job of the genetic explanation of a word or idea has been completed, meaning has been expounded. However, this is not the case, as synchronic analysis makes us aware. Words and ideas mean only what they meant to those using them in the given context under examination.

This is particularly obvious in Barr's criticisms of the use of etymology of words to establish meaning as has often been practiced in theology. However, it can also be pointed out that this applies to other instances as well. The idea of redemption used in Paul's writings means what it meant to Paul and his readers, which is not necessarily what it meant a thousand years before. Or again, their understanding of the meaning of the "spiritual rock that accompanied" the Israelites does not depend directly on what happened in terms of event but on the interpretation of the events in Exodus as understood by Paul and his readers. Synchronic analysis therefore plays the all-important role of reminding us that meaning is best approached not in terms of origins, but through a consideration of the contexts and conventions of usage.

These remarks are rather obvious, but it is as well not to make too light of Barr's contribution at this point. The satisfaction of finding where a word or idea comes from and thinking that this forms an explanation of its meaning can be a real exegetical seduction to biblical scholars. We forget that perhaps the people using the expressions knew little or cared little of their origin, and yet these words and ideas were used by them in meaningful communication.

On a more theological level, Barr's distinction of synchronic and diachronic analysis of meaning can also prove helpful in so far as discussions concerning the form and content of Scripture are concerned. It has been quite current to point to the fact that divine revelation comes to us clothed in human words. The temptation is then to seek a content of revelation, a divine element, which can be separated out from the language and concepts of the Bible which constitute its human form. In some cases the context of revelation is identified with the history of salvation conceived of as a diachronic process. In such a setting the tendency was to see the diachronic description of the *magnalia Dei* as being the normative element of Scripture, the real goal of exegetical description. The formal aspects of Scripture were then separated from the normative as fallible expressions of the real content of revelation.[5] In the light of reflexion of the relation of the meaning of Scripture in synchronic and diachronic analysis it is by no means evident that such a straightforward distinction between the history of revelation and the written form of Scripture can be made. As has been pointed out, we have no direct access to events in the history of revelation, such as, for example, the Exodus event. All we have is the Exodus story, in which the event comes to us in the linguistic and cultural structures of a particular point of time. Thus it is evident that no diachronic structure of salvation history can be read off from the text apart from the necessary preliminary synchronic analysis of the phenomena of the given time. In this analysis language structure and cultural structure which enter into the analysis are those of this instant of time. The (theological) content of Scripture depends for its expression on particular forms. If it can be distinguished from these forms it is not separable from them.

It would seem that divine content and human form are a good deal more closely interwoven than has been allowed in some theological constructs and that if revelation is still spoken of, it must be as revelation in these particular historical forms. Rather than being different from the word of man, the Word of God in this respect might be considered as coming in the form of these words of men.

Another value of the synchronic analysis proposed by Barr, which is correlated to the individuality of situations in the time process, is the diversity of the biblical materials which it uncovers. Exegesis which takes synchronic analysis seriously permits the rich diversity of the texts to come to light. In Barr's work it is true that this diversity seems to function in a way detrimental to the unity of Scripture. However, this does not mean that it is necessarily the case. The question raised here refers to the elements which enter into defining the relations between the particular text and the ensemble of traditions.

---

5. See on this H. N. Ridderbos, in *International Reformed Bulletin* 32, 3:37; and B. J. Oosterhoff, "Schriftkritiek en schriftgezag in de 19e en 20e eeuw (O.T.)," *Rondom het Woord* 10:247f., and "De prediking van het oude Testament," *Rondom het Woord* 8:117.

In the diachronic approach historical continuities were above all sought and explained. The tendency was that the particular aspects of the biblical tradition grew pale in the context of the whole. The unique character of the texts in their different situations was absorbed into a panorama of biblical traditions. In extreme cases where the synthetic view predominated in such a way as to remove the unique flavour of the individual texts, much was lost in the understanding of the text. Barr constantly warns in his work against facile syntheses which do violence to the diversity of the materials. To the extent that the possibility of innovation is overlooked in exegesis, the creative human characteristics of the texts are lost. In exegesis, as in life, what is above all fascinating is not the common, but the individual. Barr gives us a taste in his exegetical reflexions of the interest of the individual discerned in synchronic interpretation.

As we have seen, Barr is very conscious of the tradition-historical character of the Bible. Within the context of this progressing tradition, synchronic exegesis can indicate the meaning of the text within various stages of the development of the biblical tradition. In order to bring out this uniqueness of meaning in analysis, exegesis should concentrate on the sentence and larger units of sense, not the study of individual words. As Barr says, the sentence, unlike the word, is unique and non-recurrent. Barr refers to a certain number of processes which can be used by the exegete for studying the Bible. Of particular interest are his remarks on the study of the mind of the writers and the literary study of the text as it stands. Thus exegesis might consider in the context of a synchronic approach the intention of the writer and the discourse which the writer/speaker produces. It may be wondered whether Barr's discussion of the processes of studying the Bible has given enough place to the analysis of the audience which is united to the speaker in the world of discourse. However, consideration of the audience might be included in the intention of the writer and in the study of the actual form of the text. The intention of the writer reveals something of his understanding of the nature of the audience, or, in some cases, his lack of understanding. Again, when studied as literature, the Bible reveals something of the thought-world shared by the coder and the de-coders of the text. Also, Barr's distinction of what the text meant and what it means is based on the historical difference of audiences.

These considerations from Barr's work aid the exegete as he concentrates on a unit of meaning to centre attention on the various processes of interpretation which permit an examination of the writer, the text, and the audience. Barr is most interested by a fully literary approach to the text which seeks the meaning of the text as it stands. He is aware of the fallacies produced by an exegesis which is purely intentionalistic, yet retains the usefulness of considering the intention of the author. Barr is reticent to abandon the positive contributions which examination of intention has made in the fields of redaction or form criticism. It would seem to be quite correct in exegesis to see a complementarity between the historical considerations related to the intention of the writer and the literary features of the text produced. Otherwise it seems one would presume that the writer did not say what he wanted, or was unable to because of the inadequacies of his means of expression or the difficulties of the situation.

The interest of synchronic analysis in the light of the processes described by Barr touching writer, audience, and literary text, is that it permits the exegete to investigate why a certain idea or expression was used rather than another one, given the common cultural ground between the parties associated with the text. Thus the meaning expressed by the text can be seized in its specificity. A competent exegesis should then seek to understand the text involved by means of a consideration of the common context shared by writer and reader: culturally, linguistically, and historically. Were the interpreter a member of the cultural group and contemporaneous with writer and recipient, there would probably be but slight difficulty in understanding the text. Problems arise in exegesis because of distance from the situation and the limitations of our linguistic and cultural knowledge. According to Barr, the major difficulty facing the exegete is primarily the one of the relation of the past and the present, rather than one concerned with the divine and the human aspects of the text. This observation is a salutary one, and even if the exegete is concerned with the relation of the human aspects of the text and revelation in a way which Barr is not, it must be considered doubtful whether this problem can be approached other than by application of the synchronic analysis suggested by Barr. In fact, should one continue, for theological reasons, to work within a framework of divine-human revelation, the synchronic method might be considered essential for a better apprehension of the situations in which the revelation is humanly received.

Perhaps the most pertinent feature of Barr's exegetical insight concerns his emphasis on the literary character of the text of Scripture. As he remarks, theologians are often outdated in their methods of work, which have tended to neglect the Scripture as text and concentrate on historical questions. Barr is quite correct in indicating that historical criticism and description of intention do not explain the meaning of the *text* as such, although they may be a useful first step. Interpretation cannot afford to stop short at historical questions, but must recognise the primacy of the text as such in the search for meaning. This centrality of the actual form of the text has long been insisted upon in interpretation. Yet in practice, commentary on the text has tended to concentrate on the introductory historical descriptions. A separation between historical and theological reflexion becomes a real problem. As a corrective, it is worthwhile to heed Barr's comments on the relative autonomy of the text. The problem with a one-sided view of the text centring on historical description may be that this autonomy is forgotten. The author and the text are identified in such a way that an explication of the author's intention is taken for an explanation of the text. This seems to overlook the possibility that the author may not have said *exactly* what he wanted to in his work. We all know of certain situations where the text has given an impression which is contrary to the writer's intention. Thus the initial question for exegesis is not what the writer wished to say but what the text as it stands actually does say.

In this perspective, a closer scrutiny of the text in its literary form may well permit a clearer vision of the relation of the structures of the text and its theological content. Thus theological reflexion in direct contact with the text itself, can become a central concern of the exegete. This approach, which accounts for the relative autonomy of the text with respect to both author and audience, creates a possibility for interpretation which avoids the simple identification of meaning with the intention of the author or the reaction of the audience. These might both be taken into account and furnish relevant information, but cannot be embroidered upon at the expense of the meaning of the text itself.

A further element for thought which arises from Barr's work can now be added to these considerations. Considering Scripture in relation to the historical unfolding of the tradition of the people of God, this process can be evaluated by analysis of the diachronic progression of successive synchronic states. This is an important aspect of exegetical work, as through diachronic analysis the relation of different stages of the tradition can become apparent. Thus a diachronic analysis of two synchronic states of the tradition can permit a comparison of the texts involved which might reveal a connection. Thus the prehistory of a certain element in the blossoming tradition and its later transmission can be investigated and the changes of meaning examined for their significance. In examining the various diachronic states of the tradition, the categories of text (discourse), audience, and writer (speaker) enter into the analysis of the transmission of the tradition. In the case of written transmission the scribe seeks to reproduce exactly the original text handed down. In oral transmission a member of the audience becomes the speaker in a new situation. The original discourse may be reproduced en bloc, or it can be modified in view of the audience. The amount of variation of the original discourse can become very great. The complication can be increased, as students of the Synoptics know, where there are several lines of transmission. The question is also one which is relevant for modern preaching. If, as on Barr's terms, tradition is considered to run on down to the present, what constitutes an adequate transmission of an element of the tradition to a present audience?

However, as far as exegesis is concerned, the importance of Barr's remarks on synchronic and diachronic analysis of the biblical tradition will concern the possibility of a better comprehension of the factors involved in the transmission which contribute to the meaning of the message. Thus a text can be related to its sources, written or oral, which can also be analysed with reference to the synchronic context common to speaker and audience. Also the transmission of the same text, its post-history, can also be traced. In the latter case a reinterpretation of the text or a reactualisation can be discerned within the Scripture. Diachronic comparison of the state of an element of the tradition at various stages helps an understanding of the living character of the tradition as it is applied in new situations. A consciousness of these developments and reinterpretations gives access to the meaning of the tradition through a consideration of the factors involved in its application.[6] The tradition is a living word which is applied and explained anew. The NT also can be interpreted in this light as an application of the OT in a new situation. In this case, however, rather than reinterpretation, perhaps "new interpretation" should be the expression.[7]

The foregoing methods of exegesis which have been hastily sketched on the basis of the complementarity of synchronic and diachronic analysis raise some vital questions concerning the origin and nature of the Scripture. Barr has remarked in accordance that the traditional doctrine of inspiration is no longer compatible with the methods of exegesis practiced in modern study. He proposes to consider the inspiration of Scripture in a human way, which would account for the various aspects of the development of the tradition. Likewise, it has been suggested that inspiration should be applied to the whole tradition process by various modern scholars, rather than simply to the graphic aspects of the tradition. A whole new problematic is posed by these considerations; theologians have scarcely begun to grapple with this in any consequent fashion. When the various elements in the tradition are analysed in terms of text, writer, and audience, which are the authoritative/inspired factors in the tradition? Do these apply to the writer-meaning, the text-meaning, the audience-meaning, or all three in some way? When a community recognises a text as canon and thus distinguishes it from presumably spurious reinterpretations of the tradition, separating true and untrue tradition, how is the canon constituted? Is it considered canonical as text in itself, in reference to its writers and their intentions, or because of the way the canonising community understands the text to function? These questions are construed as being more or less complicated according to the distance or proximity between writer, text, and audience. Or, as is often the case, if the discussion of the tradition process is undertaken without reference to canonicity, do the sources behind the text have greater importance than the text itself? For instance, do the *ipsissima verba* reconstructed from the gospel traditions have greater authority than the traditions themselves? Is this authority of

---

6. Thus B. J. Oosterhoff has pointed to the reinterpretation and actualisation of the previous traditional materials in all parts of the OT in "Hereinterpretatie in het Oude Testament," *Rondom het Woord* 15:95-117.

7. Art. cit., p. 96; "De prediking van het Oude Testament," ad loc.

historical and/or theological nature? Such are some of the questions raised by the methods of anaysis examined here which theologians must face.

To begin to answer such questions, it may be pointed out that the
methods of analysis described are not *in themselves* a means to tell
us which meaning of Scripture can be considered as authoritative.
The different processes which enter into exegesis uncover many different levels of meaning of a text with relation to writer, literary form,
and audience as well as the pre- and post-histories of the text. But
these descriptions of different meanings do not necessarily constitute
an indication of the meaning of meaning. The normative aspect
which is discerned with reference to the text will probably depend
on factors far more wide-ranging than a consideration of the methods of describing the various elements which go into making up the
meaning of the unit. This consideration does not constitute a justification of Barr's description of the different levels of biblical studies
which separates the descriptive from the theological-normative. Even
if it were argued that methods in themselves were neutral, this does
not mean that they are used in a neutral way. No doubt the exegete
who attaches a certain authority to the text will use the methods described in such a way as to get at that authority. Nor is the exegete
who is not seeking a particular form of authority in the text totally
free of the influence of authorities: He is no doubt in some way under
the aegis of the authority of scholarly opinions.

Maybe the question of the authority is best considered in the context of what is discerned to constitute the authority of the tradition.
In Barr's thought the biblical tradition would seem to have a certain
authority as model of faith of the people of God in its continuing
experiences. The authority is a religious one which, while related to
the one God, can be discribed through an historical analysis of the
human faith. Tradition is generated by and expressive of faith in
different historical situations. Tradition has authority as that which
is expressive of the life of faith of the people of God in a previous
generation, and faith, in order to maintain the continuity of the tradition, must seek to relate itself to the insights of the oral or textual
tradition. The written traditions are paradigmatic of faith. As such
it may be said that they are expressive of the normativity of faith, but
they are not the ground of faith as in a view which relates faith to

the *sola Scriptura*. Thus continuity in the tradition is not sought with reference to the past revelation of the Word of God—to the OT in order to show the accomplishment of salvation in Christ in the case of the writers of the NT, or to the OT and NT in the case of the ground of faith of the church. The continuity is provided by the fact that the faith of the OT is directed to the God of Israel, who in the NT is believed to be the Father of Jesus Christ, in whom the church today has faith.

Whether this attempt to account for what is discerned as constitutive of authority in the biblical tradition is correct depends on whether it is thought to account adequately for the features of the tradition. Is the way in which Barr refers to the events of salvation history in the Bible as running closer to myth than might first meet the eye, as being "non-events" featured in the literary tradition, an acceptable way of handling this element in the tradition? At any rate, it would seem apparent that in this scheme the story-character of the tradition is illustrative of a religious principle. The OT could be considered as an extensive example of an exemplary sermon. If the tradition is something that is illustrative of faith in the context of an historical situation, is not this faith something apart from the history and abstracted from it? Does this not run the risk of reducing the tradition to the role of an edifying moral on the theme of the application of redemption apart from questions concerned with its accomplishment?[8]

H. N. Ridderbos construes the character of the biblical tradition as described by the NT writers in a wholly other way. The *paradosis* here is not simply a human witness of faith. "Tradition is the word of God which the community heard from the apostles and which they accepted not as the word of men but as what it really is, the word of God."[9] Tradition is not the stage at which the message goes beyond a history of revelation and becomes human. If this were so, the tradition would be the human form imposed on the gospel by the church. Nor

---

8. See the interesting discussions concerning the exemplary and redemptive historical preaching debate in Holland in S. Greidanus, *Sola Scriptura* (Kampen, 1970), pp. 134, 192ff. Also J. Veenhof, *Revelatie en Inspiratie* (Amsterdam, 1968), pp. 468ff., for H. Bavinck's approach to Scripture as *historia revelationis*.

9. H. N. Ridderbos, *When the Time Had Fully Come* (Grand Rapids, 1957), p. 86; also *The Authority of the New Testament Scriptures* (Philadelphia, 1963), pp. 17ff.

is tradition simply the authority from the previous generation. The tradition is part of revelation and of the history of revelation itself. For Paul, says Ridderbos, the holy tradition (Gal. 1:14) was derived from Moses, thus from God himself. The apostolic authority is a prophetic authority in the Mosaic tradition and is thus to be accepted as having authority as tradition received from the Lord (I Cor. 11:23).[10]

It seems that the task of exegesis is to seek a way between the evaluation of the tradition as a human word and the witness of the tradition to its own character. Both aspects must be taken into consideration. Interpretation cannot afford to overlook the *sola Scriptura* at the risk of losing sight of the fact that this tradition is part of revelation. The history it recounts and transmits, if it is tendencious, is no less historical than the tradition itself. Revelation is woven into the history of ancient Israel and its traditions receive their significance from this history.[11] If this is the case, the search for the message of revelation in the tradition and the consciousness of the human development of the tradition in specific cultural forms, rather than being seen as mutually exclusive, may be considered complementary tasks. Revelation takes form within the development of a religious tradition, and this tradition bears witness to revelation. To speak of the Scripture as an unfolding tradition and as the norm of faith, *sola Scriptura,* does not involve contradiction, if we can keep in view the fact that there is no competition between the human and the divine revelation which is the content giving form to the human witness of the prophets and apostles.

Barr's evaluation of the biblical tradition in purely human terms seems too extreme in its rejection of the revelational context in which the tradition is formed. For this reason Barr can give little help to those who in their exegesis wish to do justice to this particular context which the *sola Scriptura* confesses. However, many of the questions he raises about the human character of the Scripture cannot

10. Ridderbos, *The Authority of the NT Scriptures,* p. 21. See also P. Jones, "The Apostle Paul: Second Moses to the New Covenant Community," in *God's Inerrant Word,* ed. J. W. Montgomery (Minneapolis, 1973), pp. 219-42.

11. See H. M. Kuitert, *The Reality of Faith* (Grand Rapids, 1968), pp. 160ff., and Oosterhoff, *Rondom het Woord* 8:117, 119, and 15:102ff., for many examples.

be bypassed and will be helpful in provoking the thought of those who do not share his theological presuppositions.

All the features we have sought to bring out as they exist in the reflexion of Barr may be evaluated as having greater or lesser significance in his thought and varying interest for present theological discussion in general. The real question, or so it seems to us, is not so much the presence of a certain number of positive or interesting elements in Barr's works. It concerns the basis on which he reaches the positions he proposes in the critique of present interpretations and theologies and on which his own theological propositions are formulated. We are not talking here of some hidden presupposition which could be claimed to have been excavated from hidden depths in Barr's thought, but of the fundamental perspective present in Barr's early work and progressively unfolded in the various aspects of his writings. It seems to us that the starting point for understanding the various aspects of Barr's work which have been lengthily described, is his fundamental critique of the validity of the revelational model which considers the Scripture along the lines indicated by a christological analogy. Barr proposes from the early review of J. K. S. Reid's *The Authority of Scripture* that we consider the biblical text as Word of Israel and the church, a human word having authority, bearing revelation in its human character. The Scripture is not of two elements, divine and human, but strictly speaking is of one element, the human.[12] This perspective, which is fundamental, finds its detailed development in *ONI,* perhaps Barr's most creative book, where the biblical corpus is considered as the crystallisation of the traditions of Israel and the church.

Thus Barr affirms the centrality of the human element, the "one" element of the Bible for describing the status of Scripture and properly understanding the material as a human document by normal procedures of interpretation. Granted that one believes in a God who entertains some relations with material reality and more particularly with a specific history, when we say that the Scripture is a human word, the problem still remains of the way in which this word is to be related to God. This brings us to the central problem, and to what appears to be the fundamental issue of Barr's work as a whole,

---

12. *SJT* 11:90.

namely, the problematic of the relation of the divine and human in so far as Scripture is concerned.

5.2. *The divine-human duality in Barr's thought*

The basic thesis of this conclusion to our examination of Barr's theological activity can be stated concisely here and illustrated with some specific examples. Barr rejects the christological analogy as an adequate model for illuminating the nature of the Scripture. This analogy mitigates the centrality of the human nature of the Bible. Barr then proposes that the Scripture be considered as a completely human document, with the possibility of seeing this as expressive of the faith of the people of God. The way this faith in God is related to its object is not by means of a revelational construct, but rather in terms of a model based on the idea of presence. The Holy Spirit accompanies the people of God in their history. God, through the Spirit, is present and accompanies the tradition process. This can be explained in human terms without reference to special divine interventions. The true analogy is not therefore the incarnational one, but the relation of the Spirit of God to the people of God in the election and inspiration of their tradition.[13]

The fundamental problem which can be discerned in this change of theological models is that even though there is a shift from a God-to-man movement and from a christological analogy of revelation to an evaluation of the Bible in immanent terms, the basic polarity remains between the divine and the human in explaining their relation with reference to Scripture. Thus, although Barr may have made quite an alteration in suggesting that Scripture be considered as human rather than as union of divine and human elements, the problem still remains unsolved as far as the relation of the divine and the human elements is concerned. This is so because the ground motive of Barr's thought would still appear to be a duality of the divine and

---

13. Ibid., pp. 89, 91. Barr speaks of God electing the tradition of his people in electing them into existence as his people. The problem of the guidance of God in relation to the development of the tradition is an aspect of the relation of divine sovereignty and human freedom. I am not aware of Barr's having related the development of the tradition as a human process to the question of election and human freedom elsewhere in his work, though had this been attempted it might have made the whole question of the human character of the tradition in relation to the divine a lot clearer.

the human factors, even though he modifies the way the relation is to be perceived. Barr's construction is limited by the confines of a polarity of God and man, in terms of which the relations of God and the Bible are discussed. In fact, it may even be thought that the discontinuity which existed between the divine and human elements in discussions of the doctrine of Scripture in neo-orthodoxy prior to Barr's time, becomes almost a dualism in the construction Barr presents. This thesis concerning the duality of the divine and human with reference to Scripture can be underscored by means of the following observations.

A perennial problem in theological reflexion concerning the relation of the divine and human aspects with respect to Scripture is illustrated in the various ways the Bible and revelation have been defined in reference to each other. How is Scripture to be considered as the Word of God? The traditional way seemed unproblematic as the Scripture was seen as a divine revelation and this permitted justice to be done to the affirmation that the Bible *is* the Word of God. Revelation in this formulation was taken together with inspiration as revelation of truths by God in the inspiration of Scripture.[14] Emil Brunner made his well-known judgment relative to this aspect of the traditional view of the relation of revelation and the Bible when he declared that "The theology of the Reformation was right in setting the doctrinal authority of Scripture above that of the church as its norm; but it was wrong when it made the Bible a final court of appeal, since it simply identified the word of the Bible with the Word of God."[15] With the growing interest in critical research the correlation between revelation and inspiration through which the Bible was identified with the Word of God was often abandoned. Revelation was no longer revelation of inspired truths of Scripture. In this situation two possibilities seemed to lie open. Either it would be possible to point to a partial identity of revelation and Scripture in positing that the Bible contains the Word of God, in an inner canonical fashion, or it could be said that the Word of God is a simple metaphor and the Bible is a record of man's religious aspirations as he searches for God. Inspiration in this instance could be referred to as a spiritual insight.

14. See J. I. Packer, *God Has Spoken* (London, 1965), pp. 16ff.; G. S. Hendry in *SJT* 1:30ff.
15. E. Brunner, *Dogmatics,* I:63.

In both these lines of approach Scripture and revelation become distinct entities. The difficulty lies in the problem of distilling revelation from the Bible or, on the other hand, of indicating the relation of Scripture to the mediacy of subjective inspiration.

To resume the sense of this development in a general way: When the union of the divine and human factors contributing to the formation of the Scriptures as revelation is dissolved, the relation of these factors is seen in terms of a polarity in which the presence of one of the elements excludes the other. In other words, there is no historical union of the divine and human factors in the case of the Scriptures which would permit the Bible itself to be considered as Word of God while it is also manifestly human. On the basis of the formulations of the problem which seek to go beyond the traditional "theandricity,"[16] where the Bible is said to *contain* the Word of God, an attempt is made to separate this element from the rest; it is therefore distinguished from the other material and provides a key for a normative formulation of revelation. On the other hand, where Scripture is considered inspired as indicative of an exemplary human seeking after the Absolute, it is obvious that this Absolute always lies beyond the capacity of human formulation. The ultimate is sensed beyond man and the divine is therefore different from the humanity expressed in man's aspirations. G. S. Hendry, commenting on these two approaches, says that each is wrong in itself, but relatively right over against the traditional formulation which maintained an identity between the Bible and the Word of God.[17]

In the movement which revived biblical authority in the first part of our century, which has been incisively criticised by Barr, there was an effort made to surmount the problem of the non-identification of Bible and Word of God and the polarity of the divine and human elements which remained unsolved in terms of the previous solutions. J. K. S. Reid, describing Karl Barth's view of the authority of Scripture, seems to put the issue rather well:

> In standing before Holy Scripture, we do not stand before authority itself. Rather we stand before that in which, as we hear it, we hear God himself speaking. The authority of Holy Scrip-

---

16. Cf. J. Levie, *The Bible, Word of God in Words of Men* (London, 1964), pp. 203ff.

17. G. S. Hendry, art. cit., p. 36.

ture is not a possession of Holy Scripture, not even a gift be-
stowed by God Himself. Holy Scripture is authoritative because
God Himself takes it and speaks through it.[18]

Some comment has already been made on this point (sec. 1.2), and it
is hardly necessary to go beyond a recapitulation of the main point as
far as the relation of the divine and human is concerned. The neo-
orthodox solution regarding Scripture and revelation made something
of a virtue out of a necessity. A dialectical solution was sought to the
problem of the polarity of the divine and the human elements connected with revelation, as no natural unity between God and man is
attainable. Between the divine absolute of God and human relativity there lacks the continuity necessary to posit an identity in revelation. As the complement of this bi-polarity of the divine and human
there stands the possibility of the resolution of this separation in a
connection established by God. Thus T. F. Torrance says that Barth
seeks to make clear the separation and the connection which the act
of revelation effects, as in this, God in his Godness comes to man in
his humanity.[19] The unity which is established in revelation is therefore not a direct one, but it depends on the decision of God and his
will to make himself known to man in the act of his self-revealing.
No revelatory nature, inherent inspiration, or authority can be
claimed for the Bible apart from the decision and act of God in his
revelation. The Bible is not the Word of God in the sense of a direct
identity but only in an indirect way in virtue of the divine act.

G. Wingren has proposed in his discussion of Barth's view of revelation that in Barth's early thinking anthropology determines hermeneutics on the presupposition that there is a polarity between God
and man. This is fundamental to his approach to Scripture.[20] Wingren thinks that Barth's doctrine of revelation is based on the an-
tithesis of God and man and states:

18. J. K. S. Reid, *The Authority of Scripture* (London, 1957), p. 221. Reid
commenting on Calvin also claims that the Reformer was no verbal inspiration-
ist and saw no direct identity between Scripture and Word of God but only an
indirect one. But see Runia's criticisms of this in *Karl Barth's Doctrine of Holy
Scripture* (Grand Rapids, 1962), pp. 42ff. Also J. I. Packer in *God's Inerrant
Word,* ed. J. W. Montgomery (Minneapolis, 1973), pp. 95ff.
19. T. F. Torrance, *Karl Barth: An Introduction to His Early Theology,
1910–1931* (London, 1962), pp. 81f.
20. G. Wingren, *Theology in Conflict* (Edinburgh, 1958), pp. 108f.

He has not penetrated beneath the liberal period. . . . At the very start he has simply turned liberal theology upside down; he has moved the accent within liberal theology from "man" to "God," but he has not been able to break up the structure of the problem.[21]

This view of Wingren's might well be contested as to its interpretation of the relation of Barthianism and liberalism.[22] However, what seems to be somewhat more incontestable is the fact that Barth's thought about the relation of God and man with respect to revelation does seem to run along the lines of a marked difference of the divine and human. This disjunction which contrasts the divine and the human does not resolve the tension of the elements which arose in liberal theology following the demise of the traditional unity of revelation and Scripture. Although it is true that in neo-orthodoxy there is a special accent on the freedom and grace of God rather than on the freedom and autonomy of man, the basic structure of polarity between God and man remains. The knowledge of the modern man seems to be unreconstructed in neo-orthodoxy, as revelation being an act of God's grace is tangential with historical realities and is not subject to the same criteria of evaluation as those which apply in the temporal domain. In fact, it may be that the dialectical tension of the bi-polarity between God and man is heightened in neo-orthodoxy through its critique of human culture in terms of sin and guilt rather than unbounded optimism. As D. Tracy remarks: ". . . the neo-orthodox, by their profound analyses of the negative elements in the human situation allow a more dialectical, a more contemporary, and most importantly, a more accurate understanding of the actual human condition than did most of their liberal or modernist forebears."[23] If this is indeed the case, it would seem that Wingren's opinion about neo-orthodoxy remaining in the same frame of structural tension of a contrast between man and God may not be far from the mark.

Langdon Gilkey has formulated this in similar fashion in his book, *Naming the Whirlwind.* He points out that neo-orthodoxy grounded its theological affirmations in a way which was autonomous in re-

---

21. Ibid., p. 25.
22. See also, D. Tracy, *Blessed Rage for Order: The New Pluralism in Theology* (New York, 1975), pp. 27ff.
23. Ibid., p. 28.

lation to secular culture, but remained half-secular, after a liberal pattern, in many of its attitudes. In particular it remained in the liberal line as far as the interpretation of history in spatio-temporal reality is concerned. As such it created a duality between a this-worldly account of reality in the modern terms of secular man and the religious account of the contact of God with the world which lies in the domain of faith. Gilkey claims that its attitude was secular in that the revelation of God was not in the frame of ordinary secular life, which is accounted for in a naturalistic way. On another level a religious meaning is given to this naturally interpreted life in terms of a faith in a transcendent word. As Gilkey says, neo-orthodoxy "attempted to accept the secular world secularly, but to retain the Biblical and orthodox worlds religiously. . . . this dual posture, while the source of considerable power, proved its undoing in the end."[24]

These remarks serve to illustrate the polarity of the divine and human elements in revelation which was fundamental to the model proposed by neo-orthodoxy. The separation and connection between God and man effected by the divine act of revelation in which God is known as the Wholly Other, if it highlights the gracious nature of revelation, also preserves this act in discontinuity with historical realities. Even where the revelation touches history, it does not take the form of a structure of truth within the milieu of historical reality. In the case of Scripture too, revelation lies beyond the textual corpus which points away from itself to the act of God. What Oscar Cullmann says about this is quite representative:

> The human way, with all the elements of "scandal" in which the books of the New Testament were written and the canon constituted, is the necessary "rock of offense" which God desired, and on which alone the true faith and divine inspiration of the Bible could be founded. Within this process, containing as it did all human defects and every kind of secular influence, the Holy Spirit was at work, so that the word of God might be revealed to humanity.[25]

This is standard fare in the movement which sought to renew biblical authority. The Spirit of God is said to be at work, to "inspire," but

---

24. L. Gilkey, *Naming the Whirlwind: The Renewal of God-Language* (Indianapolis, 1969), p. 84.
25. O. Cullmann, *The Early Church* (London, 1956), p. 10.

in such a way as to leave the human aspects of the scriptural witness unreconstructed as "rock of offence." The polarity of the divine work in revelation and the human witness is quite plain here. The ordinariness of the temporal and human imperfect character of the Bible is of a kind with the way in which God becomes flesh in revealing himself to men. The very ordinariness of the human "is part of divine revelation."[26]

Barr himself has been quite critical in more than one instance of the "scandals" of neo-orthodoxy. He has pointed to the fact that some such scandals are in fact readily acceptable and mitigate the difficulties of elements which are a lot more problematic. "Conventional wisdom" can masquerade as scandal.[27] Revelation in history is a lot easier to negotiate with in terms of the modern mind than revelation as verbal communication. Along similar lines it could be added that in the context of a bi-polarity of divine and human elements in revelation, it does seem quite feasible to affirm the human-imperfect character of the Scripture, and this does not really give too much offence as the revelation is safe in another domain.

However, this duality, as Gilkey ably indicates, has its drawbacks as well as its attractions. Without a rooting in the reality of this world, the epistemological status of faith affirmations about the divine revelation remain conjectural.[28] The polarity of the divine and human in revelation leaves the way open for a critique of the reality of the religious affirmation founded in faith on the basis of the observation of the processes of spatio-temporal reality. In these conditions the polarity of the divine and human which in neo-orthodoxy was complementary is modified to a duality of opposition. The pole of the dialectic which emphasised the divine undergoes a reality-loss as a result of a critique based on the reality structures of this world; thus the separation of the divine and human elements with reference to the Scripture is totalised. The human becomes again the centre of theological thinking, as man begins to construct his view of reality

26. Ibid., p. 9.
27. Barr in *New Theology no. 1,* ed. M. E. Marty and D. G. Peerman (New York, 1964), p. 70.
28. See on this Gilkey's article, "Cosmology, Ontology and the Travail of Biblical Language," *JR* 41:194ff.; also G. D. Kaufman, "On the Meaning of 'Act of God,'" *Harvard Theological Review* 61:175-201, and S. M. Ogden, "What Sense Does It Make to Say 'God Acts in History'?" *JR* 43:1-19.

from within the historical process. In other terms, the connection between the human and the divine assured in neo-orthodoxy by the revelational act of God, not entering itself into the domain of this-worldly realities as a structural principle, is dissolved; the separation inherent in the ontological distinction of God and man is realised. As William Hamiliton has remarked, it is "a short step, but a critical one, to move from the otherness of God to the absence of God."[29]

The movement of thought in the post-neo-orthodox generation has been in this direction in the radical theologies which arise from a uniting of the secular affirmation of the reality of this world with the negation of the cognitive certainty founded on a faith in God tributary of a divine act of revelation.[30] It is at this point that we can direct our thought again to the basic structure of the work of James Barr. Far from wishing to say that Barr is a radical theologian—his ideas and fields of study are well away from those of the radicalism of the 1960s—Barr's work does portray some of the characteristics of the post-neo-orthodox situation, both in his critique of the incongruities of the former theology and in the general approach he takes to the question of revelation and the Bible. This point will be developed briefly and then illustrated in three ways.

For Barr, as for Barth, there is no objective union of the divine and human in history in terms of a biblical revelation. Barr accepts the same basic duality of divine and human in his thinking about revelation as Karl Barth, his theological forerunner, but criticises this dialectic from within. He affirms that the christological analogy is not a profitable model for understanding the nature of Scripture and its interpretation; such an analogy breaks down in the light of a thorough-going consideration of the human nature of Scripture. Thus Barr approaches the question of the character of the Scripture as a tradition developed in Israel and in the church in terms of a normal historical approach. The texts are interpreted as human documents without any special appeals to a salvation history with a particular moulding influence on language patterns which would be indicative of the divine revelation beyond the texts. It would seem that Barr has radicalised the centrality of the human nature of Scripture which

29. W. Hamilton, *The New Essence of Christianity* (New York, 1961), p. 55.
30. See Tracy, op. cit., pp. 31f., and Gilkey, pp. 107ff.

tended to be a preliminary consideration in the neo-orthodox structure of revelation. In this perspective he criticises the object-centred
exegetical principle proposed by neo-orthodoxy.[31] The goal of interpretation is not to see the text in analogy with a revelatory activity
of God in such a way that the human is related to the divine act of
revelation; such an approach tends to make the human character of
the Bible a preliminary. In an historical approach to the Scripture
as a human document, we are dealing with man's word to man; biblical study spends time mostly making "assertions about human relations."[32]

However, having affirmed the human character of the Scriptures in
this immanent fashion, if faith is going to have any reference at all to
the Bible, it is necessary to maintain a relation between the human
Scriptures and the God of whom they speak. The problem would
seem to consist in the fact that once the connection of the human text
of the Bible and the divine revelation is made tenuous by an insistence
on the one-element character of Scripture, it is difficult to formulate
the relation of the human text with the divine about which the texts
speak. Barth was able in his dialectic to maintain a sort of relation in
terms of the priority of God and his act of divine grace which relates
the human text to the divine revelation. Barr on the other hand,
choosing to approach the text on the level of the word of man, the
one element, shuts off the way to relating the human to the divine in
this fashion. Such an appeal would put the ball back in the courts of
the christological analogy. Barr is consistent with his approach to
Scripture as human by seeking to make an historical description of the
nature of the Bible without falling back on supernatural interventions.

Such a description "appeals to" Barr.[33] The solution which Barr
proposes is that the Scripture tradition should not be seen as a revelation but in relation to the accompanying Spirit of God, who guides
the people of God. The Bible gives a model of faith formed by the
church "in the Spirit." This presence and accompaniment continue
in the development of the church today. The spiritual presence is the
link of continuity which Barr introduces in two dimensions: It links
the past of the people of God to the present through the reference to

31. *ONI*, pp. 90ff.
32. "Does Biblical Study Still Belong to Theology?," p. 8.
33. *BMW*, p. 132.

the notion of a classic model, but also it relates the human history to a divine leading. The model of presence, or the analogy between the people of God and the Spirit of God, is Barr's way of seeking the relation of the human and the divine in theology. Through it, Barr refers a process which is described in a totally human way as an historical tradition to a notion of transcendence. The immanent evaluation of the human character of Scripture is counterbalanced by an affirmation of the transcendence of God, who is truth in unity beyond the diversities of the historical process. It remains to be seen whether Barr's models of presence and accompaniment can establish a meaningful contact between the human and the divine.

If we compare the model suggested by Barr to describe the status of Scripture with that of Barth based on the christological analogy, it would appear that Barr remains in the same basic framework as Barth. The difference is that the roles are reversed. In Barth's dialectic the accent is on the divine priority and the human is related to the divine in terms of a revelational model. In the case of Barr the accent falls rather markedly on the human nature of the Bible and the model for the relation of the human word to the divine is non-revelational. In spite of this difference of approach which changes many points in the doctrine of Scripture and in its interpretation, the same basic polarity of the divine and human remains in both models, together with the problem of articulating the relation between the two diverse elements. If we were to refer to the comment of G. Wingren concerning the fact that the relation of "man" and "God" of liberal theology has been turned upside down by Karl Barth but that the essential structure has not been broken up, the same might be said concerning Barth and Barr. Barr turns over Barth's relation of the divine and the human with reference to revelation, but the structure remains one which works within a duality of the divine and the human. In this movement, Barr returns to something more like the preceding liberal models of theology, which is not to say his thought is the same as liberalism or that he himself should be classed as a liberal. However, certain points can be indicated in his theology which show some affinity with liberalism.

On the question of authority, Barr seems quite close to the attitude often characteristic in liberalism. We said in our Introduction that Barr's critique of the interpretation and revelational based doctrines of the status of Scripture was "profoundly anti-authoritarian." This is not, it seems, because Barr is an iconoclast who has as a goal the dismantling of authority structures. In fact, Barr's work in many places shows great moderation. The critique of authority in Barr's work is better seen, perhaps, as a correlate of his understanding of the human nature of Scripture and his desire to do justice to this fact in terms of normal scientific procedures. This does lead Barr into a polemic with various systems of thought which make unsubstantiated appeals to authority in theological construction. This is the mainspring of Barr's criticism of the BTM or of fundamentalism. These build up authority structures on the basis of unproved assumptions which cannot do justice to the text of Scripture; they ignore its fundamental character by sublimating its humanness in a doctrine of revelation. Commenting on the breakdown of the idea held widely in the BTM that Hebrew mentality provided a distinctive approach ot biblical thought as a mandatory mental structure for faith and theology, Barr says:

> The present writer's *SBL* has been only one of the factors making for the breakdown of this type of argumentation, a breakdown which has become increasingly evident during the sixties and which is allied also, and more widely, with changing conceptions of biblical authority itself.[34]

Barr's work, which emphasises the human aspects of the Scripture and its interpretation, goes together with a changing view of the authority of Scripture. In a reference to the first edition of *BWT* (1962) in the second edition seven years later, Barr states that the book was more conservative than it need have been. The situation has since changed, which is not for Barr an indication of the success of his argument but points to the decrease in confidence that there is a unitary Bible view on certain topics. The unity of the Bible in the new situation, says Barr, is "no longer considered to be a decisive principle either for strictly exegetical problems or for the application of the Bible to questions of our own time."[35] Barr says that in 1969 he has come to accept a greater degree of theological tension and contradiction in the biblical tradition. The loosening of the authority structures con-

---

34. "Old Testament Scholarship in the 1960's," *Church Quarterly* 2:203.
35. *BWT*, pp. 170ff.

nected with revelation is implied in the approach to Scripture which wishes to do full justice to its humanity.

This critique of the interpretation and the status of the Bible based on an appeal to the authority of revelation which is the negative part of Barr's work is matched by a positive intention, namely, that of an open exegesis related to an understanding of the human nature of Scripture. To do justice to this fundamental character of Scripture is to "encourage the Scripture to speak freely." This implies the relative independence of biblical studies over against theology, or the freedom of historical enquiry into the Scripture as a human document apart from considerations of theological normativity. Therefore Barr breaks with interpretation which sees the biblical history as a salvation history which witnesses to special revelation. The biblical stories are to be approached in terms of our understanding of history and their relation to that which we call history is found to be variable. Their meaning is internal to the development of the tradition of Israel, and they function in this context, which is a human one. If, therefore, Barr seeks to maintain a continuity between historical research and theology, it is important that theological structures are not imposed arbitrarily on the historical material in such a way as to predetermine its interpretation. This independence of historical enquiry and the corresponding need of theology to integrate in its constructions the material historical research presents to it, marks the way in which Barr moves away from Biblical theology as it was conceived (perhaps rather unreflectingly) in the neo-orthodox period. The emphasis on the primacy of the historical concerns of the Biblical theologian would seem to place Barr in line with the enterprise of the History of Religions approach, at least in a formal sense. It is not therefore surprising that one of Barr's reiterated criticisms of the BTM and a reason for its decline is that it did not pay sufficient attention to the legacy of liberalism. In spite of the fact that the BTM passed them by, philosophical theology and the History of Religions approach did not disappear, but emerged in strength at the end of the intermezzo of the BTM.[36]

Langdon Gilkey has indicated that one of the features of the nineteenth-century liberalism was that " it accepted as normative cri-

---

36. See, for example, *IDB*(S), pp. 105f.

teria for theology the dominant scientific, philosophical, historical and moral ideas of its culture."[37] It would doubtless be incorrect to apply such a description to Barr's theological constructions. However, in one respect Barr approaches this kind of theological attitude. Theology is not constructed, for Barr, on an application of the biblical message taken as normative for the present. Nor is interpretation a translation of the biblical content into present terms. For Barr, as we have seen, theology is the statement of what the church believes now. Its assertions must be fresh.[38] This is linked with the consideration of the Bible as the tradition of the people of God, which tradition runs on to the present. The Bible is the classic model of the faith of the people of God in the past, which is illuminating for our faith in the present. As a model of faith its function is to call forth faith with reference to a new situation. For this reason theology is constructive in the present in terms of the expression of faith in this situation. In relating itself to the Bible, a theology must decide how the biblical material can be affirmed today. Barr's emphasis on the need that theology be present affirmation of what is now believed by the church does bear a certain relation with the standpoint of liberalism, and Barr's attempt to state a doctrine of Scripture in terms of present academic criteria in a "rational" way seems to fit this pattern. However, Barr's position is far from being simply world-affirming. To Barr's desire for a present theology corresponds the notion of the presence of the Spirit, who leads the people of God in this task. This mode of the divine accompaniment gives a continuity to the people of God and places the affirmation of the church today in relation to the model of faith expressed in the Bible. Thus the theology must be related in some way to the God of Israel and to Jesus of Nazareth.

Referring to the title of Auguste Sabatier's well-known book on different types of religion, Barr's work could be described as a criticism of religion of authority in favour of a religion of the Spirit. In taking the human nature of the Scripture as a central consideration for interpretation and theological construction, Barr criticises theological structures based on the appeal to the authority of revelation.

37. L. Gilkey, op. cit., p. 76.
38. *BMW*, pp. 133ff.

The human character of the text is recognised in the development of an historical process of tradition. The human is related to the divine through the accompaniment of the spirit with the people of God in a way that respects the integrality of human nature and history. Faith expresses the belief that God works in relation to this human process through the presence of the Spirit. This theological perspective proposed by Barr represents a substantial difference from the prior neo-orthodox approach to Scripture and theology. The critique of neo-orthodoxy developed by Barr in his work is situated in the context of a more general move away from the conceptions of neo-orthodoxy in recent years. Peter Berger has described this general evolution of attitudes in this way:

> The new liberalism "subjectivizes" religion in a radical fashion and in two senses of the word. With the progressive loss of objectivity or reality-loss of the traditional religious definitions of the world, religion becomes increasingly a matter of free subjective choice. . . . Also, religious "realities" are increasingly "translated" from a frame of reference of facticities external to the individual consciousness to a frame of reference that locates them *within* consciousness.[39]

While it would be wrong to state simply that this quotation gives a description of what happens in Barr's theology, it does probably describe quite accurately the theological drift of recent years within which the ideas of Barr can be contextualised. We do see in his work a criticism of the traditional religious definitions concerning Scripture which relate the text to an objective revelation and seek an object-centred exegesis. In his thought also there is an increased consciousness of the subjective aspect of religion, in that the Scripture is not seen as a transcript of divine revelation, but as the developing faith of the people of God. Barr does seem, in his theological reconstruction, to translate a certain number of the traditional doctrines concerning Scripture into a new theological frame of reference. So, the unity of the Bible is sought in relational centres, but such centres are a matter of personal choice and may be of only temporary value. As far as the canonicity of Scripture is concerned, Barr doubts that it can be used as a norm for exegesis in the way suggested by B. S. Childs; it is a question of a prior decision of the

---

39. P. L. Berger, *The Social Reality of Religion* (London, 1973), p. 168.

church and a contingent decision at that. That tradition is no longer a secondary consideration under the authority of Scripture shows a change of attitude as well. Tradition forms the Scripture as an expression of the faith of the people of God. Here it is within the consciousness of the people of God that the tradition itself is formed. The relation between the church and God then and now is not a fundamentally different one. God relates to the listening church today in a similar way as in the time of the formation of the classic model. Inspiration is not limited to the canonical Scriptures, but it is more like the inspiration associated with literary insight and does not exclude human error, theological and other, from the tradition.

In interpretation too, external facticities tend to disappear from view as the significance of the text is evaluated in terms of a literary model or according to the intention of the author. The fundamental approach is not then to locate the revelation in word or act referred to by the text, but to find its meaning in the human dimension and interpret this historically. These considerations can hardly avoid to recognise the relativity of the biblical message, which does not give a model of truth but a paradigm of faith working itself out in particular situations. When the status of Scripture is so defined and interpreted as an expression of the religious consciousness of the people of God, it follows that faith in God today, which has no reference to a given objective truth, is construed in terms of a pluralism which expresses the variety possible for faith within the framework of Christianity. Religion in the context of the reality-loss of the traditional formulations of truth expresses itself in a pluralism of theological assertions which depend largely on the personal choice of the individual. Barr's thought would seem to combine a very high objectivity in terms of historical research into the Scriptures, counter-balanced by a good measure of subjectivity in the expression of the faith.

The problem we have sought to present lies, then, in the fact that in radicalising his approach to the human nature of Scripture, Barr does not avoid the duality of the divine and the human present in Barth's theology. The question of a possible relation is placed on another level. In Barr's thought this discontinuity is expressed in terms of the relation between the Spirit of God and the people of God and is seen in several aspects of Barr's work, three of which can be considered now.

Barr's thought is wide-ranging and it is necessary to select certain central areas to illustrate this point concerning the polarity of the divine and the human in his theology. One level at which it seems to operate is in the description of the relation of God to the formation of the tradition. A second level at which such duality appears is in the interpretation of the tradition between historical knowledge and the faith founded on this knowledge. A third aspect would follow on from these two: Granted a duality between God and the developing tradition and between knowledge and faith in interpretation there arises a duality between the objective reality of faith and the subjective grounding of faith. The basic problem in these three areas is that of establishing a connection between the faith expressed in the formation of the tradition and in theological assertions interpreting it as a classic model and the God who transcends but who is spoken of in the traditions. The question is whether a satisfactory form of mediacy between God and his people can be established once the revelational model of the christological analogy is left behind.

5.3. *God and the biblical tradition*

In neo-orthodoxy mediacy between God and man was sought in terms of God's acts in history and his Word of revelation.[40] In both these cases a duality was apparent between the secular view of the spatio-temporal process which was held and the biblical world view which spoke of God's act and his Word. Thus the acts of God were assigned to a special domain of salvation history and the Word of God to the sphere of the personal experience of faith. This duality opened neo-orthodoxy to the accusation that its use of God-language was lacking in cognitive content. If nothing happened in history, it may well be that to speak of God's acts is not meaningful; again, if the Word of God as revelation was to be meaningful, it would appear that some connection would need to be forged with the words of the Scripture. Failing to find a definite continuity between the acts and words of God confessed in faith and the wonders and word revelations of Scripture which appear in the text as historical realities, it is natural that theologians should seek continuity on another level.

The most obvious possibility open is to seek a continuity in the

---

40. I follow the account of Gilkey, op. cit., pp. 91ff., at this point.

tradition of the Jewish religion as an expression of the historical life in faith of the people of God. This avoids the incongruity of an appeal to events and word-encounter, which do not seem wholly historical, or to events as actually having taken place or words of God as having actually been uttered. Barr's criticisms of the acts of God and the notion of the Word of God in neo-orthodoxy and his view of the relation between God and the tradition move in this sense, away from the search for continuity between God and the historical process in divine interventions to an understanding of the tradition process as expressing a continuity of faith in God, who lies beyond the expressions of the tradition. Thus Barr doubts that the acts of God can be a key for understanding the origin of the biblical material as an interpretation in faith of such events. The words of God are just as central an element in the biblical texts. However, as we have seen in our exposition, when Barr speaks of the words of God, this does not necessarily mean for us audibility of divine communication. It can signify something other for us than for the prophets of old. Barr considers the words and acts of God presented in the tradition to function not in a referential fashion as actual occurrences, but as elements in the tradition, which have their role in the ongoing story.

This is indicative of the way God and the tradition are related in Barr's construction. The speaking and acting of God are elements within the tradition. Rather than expressing a faith based on the reference to an act or word of God in history, they are significative of a faith which develops its forms of expression in the context of history. The tradition is a process of historical development and the different elements are seen as functional within this tradition-context. This intra-traditional method of interpreting the various elements of the biblical stories can also be illustrated in the way in which Barr speaks of the relation between the tradition and revelation. In the progressive tradition of the people of God, the creation story is the starting point which has priority in the cumulative progression of the story. However, Barr makes no appeal to a particular revelation at the inception of the tradition process. Certain facts and thoughts from antiquity blend together to provide a framework of understanding which is referred to and reinterpreted as the tradition develops. There is no revelation of God as Creator in the sense of a special communication to man concerning the nature of God. The mode of the divine influence in relation to the origin of the tradition is left vague (cf. sec. 4.1.1).

Since no divine intervention is appealed to in the origin of the tradition process in which God is revealed as Creator in communion with man, it cannot be affirmed as definitely as often thought in Christian theology that there is a revelation of man's sin in the early chapters of Genesis. There is, to be sure, the consciousness of a certain disturbance in the relation of God and man and that man has done what God forbade. After the crisis, human life went on, "contrary to the assertion of God . . . and in agreement with the words of the serpent. . . ."[41] Sin is not mentioned in Genesis 3, nor is salvation; Genesis 3:15 is too vague for anything of this magnitude to be deduced from it. Salvation is not therefore necessarily a central aspect of the tradition of the OT, although this tradition is soteriologically functional with reference to Christ. The tradition is the faith response of the people of God expressive of the life of communion with God in which faith is seen in an historical progression. In this account there are no divine interventions in revelation at the start of the tradition process either with reference to God as Creator or as to the nature of man's "original" sin.

On this basis nothing so precise as *salvation history* can be used to describe the developing tradition. The absence of historical acts of revelation of God in the development of the tradition corresponds to a similar absence at its beginning. Barr seems to describe the formation of the tradition in an imprecise formulation which allows for the coming together of certain elements of thought which express faith in the Creator-God and a certain consciousness of disturbance in relation to Him."[42]

This perspective is clearly represented in the following way:

> There is no "history" of the acts of God alone, but a history in which the tradition grows and suffers change, in which the tradition itself is affected by the impact of events; and these events may be in some cases acts of God, in others not. . . . the function

---

41. "An Aspect of Salvation in the Old Testament," *Man and His Salvation*, ed. Sharpe and Hillells (Manchester, 1973), p. 46.

42. In saying this it must be pointed out that Barr has not attempted any synthetic presentation of the origin of the tradition process in a detailed way at any point in his works. The elements which could make up such a description are dispersed and therefore their synthesis is rather conjectural.

of the Old Testament tradition is not mainly to point back to a
series of events from which the tradition has originated, but also
to form the framework within which an event can be meaningful.[43]

The tradition does not depend on a preceding revelation for its development. Revelation of God does not generate the tradition of the
people of God as a prior factor to the tradition. Rather the tradition
is the process in which God is known. It is in communion with God
that he is known. The tradition makes God known through the framework of interpretation which it proposes. Revelation follows on from
this tradition in subsequent generations. It may be said in this respect that God adopts the tradition and makes it his own message.
In these formulations the duality of the divine and the human is evident when Barr speaks of tradition and revelation. The knowledge of
God that his people has is formed in their human consciousness, in a
way which can be described in human terms without reference to
revelation. In communion with God, there is a knowledge of him
which is expressed by man in the formation and development of the
tradition. Scripture does not come into existence by a divine revelation but out of the human reflex arising from contact with God. Man
knows God through the consciousness arising from the fellowship
with God. This is expressed in a human way, as a human consciousness of communion with God is in view. God does not "reveal" the
tradition, but is known through it by his continuing presence.

In this matrix, when inspiration is spoken of it does not refer to
the theopneustic action with respect to the text of Scripture or its
writers or readers. Inspiration as an expression of the life of the
people of God in communion with God, relates to a fallible document.
It speaks to us who are sinful men precisely for this reason. Thus
God uses sin to conquer sin through the fallible process expressed in
the tradition-production of the Bible. The inspiration is not a divine
influence, but is seen in the formation of a tradition along human lines
in which man expresses his struggle for communion with God. The
inspired tradition is an ambiguous human one at once showing a
faithfulness to God and a propensity for sinfulness.

Similarly, when the unity of the Scripture as a process of tradition
is referred to, this unity is approached in terms of an historical de-

---

43. *ONI*, pp. 19f.

velopment, which is related to a unity of God. The establishing of this relation is, however, an affirmation which belongs to the realm of faith, rather than that of historical demonstration. It does not illustrate the unity of the Bible, but it refers to a unity of the one God, the God of Israel and the Father of Jesus Christ, beyond the tradition process itself. Once again in this case there is a duality between God and the tradition process, between the divine unity of purpose and the multiplex nature of the historical tradition by which this purpose becomes evident in the work of salvation.

The problem which seems to arise in these formulations is that of relating statements concerning the Scripture tradition defined in terms of "one element" to the divine reality. Can what is affirmed in a human way as a statement of faith be taken as an expression of the truth about the eternal God? Israel and the church form the tradition in communion with God as an expression of faith. Thus God is confessed in Israel as Creator and Saviour, as the one God who is known in communion with his people. The tradition is inspired as expressive of this human faith and adopted by God as the vehicle of his revelation for later generations. The Bible is recognised as a classic model of the faith of the people of God by the church. But whether we speak of the biblical tradition in terms of its origination, inspiration, classic status, the facticity of its canonical recognition, or as developing story, all of these aspects describe immanent historical processes capable of description in human terms. It might be said that they are accompanied by a divine presence, but the fact of their humanity is central. These are human historical processes governing the formation of tradition which do not tell us anything about the purpose of God in himself. The tradition gives us a key as to how this purpose might be transparent to faith which deciphers the divine will in contact with the historical movement.

The following section from *ONI* is quite illuminating as illustrative of this point:

> God was known in Israel. We believe that his work with Israel worked also for the purpose which we see fulfilled in Jesus Christ. But the way he worked for this purpose was by contacts with Israel which were real in themselves. These contacts worked also afterwards through the after-effects in later interpretation of the texts which they produced. But our interest in the original setting of the texts is an interest in the reality of God's original contact

with Israel. The process of salvation was not, even theologically
seen, a wholly pre-planned scheme; in such sense as we can see
planning, purpose and foreknowledge, it is always done through
real contacts with real people who have real choices.[44]

Barr's conception of the relation of God to historical reality is a
very discreet one. The biblical texts are reflexes produced by contact with God. God and his purpose are not directly revealed in the
biblical tradition. They come to expression in the text in so far as the
faith of the real human persons in actual situations gives expression to
the reality of the relation with God.

The mediacy between the divine and the human is provided in this
context by the "original contact" between God and his people. The
reality of this contact is given form in the faith reflex of the tradition
forming process. Scripture points beyond itself as a model of faith to
the fellowship with God in which the purpose of God is discerned with
relation to the historical situation. The purpose of God, his will and
salvation are expressed not in the revealing of truths by God about
himself, but are revealed in the formulations that are given to them
by human faith which discerns God's presence. Man is complementary to God in the revelation process. God does not pre-plan
salvation, but brings it in connection with the real human reactions
to contact with himself. In a sense it would even appear that God is
dependent on the faith of man fostered by the relation with God in
order that he be known in the tradition. The tradition process is
describable in terms of historical development as a human process.
However, in this human context, faith in God is expressed by man.
This points to a contact with God in faith which cannot be described
by historical enquiry, but for which historical research must allow. As
a model of faith the Bible points us to the belief that God is working
in the historical movement, though without a direct self-identification
in this sphere. Nothing very precise is said about the mode of this
presence of God which faith discerns.

There is no doubt that with this historical approach to the biblical
tradition, Barr can tell us a lot about what Israel believed God to be
up to in connection with the development of her history, or what the
church believed to have happened in Jesus Christ. Faith discerned

44. Ibid., p. 155.

the things of God in the situation, the way God established contact. It is one thing for faith to believe this, however, and another to affirm that this is what God was really up to. To speak of the Bible as a classic model of the faith of the people of God tells us how it saw the situations as they developed, but does not tell us how God saw them. Nor does it assure us that the people of God always got it right. In fact, Barr tells us that they didn't, as inspiration is with fallibility. To really affirm that the faith of the people of God is in conformity with the reality of what God is and what he wants to do, it is not sufficient to appeal to how the people of God saw it in faith. Only God can tell us who he is and what his intentions really are. But this is precisely what God does not appear to do on the basis of Barr's formulation. This would amount to a revelation in history made by God, which is more precisely what Barr refuses, even though he is prepared to talk in more vague terms of a real contact of God in history. It may be that the people of God in their communion with God did get it right, if not all of the time, but this is not really the question. The problem is as to whether man's faith-expression of what he believes God to be or to do is ever adequate to express what God is and what he does. If the modicum of fallibility, in theological and other senses to which Barr points, is present in the Bible, can it really merit the expression of "classic model" of faith? At most we could perhaps talk of some classic models of faith within the Bible with relation to some particular situations. In this case too the problem would arise of indicating the criteria by which such diverse models were judged to be correct.

There is, I conclude here, an irreducible chasm in Barr's approach between the divine and the human, between God and the tradition. It cannot be denied that God is in contact with man on Barr's terms of interpretation. What is not sure is that what the tradition expresses about God is, in fact, what ought to be said about him. God is spoken of in the biblical tradition, he speaks and acts, but these are elements of the tradition which explicate the contact God originally had with his people as seen by their faith. They are not revelations of God in the Scriptures. Even if God has a contact with history, we cannot conclude from this that God reveals himself in Scripture. This is how the people of God expressed it in faith. To return to the question of the christological analogy, the issue could be formulated in this fashion. Barr replaces the mediacy of the union of the divine and human elements of christological analogy by a dynamic mediacy on the grounds of the analogy of the Spirit of God and the people of God. There is no direct self-identification of God in this; the mediacy created by the divine presence is vehiculed indirectly in the tradition of the Scriptures through the expression of faith of Israel and the church. This indirect relation cannot be resolved in terms of union between divine and human in Scripture. The question remains whether in this duality between God and the tradition-formulations, Barr can say any more than Barth was able to affirm in his mysterious encounter with the Word. In the light of the little that can be said about the mode of the presence of God, it is at least legitimate to ask whether mediacy based on the analogy between the Spirit and the people of God does not finally leave us with an abstract God set over against a dynamic contingency in the growth of the people of God. Once the human element is taken fundamentally as the "one element" in the Scriptures, it is doubtful whether the analogy which appeals to the presence of the Spirit can be sufficient to establish the reality of the knowledge of God which is expressed, albeit in faith.

5.4. *Historical knowledge and Christian faith*

Let us now consider a second duality in the thought of Barr, more particularly with reference to interpretation, which appears between the historical knowledge of the tradition and Christian faith. This second aspect in the thought of Barr corresponds to the fundamental duality of the divine and the human which we have tried to illustrate with reference to the relation between God and the tradition of the people of God. Given that the contact between God and the tradition is indirect and is described in terms of a presence of God which is discerned in faith, but does not express itself in a revelation which organically unites itself with the witness of Scripture, the biblical texts are interpreted by normal hermeneutic procedures. No special hermeneutic is involved, and biblical hermeneutics could be considered as an extension to the examination of the Bible of methods used in other domains—historical, scientific, linguistic, sociological, etc. Being a document of human origin, it is possible to undertake a study of its meaning without any immediate reference to questions of normativity.

A similar question to that raised in preceding paragraphs can be asked in this connection, namely, in what respect the interpretative procedures which are normal ones, making no appeal to normativity, can be related subsequently to faith questions.

Four areas can be broadly considered in the work of Barr in which this duality in interpretation can be considered. It applies firstly to the method of theological study in general; to the relation of the different levels of study which are observed in theology; to the issue of the diverse functions of the biblical materials and the problem of their unity; finally to the question of the nature of biblical language and its relation to faith.

Concerning first of all the nature of theological method, we have remarked that Barr proposes that there is no pure method, which is specifically theological and would serve to distinguish theology, in so far as methodology is concerned, from other branches of academic study. In particular, the historical character of the biblical stories requires that these be interpreted in conformity with the canons of historical and literary studies. The historical and literary study of the Bible can be carried on without reference to theological presuppositions. In fact, it is to the advantage of theology that it should be so, as this avoids the injection of theologico-normative assumptions into biblico-historical description. There is no pure theological method, either for Biblical theology or for theology in a more general sense. Therefore, in systematic theology, a framework which is constructed must leave freedom for the methods of exegesis and take into account the possibility that the results of exegesis can be revised. However, such a revision does not depend uniquely on theological considerations, since exegesis uses methods which lie beyond its own province. These methods are elaborated independently of theological concerns, and they are held in common by biblical study with other neighbouring fields of enquiry. Theology is not governed by its own self-appointed procedures, and the methods which determine its way of working and its shape do not lie totally within the sphere of its jurisdiction. The methods of theological study as a whole are determined non-theologically.[45]

---

45. See Barr's statements in *JTS* 25:281f.; in *Weerwoord* (Nykerk, 1974), pp. 9ff.; and "Does Biblical Study Still Belong to Theology?"

This thought is illustrated in the following way:

> . . . theology . . . is not a single subject in the sense in which economics or philosophy or English, is a single subject. Rather, it is a constellation of different fields and subjects held together by the fact that they are studied as they relate to God, to the church, its work and its tradition, and to the Bible. There is no specific theological method or methodology that covers all the ground: on the contrary, the methods are in large measure drawn from principles of method already standard within [other disciplines] . . . and these are applied as is appropriate to much of the material that is agreed to come within the purview of a faculty of theology.[46]

Barr is not just saying in this that there is no one theological method which can claim ultimately to be the right one. His conception of the matter is a criticism of the idea of the possibility of attempting to state a method which can cover all the disciplines involved in a unified theological statement of approach. Theology is a collection of different processes, and there is no principle held in common among them all which would permit the formulation of a statement of theological method. Fundamental to this perspective is Barr's conception that theology as such in a proper sense involves a statement of faith. A theological statement of faith is to be distinguished from a descriptive statement which states the evidence without making a normative formulation of it. The general term "theological" can be used in a comprehensive sense to cover both the descriptive process and the normative statement of faith. In the strict sense a theological statement is one which involves an affirmation which goes beyond a description of the evidence.[47]

When Barr states the opinion that there is no one theological method, it may be understood that he is using "theological" in the general sense. There is no method which is common to the ensemble of processes in the broad theological field. Moreover, there is no one approach which may hold together the descriptive and the normative aspects of theological work. Barr sees these as lying on different levels which, though separate, may be related one to another. They are characterised by a relation of relative independence which does not exclude a certain complementarity. Such complementarity as may

---

46. "Does Biblical Study Still Belong to Theology?," p. 4.
47. Ibid., pp. 7f.

exist does not, however, permit the statement of a common theological method.

Two remarks can be made concerning Barr's statement on theological method. Fundamental to this is the idea that faith is limited to the domain of normative statements about God. Because of this limitation of faith and its confinement in the domain of religious affirmation of personal or ecclesial belief, there is no common method for theology in the broad sense. To this limited concept of faith and its function in theological work as a whole there corresponds the idea that it is not necessary in the domain of descriptive study to have any faith commitment. Truth is attained in terms of correspondence to the evidence in the interpretation given to the facts available. In the area of descriptive study in theology in the broad sense the work can be done by believer and unbeliever alike. The principles of the descriptive study are determined not theologically in the light of questions of normativity, but by other disciplines. The aim of this study is to reach a high degree of objectivity in the stating of the evidence. To the extent that this is achieved, it may be concluded that the scholar has satisfied the criteria of veracity in his presentation. In this domain faith is not in question, as the matter can be properly stated without reference to faith concerns. Objectivity stands here apart from faith.

This illustrates quite well the consequences in theological interpretation of Barr's view of the biblical tradition as a developing human process which can be approached without appeals to revelation or supernatural interventions. There is an interplay between how Barr conceives of the tradition and how he considers its interpretation. The formation of the tradition is interpreted in terms of principles which are not strictly "theological." Man interprets man. Just as there is a duality between God and the tradition process, so also there is a duality between the high degree of objectivity of historical research and normative faith affirmations. There is no organic unity of the divine and human in history in revelation; also there is no unity of theological method, but different levels of study. To be sure, Barr seeks to overcome this duality. God is present as the tradition process unfolds "in the Spirit"; faith seeks to relate itself to the results of descriptive study by using the material provided by it in normative formulations. What is not totally reassuring in both cases is the way

Barr relates the divine and the human. In both cases there appears to be a marked limitation of the divine elements to the scope of the human factor. God's purpose is limited by the human factors of the situation, and in spite of his "contact" with the situation, this receives no interpretation other than the human. Likewise, in the interpretation of the texts the faith affirmation which is possible depends on the results of lower levels of study and is made accountable to these. Faith is restricted to what is historically possible in terms of descriptive reconstruction.

The question which is not really faced in Barr's work is as to whether this restriction of faith to the religious domain is in fact justified. Barr seems to take it for granted that such a restriction is justified and necessary and also that faith does not enter into the domain of descriptive study. The quality of descriptive study is not determined by a faith commitment, but by the fact that a high degree of objectivity is obtained, even though this is never total. Barr does not seem to entertain the possibility that on the level of descriptive study some kind of faith commitment of one sort or another may be in fact present. Yet, as soon as it is held that in descriptive study a statement of the evidence which corresponds to the reality of the situation is achieved, this would seem to imply that this is in fact possible and that there is some kind of morality operative in distinguishing truth from error. What is the basis of this possibility? Does man possess a basic propensity for truth in an autonomous sense, or is there some transcendent foundation for truth to be taken into account? As a Christian theologian, Barr might have asked the question as to whether man is capable of truth apart from faith in God. But because such a question is apparently not raised, the duality between faith which is personal belief and knowledge of truth objectively held remains. This means that there is no pure theological method, as theological statements which are faith qualified are not called upon to establish the criteria of truth in the realm of descriptive study.

These considerations of theological method have already directed us into the second aspect of the duality of the divine and human in interpretation. This concerns the relation Barr sees between the various levels of theological activity. It is already implied in the affirmation that there is no pure theological method. The lower levels of theological study which use the methods of linguistics or history, for example, can work without involvement in theological decisions. Yet they are essential to the statements made on the higher (theologico-normative) level:

> . . . the viability of proposals made on these higher levels never rests on theological considerations alone, but rests on the data of the lower levels where it is subject to non-theological control.[48]

Obviously, for Barr, to talk of the lower levels of study implies no disparagement. On the contrary, to the extent that theology must relate itself to them, theology depends on them for its material. They determine their own criteria of veracity independently of theological considerations. This situates Barr's attitude to the historical critical method. There is a certain autonomy of the historical method over against theological constructions. It is not that the method is taken by Barr as axiomatic in itself. However, its validity is independent of theological considerations. The criticisms of Barr are made not on the grounds that the method clashes with a view of the Bible's normativity, but rather that it has been too narrowly applied. The intentionalism characteristic of historical criticism must be broadened to include other perspectives.[49]

In fact, from a critical point of view, Barr's distinction between the historical and the theological levels of study has the great value of freeing the historical aspect of study from theological decisions which prevented its being used in a positive way. Independently of normative considerations it can, on a different level of study, be used in a more beneficial way for theology. In reconstructing the development of Israel's traditions in an historical sense, without the pressure of normative considerations, it uncovers historically the situations in which Israel knew God. In this sense it contributes to the understanding of the Bible as classical model of the faith of the people of God through the reconstruction of the situations in which that faith was developed. Thus historical reconstruction is integrated into the theological understanding of Scripture as a model of faith. Barr's approach could be stated something like this:

— the Bible as a human document expressing the faith of Israel

---

48. Ibid., p. 16.
49. *ONI*, pp. 147f., 180f.

and the church is to be approached as other texts are.
— historical criticism aids in the reconstruction of the development of the various traditions of Scripture.
— theological significance can be seen in the light of the connections established by historical research.
— thus historical reconstruction aids in the consideration of the
Bible as a paradigm of faith.[50]

This attempt to relate historical study and theology is certainly a
very stimulating one by comparison with other approaches which
paid lip service to historical criticism but did not seek to unite it with
theological statement on the one hand, or which made historical research an end in itself.

However, it may still be asked whether Barr has succeeded in integrating the historical approach and theologico-normative statements
in a way which is theologically meaningful. In his statement, Barr
affirms the necessity of a literary-historical approach to the biblical
texts without reducing the sense of the biblical tradition to a supra-
temporal kernel of redemptive history or dissolving history into a
historicity of existence.[51] Even though the dichotomies between the
historical study of the biblical texts and the object of faith inherent in
these positions are avoided, there remains in Barr's interpretation of
the biblical texts through his modified historical method a certain
duality between the two forms of "theological" statement. The lack
of integration of the divine and the human factors with reference to
the Scriptures is reflected in Barr's discerning different levels of study.
The limitation of faith affirmations to a "higher" domain different
from that of descriptive study is predicated on Barr's supposition that
there is no divine revelation of truth in the human domain on the
level of historico-temporal realities. This being so, historical research
and/or literary description are concerned largely with human situations. They may indicate the way Israel or the church expressed
faith in God and the situation in which this faith was operative, but
they do not disclose the object of faith in terms of an objective truth-
content.

The normative statement lies, therefore, on a level other than

---

50. Ibid., p. 198; *BMW*, pp. 162ff.
51. Cf. also on this the remarks of W. Pannenberg in *Basic Questions in
Theology* (London, 1970), I:15-80.

that of the historico-literary examination of the texts. The "lower" level study does not give a normative formulation to which faith relates itself. On this level truth is sought in terms of the high level of objectivity in historical or literary research, but this is something other than the truth which is sought by faith in the theological normative domain. In other words, Barr's distinction of the levels of study of Scripture would not seem to get over the problem of relating the results of historical study to the way faith assertions refer to an object beyond themselves. For if the lower level of study is descriptive and limited to the human situation, it cannot found faith in an objective way with reference to a reality beyond itself. Criticism does not serve to provide a foundation for faith in God. This being the case, when faith is spoken of in terms of normative theological declarations, these are not integrated with the historical material itself, but something which lies on another plane. Faith tacks on its belief in making reference to the historical material, but without seeking any verification from an appeal to an objective historical truth which would provide a foundation for faith.

The differentiation of the historico-descriptive from the theological domain proper on different levels and the improbability of integrating these in such a way to give faith a positive truth content with reference to history is illustrative of the duality in interpretation which arises in the context of the fundamental duality of the divine and the human in Barr's thought. Once the Scripture is considered as a human document and the human factor is made the primary one in its interpretation, the inevitable result is that faith can find no grounding in a truth of God which can be located in Scripture or in the revelation of which Scripture speaks. It has no transcendent foundation which becomes transparent in the context of this-worldly realities. Barr attempts to meet this problem by treating faith in a human way. The Bible expresses the faith in God of Israel and the church in the course of history, and as such is a paradigm of Christian faith. It does not reveal an objective grounding of faith but discloses a model of what faith in God might be which is illuminating for another situation. This faith is related to the presence of the Spirit guiding the people of God. This, however, does not provide an assurance that the expression of faith is adequate to its object, nor would it seem to be possible to accomplish this without referring faith to a revelation of God.

Thus it may well be considered, in spite of Barr's reference to the
Bible as a model of faith, and the idea that this model is formed in
the presence of the Spirit who continues active among the people of
God today, that the human subjectivity of this faith lacks correspondence with a reality outside of itself. J. I. Packer's evaluation of
Barr's theology in the following way might well come quite close to
the mark:

> Barr is opting for a theological programme which sees Christianity
> as an historical phenomenon of which biblical and theological
> study is one continuing aspect, and he views the theological task
> humanistically as a venture in analytical description and free con-
> struction. On his programme, what authority the end-product has
> will presumably be decided by estimating its coherence as an
> historical analysis on the one hand and its vitality as a stimulus to
> discussion on the other; and the question of its *truth,* in the sense
> of whether it squares with God's view of things or not, will never
> be raised.[52]

Packer is quite right in indicating this fundamental problem of the
nature of the truth of the theological constructs elaborated in the context of a view which centres on the analysis of the material in terms
of a human model of faith and seeks a reconstruction of that model in
today's terms. Ultimately, when Scripture is considered as a human
document and theology is conceived of as analysis and theological reconstruction, even though reference to the analogy of Spirit and people
of God is made, very little can be said about truth as such, but only what
we believe to be true by faith. But on these terms it is hardly possible
to say that what the church or the individual believes to be true in
faith actually bears any reference other than a subjective one to a
reality which lies beyond the subjective statement of belief.

The duality of the divine and the human in Barr's conception of
Scripture has its issue in a duality of historical and theological statement in which the historical knowledge as a descriptive field of enquiry is divided from faith considerations. Conversely, faith no longer
seeks its foundation in relation to certain truths which can be stated
in an objective way by reference to spatio-temporal contingencies.
In seeking to give "a rational account" of the status of Scripture,

---

52. J. I. Packer, in *God's Inerrant Word,* ed. J. W. Montgomery (Minneapolis, 1974), p. 58.

Barr seems to have separated faith and knowledge from each other. When man's ability to approach the questions of Scripture in a rational sense centred on the primacy of human analysis is taken as the way of doing theology, considerations of faith seem to be sublimated into a non-objective realm.

When faith in a Christian theology is situated in a non-objective realm over against that of spatio-temporal realities, the status of the judgments made about historical reality can scarcely be avoided. Barr, as we have pointed out, rejects a referential view of the content of the Bible and thus the possibility of an objective content for faith based on the references of Scripture to objects beyond itself—God, the world, historical events of salvation. He criticises fundamentalists who seek to maintain some sort of consistency between the form of the texts and external realities involved. Inerrancy seeks correspondence with the facts of the external world. Fundamentalism still works with a philosophical view derived from "a pre-Kantian eighteenth century rationalism."[53] Yet Barr's own position concerning what constitutes objectivity remains far from certain. Barr seems to propose a view of objective truth which can be constituted on the basis of critical research. Thus Barr says in a footnote tucked away in *BMW*: "Perhaps theology has to regard philosophical thoughts as something 'that has been given given to us' through the actuality of the world and of the human mind."[54] The matter does not seem to be pursued further. Barr gives the impression of taking for granted that man can in critical enquiry reach a sufficient conception of the truth and that such an approach can also be applied to the theological material of the Bible. The modern consciousness is the key to questions of what is possible and not possible in the domain of knowledge. The basis of this implicit epistemology is not clarified and the attempt to critically review the assumptions of such an epistemology in the light of faith in God is nowhere accomplished. Perhaps the main difference between Barr and the fundamentalist after all is that Barr is "a post-Kantian twentieth-century rationalist."[55]

---

53. *F,* p. 272.
54. *BMW,* p. 94, n. 7.
55. Barr, in a rather tongue-in-cheek rejoinder to some arguments of D. Hill in his *Greek Words and Hebrew Meanings* (Cambridge, 1967), refers to an element in his thought, namely, the tradition of Scottish common sense philosophy. His difference with Hill might be *within* this tradition. Barr also points out that

A third way in which the fundamental duality of the divine and human in Barr's thought is reflected in terms of interpretation is in the dichotomy which exists between the diversity of the tradition and the diversity this implies for interpretation, over against the oneness of God which transcends the tradition history but lies behind it as an ultimate form of unity. The unity of the various elements is thus the unity of the one God who "has a history." In this respect once again we are faced by a duality between the historical knowledge of the tradition as diverse, and the faith in the unity of the one God who is above the historical diversities.

Barr has pointed out that the christological analogy, though theologically impressive, is little use in solving the interpretative problems of biblical scholarship. The focus of study has moved from the question of the divine and human with reference to Scripture to the difference between ancient and modern.[56] This shift of focus implies a move away from the centrality of ontological categories to the predominance of historical considerations. In this respect the biblical texts are interpreted as a developing historical tradition in a human sense and the question concerns the relation of the human point of view as it was then in distinction from our point of view in the twentieth century. The move from the category of the unity of the divine and human results in considering the Bible as a human document, therefore diverse in its historical moments and above all different from our situation today. In advocating such an approach, which takes the human aspect of Scripture as the one we interpret, Barr posits a diversity of human expression in the biblical tradition; to this corresponds a diversity of interpretation of the material in terms of processes of study and a diversity of possible theological construction today. J. I. Packer is to the point, once again, when he proposes that

---

it is important to discover why common sense rules out certain interpretations when it does so, not simply that it does. See *Biblica* 49:384f. It could be remarked that Warfield, the Princeton theologian, also stands in the common sense tradition (*F,* pp. 270ff. See also J. C. Vander Stelt, *Philosophy and Scripture* [Marlton, N. J., 1978], passim). The difference between Barr and Warfield could also be one in the common sense tradition. Yet Barr does not seem to have avoided doing what he accuses Hill of indulging in, as he has not really stated on what grounds his common sense rules out the interpretation of Warfield et al. That he does so on the basis of the criteria of modern criticism does not constitute a reason why this should be so.

56. *IDB*(S), p. 795.

"current exegesis, which has theological pluralism in its presuppositions and its method, has such pluralism in abundance in its conclusions."[57] We are, according to Barr, in the same unbroken line of tradition which continues to the present. Diversity in the human model of Scripture tallies with one diversity of present theologies. The methods of interpreting the classic model are similarly diverse.

We have made the point (sec. 4.2.1) that there is a kind of hermeneutical circle operational in Barr's presentation of the Scripture and its interpretation. Diversity is present in the biblical material, its interpretation, and in the church tradition today. The question remains as to the point at which one joins this particular scheme of interpretation. This would appear to be, as Packer puts it, a question concerning a presupposition. Neither the diversity of the scriptural material itself, nor the diversity of possible interpretations, nor even the different possibilities of method of interpretations necessarily indicates that the Bible is in fact the crystallisation of a human tradition rather than a revelation of God in human language. The constitutive factor in Barr's approach, then, is not the decision to treat the Bible from the standpoint of its diversity, but the connection of the diversity to an immanent human process in a way exclusive of a revelation in Scripture. This point itself would seem to be an assumption on Barr's part which is implied in his rejection of the model provided by the christological analogy.

It is quite expected that on these grounds Barr should reject the older notion that Scripture is self-interpreting as the Word of God. This is replaced by the differentiation between the meaning of the Scripture as it was understood then and its meaning today. Thus history is what we understand by history now. The history of tradition is therefore constructed in such a way now to make it different from the way it was considered in biblical times. This historical construct creates a picture of the biblical situation different from that which is found on the surface of the text, but also indicates the historical difference between that situation and our present one. In this setting there is not much likelihood of producing a view of the unity of the biblical tradition. If this were achieved, it would not be applicable to a different historical moment as normative. The

---

57. Packer, art. cit., p. 59.

tradition is therefore diverse in itself and distant from our historical situation. The unity of the tradition cannot be stated in terms of historical constructions which tend to uncover a great diversity. Unity in respect to this process is found in the one God, the God of Israel and Father of Jesus. This is appropriated in faith. Faith perceives the presence of God, who is beyond this diversity, yet in whom there is a unity of the whole diverse process. However, this unity cannot be apprehended in the multiplex character of the tradition, where it is perceived only fractionally. On this issue, once again, we can discern the same fundamental duality in Barr's thought between the human diversity of the historical tradition and its interpretation and the integral unity of God which is not constitutive of the historical unity of the tradition, the biblical message, but which is beyond the historical contingencies. But if this is the case, on what grounds do we proceed to posit the oneness of divine unity from the multiplicity of historical situations?

A fourth aspect of the question under discussion concerns the nature of biblical language and its relation to revelation. No attempt has been made in this work to criticise Barr's earlier work in semantics on the basis of more recent advances in the discipline. Barr's contribution to the discussion of the nature of biblical language is not to be measured by reference to such later advances, but rather in the context of the discussion which preceded Barr's critique. It is in consideration of this that full credit must be given to Barr for the innovative nature of his critique in the field of theology, even though this critique be articulated on the basis of quite limited principles.[58] Barr's emphasis on the need to direct the search for meaning to the examination of larger units of sense rather than to the atomistic consideration of words as bearers of meaning and on the usefulness of translation were positive propositions. The affirmation that the distinctiveness of biblical thought is on the level of what the writers say, not in the words as individual units, provided a useful corrective to the then current biblical concept theology. The proposition that a fuller examination of the contexts was needed in exegesis could be positive only in terms of biblical interpretation.

The arguments advanced against Barr's work which criticised it

---

58. See the remarks of C. Payot in *Revue de Theologie et de Philosophie* (1968), pp. 230ff.

of being formalistic and negative and of cutting through the positive relation of language and thought very often seem to have missed the mark.[59] Barr's position stated in *SBL* does not constitute a denial that thought and language are related, but situates the relation at another level than that which is accepted by his critics. Thus Barr proposes that there is no direct relation between the words used and the message. The social convention of language must be taken into account as the middle term between linguistic material and the message proclaimed. The mind of the writer, his linguistic consciousness, is formed by the social convention of language, which itself is an arbitrary convention.[60] This accent on the link of the human mind and the social convention of language has certain consequences for interpretation which Barr has followed through. It means that theology cannot be read off from the text of Scripture, but the mind, the intention, of the author must be taken into account in establishing interpretation. Thus Barr's use of structuralism as a means of interpretation is limited and eclectic.[61] Barr does not adopt a totally structuralist approach to interpretation as he does not seem to want to deny the relevance of the intentionalism of historical criticism. He rather tries to adapt insights from both methods in admitting the validity of various different processes for reading the Scripture. In fact, in this respect Barr seems to perceive a certain complementarity in interpretation between the linguistic implications of a structuralist method and the historical implications of the intentionalism of historical criticism. Both of these function in their domain against a referential way of reading theology from the lexical structure and relating the events of the text directly to historical reality. To understand the meaning of the linguistic form of the text it is necessary to take into account the fact of the arbitrary convention of language; likewise the historical reference of the text must be understood in the light of the writer's intention and milieu.

Taken together, these considerations from the two different disciplines constitute a fundamental criticism of biblical concept theology

---

59. See, for example, T. Boman, *SJT* 15:319ff.; M. Sekine in *VT*(S), 9:74; G. E. Wright in *Int* 22:83ff.; D. Hill, op. cit.,; also Barr's replies in *BWT*, pp. 170ff., and *Biblica*, loc. cit.

60. *SBL*, pp. 213f.; *BWT*, pp. 204f.

61. As pointed out by Payot, art. cit., and Tångberg, in *The Bible Translator* 24:306.

based on a pattern of redemptive events. It is no longer possible to use redemptive event as a central category for the interpretation of the biblical material. This recognition of the fact of the arbitrary nature of language as a social convention and of the intention of the writer is an element within the context of Barr's view of the Scripture as a human text, which favours the acknowledgment of the diversity of the Scripture as the product of the human mind. The factors appealed to in the BTM as illustrative of the unity of Scripture, namely, the concepts and events connected with revelation, cease to be compelling factors in interpretation. This criticism opens the way to a reformulation of the notions of inspiration and revelation in the context of a consideration of the Scripture as an expression of the multiplex tradition of the people of God.

If Barr can hardly be justly accused of formalism or positivism in so far as his definition of the relation of thought and language is concerned, there is perhaps another level on which a question may be raised. If the relation between words or linguistic structure and the message or the reality referred to is an indirect one through the social linguistic conscience, the question remains as to what are the particular influences present in the formation of this social conscience. The limitation of Barr's study of biblical semantics may lie in the fact that it makes little effort to place the formal study of the meaning of biblical language into contact with the particular socio-cultural setting in which *this* language functioned meaningfully. It might be said that this limitation of Barr's study of semantics is self-imposed. In the first pages of *SBL* Barr refers to his procedure in these terms:

> . . . traditional philosophical (and of course theological) beliefs have been an obstacle to the accurate evaluation of linguistic phenomena, [but] I shall make no attempt to suggest a better philosophy of language. I do not suppose that one can make linguistics a substitute for a philosophy of language, but I assume that by studying language linguistically one is making a genuine and valid contribution to the understanding of it, however much more remains to be done . . . in the area of philosophy.[62]

In the same place Barr says of his work: ". . . there is no intention here to separate the biblical language from other language as belonging to a different kind—quite the reverse." These quotations indicate

---

62. *SBL*, p. 2.

the limitations of Barr's approach to biblical language. His linguistic comments, although having implications for theology, tend to be of a descriptive nature centred upon questions of usage, and for this reason fail to reach a statement of what might be the particular character of biblical language.

Barr does, it is true, make some allowances that the semantics of a theological tradition may have a special aspect, on the basis of two considerations. A particular religious tradition may have certain semantic developments peculiar to it beyond the characters of everyday speech. Also the semantics of a religious tradition will be more axed on past usage than daily speech is, as the use of particular expressions is related to prior usage, and continuity of belief in the tradition is important.[63] However, beyond these very basic considerations, little effort has been made by Barr to integrate semantic usage with the behavioural patterns of the religious community. Perhaps it may be said that Barr does not carry these two above considerations far enough in their practical application. Barr's positive contribution to biblical semantics might have been greater had he sought an integration of the linguistic patterns of the text with the field of religious behaviour which provides the context in which the texts have their meaning.

Recently this factor has been pointed to by J. Lyons:

> Any meaningful linguistic unit . . . has meaning in context. The context of the utterance is the situation in which it occurs. . . . The concept of "situation" is fundamental for semantic statement. . . . Situation must be given equal weight with linguistic form in semantic theory.[64]

K. Pike points out that since language is a form of human behaviour, a structure must be sought which will permit the explanation of the verbal and non-verbal aspects of behaviour in a single framework as complementary elements.[65] In this perspective the function of semantics would be not to regulate the function of words in sentences, but the structural organisation of discourse in terms of large unities[66]

---

63. Ibid., pp. 3f.
64. J. Lyons, *Structural Semantics* (Oxford, 1963), pp. 23f.
65. K. L. Pike, *Language in Relation to a Unified Theory of the Structure of Human Behavior* (The Hague, 1967), chaps. 1–5.
66. See A. J. Greimas, *Sémantique Structurale* (Paris, 1966), and E. Benveniste, *Problèmes de Linguistique Générale* (Paris, 1974), II:91ff.

perhaps incorporating a consideration of the *Sitz im Leben* of the discourse.[67]

It is in this sense that B. S. Childs has made some criticisms of Barr's semantic approach. In particular he thinks that Barr's descriptive effort is weakened by the fact that it is not related to an historical method which would take account of the tradition in its development in exegesis. On these lines Childs remarked:

> . . . it is doubtful whether the proposed method of procedure can make a positive contribution, since it tends to remain almost entirely on the level of descriptive semantics with little cognizance of the depth of dimension which form-critical analysis has opened up in the study of words.[68]

K. Koch has pointed to the same possibility offered by the form critical approach of establishing the correspondence between the literary types of the biblical text and the sphere of existence in which they were formed. This proposes an integration of literary study and the study of the socio-cultural milieu. The literary forms correspond "with regularly recurring events and needs of a particular way of life, out of which the literary types arose naturally."[69] Barr's approach to biblical semantics might have been rather more constructive if an attempt had been made to coordinate in similar fashion the verbal and non-verbal aspects of meaning.[70]

However, if this criticism can be made concerning the lack of a broader perspective in Barr's work, it would be a wrong interpretation of Barr's intention to carry it too far. If Barr himself does not

---

67. Payot, art. cit., ad loc., thinks Barr does not give sufficient place to units of discourse which are longer in *SBL* and *BMW*. His approach is too eclectic and empirical. Thus Payot thinks Barr falls back into a modified lexical approach. Barr is well aware of the need to work with longer units of discourse. For example, in an earlier article, "Christ in Gospel and Creed," *SJT* 8:233, we read that the whole book of Mark is a christological text, narrating Jesus' dealings with men. Barr does not seem to have developed this insight in any detail in his semantic work.

68. B. S. Childs, *Memory and Tradition in Israel* (London, 1962), p. 84n. See also his review of *SBL* in *JBL* 80:374ff.

69. A. Alt, quoted by K. Koch, *The Growth of Biblical Tradition* (London, 1969), p. 27.

70. D. Hill makes a similar criticism, op. cit., pp. 6ff. See also P. R. Ackroyd, "Meaning and Exegesis," in *Words and Meanings,* ed. Ackroyd and B. Lindars (Cambridge, 1968), and J. F. A. Sawyer, *Semantics in Biblical Research* (London, 1972), pp. 112ff.

COMMENTS ON SOME BASIC ISSUES OF BARR'S WORK 331

attempt in his linguistic analyses to develop a study of meaning which combines linguistic and non-linguistic aspects, it is not that he does not account for this as a specific possibility. In the conclusion of *SBL* Barr explicitly states: "The valid and correct analysis and description of religious structures is an essential correlate of linguistic progress in much of the semantic field."[71] The criticisms of formalism with reference to Barr's work can apply only to the actual way Barr carries through his argument, but not to his theoretical perception of the nature of semantic analysis. If Barr's linguistic criticisms have remained largely on a formal level, this may have been the approach best adapted to Barr's intention and also to the pioneering nature of his semantic reflexions in a theological context.

Nevertheless, in spite of these considerations, there appears in the same passage of *SBL* an illustration of the duality between the divine and human elements in Barr's thinking in the field of linguistic interpretation. It could be termed to be a duality between the nature of language as human and revelation. We have seen above that Barr thinks that traditional philosophical and theological beliefs have been an obstacle to the exactness of the evaluation of linguistic phenomena. Barr does not propose a new philosophy (or theology) of language. This is true in a way, but in another way it is not true, as it is quite plain that were Barr to propose a philosophy of language or adopt another in modified form for theological application, this would be a philosophy based on purely immanent considerations. In a certain way, Barr has a philosophy and a theology of language just as soon as he supposes that language as a human phenomenon can be meaningful apart from its rooting in the divine transcendence of meaning. The duality we are speaking of comes to light in this affirmation:

> It seems to me that the modern movement towards biblical theology has made it rather harder for the non-theological linguist to make this correlation [i.e., between religious structures and linguistics]. It is for theologians here, it seems to me, to make it clear that, whatever their own ideas about biblical theology may be, what they ask from the non-theological linguist is not what the latter would understand as "theology," but rather a description of religious phenomena. This should be all the easier inasmuch as a very large area of biblical theology is in fact religious description, however much it differentiates itself in theory. It is

---

71. *SBL,* p. 293.

reasonable for the theologian on the other hand to ask that the non-theological biblical scholar be prepared to give an account of what a Jeremiah or an Ezra was saying and what, as he sees it, was in his mind. The thought of such men, and this means their religious and theological thought, is a foremost part of the facts of the culture, the linguistic aspect of which it is the task of the linguist to understand.[72]

This makes it evident that Barr's linguistic critique is articulated on the assumption that the language as an aspect of human culture can be studied in a descriptive way without reference such as was made in the BTM to considerations of revelation. The descriptive approach to the domain of human biblical language is possible without reference to theological considerations of normativity. That is, when Barr refers to the correlation of linguistic meaning and cultural situation, he is thinking of a description of biblical language on a purely immanent basis, without reference to revelation. The mind of the writers is part of the cultural matrix, not a mind revelatory of the divine mind. In this respect we recall Barr's discussions about the expression, "Word of God," and his remark to the effect that we have no idea what the speaking of God might mean, our understanding of this being other than that of the prophets. There is no special revelation of truth in linguistic form in Scripture; the Bible is described linguistically in human terms.

Once again, Barr's considering the Scripture in "one element" human terms produces a duality between the text as expressive of the human mind of the writers and the reality of God. Language in the Bible has no special status owing to a connection with revelation. Theologians who do not accept Barr's view of the Bible may well doubt that Barr's semantics can really attain the correlation with the situation he seeks because of the elimination of situations in which God makes himself known in history.

5.5. *The question of the reality of faith*

The third aspect of the duality in Barr's work which is a consequence of the two aspects discussed has been indicated at several points in the preceding exposition. Once the tradition of Scripture is considered a classic model of faith and interpreted as such, there arises

---

72. Idem.

a duality centred on the problem of the nature of faith in relation to the reality of God and of salvation. A duality exists between the subjective aspect of faith and the reality of its object. Where, then, might certainty be said to be found by Barr?

The answer to this question is not given in any place in Barr's work in a straightforward discussion of the nature of faith. It can be given only in an indirect way on consideration of the structure of Barr's general theological approach and of various remarks made in reaction to fundamentalist doctrines. In spite of these difficulties, some basic aspects of the nature of certainty can be indicated.

For Barr it is apparent that the fundamentalist approach to the object of faith is unsatisfactory. Faith is not grounded by reference to truth sought objectively in terms of historical and doctrinal correspondence. The former way of locating the certainty of faith in the revelation of truth in the Bible which assured rooting in the external realities of history is roundly criticised by Barr. The biblical texts cannot be taken as fundamentalists see them, as "close transcripts of divine reality."[73] Modern criticism has modified the way we consider the Bible and implies changes in the traditional doctrines such as the doctrine of God, of the person of Christ, or our idea of miracle.[74] Greater changes are to come, and these are not for the worse, as the reactionary fundamentalist fears, but for the better. In the sphere of these changes, the work of criticism has been the means of advancement and liberation from the view of faith as functioning with reference to factual certainty. Barr's confidence in the correctness of the enterprise of critical reconstruction of Christian faith is quite impressive in its own way. He writes: "Such things as the rise of liberal theology or the rise of biblical criticism at the least may be positive elements in the movement of the world process towards its consummation."[75]

Some of the changes Barr's work indicates have been already mentioned. The standard image of the perfection of God is less satisfactory than one which proposes a God involved in history who "can be argued out of positions he has already taken up";[76] the classic formulations of christological orthodoxy are not necessarily com-

---

73. *F*, p. 334.
74. *F*, pp. 185f.

75. *F*, p. 340.
76. *F*, p. 277.

patible with present discussion which may be unorthodox or heretical in terms of them;[77] revelation and authority are not the first things to be stated in Christian belief, from which theology is derived. Such alterations as are to be made on the basis of the freedom of biblical criticism are both legitimate and necessary.[78] The main change of perspective in Barr's work by comparison with the former way of basing theology on a consideration of revelation, is the function Barr attaches to Scripture as a model of faith. The transformations undergone in a more general theological way are applications of this fundamental difference in the doctrine of Scripture.

By taking the Bible as the crystallisation of the processes of development in a human tradition, the central function of Scripture is located in the religious aspect of the text. The Bible is not primarily a source book of doctrine or a record of saving events, but above all a witness to the faith of the people of God which bears witness to the contact with the living God. The significance of Scripture as model of faith is not found in that it conveys essential information which provides a cognitive foundation for faith, but in that it illuminates us as to the nature of faith as dynamic trust in God. As a paradigm of Christian faith the Bible points to the nature of faith in terms of the significance of the relationship of trust in God which forms the life of the people of God.

It is perhaps superfluous to point to the difference between this conception of faith and the classic formulations, such as that of the Westminster Confession: "By this faith, a Christian believeth to be true whatever is revealed in the Word, for the authority of God Himself speaking therein" (XIV.2). Barr turns the nature of faith around from being something whose substance is revealed by God and therefore a "grace" given in connection with God's enabling, to the expression of a dynamic human trust in God through contact with the Spirit. The Bible bears witness to this renewing faith in contact with the Spirit; as a model it functions to give significance to the correlation the believer of the present makes with the past experience of faith of the people of God. The significance of the Bible is not in the information it provides on the level of correspondence with fact, but

---

77. *F*, p. 172.
78. *F*, pp. 106f.

in the significance of the human act of faith in contact with the Spirit which is portrayed.

This effort to account for the status of Scripture as a model of faith which can be correlated with like transforming faith in the present life of the church "in the Spirit" cannot but raise the issue of the reality of faith in relation to the object of faith. What measure of parity between a formulation of faith as human trust and the object to which trust is directed can be expected on Barr's terms? This issue has not been given a very concise airing in Barr's work. Either it does not seem to present a very real problem for him, or perhaps more precisely it might be answered in terms of the general notion of the guidance of the Holy Spirit, whereby the people of God are led in new situations through obedience by reference to the classic biblical model. The accent is on obedience and trust in different historical situations rather than the rightness or wrongness of our ideas of God. In the developing tradition there is a struggle of the people of God with each other and with God which can be described as obedience or disobedience of sinful human individuals with reference to the leading of the Spirit. The Bible witnesses to this struggle and to the life-renewing power of faith in God, which we might seek to know in each new situation.

Few Christians, even fundamentalists, will deny that the Bible gives models of faith or that its primary function is religious. The Bible is more than a book of objective information; it does bespeak the importance of life-renewing power. Carl Henry, in his review of *Fundamentalism,* has recognised this but has seen also the problem beyond this aspect of the matter by saying: "What evangelicals reject is the practice of reducing the Bible's authoritative function to its life-transforming impact alone and of pushing aside its role as the bearer of divinely revealed ideas (propositional truths guaranteed by God)."[79] What Barr fails to do is to provide a foundation for the obedience of faith in the life-transforming truth of God which is known to man because made known by God. Because of this, faith lacks the reality of a contact with the object to which it is directed. Its only reality can be the human subjective expression of faith which lacks in corres-

---

79. C. Henry, "Those Incomprehensible British Fundamentalists," *Christianity Today* 22:1207.

pondence to the object of faith. Ultimately it is not able to tell us whether its object really exists or whether its perception of the object of faith is in accordance with the object itself. It can speak of of life-renewal in the contact with the Spirit, but not necessarily with reference to the finished work of redemption of God in Jesus Christ. To do this would be to return to a view of faith based on revelation.

What this seems to run out to is that instead of a christological analogy, here we end up with pneumatological duality. The Spirit works in human situations and traditions, but his presence is so imperceptible that it leaves us with a mere conviction of his work. This stops short of a statement of truth which would serve as a ground of faith. But because this faith is not rooted in the truth borne by the witness of the Spirit, it is not only lacking in objective rooting with reference to truth in terms of objective realities, but also with reference to its divine object. To separate faith from truth revealed by God in history is also to uproot it from its foundation in God as Lord of history. Faith stands here in a dual relation both to the possibility of a historical reference, and to the reality of which it speaks. The leading of the Spirit which results in faith does not provide a foundation for faith which is grounded in the reality of the object of which faith speaks. This is the inevitable consequence of a system which wishes to make no appeals to supernatural interventions in historical reality, but to explain the function of Scripture in terms of a human document.

5.6. *Résumé of the problem*

Barr's work, as we saw in our first chapter, included at an early stage of its development a penetrating critique of the christological analogy. The way of considering Scripture with reference to a correlation of the divine and human elements has broken down. Barr's own suggestions regarding the status and the interpretation of Scripture are predicated on the assumption that the Scripture can be described and exegeted in a way which makes no appeal to the presence of a divine element in the texts. "Scripture does not come into existence by direct action of God, but a human action which is a reflex of contact with God."[80] Thus when Barr aims at "encouraging the

---

80. *ONI,* p. 163.

Scripture to speak freely," this can be taken as an attempt to listen to the message of faith which comes to us as a human statement in the Scripture. The human elements of the Bible are freed from the compulsion to explain them as aspects of an entity whose meaning originates in the divine will. In interpretation the text speaks freely in a human sense when its meaning is liberated from the connection with a revelation which is the object of the witness. Barr proposes that it is beneficial to theology when we approach the Scripture in terms of this sort of freedom of analysis and construction. This emphasis on the humanity of the text constitutes a rejection of analogical thinking in general, but of the christological analogy which was the most popular form of analogical thinking in Protestantism in recent years. To this turning away from an analogical approach corresponds an increased sensitivity to the mythico-literary aspect of the Scripture.[81]

The problem of biblical interpretation is therefore no longer that of the divine and human elements, but of the past and the present. Barr seeks to overcome this particular historical difficulty in terms of the human witness to contact with the Spirit which gives the tradition a unity in the presence of the Spirit. To the freedom of analysis and interpretation of the Scripture as human document, corresponds the freedom of faith in its models expressing contact with the Spirit. In a sense analogy has not been avoided here, but turned on its side, from being a vertical analogy between the divine and human to a horizontal one between a past model of faith formed in contact with the Spirit and the present formulation of faith illuminated by the classic model. The weakness of this perspective is that a fundamental duality remains in the relation between the formulation of faith and the presence of the Spirit. On these terms, it may be that the appearance of oppositions in the expressions of the faith in past and present is inevitable; thus it may no longer be clear in what sense the Scripture remains a model for faith today. In other words, the duality of the presence of the Spirit and the purely human expression of faith does not permit a formulation of faith which provides an adequate foundation on which the duality of past and present formulations of faith can be bridged.

---

81. Paul Ricoeur, *Le Métaphore Vive* (Paris, 1975), pp. 344ff., 353, points out that analogical thinking refuses compromise with the poetic in its constructions and makes the distinction between analogy and metaphor.

In résumé: Barr provides no theoretical justification as to why a Christian theologian should take his starting point in the affirmation that the Scripture is a human document other than stating the breakdown of the christological analogy. In this respect Barr as good as states that this is a very different position from the point of view of the biblical writers. In speaking of the OT quotations in the NT, Barr refers to the view that the NT writers lived in "an atmosphere of revealed religion which regards scriptural statements as true both in whole and in various sized parts."[82] This, he adds, is close to his own interpretation of the NT view. Here, at least, there is a substantial divergence between the model of faith and the faith of today. No doubt the NT writers were only expressing a human belief when they thought this and as such this is no longer valid as over against what we might believe about the Scripture today.

The problem that I can see with this whole position seems to be as follows. Scripture is a model of faith in the sense that it expresses man's faith in God in contact with the Spirit in a human way. As such it gives no objective revealed truth about God. This human faith expressed in Scripture remains on the level of *fides qua,* an act of believing in contact with the Spirit, which is a reflex to this contact. It does not attain to the status of *fides quae* in the sense of being faith grounded in a revealed knowledge of the object of faith. However, this would seem to mean that the faith expressed today following this model is of the same sort. This consideration, if correct, points to the fact that assertions which are made about Scripture as model of faith in terms of human reaction cannot *themselves* claim to any status as objective truth. In practical terms this means that Barr's assertions about the human status of Scripture are self-defeating, as Barr cannot claim that his assumption that Scripture is a human document expressing a model of faith is in any way demonstrably true. Certainly the status of Scripture as classic model of faith is not demonstrable in terms of historical research; the contact with the Spirit is not susceptible of historical proof. To accept Barr's assumption that the human Scriptures give a classic model of faith through the contact with the Spirit is itself a position which requires an act of faith. This act seems to have no substantial support, and it may be wondered

82. *ONI,* p. 142, n. 2.

whether this is not more incongruous than the neo-orthodox models Barr criticised. Certainly it hardly provides a coherent position from which to criticise the contradictions of neo-orthodoxy or fundamentalism. It may be wondered whether Barr's rationalism in the interpretation of fact does not lead him to an irrationalistic faith in the area of meaning. We are left with a dualism between the nominalistic rationalism of free human analysis and construction on the one hand and a realism of faith in the subjective domain of the contact with the Spirit. Faith as the mode of the Spirit's presence is not grounded in the objective statement of truth; nor is the interpretation of historic fact dependent on the condition of faith.

The dualism we have repeatedly sought to illustrate in the thought of Barr is a problem generated by a problem. The duality which was expressed in neo-orthodox thought centred on the relation of the divine act of revelation and the witness of Scripture to that revelation in terms of the pointing away from itself to the Word of God. The inadequacy of the revelational model of the Word of God is criticised by Barr: ". . . an incarnational analogy is not an adequate substitute for a doctrine of inspiration."[83] However, Barr's reconstruction of the inspiration doctrine outside of the context of revelation leads to an even more marked duality between the divine and the human than the incarnational analogy. Even though Barr may be inclined to think that he has given a rational description of the status of Scripture, as far as overcoming the fundamental duality between God and man is concerned, his construction remains unsatisfying. This is perhaps a sufficient reason for looking again at the basic structure of the problem which is raised by the christological analogy and commenting briefly on this in conclusion to this study.

---

83. *SJT*, 11:90.

6

Conclusions and Suggestions

6.1. *Problems of the christological analogy*

The first question which may be raised is as to the suitability of seeking to establish an analogy between the relation of the divine and human in the hypostatic union and the divine and human elements in Scripture. Even if the parallel seems to be suggestive and the power of this suggestion is heightened by reference to the expression "Word of God," the question remains as to whether it is proper to speak of the Bible as standing in a relation of analogy with Christ. It has been pointed out that the role of analogy in the formulation of hypotheses is to note how previous knowledge can be applied to new settings. Analogies are established between the facts we are trying to explain and other facts whose explanation is already known.[1] The unclear and the unfamiliar are made clear by the familiar.[2]

Already this general acceptance indicates something problematical about the establishing of a christological analogy for illuminating the doctrine of Scripture. The nature of the union of the divine and human elements in the person of Christ is just one thing that is not familiar or known to us. There is a mystery about the union of the two natures of Christ in the one person, which if it is confessed by faith, hardly enters into the field of that which is explicable to us. As has been indicated by theologians making a general use of the analogy, if the Bible as the Word of God and word of man contains a similar formal reference to two elements, the mystery is not of the same sort as the mystery of Christ. Hypostasis is absent in the case of the Bible,

---

1. M. R. Cohen and E. Nagel, *An Introduction to Logic and Scientific Method* (London, 1966), pp. 221f.
2. T. Fawcett, *The Symbolic Language of Religion* (London, 1970), pp. 48ff.

and the parallel with Christ cannot be used to explain the mode of union of the elements of the Bible. R. Preus, commenting on the doctrine of inspiration of the orthodox theologians of seventeenth-century Lutheranism, remarks on their lack of a christological analogy. This he attributes to the inadequacy of the analogy in the light of the hypostatic union in Christ, which is unique and without analogy: ". . . inasmuch as it was a union between God and man, [it was] a union between *disparata* which were mutually exclusive."[3] This reserve concerning the usefulness of the analogy found in theologians whose thought cannot be described as unconservative, from the scholastic Lutherans to B. B. Warfield and more recently G. C. Berkouwer, is a warning that too much should not be expected from a christological analogy in the explanation of the nature of Scripture.

Another consideration about the suitability of the analogy can be related to the following remark: ". . . analogical reasoning . . . is a case of probable inference which depends on fair sampling."[4] To this observation we can add the reflexion of A. Farrer, who points out that the comparison in analogy is drawn by the mind which makes the comparison and is not in itself a real character in the thing: ". . . analogy is a relation between objects capable of being classed as a species of 'likeness.' . . . it is not a real relation but *ordo rationis cum fundamento in rebus.*"[5] These considerations may lead us to reflect on the method of sampling employed in establishing the analogy between the two natures in Christ and the divine and human in Scripture. The prior reflection on the uniqueness of the mystery of the union of the two natures in the one person of Christ would seem to illustrate the remark of Farrer that analogy is not indicative of a real relation but a likeness established by our mind's ordering. In establishing the analogy between Christ and the Scripture in terms of the divine and human, is this sampling a fair one?

Barr has touched on this aspect of the question when he refers to the function of the Scripture as human witness to the Word of God as revelation in neo-orthodoxy. "The finger of John the Baptist should

---

3. R. Preus, *The Inspiration of Scripture* (Edinburgh, 1955), pp. 201ff. Preus points out that the analogy is prevented by the Lutheran conception of the anhypostatic human nature of Christ; in Scripture the human nature exists before the divine act of inspiration.

4. Cohen and Nagel, op. cit., p. 288.

5. A. Farrer, *Finite and Infinite* (London, 1943), p. 88.

be given a rest; he is simply not an adequate analogue for the whole range of biblical statement."[6] Barr argues in this place that the use of a christological analogy in dealing with the Scripture witness results in the human aspect of Scripture being considered as part of the movement of revelation from God to man; this is not adequate to account for the full human character of the text as word from man to God. In this application of the analogy to Scripture, there is a sampling of the material which does not do justice to it.

Along similar lines it can be indicated that when the analogy between Christ and Scripture is used, a certain form of sampling is involved and it can be asked whether this represents properly the two realities involved. In particular the analogy involves a selection which centres on a question concerning the mode of being of Christ and the Bible. G. C. Berkouwer has made this quite evident in his recent discussion, where he indicates the prominence of the element of union of the divine and human natures as important for the parallel between incarnation and inscripturation. Berkouwer sees the risk in this sampling of divine and human factors of rationalising the mystery of Holy Scripture, but also that of the person of Christ. Concerning the theme of union of the elements he remarks: ". . . it is difficult to understand how such a theme can do justice to the mystery of Scripture and the confession 'Sacred Scripture *is* the Word of God.' For this confession does not say that Scripture originates from a union of divine and human factors, but points to the mystery of human words *as* God's Word."[7]

When the union of the divine and human factors is appealed to in the parallel of Christ and Scripture, the structure of the relationship between these elements constitutes the fundamental resemblance in the analogy. This is developed in terms of the mode in which the divine element enters into relation with the human form. The focus is on the entrance of God's Word into creaturely relations through incarnation and inscripturation. Berkouwer makes this point with reference to the work of A. Kuyper and H. Bavinck. In another instance, T. F. Torrance suggests that in B. B. Warfield the account of inspiration is parallel to the Romanist doctrine of the virgin birth. Torrance,

---

6. *SJT* 11:88.
7. G. C. Berkouwer, *Holy Scripture* (Grand Rapids, 1975), p. 203.

who himself thinks that a christological analogy is useful for indicating the derived relation between Word of God and word of man in Scripture, speaks of a double limitation in the analogy. In Christ there is perfect union between God and man, but in Scripture the Word of God is given in the limitations of our fallen humanity, in conditions of imperfection and limitation. There is no incarnation in Scripture, even though Scripture is grounded in a unique relation between God and man in Christ. Torrance thinks that Warfield's view of verbal inspiration amounts to an incarnation of the Holy Spirit.[8] Torrance's judgment of Warfield may well seem exaggerated, but quite apart from this his own description of the double limitation points to the difficulty of an analogy which relates Scripture and Christ in terms of a parallel between two natures. When Torrance's limitations are respected, it may be wondered whether the dissemblances are not greater than the resemblances. As far as the central issue is concerned, the difference in relation founded on the consideration of hypostatic union in the person of Christ means that the union of the divine and human in Christ has only slight suggestiveness for indicating the relation as far as Scripture is concerned.[9]

These two factors, then, may be indicative of the difficulties involved in speaking of the christological analogy. In the case of the Bible, we do not illuminate the unknown by the known in making the analogy with the two natures of Christ. When the analogy is centred on the question of the two natures, the hypostatic union of the God-man is not explicative of the union of the natures in Scripture. The mystery is not the same: In Christ it concerns the union of the two natures in one person, but in the Scripture there is no such union; the mystery is rather as to how God's word comes to us in the

---

8. T. F. Torrance in his review of B. B. Warfield's *Inspiration and Authority of the Bible*, in *SJT* 7:106f. I think Torrance has gone beyond what the writings of Warfield permit in his review. The Princeton theologian shows an extreme reserve for the usefulness of the christological analogy. Also he emphasises the humanness of Scripture alongside his affirmation of verbal inspiration. Warfield states that the Spirit does not supersede the activities of the writers but works confluently with them. Thus "the whole Bible is recognized as human, the free product of human effort, in every part and word." See "The Divine and Human in the Bible," in *Selected Shorter Writings of B. B. Warfield*, ed. J. E. Meeter (Nutley, N. J., 1973), p. 547.

9. See the discussion of the mechanics of analogies in L. S. Stebbing, *A Modern Introduction to Logic* (London, 1930), pp. 250ff.

inspired witness, which is a human word.

The danger of the christological analogy applied to the Bible would be that in considering Scripture in terms of divine and human elements doctrinal formulation tends to identity or duality in the way these are related. The risk of identifying the human text in terms of a divine word issuing from mechanical inspiration is perhaps the lesser of the dangers. More common is the duality which results when the Bible is considered along the lines of the relation of the divine and the human in which the human element is seen as an imperfect witness to a revelation beyond the text. Scripture becomes the Word of God; the human word is the instrument used in revelation. This risk of identifying the human word with the divine or distinguishing them in dual fashion is inherent in theological formulations which consider the doctrine of Scripture in the light of a divine-human polarity. A theology of revelation which seeks to describe Scripture in terms of such a polarity by analogy with Christ's natures will inevitably fail to find a point of unity between the diverse elements, and not wishing to make a simple identity of the human word of Scripture with the Word of God by means of a dictation doctrine, will be forced to a duality of the divine and human.[10] In this case the problem is to establish a point of contact with the divine action which assures a real continuity between the elements.

Therefore, we may wonder whether to speak of *analogy* in this instance is really suited to the relation of the cases considered. This is not to say that no comparisons can be made between Christ and the Scripture, but these will be of a lower order than an analogy which seeks a statement of the relation of the divine and the human elements by the parallel. It would be quite possible to say, for example, with K. Rahner that the free spontaneity of Christ's humanity was not lessened by the divine person to whom this human nature belonged, and that likewise inspiration does not lessen the humanity of the authors of Scripture.[11] Or, to say that there is a resemblance between the *kind* of evidence for the divinity of Christ and the divine

---

10. An exception might be Origen, who, according to some recent interpreters, conceived of Scripture as an incarnation of the Word. See H. Urs von Balthasar, *Origenes* (Salzburg, 1938), pp. 121ff., 210ff., 247ff.; H. de Lubac, *Histoire et Esprit* (Paris, 1950), pp. 336ff.; R. P. C. Hanson, *Allegory and Event* (London, 1959), pp. 193ff.

11. K. Rahner, *Inspiration in the Bible* (Freiburg and London, 1961), p. 14n.

inspiration of Scripture and likewise in the case of the human aspect.[12] These are rather comparisons which are legitimate or not in their own right on the basis of the evidence called upon to establish the similarity. They do not seek to explain the mode of union of the two elements in terms of a christological analogy.

A second consideration which would seem to be apropos in this discussion concerns the nature of the analogy which is being used. In spite of the widespread and seemingly persuasive references to the christological analogy among theologians influenced by the theology of the Word, there seemed to be little detailed examination of the sort of use made of analogy in this case. The general attitude is well illustrated by Torrance when he says: ". . . there is no question about the fact that a proper doctrine of Scripture must be grounded analogically upon the birth, life, death and resurrection of Jesus Christ. . . ."[13]

This rather loose use of analogy in recent theology has been criticised in an important article by J. McIntyre, who has indicated several ambiguities.[14] In particular, McIntyre points out that Barth's use of analogy takes its point of departure in Quenstedt's replacement of the analogy of proportionality of Thomism by an analogy of attribution. McIntyre discerns in Protestantism a misunderstanding of the Thomist *analogia entis,* which as an analogy of proportionality does not imply the ontological continuity of God and man, as has been thought.[15] Barth with Quenstedt rejects the analogy of proportionality, but criticises him for the way he uses the analogy of attribution in so far as man's knowledge of God is concerned. For Quenstedt would appear to speak of an analogy of intrinsic attribution. Barth maintains that any analogy which can be spoken of here is not intrinsic: ". . . the analogy between God and man is not something that is ever *proper* to man. . . . the attribute is never *intrinseca* but always *extrinseca.*"[16] The creature is created into an analogue by virtue of an act of divine grace and not on the grounds of an in-

---

12. As in J. Bannermann, *Inspiration* (Edinburgh, 1865), pp. 438ff.
13. Torrance, art. cit., p. 106.
14. J. McIntyre, "Analogy," in *SJT* 12:1-20. McIntyre's contribution to Barr's thought is indicated in *ONI,* p. 12.
15. Ibid., pp. 11f.
16. Ibid., p. 14. Barth's exposition is in *Kirchliche Dogmatik,* 2.1, 267ff.

herent property. The analogy which can be spoken of is an analogy of grace founded on the act of God and is as such an extrinsic one. McIntyre thinks that Barth has been misled in his rejection of the analogy of proportionality. He remarks that "despite his overt allegiance to analogy of attribution, [Barth] in fact is implicitly committed not only to a seriously modified form of this analogy, but also to another type of analogy which he explicitly rejects."[17] McIntyre claims that Barth's *analogia gratiae* is an analogy of *relations* rather than one of attributes or of attribution and as such fits in with the classic definition of the analogy of proportionality.[18]

Regarding the christological analogy: The question may be put as to whether either Barth's analogy of extrinsic attribution or his implicit analogy of proportionality, claimed by McIntyre, can provide the necessary conditions for the construction of an analogy between Christ and the Bible. The analogy of attribution would not seem to justify the parallel drawn between Christ and the Scriptures. This analogy "is applied to those entities which, while different in other respects, are the same in that they are related, even by different relations to one identical thing."[19] The problem would appear to be that if we wish to relate the divine and the human in Scripture and Christ, the union in the two cases is not identical. The mode of union in the hypostasis of the God-man is different from that of Scripture. The principal property of the union in Christ cannot be predicated to the analogate even by an extrinsic denomination. Nor would the analogy of proportionality seem to fare any better in the light of McIntyre's analysis. This analogy concerns relations, but it does not show the way in which the divine and human are related in Christ to be the same as the way they are related in Scripture. To illustrate:

$$\frac{\text{Divine in Christ}}{\text{Human in Christ}} = \frac{\text{Divine in Bible}}{\text{Human in Bible}}$$

The relation of the elements in Christ in an analogy of proportionality tells us nothing about how the elements are related in the Bible.

---

17. Ibid., p. 19. Also H. Urs von Balthasar, *The Theology of Karl Barth* (New York, 1971), pp. 93ff., 148ff.; H. Chavannes, *L'analogie entre Dieu et le monde selon Saint Thomas d'Aquin et selon Karl Barth* (Paris, 1969).

18. Ibid., p. 16.

19. Ibid., p. 8.

Concerning this McIntyre remarks that "because the analogy of proportionality is an analogy of *relations,* it requires to be supplemented by some form of analogy which relates the *terms* of the analogy."[20] This use of analogy provides no criterion for distinguishing the ways the terms associated with Scripture resemble and differ from the terms of the primary analogate. As such, it does not establish an effective analogy *between* Christ and the Bible.

The fundamental difficulty in the use of the analogy of the *unio hypostatica* with Scripture would appear to be that when such an analogy is constructed in terms of attribution or proportionality there lacks the ontological underpinning necessary to support the analogy. To provide such an ontological foundation to the analogy Christ-Bible it would be necessary to consider the secondary analogate as being a particular instance of the prime analogate. In this case another different analogy would be appealed to—the analogy of inequality. Here an ontological foundation for the analogy is furnished, but the principle of the analogy of proportionality is put aside. Where the analogy of proportionality which claims resemblance of relation or properties is appealed to, there lacks a real link between the *analogans* and the *analogatum.*

In the case of Barthian analogy the reference is to an extrinsic analogy of attribution. Barth wants to make an effort to distance himself from the analogy of inequality which would suggest a common being shared by the divine and the human, but also from the analogy of proportionality which is basic to the Thomist *analogia entis.*[21] Barth chooses in describing the relation of the divine and the human the analogy which steers between univocity and equivocity, the analogy of grace (or of faith). Knowledge of God is made possible by God's act of revelation rather than by a nature inherent in the creation.[22] Barth's doctrine of analogy is the foundation for a dynamic approach to the doctrine of revelation and in particular to the Scriptures which

20. Ibid., p. 14.
21. See the discussion of W. Pannenberg in *Basic Questions in Theology* (London, 1970), I:221ff., on the scholastic use of analogy. Also H. Lyttkens. *The Analogy Between God and the World: An Investigation of Its Background and Interpretation of Its Use by Thomas of Aquino* (Uppsala, 1952).
22. B. Mondin, *The Principle of Analogy in Protestant and Catholic Theology* (The Hague, 1963), chap. 7, and H. G. Pöhlmann, *Analogia Entis oder Analogia fidei? Die Frage der Analogie bei K. Barth* (Göttingen, 1965).

as part of the created world are not in themselves revelatory word, but the object of God's act of revelation. The analogy of extrinsic attribution in the context of a discussion of the christological analogy can only foster a duality between the text of the Bible and the divine act of revelation. The criticism of the analogy of attribution made above, that is, that the mode of union in the two cases is not identical, can be applied here. The mode of union in these instances is not similar. Even if Barth's analogy is one of proportionality though unacknowledged, as in McIntyre's suggestion, the analogy between Christ and the Bible does not stand. The analogy of grace which lacks a foundation in a creational revelation breaks down into a duality between the divine and the human.

These reflexions aid, perhaps, our understanding of how the duality of divine and human in the christological analogy of neo-orthodoxy breaks down into a dualism under the effect of Barr's critique. For Barr the analogy lies now on the level of the developing human consciousness which expresses faith in God. Analogy is not divine and human but past and present. Contact with the divine is sought by reference to the presence of the Spirit.

A third matter can be briefly referred to concerning the problem of the analogy with the hypostatic union. This has already been touched upon and concerns the relation between the prime and secondary analogates in question. In the form of the analogies discussed, it would not appear that the nature of the divine and human in the person of the God-man makes the character of the divine and human elements attributed to Scripture any clearer. How is the human nature of Christ related to the human nature of the Bible? Here once again the problem of the analogy arises in connection with the particular character of the *unio hypostatica*. This implies that in the person of the mediator the human nature of the Incarnate Word is not dissociated from the unity of the divine nature. Yet if this is the case, there is a manifest difficulty of relating the humanity of Christ to that of the Bible. This is particularly apparent in some representatives of neo-orthodoxy who speak of a limitation in this respect. The sinlessness of Christ confessed in Scripture is not to be equated with the infallibility of Scripture. Nor on the other hand can the fact that the Logos dwelt among men be the basis of an inference to a permanent revelatory quality inhering the text of the Bible. The kenosis of the second person of the Trinity is here hardly an adequate analogue for an accommodation of the third person. The character of the manifestation of the divine and the taking into service of the human are not necessarily comparable in terms of an analogy.

It would appear that the analogies which have been traditionally appealed to in discussions of the person of Christ and Scripture are not adequate to illuminate the nature of the inspired Word. They do not indicate the nature of the uniting of the divine and human factors in the case of the Scripture. The union of these in Christ does not provide an analogy for the way such a uniting of elements might be effected in inspiration. Nor does the reference to the human nature of Christ make the nature of the humanity of the Bible any plainer. The problem with these analogies may lie in the use of analogy itself, in its use in the context of a duality of the divine and human or in a combination of both of these factors. Whatever the case may be, it would seem that when the christological analogy is approached in the context of a divine-human duality, the relation of the divine and human elements in Scripture is not made clearer. For if the duality can be overcome in so far as the person of Christ is concerned by a special appeal to the mystery of the incarnation, this mystery in its unique character provides no analogy for the nature of the Bible.

6.2. *Suggestions concerning the divine and human in Scripture*

Barr's fundamental criticism of the christological analogy as a model for understanding the nature of Scripture as Word of God and the implications this had in interpretation must be considered to be highly legitimate in its insight into the problem. The analogy of the Word of God is inadequate to describe the character of the Scripture when it is taken alone. Thus Barr deems it to be no substitute for a doctrine of inspiration, which tended to lack in neo-orthodoxy. It does not enlighten the nature of the union of the divine and human elements in the Bible; nor does it explain the role of the human in relation to revelation. When taken in isolation, the analogy leaves us with a duality between the divine and the human in Scripture. This was particularly so in neo-orthodoxy, which spoke of the Scripture as becoming Word of God through God's act of revelation and accounted for the human element of Scripture in terms of a witness to the revelation of God which is beyond the text itself.

However, in criticising this theology, Barr does not provide a solution to the basic problem posed by the duality of the divine and the human; his theological constructions tend to widen the split in the duality. The refusal of the possibility of considering Scripture in the context of a God-to-man movement and consequently in terms of a special revelation in history removes the possibility of any *concursus* between God and man in Scripture in concrete terms. In addition it leaves the divine-human relation juxtaposed with respect to Scripture. In Barr's analogy of the Spirit, the text is considered a human manifestation, while the mode of the Spirit's presence remains a mystery about which little can be said. The duality remains here in its integrality.

These reflections leave us with the fundamental question as how it may be possible to formulate an adequate view of Scripture, that is, one which seeks to overcome these dualities which leave man marooned in history without real contact with God. That neither the view which seeks an explanation of the status of Scripture in terms of the christological analogy, nor Barr's analogy of the Spirit and the people of God succeed in overcoming the fundamental duality of the divine and the human regarding Scripture is an indication that some broader perspective is necessary. The problem of the first is that it articulates a view of Scripture in terms of a soteric *revelational* analogy and therefore lacks the broader perspective. To relate the divine and the human aspects which function differently in Christ and the Scripture, this revelational analogy would have to provide some more general ontological foundation in the context of which incarnation and inscripturation could be accounted for. Theologically speaking, some doctrine of creation and general revelation would have to be stated in which the parallel of incarnation and inscripturation would function meaningfully.

The problem of the second position, that is, Barr's analogy between Spirit and people of God, is not quite the same. Here there is an effort to provide the broader perspective necessary to explain the status of Scripture. This is achieved through reference to the way the Spirit of God guides his people in the development of their tradition. The perspective sweeps from the formation of the elements of the creation story, which relates the meaning of reality to God, to the salvation in Christ in which the tradition is soteriologically functional. As a cumulative tradition, it provides the broad perspective for relating the various aspects of the tradition to the presence of the Spirit. Even the sinful aspects are functional in this context to reveal the truth of God. However, in this instance the difficulty lies in that this tradition is described in terms of an immanent process, which, if it has the breadth of perspective, lacks in a certain depth dimension. The God who is in contact with this history is beyond it and not revealed in a definitive way. If the presence of the Spirit is history-encompassing, there is no revelation of the divine in the human domain in the form of a uniting of the divine and human witness in Scripture.

The above considerations suggest that a proper model for the doctrine of Scripture may be provided only when the broader perspective of the relation of the Spirit of God to his people and the more particular revelational analogy are taken as inter-related. My proposition here is not that a christological analogy on the neo-orthodox lines should be re-synthesised with Barr's broader outlook. There are elements in both approaches which would seem incompatible and render such a synthesis impossible and ineffective. What I am suggesting is that the duality of the divine and human aspects of Scripture may be resolved only when the question is situated in the broader scope of the work of the Spirit of God. To place these two in a complementary relation is to achieve a different view of both approaches. For the way the work of the Spirit would be spoken of would not be similar to Barr's position in a theology which allowed the possibility of revelation in the human sphere, rather than assuming the Scripture's humanity on the basis of compatibility with modern knowledge. Nor would there appear the same chasm between divine and human elements to the broader perspective of the Spirit's work. In terms of dogmatic formulation, the complementarity of these two approaches would permit the articulation of a proper relation of the divine and human elements in Scripture by reference to the unifying work of the Spirit; conversely, the work of the Spirit enunciated in these terms could be understood as a work through which God really makes himself known to man in history. The solipsism of human knowledge is broken.

Something along similar lines has been suggested by J. McIntyre in the conclusion to his article on "Analogy," to which we have referred. If we wish to stick to the traditional theological use of analogy, Mc-

Intyre suggests that a combination of the analogies of proportionality and attribution might be positive in the description of our knowledge of God.

> By analogy of proportionality we secure for God's gracious work in Jesus Christ the dominant place in our understanding both of God's relations to ourselves and of His nature. The *analogia gratiae* becomes the prime analogate, and all is interpreted proportionally thereto. But because the *analogia gratiae* sets us in new relations, it also endows us with new being, and it is the norm of all the relations into which we enter. At that point analogy of attribution operates, to speak of the kind of righteousness, wisdom, truth . . . which may be ours. . . .[23]

The limitation in this suggestion about analogy is that it remains in the context of the renewal of man's knowledge of God in Jesus Christ in the relationships of renewal through grace. The new being is attributed to man in the context of this renewal of relations. In this illustration, however, there remains the problem concerning the character of the new relations which express the new being through grace in the context of the general world order of the "old" being. Analogies which seek to found their meaning in the grace of God and faith are obliged, if they are to be fully meaningful, to relate themselves not only to the renewal of the creation in Christ but also to the creational order as it stands, and in which new being is manifest. Failing to comply to this, knowledge of God referring solely to the analogy of grace will inevitably collapse into apposition with reference to other human knowledge. Applied to the biblical revelation, even this modified interpretation would land us back in a duality of the divine and the human aspects in revelation.[24]

In all that we have said hitherto, the fundamental contention is that when the question of revelation is contextualised within a consideration of the relation of the divine and human elements, no analogy can break down this duality. This would seem to be the case because in discussions of the relation of the divine and the human elements in Scripture, theologians seem to repeatedly use the ex-

---

23. McIntyre, art. cit., p. 19.

24. McIntyre indicates an awareness of this when he speaks of the possibility of separating the logical forms of scholastic theology and its metaphysics. "What we want is this logic without that metaphysic, and I have a feeling that we may be crying for the moon" (ibid., p. 20).

pressions "divine" and "human" in neutral fashion. The distinction comes to be a purely metaphysical one in which the *character* of the divine and the human recedes into the background. The problem consists in bringing together two metaphysically opposed elements in such a way that there is in the biblical revelation a synthesis of the two factors. Thus the attempt is made through the complementary function of a first cause and a second cause to illumine the theandric character of Scripture. Or, by contrast, on the basis of the total incompatibility of the two elements, divine revelation pertains to a domain other than that of the human witness to the text of the Bible. Even theologians who make an explicit effort to avoid a causal relation between the divine and the human elements in respect to revelation, seem to unconsciously slip into speaking of the divine and human in a sort of neutral way. For example, G. C. Berkouwer points to the dangers of "synergism" which sees Scripture as partly human/partly divine resulting from the cooperation of the two factors. Equally dangerous is an "unbiblical monergism" which lacks insight on the way in which God works in the world.[25] Berkouwer asks the question of the continuity of the Word of God with the human form which it calls into being and adopts. Thus he speaks of the "time-bound character" of Holy Scripture. A continuity is sought between the "new," the divine element, and the "old," the human character which pertains to the thought, context, speaking, and writing of the human authors. Berkouwer remarks that today the problem of accommodation concerns not so much the accommodation to human nature as such, but refers to the biblical authors in their period, from which they were not lifted.[26]

The difficulty, also in Berkouwer, would seem to me that the divine and the human are approached in a fundamentally neutral perspective. Even if the human element is spoken of in a more historical way rather than in terms of the limitation of human nature, the *character* of the "old," the human reality seems to be unanalysed. The polarity of the human as human and the divine as divine seems to persist here in an unreconstructed way. Does the divine as it enters into connection with the human leave the "old" as it is? Is this seemingly unreflective contrast of the "new" and the "old" an adequate starting

---

25. G. C. Berkouwer, *Holy Scripture* (Grand Rapids, 1975), p. 170.
26. Ibid., p. 177.

point for a discussion of the relation of the two elements? We are not hereby questioning many of the valuable and useful contributions which Berkouwer has made to the discussion of the doctrine of Scripture. His emphasis on the need to do justice to the human aspect of the biblical tradition is a necessary stimulus for theologians who continue to seek to make something of the God-breathed character of Scripture. Our question concerns the fundamental perspective in which the discussion of the human and the divine takes place. When this perspective is governed by a structure centred upon the "unassailable divine aspect" and the "relativity of the human aspect" in Scripture, we are faced with the impossibility of transcending this polarity.[27] This is so, it would seem, in theological systems which approach the question in terms of a more fundamental historical approach to the human aspect as well as those which are characterised by a metaphysical causality or an anti-metaphysical approach.

To résumé: Our basic contention is that discussions of the divine and human which relate these elements in Scripture in a neutral way fail to achieve an adequate perspective on the problem involved. Some more fundamental starting point must be discovered which will serve to relate the divine and the human aspects of revelation in Scripture in a more concrete form. Only a starting point which tells us something about the character of the divine and the character of the human can provide the context in which these can be related in a way which removes the neutrality of the elements.

This observation is basic to the suggestion made here concerning the need to place the question of the divine and the human in a broader context provided by the unity of the Spirit of God and the people of God. If this can be done, the real duality in Scripture is seen to be not between the divine and the human, but between communion with God in the Spirit and rupture of this communion in covenant-breaking disobedience. The fundamental perspective of Scripture is not centred on man as finite and God as infinite, on the human and the divine, but on the contrast of man in covenant communion and man in covenant-breaking sin. As S. Greidanus has

---

27. Ibid., p. 190. Even Berkouwer's remarks on the "servant form" of Scripture, in spite of their necessary emphasis on the character of the human form of Scripture, would not seem to go beyond the perspective of the divine and human as a neutral starting point in the discussion of Scripture.

pointed out in his discussion of redemptive historical preaching, the question is not so much as to the presence of God and man as two factors appearing in Scripture. If we must speak of two factors, perhaps we should speak of God and Satan. "On either side men come into action, but the real parties in the battle are God and Satan. . . . The place of both opponents and 'co-workers' can only be determined Christologically."[28]

Continuing this insight, it is perhaps possible to put the matter like this. It is when man no longer stands in communion with God through the Spirit that the duality of finite-infinite opens up. Opposition to God breaks the communion of man with God. It is sinfulness, not finitude, which separates the creature from the Creator. This is not to deny the distinction between Creator and creature. What we mean is that this distinction itself is no obstruction to communion of man with God. There is a real metaphysical difference between God and man. This distinction becomes division, and the relation of the infinite and the finite becomes a problem as a result of the ethical or religious separation. The fundamental present opposition of divine and human is an ethical one, and the metaphysical problem is grafted onto this root of rebellion.

This reflexion indicates that when discussions of the divine and human are carried on outside of the perspective of the communion with God, broken and restored, the order of priority of these questions has been reversed. A secondary problem, existing because of the rupture of communion, has been made primary and is taken as the starting point of theoretical discussion in a neutral fashion. When this is the case, communion with God considered in a secondary place becomes itself a real problem: What sort of communion can span the chasm of the infinite and the finite? Furthermore, to construct a doctrine of Scripture apart from the fundamental fact of the primacy of communion between God and man, in terms of man as finite and God as infinite, invariably results in an unbiblical duality. Knowledge of God is placed in a different realm from other finite knowledge. Often the consequence is that the possibility of the knowledge of God is estimated according to what is acceptable on the basis

---

28. B. Holwerda and M. B. Van 'T Veer, cited by S. Greidanus in *Sola Scriptura* (Kampen, 1970), p. 147.

of human criteria. It is supposed that man in his actual state is capable of making judgments about what does or does not constitute knowledge of God.

This approach is a blind alley for the discussion of the doctrine of revelation and Scripture. In fact, it may not be too extreme to say that a good deal of theological discussion of the subject for the last century or so has been barking up the wrong tree, in considering the categories of the divine and human in a neutral way, apart from consideration of the nature of God and the *present* nature of covenant-breaking man. An unsolvable problem has been manufactured as a result of this perspectival misjudgment.

Accepting sin as the basic opposition in Scripture opens up the possibility for considering the function of Scripture in terms of the communion of the Spirit. By this we need not understand that the doctrine of Scripture be discussed in the locus of ecclesiology.[29] There is perhaps a more fundamental consideration to be accounted for here. Scripture is not to be considered in relation to the communion of the Spirit uniquely in terms of restoration of communion, but in the first place with respect to the *original* communion between God and man. This consideration is important to insist on the fact that if we are to speak of communion with God we must do so in reference to the historical aspects of this original and restored communion.

Communion with God as the primary perspective for considering the divine and human in Scripture can be considered as something other than the abstract ethical religiosity which makes the authority of Scripture dependent on personal faith.[30] God is known in historical circumstances, in the original relation of communion and the restoration in Christ. *In principio* man's knowledeg of God's divinity and his own creaturely humanity is in the context of the Spirit of communion which seals the covenant between God and man. When man sinfully wishes to become "as God," the communion is broken, man realises the disaster of his own pretention, and the metaphysical chasm appears

---

29. Barr, *BMW,* pp. 118ff.; cf. D. Kelsey, *The Uses of Scripture in Recent Theology* (London, 1975), pp. 98, 109, 165f. See also the remarks of J. Veenhof on this, relative to the ethical theologians of the nineteenth century, in *Revelatie en Inspiratie* (Amsterdam, 1968), pp. 190ff.

30. Cf. Veenhof, op. cit., pp. 194ff.

with the consciousness of sin. This chasm is abolished in the incarnation and the mystery of the union of the two natures in the one person of the God-man. In Christ the communion between God and man is restored and sin is abolished. In this renewed communion the duality of the divine and human is removed and man, restored in the image of Christ, beholds the godliness of God and his own humanness in redemptional light.

The history of redemption is the field of differentiation in which the reality of sin and grace, thus of communion lost and recovered, finds expression. In communion with God, *God* is *known* in history; the historical reality of sin separates the human from the divine. Relating the communion with God to the history of redemption avoids the separation of the idea of communion from the fact of communion. It unites idea and fact and shuns the communion of ethical religiosity abstracted from the facts of history. Communion with God must have a fact basis in order to retain its reality. In this respect H. M. Kuitert is quite correct in pointing to the historical nature of the hard core of the biblical tradition which witnesses to the significance of historical events that happened in time past. This resists being "melted away into dimensions of subjectivity."[31]

The fundamental nature of the communion between God and man, as context for the discussion of the soteric revelation of Scripture, can be illustrated in a biblical sense by reference to a recent article by M. G. Kline. This serves to indicate that the Spirit of God functions in establishing communion between God and man, not only in redemption, but first of all in creation. Kline proposes that the Spirit of God of Genesis 1:2 is not only a creative power but a paradigm for creation: "The theophanic Glory was an archetypal pattern for the cosmos and for man, the image of God." The creation as God's temple-sanctuary and man created in the image of God bear the mark of the Glory-Spirit which is the paradigm for the creation. With his basic consideration in view, Kline indicates the relation of the Glory-Spirit, which is the effulgence of the Creator, and the Word of creation: "In creating all things, the Word of God who was in the beginning thus proceeded forth from the Spirit of God—as did also the incarnate word and the inscripturated word."[32]

---

31. H. M. Kuitert, *The Reality of Faith* (Grand Rapids, 1968), pp. 161ff.
32. M. G. Kline, "Creation in the Image of the Glory-Spirit," *WTJ* 39:254.

These considerations are important, for they bear on the fact that a doctrine of Scripture cannot be just constructed in terms of redemptive revelation or salvation history, but must be related in the first instance to the purpose of God in creation. Man created in the image of the Glory-Spirit, placed in the cosmos, which is the temple-habitation of God, was at the beginning in communion with God. Man himself as bearer of the image of the Glory-Spirit is created to be a "spirit-temple of God in the Spirit." This image is also the image of sonship as Kline suggests: "It was in his creative action as the Son, present in the Glory-Spirit, making man in his own son-image that the Logos revealed himself as the One in whom was the life that was the light of men. Not first as incarnate Word breathing on men the Spirit and re-creating them in his heavenly image, but at the very beginning he was the quickening Spirit, creating man after his image and glory."[33] What serves as paradigm for creation is also vital for re-creation in the image of the Son. As Redeemer, Christ restores man to the image of the Glory-Spirit and to communion with God in view of the eschatological Sabbath which was the goal of creation history and which is now the *telos* of redemption.

The exegetical propositions of Kline's work on the image of God point very clearly to the fact that incarnation and inscripturation are aspects of a comprehensive purpose of God expressed in biblical revelation. It is hardly viable to separate out these two aspects from the broad biblical context and attempt to forge an analogy between them as aspects of revelation in a theological matrix which has a duality between the divine and the human built into it at ground level. These attempts at analogical thinking will remain incomplete as they lack in the foundational perspective provided by the biblical doctrine of creation. Their description of revelational analogy will fail because the perspective of creational analogy is lacking. The creational analogy is provided not in terms of a contrast between finite and infinite or divine and human, but in terms of the image of God in creation and in man, which is the foundation for communion with God in the Spirit. Likewise the analogy of grace is the divine gift of the new being in analogy with the creational image of the Glory-Spirit.

Two reflexions follow from this. The first concerns the scope

---

33. Ibid., p. 261.

of the Scriptures.[34] In the context of the fundamental biblical duality of sin and grace, the question of the relation of the divine and human in the Scripture is secondary to that of the need for the restoration of communion with God. The Creator Spirit is at the origin of the original communion between God and man as the Redeemer Spirit is the author of incarnation and inscripturation. In the restoration of the image of the Glory-Spirit through the Son there is a work of redemption from sin which is essential to the renewal of communion. The Scripture as inspired by the Spirit of God has a redemptive or renewing scope. It is the new covenant contract bonded by the death and resurrection of the New Man.[35] Scripture has as its scope the renewal of the relation with the Creator, not the bridging of the divine-human duality. Its work of renewal of the covenant includes a vision of the transcendent lordship of the covenant partner, but the primary function of Scripture is to restore the covenant communion through the abolition of sin.

A second reflexion along these lines concerns our approach to Scripture as God's redemptive revelation. As the scope of Scripture is the renewal of communion with God, Scripture expresses the primacy of the Glory-Spirit in this work. The incarnate Word and the inscripturated word proceed from the Spirit of God in renewal, as the creative word proceeded from the Spirit in the creation of the world and man. This places the renewed man in a particular relation not only to God as Lord, but also to the incarnate and inscripturated word. The renewal of communion he knows through the work of the Spirit in him in the restoration of the image of God depends on and is interpreted by the new relation in which he stands with the incarnate and inscripturated words. Faith in Christ and in Scripture is of the essence of the terms of his communion with God. Here the relation of the renewed man with the Lord of the covenant is not approachable in a neutral way in terms of divine and human, but according to the prior condition of faith in God. The relation of God and man, Creator and creature, is not susceptible of neutral theoretical description, but can be described by man only in faith

---

34. On this generally see Veenhof, op. cit., pp. 459ff.; H. Ridderbos in *International Reformed Bulletin* 32, 3:29ff.; Berkouwer, op. cit., pp. 183ff.

35. On the Scripture as covenant document, see M. G. Kline, *The Structure of Biblical Authority* (Grand Rapids, 1972).

out of consideration of his fallenness and restoration to communion with God through faith.[36] Communion with God is the condition *sine qua non* which alone gives meaning to any of the relations between God and man about which we wish to speak. In addition, as the Glory-Spirit is the paradigm for creation as cosmic temple-habitation or "footstool of God," relations in temporal reality do not contain their own meaning apart from communion with God in faith. This supposes a primacy of God over our reason, and the need of a faith-communion in describing God's dealings with men and men's dealings with men in created reality.

Such a consideration must equally be operative in the construction of a doctrine of Scripture and its interpretation. If the scope of Scripture is redemptive restoration of the image of God, its interpretation can hardly be undertaken on neutral hermeneutic grounds. No theoretical description of the relation between the divine and human in Scripture can be offered which makes no account of the scope of Scripture in the context of sin and grace. When this is attempted, as we have argued is the case in Barr's thought, and this criticism could be extended to many other theologians of the present, the result is inevitably a duality in which God and man's knowledge of him are set over against each other. In the case of Barr this duality of the divine and the human also implies a duality between faith and knowledge. The Bible is approached as a human document through the neutral interpretation of biblical studies, which leave open a possibility of theological faith which lies on a level other than historical enquiry. Faith and knowledge are complementary possibilities, but no integration of these elements is sought in a comprehensive sense.

---

36. By saying that the relationship between God and man is not susceptible of *neutral* theoretical description, we do not mean that it is not susceptible of *any* theoretic description, as some neo-Dooyeweerdians seem to infer. For instance, J. C. Vander Stelt says, in *Philosophy and Scripture* (Marlton, N. J., 1978), that "it should be said that the relationship between God and the world that he made can never be understood or defined in a theoretic way" (p. 315); see a similar affirmation concerning inspiration (p. 327). What we mean is that a theoretical description is perhaps possible in the context of the primacy of the communion between God and man. In the context of this communion, God can speak to us in a theoretic way, even through the literary forms of witness, confession, or poetry. For a critique of the naive-theoretic distinction in neo-Dooyeweerdianism see J. Frame, *The Amsterdam Philosophy: A Preliminary Critique* (Phillipsburg, N. J., n.d.), pp. 6ff.

There is no "pure theological method" in Barr because the fundamental perspective in which the divine and the human are related in his thought represents a duality which cannot be synthesised.[37]

The purpose of this work has been to analyse the thought of James Barr on Scripture and interpretation. In the course of this analysis the problem of the fundamental duality of the divine and the human with relation to Scripture has been raised. The root of this problem has been located in the assumption that the Scripture can be approached as a human document, without appeals to revelation or special divine acting. The criticism has been made that this constitutes a basic error of perspective in so far as the Scripture is concerned. This fundamental error of perspective conditions the theological ensemble which is articulated in Barr's work on Scripture. The duality which sets the divine over against the human in emitting the judgment that Scripture is a human document produces secondary dualities throughout Barr's thought. This fault of perspective, in which Barr is by no means alone, fails to contextualise the discussion of Scripture with reference to creation and redemption and to sin and grace; it has been well described by Gerhard Maier in the following terms:

> In opposition to Luther's *De servo arbitrio,* the higher critical method would take human reason out of the fall into sin and use it critically, i.e., to discriminate and make judgments in matters of revelation. In actual fact this method has thereby already withdrawn reason from the claims of revelation. . . . It does not want to admit that every critique, and therefore the critical method in theology, demands a point of view from which classification and coordination follow and from which judgments and evaluations can take place. Since criticism initially wants to approach the Bible from the outside, its position toward it cannot possibly be found in the Bible even if it has immediately gained a footing there and now takes the latter as a further point of departure.[38]

Barr's rejection of the Scripture as self-interpreting, his confidence in the efficacy of human judgment implied in his use of criticism,

---

37. On the inadequacy of "secular approaches" to the biblical witness, see H. Ridderbos, *The Authority of the New Testament Scriptures* (Philadelphia, 1963), pp. 52, 66.

38. G. Maier, *The End of the Historical Critical Method* (St. Louis, 1977), pp. 23f.

the consideration of Scripture as a human tradition which excludes a prior revelation, the approach to the Bible from the outside—these all fit into the general pattern described by Maier. This withdrawal of critical reason from the revelational perspective of the Bible pointing to sin and grace in the relations between God and man produces a critical system of theology which evaluates human expressions of faith, but lacks the means to apprehend the truth of God. This duality of human faith and the truth of God isolates faith from its object and leaves us with uncertainty as to God's grace.

On the alternative approach to Scripture which has been alluded to in this conclusion, some very brief remarks can be made relating to the relation of the divine and human in Scripture within the perspective of communion with God in creation and redemption. If the approach to the question of the divine and human ends up in a duality when it is stated in a neutral perspective, when the primacy of God as Creator and Redeemer is recognised in faith some limited explanations can be made concerning the relation of the divine and human aspects of Scripture. Four aspects can be mentioned as indicative of the relation of the divine and human in Scripture in the context of the scope of renewal of communion with the Creator. In each of these aspects there is a primacy of the divine work in the renewal which associates the human agency with its work by transforming it.

*   *   *   *   *

Firstly, some comment can be made concerning the *monergism* of the divine renewal of the fallen creation, as this applies to regeneration and inscripturation. The image of the Glory-Spirit is the seal of creational communion and conformity with God. The means by which this communion is established is through the efficacious word of God, which proceeds from the Glory-Spirit. Thus there is, in the creational communion between God and man, a complementarity of created fact and creative word which functions to establish the fellowship in the Spirit of Creator and creature. The communion is in creating Spirit and creative word. For the creature this is a communion of worship and praise. Man's communion with God is worship in the cosmos-temple, in Spirit and in truth. Just as in the creation all flows from God, in the restoration of the image in fallen man there is a monergism of the renewing work of the Spirit. Restoration is creative renewal (II Cor. 4:6), by the re-establishing of the communion between God and man. In his work the Spirit, who restores according to the image of the Son, abolishes the divine-human duality which is the metaphysical consequence of man's ethical fault. This renewal is planned, executed, and applied by God himself. In renewal, the sovereignty of divine grace gives man his true freedom through regeneration. It is correct to speak of the monergism of divine grace in the renewal of the God-man communion. However, in this monergism of grace the human agency is not bypassed in redemption accomplished and applied. It is by the kenosis of the Son, his becoming like us, yet without sin, that man's sin is abolished. In regeneration, the Spirit works sovereignly in the human decision of faith in Jesus Christ.

So it is that a parallel can be drawn between the monergism of grace in renewal of communication between God and man and the inscripturation of the witness to this renewal. God inspires Scripture and speaks it as his own word of covenant renewal to man. Yet, as in regeneration, this monergism of divine grace does not eliminate the human agency, but associates it in inscripturation. God inspires his Scripture through human decisions to write, order the materials, interpret the events, and so bears witness to himself through human witness.[39]

If we wish to speak of analogies in connection with Scripture, perhaps we can find no better one than the sovereignty of divine grace expressed in inspiration and conversion. This is not to say that the inspiration of Scripture represents a higher degree of personal illumination than that common in believers in general.[40] We are speaking of the monergism of grace in renewal of communion with God, through Word and Spirit. Here also, as in the creation, communion is in Spirit and in truth. There is a complementarity of the fact of re-creation and the re-creative word of truth. The primacy of action in regeneration and revelation lies in God. The work of the renewal, it must not be overlooked, applies not to what is merely human in ap-

39. On the monergism of divine grace and human cooperation in conversion and inspiration, see Preus, op. cit., pp. 196f.; W. G. T. Shedd, *Dogmatic Theology* (1888), I:88; B. B. Warfield, *Inspiration and Authority of the Bible* (Philadelphia, 1948), p. 422.
40. Veenhof, op. cit., pp. 170-78.

position to the divine, but to man who is creaturely. God as Creator stands in a sovereign relation to the creature, both to renew him in a way conforming with his creatureliness, and to communicate truth to him without violating his fundamental character. In both instances, God's initiative of restoration is creative of the creaturely human response and witness. Nowhere is the divine sovereignty a factor which eliminates true humanity or man's liberty, but is creative of the true humanity of the creature in the liberty of the Spirit and the truth of the word.

It is in the context of this re-creative monergism that the confession of the church, *Sacra Scriptura est Verbum Dei,* can be best approached.[41] The fact, as pointed out by Barr, that the inflation of the expression, "Word of God," has not helped the discussion of the problems relating to the Scripture in our time, need not necessarily daunt us. It can indicate that we need to be more conscious of the context in which we use such an expression. My basic thought here is that the expression "Word of God" has lost its meaningfulness in modern theology for a precise reason. This is because in the context of discussions of Scripture centring around the divine and human, a duality between the Word of God and the word of man could hardly be avoided. Theologians spoke of Scripture in relation to the Word of God, when really Scripture could not be identified with that Word.

The problem of the unreconstructed duality of much modern theology in approaching the question of the divine and human might in fact be called a problem of Arminianism. The divine and the human are seen as separate but complementary aspects as far as Scripture is concerned. Just as in the doctrine of salvation, Arminianism claims the liberty of man to accept or reject divine grace, so in the doctrine of Scripture a form of Arminianism appears when the human and divine are considered as two complementary factors in revelation. Thus when Scripture is thought of simply as a human witness to a revelation-event which is revelation beyond Scripture, the human is complementary to the divine action. The doctrine of Scripture in this case will be characterised by the synergistic relation of the divine and the human.

To situate the Scripture in the context of the renewing monergism

---

41. See Berkouwer, op. cit., pp. 145ff., and Kuitert, op. cit., pp. 187ff.

of grace makes possible a positive approach to the relation between the Word of God and the Bible, in such a way as to do justice to the human character of Scripture. However, it is perhaps necessary to indicate that, firstly, speech is an attribute of God.[42] In contrast with "dumb" idols, God's nature is to be a speaking God. As an attribute of God, his speech-capacity is coterminous with his divine essence. Yet it is obvious that we cannot say that the Bible is an attribute of God, or an aspect of his essence; it belongs to creaturely reality. If speaking is necessary to the godness of God, speaking to creatures is not necessary to God's being. Like creation, speaking to creatures the Word of God is a free act of God. This word is the *free speech* of God to creatures. Nevertheless, when God speaks his word to men, this divine word is expressive of the divine faculty of speech, which is characteristic of God. If we wish to speak of Scripture as the Word of God, we must consider this word as God's free speech to man, but also as expressive of the divine capacity for speech. Thus the words of the Scripture are not separated from God himself as a product of the faculty of divine communication. In this respect the word of Scripture is a concretisation of the monergism of grace.

Such an emphasis on the monergism of God's grace in his speaking and renewing communion with man, can certainly account for the "is" which relates Scripture to the word of God in the church's confession. It is perhaps, therefore, necessary to insist on the divine monergism in connection with the origin of Scripture, particularly as it is the "is" which has lost its meaning in the increasing attention given to the humanness of Scripture. In the reaction against supernaturalism, as G. C. Berkouwer warns, the danger is that the "is" can "fade before an emphasis on the full and truly human aspect of Scripture."[43]

However, if one wishes to speak of monergism in relation to the origin of Scripture, some care must be taken to speak of this monergism in a way fully concordant with the Scriptures themselves. Berkouwer also warns of the possibility of reacting to an unbiblical synergism which sees Scripture as part human and part divine in an

---

42. I am indebted for these remarks to a course outline by J. Frame on "The Doctrine of the Word of God" (unpub.), Westminster Theological Seminary, pp. 10f.
43. Berkouwer, op. cit., p. 152.

unbiblical monergism which fails to see the way God deals with men in his grace.[44] This also ignores the true character of divine sovereignty. The true human aspect is here swallowed up in a system of causality. In such a system the secondary causes are explained with reference to the first cause, and little is said about the human origin of Scripture.

Must talk of monergism and divine sovereignty end up in an abstraction of the word of God from its human form? Will it invariably lead to a mechanical view of inspiration in which man becomes a "flute" or a "pen"? Is insistence on monergism in inscripturation incompatible with organic inspiration? Such questions can hardly be avoided. What is the relation of the true humanity of the writers of Scripture and the divine? This, as J. Veenhof indicates in his exposition of the problem in the thought of H. Bavinck, is a fundamental problem for all theological discussion.[45] If no division of labour is made between the divine and human in synergistic fashion, how can the relation be stated? There are ample discouragements for those who wish to face this question. H. N. Ridderbos tells us that Scripture itself "gives no systematic doctrine concerning the relationship of the divine and the human in the Scriptures."[46] Yet in spite of this it is plain that the witness of Scripture (*pace* Barr!) points to its character as Word of God, while its humanity is plain to see.[47] B. J. Oosterhoff remarks that up till the present no inspiration theory has given a satisfactory reply to the question, which does full justice to this human character.[48] This certainly encourages a certain modesty in theological formulation!

Perhaps it may be helpful to ask why theology stumbles again and again over this question of the relation of the divine and the human in Scripture. Three reasons, which no doubt do not exhaust the possibilities, could be given. It could be that the problem is a false one and the question should be abandoned; or that the problem has not been approached in the right way; or that we are faced here with an

---

44. Ibid., pp. 170f.
45. Veenhof, op. cit., pp. 438ff.
46. Ridderbos, *IRB* 32, 3:27.
47. For a discussion of various views of the human factor, see B. J. Oosterhoff, "Schriftkritiek en schriftgezag in de 19e en 20e eeuw (O.T.)," *Rondom het Woord* 10:247f.
48. Ibid., p. 248.

antinomy which must be stated as such. Abandoning the first consideration, since the material of Scripture itself makes the question a valid one for theology, the second two reflexions both seem to be useful for the discussion.

Our basic contention has been that to approach Scripture in terms of the problematic of the divine and human breaks down into dualities in which one or the other is predominant. The broader perspective of the communion with God is necessary to give the divine-human relation its meaning. As far as the monergism of the divine action regarding the Scripture is concerned, this has different meaning when spoken of in reference to the communion between God and man. Here the monergism does not stand over against the human, but its character of divine sovereignty is relational in reference to the human. It is in the covenant communion that God is known as God in relation to man in his true humanity. In the communion, the character of the covenant partners determines their relations.[49] To speak of monergism in the context of the primacy of communion eliminates all oppositions in which the divine would overrule the human factor of Scripture in a mechanistic doctrine of inspiration, or share a synergistic division of labour in a duality of the two factors. In a communion the monergism of a personal God is the foundation of the personal character of the creaturely nature.

In this personal communion, the word of God to man takes on the use of created means. Communion between Creator and creature which is in Spirit and in truth involves mediation by created means. Revelation takes form in created reality, in events in the visible world, in the address of words to man in human language, in the human consciousness of the prophets, and the human text of Scripture. The word of God is not known to man until it enters into a human form.[50] In this sense within the context of communion, the consideration of monergism points us to the necessity of the human character of the revelation. To have fellowship with man God takes upon himself to use human forms. The word of God is at once transcendent and immanent; transcendent as an attribute of the divine nature, immanent in the free speech act of God in which he enters language relations with his linguistically gifted image bearer. As J. Frame says:

49. See M. G. Kline, *The Treaty of the Great King* (Grand Rapids, 1963).
50. Kuitert, op. cit., pp. 158ff.

> The Word can be perfectly human because it is so perfectly divine. Because the speaker is *sovereign* over all things, he can speak human language without "dictating"; he can speak human language "naturally." The world cannot shut him out; he is not compromised by speaking human language; on the contrary, in that act he demonstrates his deity.[51]

Contrary to what might appear to be the case, a monergistic view of the Word of God does not simply permit the use of human characters, but positively requires it. The doctrine of accommodation is the necessary correlate of the monergistic inspiration of Scripture, and accommodation implies this view of inspiration.[52] Both have their places in the structure of the Creator-creature communion.

These insights may well provide us a way to do full justice to both the divine and the human character of Scripture. What has been said here is not contrary, I think, to the idea of organic inspiration developed in Reformed theology in the last century.[53] But perhaps what has been suggested can help in seeking a sense of the human character of Scripture beyond considering it as the organ of the divine or a factor taken into service. As B. J. Oosterhoff remarks, Reformed theology must seek to consider the human factor of the Scriptures in an ever more consequent way.[54] A theology which recognises the primacy of the communion of God and man could do this, it seems, as the human factor, human history, and created reality are necessary for this communion to be realised. The human is not an appendage to the divine; revelation bears an essentially human mark in establishing the communion between God and man. Thus man is not excluded from revelation, but included in order that the bond of fellowship be joined. The human history of the covenant is the history of revelation, as in it God is known to man. Covenant history includes man's response to God, his faithfulness or unfaithfulness. So in Scripture we have not only the identification of the suzerain, but also the history of covenant administration, words of man

---

51. Frame, op. cit., p. 21; see also his article, "God and Biblical Language: Transcendence and Immanence," in *God's Inerrant Word*, ed. J. W. Montgomery (Minneapolis, 1973), pp. 159-77.
52. See the remarks of Preus, in op. cit., pp. 195ff., and in *The Theology of Post-Reformation Lutheranism* (St. Louis, 1970), pp. 286ff.
53. Veenhof, op. cit., pp. 250ff.
54. Oosterhoff, art. cit., p. 249.

against God, disobedience, covenant lawsuits, blessings and curses.[55]

The word of Scripture, expressive as it is of the covenant, is therefore very human, in its form and in the descriptions of man's response to God. Yet because of the monergism of divine grace, these human expressions are the ones God wills as witness to *his* covenant faithfulness. Human response is of a piece with the Word of God as it is a part of covenant history. Scripture as Word of God bears God's own witness to his presence with man in covenant history. So it is that human faithfulness and sinfulness, even man's speaking against God, is properly part of the Word of God, and not a human admixture to it.

* * * * *

A second aspect of the doctrine of Scripture placed in the context of renewal of communion with God concerns the discussion of the relation of the letter of the Scripture and the Spirit. Do we not here face the antinomy we referred to earlier, which is encountered whenever the *how* of the relation of the divine and human in Scripture is asked? Can the perspective we have adopted make a contribution here?

In the recent theology of neo-orthodoxy and particularly in Barth's argument that the freedom of divine grace is incompatible with *Verbalinspiriertheit,* we see a duality between the letter of Scripture in the context of the human and the revelation of God on a higher level. In our discussion of Barr's view of tradition a similar dichotomy is observed. Verbal inspiration can be spoken of in a human fallible sense; it is not the mode of the Spirit's action in revelation. Here again there is a duality of the divine and the human in so far as the letter of Scripture and the Spirit are concerned. This, we have contended, lands Barr in a sort of nominalism of autonomous reason in the examination of the text, complemented by an appeal to a realism of the Spirit's presence. However, there is no way over this dichotomy. For this reason, there is an absence of a criterion by which error might be judged. Calvin had something to say about this problem: "Since 'Satan disguises himself as an angel of light,' what authority will the Spirit have among us, unless he be distinguished by a most certain mark? . . . lest under the Spirit's sign the spirit of Satan

---

55. M. G. Kline, *The Structure of Biblical Authority* (Grand Rapids, 1972), pp. 131ff.

should creep in, he would have us recognize him in his own image, which he has stamped on the Scriptures. He is the Author of the Scriptures: he cannot vary and differ from himself."[56] Calvin can overcome the duality of the divine and the human with respect to Scripture and transcend the dilemmas of nominalism and realism because the Spirit is everywhere consistent with himself in the letter of the Scripture. To speak, as Calvin does, of the Spirit as the author of the Scripture who is perfectly self-consistent and may be compared with himself, is to place the doctrine of Scripture in the context of Spirit-renewal. Fallen reason is here no judge of the truth of the Spirit.

The renewal of the Spirit is the principle governing the inspiration of the Scripture. In the letter of the Scripture this restoration finds its expression. Here also it is possible to speak of accommodation to man's limitations and precise historical situations in which communion exists between God and man. The Spirit takes men's words into service so that these words are divinely authorised to seal the covenant communion.[57] However, this accommodation or service cannot be considered in a formal way, as a problem of how the divine and human are united in the Word of God. This formal question has been placed on one side by Reformed theology as an unwarranted attempt to penetrate the mystery of the Spirit's work. Accommodation has its place in theological description to point to the divine condescension in the work of the renewal of the old (sinful) creation in the image of the Glory-Spirit. The Spirit is not accommodated to the old creation of sin and disorder but to man as renewed in communion with the Creator. The servant-form of Scripture has redemptive scope. Its human form set in new relation to the Spirit points eschatologically to the renewal of creation by the Spirit. Because of the inspiration of the communion-renewing Spirit, the Scripture is not only servant, but also lord in the servant form. The covenantal Scripture, like the covenantal Mediator, bears the characteristics of covenantal lordship and covenantal servanthood. Scripture is word of man and word of God as the treaty document of covenant communion.

---

56. J. Calvin, *Institutes of the Christian Religion,* 1.9.2., ed. J. T. McNeill and F. L. Battles (1961), pp. 94ff.

57. Kline points to the fact that the canon is constituted with the coming into existence of the people of God, op. cit., pp. 27ff.

It is in this respect too that I would wish to speak of the *witness* of Scripture. In discussions of Scripture as witness one sometimes has the impression, not without foundation perhaps, that the human character of Scripture is strongly emphasised to compensate for an impersonal conception of God. Human witness is needed to make the word of God "authentically" human or personal.[58] Here again, we encounter the problem of synergism. Such synergism with respect to the witness of Scripture is tempted to appeal to an all-sufficient Christ to compensate for an insufficient human Bible. Such tension between the divine and the human in witness can be avoided in the covenantal perspective proposed. God enters into personal communion with man in the covenant; his mercy, love, grace, and truth are known in their sovereignty. In Scripture, the witness of God and of man to the covenant are joined in one witness. The human word of witness is God's witness to himself, in the terms of his communion with man. H. N. Ridderbos has summed this up well in referring to the references to witness in John 14–17:

> The witness of the Spirit and the witness of the apostles are very closely related. . . . The witness of the Spirit is not entirely a thing other than the witness of the apostles, but it finds its expression in the witness of the apostles. . . . This does not mean that in spite of the fallibility and weakness of the human witness the Holy Spirit would nevertheless use it for His own purposes, but it means that the Spirit would enable them to speak and to write the witness of the Spirit.[59]

The nature of the NT witness is twofold; it is the witness of man and the witness of the Holy Spirit.[60] The biblical witness is formed in the communion of God and man. Yet in this communion God is sovereign, and the word of witness is in its humanity, God's witness to himself.

What, then, is the relation between the witness of man and the

---

58. I am indebted to my colleague, W. Edgar, for these remarks in a discussion relative to Vander Stelt, op. cit.

59. H. N. Ridderbos, *When the Time Had Fully Come* (Grand Rapids, 1957), pp. 84f. Cf. E. P. Clowney, in *Scripture and Confession,* ed. J. H. Skilton (Nutley, N. J., 1973), pp. 182ff.

60. Ridderbos, *The Authority of the New Testament Scriptures,* p. 66. Also R. Schippers, *Getuigen van Jezus Christus in het Nieuwe Testament* (Franeker, 1938), passim, and K. Runia, *Karl Barth's Doctrine of Holy Scripture* (Grand Rapids, 1962), pp. 25ff.

theopneustos? Hitherto we have described the nature of the relation in the broad structures, but can anything more specific be said of the character of the *theopneustos* in the human word? In recent times the tendency has been to relate the inspiration to the content of the witness of Scripture. A formal consideration of inspiration without reference to this content is rejected.[61] This is particularly so in the writing of G. C. Berkouwer. Here, we are warned against a formalistic view of inspiration which seeks to understand the relation of the Spirit and the witness of men by appeal to "instrumentality," "suggestion," and other causal categories, apart from the content of the message. The mystery of Scripture is not that of the uniting of God and man's word in the *theopneustia*. The mystery of God-breathed Scripture is that it places us before the mystery of Christ.[62] God's speaking "in the manner of men" in Scripture is not to be formalised as an instrumental problem, but is to be understood as the mode of the human witness, which is decisive for the form of Scripture. Berkouwer states that to speak formally of a suggestion of words in inspiration does not lend itself to clarity and seems, in spite of contrary protestations, to imply mechanical inspiration.[63] He wants to avoid glossing over or belittling the true human character of the God-breathed Scripture.[64] The human witness is the *modus* of *theopneustos*. It is through the human witness of Christic content and intent that the revelation of the Holy Spirit takes place.

In this light, Berkouwer criticises E. P. Clowney's rejection of the way Scripture is spoken of as human witness to Christ in the proposal to revise the confession of the United Presbyterian Church in the U.S.A. Clowney will not accept that "the Scriptures are said to be the normative witness to this revelation [i.e., of Christ], but they are not in themselves the Word of God."[65] Berkouwer sees this as a reactionary comment which relativises the human witness of Scripture from a "formal viewpoint of revelation."[66] Yet does this question of Clowney's cast an "impure dilemma" over the discussion? Clowney is asking how Christ bears witness to the Scriptures, if the Scriptures

---

61. Veenhof, op. cit., pp. 430ff.
62. Berkouwer, op. cit., p. 163; cf. pp. 145, 154.
63. Ibid., pp. 157ff.
64. Ibid., p. 195.
65. Ibid., p. 163.
66. Ibid., p. 164.

bear witness to Christ. Far from being an "impure dilemma," such a question would seem to be justified in the light of the NT concept of witness. Witness is not merely witness to Christ, but testimony *for* Christ. As witness for Christ, the Scriptures give not only the witness of man, but also the witness of God to his Son in the Spirit.[67] For this reason, it is not entirely possible to avoid the formal question, even should we wish to give priority to the content of Scripture. If the witness of Scripture is *totally* human, this does not mean that it is *exclusively* human. If such exclusivity is rejected and the human witness is seen in relation to the divine self-witness, then questions of the formal relation of the human witness and inspiration cannot be entirely avoided.

Berkouwer should be given full credit for wishing to relate the *theopneustos* and the content of the biblical message. It can never be overlooked that Scripture is God-breathed with a particular purpose—that of bringing sinners to salvation in Christ. Yet precisely for this reason, it may be wondered whether the formal question can be ignored. As sinners, for restoration of communion with God, we need not only a human witness to Christ, we need God's own witness; then the relation of the *theopneustia* and the human word must be considered. The dilemma of Berkouwer's position, or so it would seem to me, is that when *theopneustia* is understood in terms of the mode of the human witness little can be said about this *theopneustia,* unless we fall back on a complementary reference to the formal relation. Really, we are at quite a loss to say what the *theopneustia* is in relation to the witness of the writers. This problem becomes evident in the comments of J. C. Vander Stelt, who, relying on Berkouwer's discussion, says:

> Scripture is miraculous only in the sense that it is theopneustos, that is, that man's words have been legitimized by God in such a way that, through the Spirit, they can be heard as the authoritative Word of God.[68]

It is unclear in this statement how the divine action of legitimizing man's words, of "taking man into service," working "in and through

67. See. C. Trimp, in *Jerusalem and Athens,* ed. E. R. Geehan (Nutley, N. J., 1971), pp. 172ff., for a detailed discussion of "witness" in modern theology.

68. Vander Stelt, op. cit., p. 329.

him," maintaining his "full creatureliness or humanity"[69] can be called theopneustic, *God-breathed*.

The monergism of divine grace within the sphere of renewal of communion of God can be an aid for reflexion on the relation of the material and formal aspects of inspiration. The renewed communion between Creator and creature provides the personal structure in which graphic inspiration reveals the nature of the redemptive restoration of man. In this personal structure God stands as the author of salvation and also as the author of the witness to his salvation. God's witness takes human form, as salvation is achieved in man's history, for man. Scripture is Word of God in the words of his creatures. The character of God revealed in the covenant, the origin of salvation, and God's free speech to man require that graphic inspiration convey to us what God wills to speak. The character of man in relation to God, the purpose of salvation and man's response require that man speak this word. The Scripture is God-breathed, *efficienter et originaliter;* it is as well fully man's word *materialiter et subjective.* No doubt this is an antinomy, and we cannot do much to enlighten how this can be so. But neither should this surprise or trouble us overmuch, as it is our place as creatures to stand in this sort of role with God. We know that our salvation comes solely from God in his grace, *and* we are psychologically conscious and active in accepting Christ. The fundamental Christian experience of what it means for the creature to be in communion with the Lord provides us with a model for the nature of inspiration which lies within the experience of every true Christian.

If this antinomy is biblical, we do justice to Scripture not by synthesising through synergism or seeking other explanations of the relation of the formal and material, but by emphasising both aspects as strongly as possible. Having the primary nature of the communion of God and man in mind will tend, I think, to allow us to think on the antinomy in the sharpest way possible in conformity to the biblical witness.

The above comments mean that the question of the veracity of Scripture cannot be considered in isolation from the work of the Spirit in the new creation. Scripture cannot be declared errant on the

---

69. *Ibid.,* p. 328.

basis of a judgment of neutral human reason, by simply taking the criteria valid in the old creation as principial for evaluating what belongs to the new. Nor can Scripture simply be declared inerrant on the grounds of a correspondence established with certain factors accepted as true. The errancy or the truthfulness of Scripture established by correspondence with present human knowledge, set that knowledge as authority over Scripture. The old creation rises to judge the new creation of the work of the renewal of the Spirit, and in this schema the duality of the divine and the human will again impose itself on Scripture.

In discussions of inerrancy, what are frequently not established are the criteria upon which errancy and inerrancy are to become evident. The inerrancy of Scripture is not to be established or disproved by appeals to neutral human reason. The question can be properly approached only through consideration of the scope of Scripture as restorative of man to communion with God. This does not eliminate all discussion of factual correspondences, but it does indicate that this is not the central question regarding inerrancy. The problem is that the issue is perhaps not resolvable without a more general discussion of the nature of the presence of the new creation in the old, and the principles upon which knowledge is to be had in creation and redemption. Such discussion is, to my knowledge, as yet hardly inaugurated.[70]

*   *   *   *   *

Our argument to this point can be prolonged in a third topic for discussion, namely, the unity and diversity of the Scripture. To start with a consideration of the monergism of divine grace in the renewal of communion with God implies that as far as the unity and diversity of Scripture is concerned, these are no longer considered as correlates of the divine-human duality. In neo-orthodoxy the unity thought of in connection with Scripture was referred to as located in God himself beyond the Scripture or in the act of revelation of God. This also finds expression in the thought of Barr, who locates the unity desirable as being not a unity of the Bible within the Bible, but a unity found in the one God "who has a history." Here unity and diversity are cor-

---

70. A recent book on the question hardly refers to this problem. See S. T. Davis, *The Debate about the Bible* (Philadelphia, 1977).

related with God and man. Man's history is diverse and unity does not appear in the historical process but is found in God alone, perhaps in an eschatological sense. So also the unity of Scripture is no longer a leading concept in describing the status of the Bible for Barr, as Scripture, being human, is diverse. The duality between the divine and the human appears here once again in the formulation of unity and diversity with reference to Scripture. This is so even in the more moderate expressions of neo-orthodoxy, such as T. F. Torrance's explanation of the christological analogy in Barth's thought in terms of appropriation of and participation of the divine in respect to human nature.[71] The issue of the character of the human nature appropriated remains rather ambiguous. In the case of Scripture the human nature of the text implies not only diversity but also human fallibility over against the perfection found only in the unity of God.

However, if unity and diversity are considered in the contexts of the renewal of communion with God, these aspects of Scripture are no longer simply correlated with the divine and the human factors. The Spirit of God renews the unity of communion with God which was abolished by the disorder of man's sin. This unity of renewal is that of the restoration of the image of God through the Spirit of God. The unity of communion with God restores the meaning to the diversity of human existence which is no longer a disorder without centre but a centred diversity. Likewise, when Scripture is approached in the light of its redemptive scope, it is considered as a centred diversity. God's renewing Spirit everywhere creates a unity in the diversity of the human factors of the Scriptures. The human here is not separable from the organic unity of the work of the Spirit, which extends to all the authors of Scripture. Here a form of parallel can be drawn between the unity and diversity of Scripture and the unity and diversity of the person of Christ. For Scripture, like Christ, presents a true human aspect which inheres a divine substance, the human remaining distinct from and yet dependent on the divine at every point. To place the discussion of the unity and diversity of Scripture in the context of the renewal of the Spirit means that the human diversity of Scripture is denied an interpretation which makes the human factor self-contained in its meaning. The diversity of the Scrip-

---

71. See chapter 1.2.

ture is a centred one, owing to the renewing work of the Spirit. Yet this denial that the human diversity of Scripture is an autonomous diversity is not a denial of true human nature, which in Scripture, as elsewhere, receives its diverse sense in all its richness in the sphere of the renewal of the creation by God. The affirmation of the monergism of the Spirit which lends unity to Scripture is the basis on which the true value of the human diversity of the text can be maintained. In this respect, rather than speaking of appropriation of human nature and participation, it may be more fruitful to think of God in his work of recreation entering into the human realm and restructuring it from within as new creation. God creates unity in diversity by recreating humanity and thus overcoming sin.

*   *   *   *   *

The question of inerrancy and that of the unity and diversity of Scripture lead us to a final remark concerning the interpretation of Scripture.

The historical critical method, as has been applied by theologians since the last century, is practiced in the field of a divine-human duality with respect to Scripture. As B. J. Oosterhoff remarks, in this method and the view of history it often implied, there is no place for revelation *to* man, even though revelation was thought of as being in man, by and through the human spirit. For this reason, he adds, literary and historical criticism paid much attention to the human side of Scripture, but ignored its divine character.[72] This one-sided emphasis on the human character of Scripture approached the historical character of the OT in the light of presuppositions which denied its revelational character. Also it could not indicate the christological character of this history.[73]

While few would wish to deny the value of these researches for our comprehension of the human character of Scripture and its historical milieu, a real problem lies in the fact that the biblical data are isolated from the scope of Scripture and made the object of free human enquiry. Human reason is here made the arbiter of truth in the domain of things human. The truth of God appears only in correlation with what man establishes to be true according to his knowledge. Thus the identity of

---

72. Oosterhoff, art. cit., p. 241.
73. Ibid., and "De prediking van het Oude Testament," *Rondom het Woord* 8:119ff.

Scripture and the Word of God is broken down and the Word is sought beyond Scripture or by establishing a "canon within the canon" as an interpretative principle. R. Marlé says that this search for a canon in the canon is at the antipodes of fundamentalist identification of Scripture and the Word of God. He comments:

> Modern German protestant theology distinguishes between Word of God and Scripture so strictly that it runs the risk of destroying any link between them other than an accidental one.[74]

In this duality of divine and human expressed in interpretation the significance of the empirical facts under examination is separated from the ground of significance which alone can give these facts meaning. Thus T. F. Torrance speaks of the danger for modern exegetical method of processing its data in a purely empirical way which cuts it off from its intrinsic theological connections. This danger is to create an artificial framework with no ontological roots. Torrance comments:

> That hiatus will not disappear until both the biblical scholar and the theologian learn to operate with a scientific approach which does not automatically exclude the ontological unity of form and being, or of structure and material content, in their investigation and interpretation of the Holy Scriptures.[75]

To formulate this another way: Interpretation which approaches the Bible as a human expression of faith and cuts off this faith from the revelation of God leaves us without any real knowledge of God. Interpretation, as Torrance points out, when it is carried out on the half-truth of the understanding of the Bible as just a human document, "is regularly trapped within the fallacies of socio-cultural relativism and linguistic nominalism."[76] The duality of the divine and human in interpretation appears once more at this point.

This form of duality can be avoided when the Scripture is placed in the context of the renewing work of the Spirit. Interpretation in this respect would seek in the human form of the text the material content of the Spirit's work of renewal. In seeking to distinguish the impulse and content of the Bible which are divine and its human forms, the true nature of Scripture and its authority can become

---

74. R. Marlé, *Le problème théologique de l'herméneutique* (Paris, 1968), p. 97. Also G. Maier, op. cit., pp. 16ff.

75. T. F. Torrance, *Space, Time and Resurrection* (Grand Rapids, 1975), p. 7.

76. Ibid., p. 2.

more clear for us.[77] The study of the human forms of Scripture is necessary so that its revelatory nature may become materially evident.

It might be asked finally whether interpretation in the sphere of the renewing work of the Spirit does not impose an *a priori* conception on exegesis. The answer to this would at first appear to be affirmative. Yet on further reflexion this is not the case. As Ridderbos says, ". . . exegesis has to do in Scripture with the Word of God, as that has been laid down in and comes to us out of Scripture."[78] To interpret Scripture out of the context of the Word of God is, though it may not appear so at first, the real case of bringing exegesis under an *a priori*. To mistake the character of the Scripture as Word of God is to work outside the field proposed by the object of interpretation itself. Exegesis is then characterised by a dualism in interpreting the Scripture apart from its God-breathed intention.

Exegesis in the context of the renewal of the Spirit is neither *a priori* nor *a posteriori,* but covenantal. From the premise of communion with God it seeks to read Scripture as God's word. As God is covenant Lord, no *a priori* as to what constitutes the Word of God is formed apart from the witness of Scripture. In the covenantal renewal exegesis is free to hear the Word of God. This listening to the Word of God in Scripture involves a faithful understanding of the human features of the word. If Scripture is interpreted *as* Word of God, we can have no preconceived ideas of *what* the Word must say in exegesis. To impose human meanings on Scripture which are foreign to the text is a parody of man's place in the covenant order. By listening to and exegeting the Word of God in covenant communion, a view of Scripture can be formed in which the doctrine of the Bible is in accordance with the phenomena, and the *idea* of Scripture is implied in the *facts* of Scripture.

In interpreting Scripture according to its redemptive scope, we also find our salvation as men in need of the restoration of the image of the Son through the Spirit. This communion with God, in which we enter into the Creator's Sabbath-rest, is the deepest motive for the interpretation of Scripture. For it is by this renewed relation that the duality of sin is overcome in us and as new creatures we can confess: *Quidquid docetur a scriptore sacro docetur a Spiritu Sancto.*[79]

77. Oosterhoff, *Rondom het Woord* 10:248; Ridderbos, art. cit., p. 37.
78. Ridderbos, art. cit., p. 34.
79. "Whatever is taught by the sacred writer is taught by the Holy Spirit."

Select Bibliography

A. WORKS BY JAMES BARR

"The Pelagian Controversy," *Evangelical Quarterly* 21 (1949):253-64.

"Further Thoughts about Baptism," *Scottish Journal of Theology* 4 (1951):268-78.

"Christ in Gospel and Creed," *Scottish Journal of Theology* 8 (1955): 225-37.

"The Word Became Flesh: The Incarnation in the New Testament," *Interpretation* 10 (1956):16-23.

"The Problem of Old Testament Theology and the History of Religion," *Canadian Journal of Theology* 3 (1957):141-49.

"Tradition and Expectation in Ancient Israel," *Scottish Journal of Theology* 10 (1957):24-34.

"The Problem of Israelite Monotheism," *Transactions of the Glasgow University Oriental Society* 17 (1957–58):52-62.

"J. K. S. Reid, 'The Authority of Scripture, 1957,' " *Scottish Journal of Theology* 11 (1958): 86-93.

"The Meaning of 'Mythology' in Relation to the Old Testament," *Vetus Testamentum* 9 (1959):1-10.

"Theophany and Anthropomorphism in the Old Testament," *Vetus Testamentum Supplement* 7 (1960):31-38.

"The Position of Hebrew Language in Theological Education," *The International Review of Missions* 1 (1961):435-44.

The Semantics of Biblical Language. London, 1961.

Biblical Words for Time. London, 1962 (rev. ed. 1969).

"Gerhard Von Rad's 'Theologie des Alten Testaments,' " *Expository Times* 73 (1962):142-46.

"Daniel," *Peake's Commentary on the Bible,* ed. M. Black and H. H. Rowley. London, 1962. Pp. 591-602.

"Hypostatization of Linguistic Phenomena in Modern Theological Interpretation," *Journal of Semitic Studies* 7 (1962):85-94.

Articles ("Atonement," "Belief," "Blood," "Courage," "Covenant," "Evil," "Expiation," "Faith in Old Testament," "Flesh," "God," "Guilt," "Interpretation," "Life," "Messiah," "Propitiation," "Purity," "Revelation," "Sacrifice and Offering," "Samuel," "Samuel, Books of," "Soul," "Temperance"), in Hastings' *Dictionary of the Bible,* rev. ed. by F. C. Grant and H. H. Rowley. Edinburgh, 1963.

"Did Isaiah Know about Hebrew 'Root Meanings'?," *Expository Times* 75 (1963):242.

"Revelation through History in the Old Testament and in Modern Theology," *New Theology no. 1,* ed. M. E. Marty and D. G. Peerman, New York, 1964, 60-74. (Also in *Interpretation* 17 [1963]: 193-205, and *Princeton Seminary Bulletin* 56 [1963]:4-14.)

Bibelexegese und moderne Semantik. München, 1965.

"The Old Testament," *The Scope of Theology,* ed. D. T. Jenkins. Cleveland and New York, 1965. Pp. 23-38.

"Taking the Cue from Bultmann. 'The Old Testament and Christian Faith: A Theological Discussion,' ed. B. W. Anderson, 1963," *Interpretation* 19 (1965):217-20.

Old and New in Interpretation. A Study of the Two Testaments (The Currie Lectures, Austin Presbyterian Theological Seminary, Texas, 1964). London, 1966.

"St. Jerome's Appreciation of Hebrew," *Bulletin of John Rylands Library* 49 (1966):281-302.

Alt und Neu in der biblischen Überlieferung. München, 1967.

"Biblical Hermeneutics in Ecumenical Discussion," *Student World* 60 (1967):319-24.

"Den teologiska värderingen av den efterbibliska judendomen," *Svensk Exegetisk Årsbok* 32 (1967):69-78.

"St. Jerome and the Sounds of Hebrew," *Journal of Semitic Studies* 12 (1967):1-36.

"Vocalization and the Analysis of Hebrew among the Ancient Translators," in *Hebräische Wortforschung, Festschrift zum 80 Geburtstag von Walter Baumgartner, Vetus Testamentum Supplement* 16 (1967), 1-11.

"The Ancient Semitic Languages—The Conflict between Philology and Linguistics," *Transactions of the Philological Society,* 1968, 37-55.

"Biblical Translation and the Church," *New Blackfriars* 49 (1968): 285-93.

"Common Sense and Biblical Language," *Biblica* 49 (1968):377-87.

Comparative Philology and the Text of the Old Testament. London, 1968.

"The Image of God in the Book of Genesis—A Study of Terminology," *Bulletin of the John Rylands Library* 51 (1968):11-26.

"Judaism—Its Continuity with the Bible" (Montefiore Memorial Lecture, Southampton University, 1968).

"Le judaisme postbiblique," *Revue de Théologie et de Philosophie* (1968):209-17.

"Seeing the Wood for the Trees? An Enigmatic Ancient Translation," *Journal of Semitic Studies* 13 (1968):11-20.

Semantica del linguaggio biblico. Bologna, 1968.

"The Authority of the Bible. A Study Outline," *Ecumenical Review* 21 (1969):135-50.

"Semantics," *A Dictionary of Christian Theology,* ed. A. Richardson. London, 1969.

"The Symbolism of Names in the Old Testament," *Bulletin of the John Rylands Library* 52 (1969):11-29.

"Old Testament Scholarship in the 1960's," *The Church Quarterly* 2 (1970):201-06.

"Themes from the Old Testament for the Elucidation of the New Creation," *Encounter* 31 (1970):25-30.

"Which Language Did Jesus Speak?—Some Remarks of a Semitist," *Bulletin of the John Rylands Library* 53 (1970):9-29.

"The Book of Job and Its Modern Interpreters," *Bulletin of the John Rylands Library* 54 (1971):28-46.

"The Miracles," in *Jesus and Man's Hope* (Pittsburgh Theological Seminary, Festival on the Gospels), ed. D. G. Miller, D. Y. Hadidian. Pittsburgh, 1971. Pp. 305-10.

"The Old Testament and the New Crisis in Biblical Authority," *Interpretation* 25 (1971):24-40.

Sémantique du Langage Biblique. Paris-Neuchâtel, 1971. Translation of 1961 work with new introduction by J. Barr.

"Linguistic Literature, Hebrew: 5 From the 16th Century to the Present," *Encyclopaedia Judaica.* Jerusalem, 1971–72. Vol. 16, 1390–1400.

"Man and Nature—The Ecological Controversy and the Old Testament, *Bulletin of the John Rylands Library* 55 (1972):9-32.

"Semantics and Biblical Theology—A Contribution to the Discussion," *Vetus Testamentum Supplement* 22 (1972):11-19.

The Bible in the Modern World (The Croall Lectures given in New College, Edinburgh, November, 1970). London, 1973.

"An Aspect of Salvation in the Old Testament," *Man and His Salvation: Studies in Memory of S. G. F. Brandon,* ed. E. J. Sharpe and J. R. Hinnells. Manchester, 1973. Pp. 39-52.

"Reading the Bible as Literature," *Bulletin of the John Rylands Library* 56 (1973):10-33.

"Ugaritic and Hebrew šbm?," *Journal of Semitic Studies* 18 (1973): 17-39.

"After Five Years: A Retrospect on Two Major Translations of the Bible," *The Heythrop Journal* 15 (1974):381-405.

"ΕΡΙΖΩ and ΕΡΕΙΔΩ in the Septuagint. A note principally on Genesis xlix 6," *Journal of Semitic Studies* 19 (1974):198-215.

"Etymology and the Old Testament," *Oudetestamentische Studiën* 19 (1974):1-28.

"Philo of Byblos and His 'Phoenician History,' " *Bulletin of the John Rylands Library* 57 (1974):17-69.

"Philology and Exegesis," *Questions Disputées d'Ancien Testament. Méthode et Théologie* par C. Brekelmans. (Bibliotheca Ephemeridium Theologicarum Lovaniensium XXXIII). Louvain, 1974. Pp. 39-63.

"Some Old Testament Aspects of Berkhof's 'Christelijk Geloof,' " *Weerwoord: Reactiones op Dr H. Berkhof's "Christelijk Geloof."* Nykerk, 1974. Pp. 9-19.

"Trends and Prospects in Biblical Theology," *Journal of Theological Studies* 25 (1974):265-82.

" באר׳ץ — ΜΟΛΙΣ, Prov. XI. 31, 1 Pet. IV. 18," *Journal of Semitic Studies* 20 (1975):149-64.

"Jewish Apocalyptic in Recent Scholarly Study," *Bulletin of the John Rylands Library* 58 (1975):8-36.

"Biblical Theology," "Revelation in History," "Scripture, Authority of," *Interpreter's Dictionary of the Bible: Supplementary Volume.* Nashville, 1976.

"The Nature and Purpose of a Theological Dictionary: 'Theological Dictionary of the Old Testament,' ed. G. J. Botterweck and H. Ringgren," *Interpretation* 30 (1976):186-90.

"Story and History in Biblical Theology," *Journal of Religion* 56 (1976):1-17.

Fundamentalism. London, 1977.

"Some Semantic Notes on the Covenant," *Beiträge zur alttestamentlichen Theologie* (Zimmerli Festschrift). Göttingen, 1977. Pp. 23-38.

"2 Timothy 3:16," unpublished sermon preached in Keble College Chapel. Oxford, 1977.

"Does Biblical Study Still Belong to Theology?" An inaugural lecture delivered before the University of Oxford on 26 May, 1977. Oxford, 1978.

"Some notes on *ben* 'between' in Classical Hebrew," *Journal of Semitic Studies* 23 (1978):1-22.

B. SOME WORKS RELATING TO THIS STUDY

Abba, R. *The Nature and Authority of the Bible*. London, 1958.

Ackroyd, P. R. "Meaning and Exegesis," in *Words and Meanings, Essays Presented to David Winton Thomas,* ed. P. R. Ackroyd and B. Lindars. Cambridge, 1968.

Aland, K. *The Problem of the New Testament Canon.* London, 1962.

Albrektson, B. *History and the Gods: An Essay on the Idea of Historical Events as Divine Manifestations in the Ancient Near East and in Israel.* Lund, 1967.

Amsler, S. *L'Ancien Testament dans l'Eglise, Essai d'herméneutique chrétienne.* Neuchâtel, 1960.

———. "Où en est la typologie de l'Ancien Testament," *Etudes Théologiques et Religieuses* 27:75-81.

———. "Prophétie et typologie," *Revue de Théologie et de Philosophie* 3:139-48.

———. "Texte et événement," in *Maqqél Shâqédh, Hommage à Wilhelm Vischer.* Montpellier, 1960.

Anderson, B. W., ed. *The Old Testament and the Christian Faith: Essays by Rudolf Bultmann and Others.* London, 1964.

Anderson, B. W. *Rediscovering the Bible.* New York, 1951.

Antoine, G. et al. *Exegesis.* Neuchâtel-Paris, 1975.

Audinet, J. et al. *Révélation de Dieu et Langage des hommes.* Paris, 1972.

Baillie, J. *The Idea of Revelation in Recent Thought.* New York, 1967.

Baillie, J. and Martin, H., eds. *Revelation.* London, 1937.

Baker, D. L. *Two Testaments, One Bible.* London, 1976.

Balthasar, H. Urs von. *The Theology of Karl Barth.* New York, 1971.

Bannerman, J. *Inspiration: The Infallible Truth and Divine Authority of the Holy Scriptures.* Edinburgh, 1865.

Barth, K. "Autorité et rôle de la Bible," *Etudes Théologiques et Religieuses,* 23:56-66.

———. *Against the Stream.* London, 1954.

———. *Dogmatics* 1:1, 2, ed. G. W. Bromiley and T. F. Torrance. Edinburgh, [1956] 1975.

———. *God in Action.* Edinburgh, 1936.

———. *Rudolf Bultmann, ein Versuch ihn zu verstehen.* Zurich, 1953.

———. *The Word of God and the Word of Man.* London, 1928.

Barth, M. *Conversation with the Bible.* New York, 1964.

Barthel, P. *Interprétation du langage mythique et théologique biblique.* Leiden, 1967.

Barthes, R. et al. *Analyse structurale et exégèse biblique.* Neuchâtel, 1971.

Bartsch, H.-W., ed. *Kerygma and Myth,* 2 vols. London, 1972.

Batson, C. D., Beker, J. C., Clark, W. M. *Commitment without Ideology.* London, 1973.

Battles, F. L. "God Was Accommodating Himself to Human Capacity," *Interpretation* 31:19-38.

Baumgartel, F. *Verheissung: Zur Frage des evangelischen Verständnisses des Alten Testaments.* Gütersloh, 1952.

Bavinck, H. *The Philosophy of Revelation.* Grand Rapids, 1953.

Beauchamp, P. "La figure dans l'un et l'autre testament," *Recherches de Science Religieuse* 59:209-24.

Beegle, D. *The Inspiration of Scripture.* Philadelphia, 1963.

———. *Scripture, Tradition and Infallibility.* Grand Rapids, 1973.

Beker, J. C. "Biblical Theology in a Time of Confusion," *Theology Today* 25:185-94.

————. "Reflections on Biblical Theology," *Interpretation* 24:303-20.

Bellet, P. "Le sens de l'analogie, 'Verbum Dei Incarnation = Verbum Dei Scriptum,' " *Etudes Bibliques* 14:415-28.

Benoit, P. *Exégèse et Théologie,* t. III. Paris, 1968.

————. "Inspiration et Révélation," *Concilium* 10:13-26.

————. "Inspiration de la Tradition et inspiration de l'Ecriture," in *Mélanges offerts à M. D. Chenu.* Paris, 1967:111-26.

Berkouwer, G. C. "The Authority of Scripture (A Responsible Confession)," in *Jerusalem and Athens,* ed. E. R. Geehan. Nutley, N. J., 1971.

————. *Geloof en openbaring in de nieuwere duitsche theologie.* Utrecht, 1932.

————. *General Revelation.* Grand Rapids, 1965.

————. *Holy Scripture.* Grand Rapids, 1975.

————. *Het Probleem der Schriftkritiek.* Kampen, n.d.

————. *The Triumph of Grace in the Theology of Karl Barth.* London, 1956.

Betz, O. "Biblical Theology, History of," *Interpreter's Dictionary of the Bible,* ed. G. A. Buttrick et al. New York/Nashville, 1962.

Blocher, H. "L'herméneutique selon R. Bultmann," *Hokhma* 2:11-35.
————. "L'herméneutique selon Paul Ricoeur," *Hokhma* 3:11-58.

Black, M. "The Christological Use of the Old Testament in the New Testament," *New Testament Studies* 18:1-14.

Blackman, E. C. *Biblical Interpretation: The Old Difficulties and the New Opportunities.* London, 1957.

Blaikie, R. J. *"Secular Christianity" and God Who Acts.* Grand Rapids, 1960.

Boer, H. R. *Above the Battle? The Bible and Its Critics.* Grand Rapids, 1975.

Boisset, J., ed. *Le Problème Biblique dans le Protestantisme.* Paris, 1955.

Boman, T. *Hebrew Thought Compared with Greek.* London, 1960.

————. "Hebrew and Greek Thought Forms in the New Testament," in *Current Issues in New Testament Interpretation,* ed. W. Klassen and G. F. Snyder. London, 1962. Pp. 1-22.

————. "James Barr: 'The Semantics of Biblical Language' and 'Biblical Words for Time,'" *Scottish Journal of Theology* 15: 319-24.

Bouillard, H. *Karl Barth,* 3t. Paris, 1957 ss.

————. *Logique de la Foi.* Paris, 1964.

Braaten, C. E. "The Current Controversy on Revelation: Pannenberg and His Critics," *Journal of Religion* 45:225-37.

————. *History and Hermeneutics.* Philadelphia, 1966.

Branton, J. R. et al. "Our Present Situation in Biblical Theology," *Religion in Life* 26:5-39.

Bright, J. *The Authority of the Old Testament.* London, 1967.

Bromiley, G. W. "The Authority of the Bible: The Attitude of Modern Theologians," *Evangelical Quarterly* 19:127-36.

————. "The Church Doctrine of Inspiration," in *Revelation and the Bible,* ed. C. Henry. Grand Rapids, 1959.

Brown, C., ed. *History, Criticism and Faith.* London, 1976.

Brown, R. E. "The History and Development of the Theory of the Sensus Plenior," *Catholic Bible Quarterly* 15:141-62.

————. "The Problems of the 'Sensus Plenior,'" *Ephemerides Theologicae Lovanienses* 43:460-69.

————. "The 'Sensus Plenior' in the Last Ten Years," *Catholic Bible Quarterly* 25:262-85.

Brunner, E. *Revelation and Reason.* London, 1947.

————. *Truth as Encounter.* London, 1964.

Bryant, R. *The Bible's Authority Today.* Minneapolis, 1968.

Bultmann, R. *Existence and Faith.* London, 1964.

Burnaby, J. *Is the Bible Inspired?* (the Colet Library of Modern Christian Thought and Teaching, N° 9). London, 1949.

Burnier, E. *Bible et Théologie.* Lausanne, 1943.

Burrows, M. *An Outline of Biblical Theology.* Philadelphia, 1946.

Burtchaell, J. T. *Catholic Theories of Biblical Inspiration Since 1810.* Cambridge, 1969.

Cadbury, H. J. "The Peril of Archaizing Ourselves," *Interpretation* 3:331-37.

Camfield, F. W. *Revelation and the Holy Spirit: An Essay in Barthian Theology.* London, 1933.

Campenhausen, H. von. *The Formation of the Christian Bible*. London, 1972.

Childs, B. S. *Biblical Theology in Crisis*. Philadelphia, 1970.

———. *Memory and Tradition in Israel*. London, 1962.

———. *Myth and Reality in the Old Testament*. London, 1960.

———. "Prophecy and Fulfilment: A Study in Contemporary Hermeneutics," *Interpretation* 12:259-71.

———. "A Tale of Two Testaments," *Interpretation* 26:20-29.

Christian Reformed Church. "The Nature and Extent of Biblical Authority," Board of Publications of the Christian Reformed Church, 1971.

Clavier, H. *Les variétés de la pensée biblique et le problème de son unité*. Leiden, 1976.

Clowney, E. P. *Preaching and Biblical Theology*. Grand Rapids, 1961.

Coleman, R. "Biblical Inerrancy: Are We Going Anywhere?," *Theology Today* 31:295-303.

Congar, Y. M-J. "Inspiration de Ecritures canoniques et apostolicité de l'Eglise," *Revue des Sciences Philosophiques et Théologiques* 45: 32-42.

———. *La tradition et les traditions*. Paris, 1960.

Coppens, J. "Comment mieux concevoir et énoncer l'inspiration et l'inerrance des Saintes Ecritures," *Nouvelle Revue Théologique* 86: 933-47.

———. *Les harmonies des deux Testaments. Essai sur les divers sens des Ecritures et sur l'unité de la Révélation*. Paris-Tournai, 1949.

———. "L'Inspiration et l'inerrance bibliques," *Ephemerides Theologicae Lovanienses* 33:36-57.

———. "Nouvelles réflexions sur les divers sens des Saintes Ecritures," *Nouvelle Revue Théologique* 74:3-20.

———. Le problème des sens bibliques," *Concilium* 30:107-18.

Crespy, G. "L'Ecriture de l'écriture," in *Parole et dogmatique,* hommage à Jean Bosc. Paris/Genève, 1971. Pp. 96-119.

———. "Une théologie de l'histoire est-elle possible?," *Recherches de Théologie et de Philosophie* 13:97-123.

Courtade, G. "Les Ecritures ont-elles un sens 'plénier'?," *Recherches de Science Religieuse* 37:481-97.

————. "Inspiration et Inerrance," in *Dictionnaire de la Bible, Supplément, IV*, columns 482-559.

————. "Le sens de l'histoire dans l'Ecriture et la classification usuelle des sens scripturaires," *Recherches de Science Religieuse* 36:136-41.

Crehan, J. H. "The Analogy between 'Verbum Dei Incarnatum' and 'Verbum Dei Scriptum' in the Fathers," *Journal of Theological Studies* 6:87-90.

Cullman, O. *Christ and Time*. London, 1962.

————. "The Necessity and Function of Higher Criticism," in *The Early Church*. London, 1956. Pp. 3-16.

————. *Salvation in History*. London, 1967.

————. *La Tradition*. Neuchâtel-Paris, 1953.

Culley, R. "Structural Analysis: Is It Done with Mirrors?," *Interpretation* 28:165-81.

Cunliffe-Jones, H. *The Authority of the Biblical Revelation*. London, 1945.

Dantine, W. "Christologische Grundlegung einer Lehre vom Worte Gottes," *Theologische Zeitschrift* 12:471-78.

Davies, P. E. "Unity and Variety in the New Testament," *Interpretation* 5:174-85.

Davis, L. "Typology in Barth's Doctrine of Scripture," *Anglican Theological Review* 47:33-49.

Davis, S. T. *The Debate about the Bible*. Philadelphia, 1977.

Dentan, R. C. "The Unity of the Old Testament," *Interpretation* 5:153-73.

Descroches, A. *Jugement pratique et jugement spéculatif chez l'Ecrivain inspiré*. Ottawa, 1958.

Diem, H. *Dogmatics*. Edinburgh, 1959.

————. *Das Problem des Schriftcanons*. Zurich, 1952.

Dinkler, E. "Die ökumenische Bewegung und die Hermeneutik," *Theologische Literaturzeitung* 94:482-90.

Dodd, C. H. "Autorité et rôle de la Bible," *Etudes Theologiques et Religieuses* 23:11-15.

————. *The Authority of the Bible*. London, [1938] 1960.

————. The Bible and the Greeks. London, 1935.

Downing, F. G. *Has Christianity a Revelation?* London, 1964.

Duchrow, U. "Die Klarheit der Schrift und die Vernunft," *Kerygma und Dogma* 15:1-17.

Dugmore, C. W., ed. *The Interpretation of the Bible.* London, 1944.

Ebeling, G. "The Meaning of Biblical Theology," *Journal of Theological Studies* 6:210-25.

————. *Word and Faith.* London, 1963.

————. *The Word of God and Tradition.* London, 1968.

Eichrodt, W. "Offenbarung und Geschichte im Alten Testament," *Theologische Zeitschrift* 4:321-31.

————. "Les rapports du Nouveau Testament et de l'Ancien Testament," in *Le Problème Biblique dans le Protestantisme,* ed. J. Boisset. Paris, 1955.

Ellis, E. E. "The Authority of Scripture: Critical Judgments in a Biblical Perspective," *Evangelical Quarterly* 39:196-204.

Evans, C. *Is "Holy Scripture" Christian?* London, 1971.

Evans, D. "Protestant View of Revelation," *Canadian Journal of Theology* 10:258-65.

Farmer, H. H. "The Bible: Its Significance and Authority," in *The Interpreter's Bible,* ed. G. A. Buttrick et al. New York/Nashville, 1952–1957. 1:3-31.

Farrer, A. M. *The Glass of Vision* (Bampton Lectures for 1948). London, 1948.

————. "Inspiration: Poetical and Divine," in *Promise and Fulfilment,* essays presented to Professor S. H. Hooke, ed. F. F. Bruce. Edinburgh, 1963.

————. "Revelation," in *Faith and Logic,* ed. B. Mitchell. London, 1957.

Filson, F. V. "Method in Studying Biblical History," *Journal of Biblical Literature* 69:1-18.

————. "The Unity of the Old and New Testaments: A Bibliographical Survey," *Interpretation* 5:134-52.

Finlayson, R. A. "Contemporary Ideas of Inspiration," in *Revelation and the Bible,* ed. C. Henry. Grand Rapids, 1959.

Flesseman-van Leer, E. "Present Day Frontiers in the Discussion about Tradition," in *Holy Book and Holy Tradition,* ed. F. F. Bruce and E. G. Rupp. Manchester, 1968. Pp. 154-70.

Fohrer, G. "Twofold Aspects of Hebrew Words," in *Words and*

Meanings: Essays Presented to David Winton Thomas, ed. P. R. Ackroyd and B. Lindars. Cambridge, 1968.

Forestell, J. T. "The Limitation of Inerrancy," *Catholic Biblical Quarterly* 20:9-18.

France, R. T. *Jesus and the Old Testament: His Application of Old Testament Passages to Himself and His Mission.* London, 1971.

Frei, H. W. *The Eclipse of Biblical Narrative.* New Haven and London, 1974.

Friedrich, G. "Pre-history of the Theological Dictionary of the New Testament," in *Theological Dictionary of the New Testament,* X, compiled by R. E. Pitkin. Grand Rapids, 1976.

————. "Semasiologie und Lexikologie," *Theologische Literaturzeitung* 94:802-16.

Fuller, D. P. "The Fundamental Presupposition of the Historical Method," *Theologische Zeitschrift* 24:93-101.

Funk, R. W. *Language, Hermeneutic and the Word of God.* New York, 1966.

Geiselmann, J. R. *The Meaning of Tradition.* New York, 1966.

————. "Scripture, Tradition and the Church: An Ecumenical Problem," in *Christianity Divided,* ed. D. J. Callahan, H. A. Obermann, and D. J. O'Hanlon. New York, 1964. Pp. 35-72.

Gese, H. "Erwägungen zur Einheit der biblischen Theologie," *Zeitschrift für Theologie und Kirche* 67:417-36.

Gilkey, L. B. "Cosmology, Ontology and the Travail of Biblical Language," *Journal of Religion* 41:194-205.

————. *Naming the Whirlwind: The Renewal of God Language.* Indianapolis, 1969.

Glen, J. S. "Jesus Christ and the Unity of the Bible," *Interpretation* 5:259-67.

Goguel, M. "Autorité de Christ et autorité de l'Ecriture," *Revue d'histoire et de Philosophie Religieuses* (1938):101-25.

Goldingay, J. " 'That You May Know That Yahweh Is God': A Study in the Relationship between Theology and Historical Truth in the Old Testament," *Tyndale Bulletin* 23:58-93.

Grelot, P. *La Bible, Parole de Dieu.* Paris, 1965.

————. "L'inspiration scripturaire," *Recherches de Science Religieuse* 51:337-82.

————. "La Tradition, source et milieu de l'Ecriture," *Concilium* 20:13-29.

Grobel, K. "Biblical Criticism," in *The Interpreter's Dictionary of the Bible*. New York/Nashville, 1962.

Hahn, F. "Probleme historischer Kritik," *Zeitschrift für die neutestamentliche Wissenschaft und die Kunde des Urchristentums* 63: 1-17.

Hamer, J. *Karl Barth*. London and Glasgow. 1962.

Hamilton, K. *Words and the Word*. Grand Rapids, 1971.

Hanson, R. P. C. "The Inspiration of the Holy Scripture," *Anglican Theological Review* 43:145-52.

———. *Tradition in the Early Church*. London, 1962.

Haroutunian, J. "The Bible and the Word of God: The Importance of Biblical Theology," *Interpretation* 1:291-308.

Harrington, W. *The Path of Biblical Theology*. Dublin and London, 1973.

Harrison, E. F. "Criteria of Biblical Inerrancy," *Christianity Today* 11:16-18.

Hartvelt, G. P. *Over Schrift en Inspiratie*. Kampen, 1967.

Harvey, J. "L'avènement de la théologie biblique diachronique de l'Ancien Testament," *Bulletin de Théologie Biblique* 1:5-31.

Harvey, Van A. *The Historian and the Believer*. Toronto, 1966.

Hauter, Ch. "Christologie et inspiration des Ecritures," *Revue d'histoire de Philosophie Religieuses* 39: 83-96.

Hebert, A. G. *The Authority of the Old Testament*. London, 1947.

———. *The Bible from Within*. London, 1950.

———. "Fundamentalism," *Interpretation* 11:186-203.

———. *Fundamentalism and the Church of God*. London, 1957.

Helm, P. "Revealed Propositions and Timeless Truths," *Religious Studies* 8:127-36.

———. "What Is 'Self-Authentication'?" Unpublished paper, 1971.

Hendry, G. S. "The Exposition of Holy Scripture," *Scottish Journal of Theology* 1:29-47.

Hengel, M. "Historische Methoden und theologische Auslegung des Neuen Testaments," *Kerygma und Dogma* 2:85-90.

Henry, C., ed. *Revelation and the Bible*. Grand Rapids, 1959.

Henry, C. *God, Revelation and Authority*, 2 vols. Waco, 1976.

———. "Those Incomprehensible British Fundamentalists," *Christianity Today* 22:1092-96, 1146-50, 1205-08.

Hill, D. *Greek Words and Hebrew Meanings: Studies in the Semantics of Soteriological Terms.* Cambridge, 1967.

Hodge, A. A. and Warfield, B. B. "Inspiration," in *Presbyterian Review,* April, 1881:225-60, and tract. Philadelphia, 1881.

Hodgson, L. et al. *On the Authority of the Bible.* London, 1960.

Hunter, A. M. *The Unity of the New Testament.* London, 1943.

Hyatt, J. P., ed. *The Bible in Modern Scholarship.* Nashville-New York, 1965.

Jacob, E. "A propos de l'interprétation de l'Ancien Testament: Méthode christologique ou méthode historique?" *Etudes Théologiques et religieuses* 20:76-82.

―――. "Considérations sur l'autorité canonique de l'Ancien Testament," in *Le Problème Biblique dans le Protestantisme,* ed. J. Boisset. Paris, 1955.

―――. "Possibilités et limites d'une théologie biblique," *Revue d'histoire et de Philosophie Religieuses* 46:116-30.

Jacobson, R. "The Structuralists and the Bible," *Interpretation* 28:146-64.

Jenkins, D. *Tradition and the Spirit.* London, 1951.

Johnson, R. C. *Authority in Protestant Theology.* Philadelphia, 1959.

Jüngel, E. et al. "Four Preliminary Considerations on the Concept of Authority," *Ecumenical Review* 21:150-66.

Kaiser, C. B. "Christology and Complementarity," *Religious Studies* 12:37-48.

Käsemann, E. *Essays on New Testament Themes.* London, 1964.

―――. *Das Neue Testament als Kanon.* Göttingen, 1970.

―――. "Thoughts on the Present Controversy about Scriptural Interpretation," in *New Testament Questions of Today.* Philadelphia, 1969.

Kaufman, G. D. "On the Meaning of 'Act of God,' " *Harvard Theological Review* 61:175-201.

―――. "What Shall We Do with the Bible?," *Interpretation* 25:95-112.

Kelsey, D. H. "Appeals to Scripture in Theology," *Journal of Religion* 48:1-21.

―――. *The Uses of Scripture in Recent Theology.* London, 1975.

King, W. L. "Some Ambiguities in Biblical Theology," *Religion in Life* 27:95-104.

Kistemaker, S., ed. *Interpreting God's Word Today*. Grand Rapids, 1970.

Klein, R. W. *Textual Criticism of the Old Testament*. Philadelphia, 1974.

Kline, M. G. *The Structure of Biblical Authority*. Grand Rapids, 1972.

Knight, D. A., ed. *Tradition and Theology in the Old Testament*. London, 1977.

Koch, K. *The Growth of the Biblical Tradition: The Form Critical Method*. London, 1969.

Koole, J. L. *Verhaal en Feit in het Oude Testament*. Kampen, 1966.

Kraus, H.-J. *Die biblische Theologie, ihre Geschichte und Problematik*. Neukirchen-Vluyn, 1970.

————. *Geschichte der historisch—kritisch Erforschung des Alten Testaments von der Reformation bis zur Gegenwart*. Neukirchen, 1956.

Krentz, E. *The Historical Critical Method*. Philadelphia, 1975.

Kuitert, H. M. *Do You Understand What You Read?* Grand Rapids, 1970.

————. *The Reality of Faith*. Grand Rapids, 1968.

Kung, H. *Infallible? An Enquiry*. London, 1972.

Ladd, G. E. "The Search for Perspective," *Interpretation* 25:41-62.

Lampe, G. W. H. and Woollcombe, K. J. *Essays on Typology*. London, 1957.

Latourelle, R. *Théologie de la Révélation*. Bruxelles-Paris, 1969.

Lee, W. *The Inspiration of Holy Scripture, Its Nature and Proof*. Dublin, 1865.

LeFrois, B. J. "Semitic Totality Thinking," *Catholic Bible Quarterly* 17:195-203.

Lehmann, P. L. "Karl Barth and the Future of Theology," *Religious Studies* 6:105-20.

Leon-Dufour, X., ed. *Exégèse et Herméneutique*. Paris, 1971.

Levie, J. *The Bible, Word of God in Words of Men*. London, 1961.

Lloyd-Jones, M. *Authority*. London, 1958.

Lohfink, N. *The Christian Meaning of the Old Testament*. London, 1968.

————. "Ueber die Irrtumslosigkeit und die Einheit der Schrift," *Stimmen der Zeit* 84:161-81.

Lønning, I. *Kanon im Kanon.* München, 1972.

Loretz, O. *Quelle est la vérité de la Bible?* Paris, 1970.

Lubac, H. de. *L'Ecriture dans la tradition.* Paris, 1966.

————. *Exégèse médiévale: Les quartre sens de l'Ecriture.* Paris, 1959–64, 3t.

————. " 'Sens spirituel,' " *Recherches de Science Religieuse* 36: 542-76.

————. " 'Typologie' et 'Allégorisme,' " *Recherches de Science Religieuse* 34:180-226.

Lys, D. *The Meaning of the Old Testament: An Essay on Hermeneutics.* Nashville/New York, 1967.

McCarthy, D. J. "Personality, Society and Inspiration," *Theological Studies* 24:553-76.

McCasland, S. V. "The Unity of the Scriptures," *Journal of Biblical Literature* 73:1-10.

McConnachie, J. "The Uniqueness of the Word of God," *Scottish Journal of Theology* 1:113-35.

McDonald, H. D. *Ideas of Revelation: An Historical Study A.D. 1700 to 1860.* London, 1959.

————. *Theories of Revelation: An Historical Study, 1860–1960.* London, 1963.

McIntyre, J. "Analogy," *Scottish Journal of Theology* 12:1-20.

McKenzie, J. L. "The Social Character of Inspiration," *Catholic Bible Quarterly* 24:115-24.

————. "The Word of God in the Old Testament," *Theological Studies* 21:183-206.

MacKenzie, R. A. F. "Some Problems in the Field of Inspiration," *Catholic Bible Quarterly* 20:1-8.

Mackey, J. P. *The Modern Theology of Tradition.* New York, 1963.

Maier, G. *The End of the Historical Critical Method.* St. Louis, 1977.

Malevez, L. *Histoire du Salut et Philosophie.* Paris, 1971.

Marcel, P. "Christ expliquant les Ecritures," *Revue Réformée* 9: 14-46.

Marlé, R. *Le Problème théologique de l'herméneutique.* Paris, 1968

Marshall, I. H., ed. *New Testament Interpretation*. Exeter, 1977.

Marxen, W. *The New Testament as the Church's Book*. Philadelphia, 1972.

Mascall, E. L. *Words and Images*. London, 1968.

Mavrodes, G. I. "The Inspiration of the Autographs," *Evangelical Quarterly* 41:19-29.

Mendenhall, G. E. "Debate over Linguistic Methodology: 'Comparative Philology and the Text of the Old Testament,' by James Barr," *Interpretation* 25:358-62.

Meuleman, G.-E. "Autorité et Inspiration de l'Ecriture Sainte," *Etudes Evangéliques* 18:1-43.

Michaeli, F. "Grammaire hébraïque et théologie biblique," in *Maqqél Shâqédh Hommage à Wilhelm Vischer*. Montpellier, 1960.

Mildenberger, F. "The Unity, Truth and Validity of the Bible: Theological Problems in the Doctrine of Holy Scripture," *Interpretation* 29:391-405.

Minear, P. S. "Between Two Worlds: Eschatology and History," *Interpretation* 5:27-39.

Montgomery, J. W., ed. *God's Inerrant Word*. Minneapolis, 1973.

Montgomery, J. W. "Inspiration and Inerrancy—A New Departure," *Crisis in Lutheran Theology,* vol. 1. Minneapolis, 1967. Pp. 15-44.

Moran, G. *Theology of Revelation*. New York, 1966.

————. "What Is Revelation?" *Theological Studies* 25:217-31.

Moule, C. F. D. "Fulfilment—Words in the New Testament: Use and Abuse," *New Testament Studies* 14:293-320.

Mowinckel, S. *The Old Testament as Word of God*. Oxford, 1960.

Mueller, J. T. "The Holy Spirit and the Scriptures," in *Revelation and the Bible,* ed. C. Henry. Grand Rapids, 1959.

Murray, J. "The Attestation of Scripture," in *The Infallible Word,* ed. N. B. Stonehouse and P. Woolley. Grand Rapids, 1946.

————. *Calvin on Scripture and Divine Sovereignty*. Philadelphia, 1960.

Nelson, R. A. "Scripture, Tradition and Traditions," *The Ecumenical Review* 16:158-64.

Nicholas, T. A. "The Current Quest for the Meaning of the Text of the Old Testament," *Westminster Theological Journal* 34:118-36.

Nicholls, W. *Revelation in Christ*. London, 1958.

Nicole, R. "Induction and Deduction with Reference to Inspiration," in *Soli Deo Gloria,* Festschrift for John H. Gerstner, ed. R. C. Sproul. Nutley, N. J., 1976.

Nida, E. A. "Implications of Contemporary Linguistics and Biblical Scholarship," *Journal of Biblical Literature* 91:73-89.

Niebuhr, H. R. *The Meaning of Revelation.* New York, 1960.

Nineham, D. E., ed. *The Church's Use of the Bible: Past and Present.* London, 1963.

Nineham, D. E. *The Use and Abuse of the Bible.* London, 1976.

———. "The Use of the Bible in Modern Theology," *Bulletin of the John Rylands Library* 52:178-99.

Ogden, S. M. "The Authority of Scripture for Theology," *Interpretation* 30:242-61.

———. "What Sense Does It Make to Say, 'God Acts in History'?," *Journal of Religion* 43:1-19.

Oosterhoff, B. J. *Feit of Interpretatie.* Kampen, 1961.

———. "Hereinterpretatie in het Oude Testament," *Rondom het Woord* 15:95-117.

———. "De prediking van het Oude Testament," *Rondom het Woord* 8:115-22.

———. "Schriftkritiek en schriftgezag in de 19e en 20e eeuw (O.T.), *Rondom het Woord* 10:237-50.

———. *De vrijheid van de exegese.* Kampen, 1976.

Orr, J. *Revelation and Inspiration.* London, 1910/Grand Rapids, 1969.

Packer, J. I. *Fundamentalism and the Word of God.* London, 1958.

———. *God Has Spoken.* London, 1965.

———. "Hermeneutics and Biblical Authority," in *Jerusalem and Athens,* ed. E. R. Geehan. Nutley, N. J., 1971.

———. "Revelation," in *New Bible Dictionary,* ed. J. D. Douglas. London, 1972.

———. "Revelation and Inspiration," in *New Bible Commentary Revised,* ed. D. Guthrie et al. London, 1970.

Pannenberg, W., ed. *Revelation as History.* New York, 1968.

Pannenberg, W. *Basic Questions in Theology,* 3 vols. London, 1970–.

Patte, D. *What Is Structural Exegesis?* Philadelphia, 1976.

Payot, C. "Les infortunes de la théologie biblique et de l'herméneutique: A propos de quelques ouvrages récents de James Barr et
Robert W. Funk," *Revue de Théologie et de Philosophie,* 1968:
218-35.

Peter, J. "Salvation History as a Model for Theological Thought,"
Scottish Journal of Theology 23:1-12.

Piepkorn, A. C. "What Does 'Inerrancy' Mean?," *Concordia Theological Monthly* 36:577-93.

Pinnock, C. *Biblical Revelation—The Foundation of Christian Theology.* Chicago, 1971.

―――. *A Defense of Biblical Infallibility.* Philadelphia, 1967.

Piper, O. "Biblical Theology and Systematic Theology," *Journal of
Bible and Religion* 25:106-11.

Porteous, N. W. "Magnalia Dei," in *Probleme Biblischer Theologie:
Gerhard von Rad zum 70 Geburtstag,* ed. H. W. Wolff. München,
1971. Pp. 417-27.

―――. "Second Thoughts: The Present State of Old Testament
Theology," *Expository Times* 75:70-74.

Prenter, R. "Dietrich Bonhoeffer and Karl Barth's Positivism of Revelation," in *World Come of Age,* ed. R. G. Smith. London, 1967.
Pp. 93-130.

Preus, R. D. "The Doctrine of Revelation in Contemporary Theology," *Bulletin of the Evangelical Theological Society* 9:111-23.

―――. *The Inspiration of Scripture: A Study of the Theology of the
Seventeenth Century Lutheran Dogmaticians.* Edinburgh, 1955.

―――. "Notes on the Inerrancy of Scripture," in *Crisis in Lutheran
Theology,* ed. J. W. Montgomery. Minneapolis, 1973. II:34-47.

Rad, G. von. *Old Testament Theology,* 2 vols. London, 1975.

Rahner, K. "Inspiration," in *Encyclopaedie de la Foi,* t.II. Paris,
1967.

―――. *Inspiration in the Bible.* Freiburg and London, 1961.

Rahner, K. and Ratzinger, J. *Révélation et Tradition.* Paris, 1972.

Ramm, B. *Special Revelation and the Word of God.* Grand Rapids,
1961.

Rast, W. E. *Tradition History and the Old Testament.* Philadelphia,
1972.

Reid, J. K. W. *The Authority of the Scripture.* London, 1957.

Rendtorff, R. and Koch, K., eds. *Studien zur Theologie der alttestamentlichen Überlieferungen.* Neukirchen, 1961.

Resweber, J.-P. *La Théologie face au défi herméneutique.* Louvain, 1975.

Richardson, A. *The Bible in the Age of Science.* London, 1961.

———. *Christian Apologetics.* London, 1947.

———. *History Sacred and Profane.* London, 1964.

———. "The Nature of Biblical Theology," *Theology* 39:166-76.

———. *A Preface to Bible-Study.* London, 1943.

———. "The Rise of Modern Biblical Scholarship and Recent Discussion of the Authority of the Bible," *Cambridge History of the Bible,* ed. S. L. Greenslade. 1963. III: 294-338.

Richardson, A. and Schweitzer, W., eds. *Biblical Authority for Today.* London, 1951 (World Council of Churches Symposium).

Ricoeur, P. *Le Conflit des Interprétations.* Paris, 1969.

———. "Philosophy and Religious Language," *Journal of Religion* 54:71-85.

———. "Problèmes actuels de l'interprétation," *Centre Protestant d'Etudes et de Documentation* 148 (1970):163-82.

Ricoeur, P. et al. *La Révélation.* Bruxelles, 1977.

Ridderbos, H. N. "An Attempt at the Theological Definition of Inerrancy, Infallibility and Authority," *International Reformed Bulletin* 32/33:27-41.

———. *The Authority of the New Testament Scriptures.* Philadelphia, 1963.

———. "The Canon of the New Testament," in *Revelation and the Bible,* ed. C. Henry. Grand Rapids, 1959.

———. *Studies in Scripture and Its Authority.* Grand Rapids, 1978.

Ridderbos, N. "Is het hebreeuws één van de Bronnen van de Openbaring?" *Gereformeerd Theologische Tijdschrift* 64:209-29.

Ritschl, D. "A Plea for the Maxim: Scripture and Tradition," *Interpretation* 25:113-28.

———. "Spring Cleaning: 'Biblical Words for Time,' James Barr," *Interpretation* 17:206-09.

Robinson, H. W. "Canonicity and Inspiration," *Expository Times* 47:119-23.

———. *Inspiration and Revelation in the Old Testament.* Oxford, 1946.

Robinson, J. M. "Interpretation of Scripture in Biblical Studies Today," in *Ecumenical Dialogue at Harvard: The Roman Catholic-Protestant Colloquium,* ed. S. H. Miller and G. E. Wright. Cambridge, Mass., 1964. Pp. 91-109.

———. "Scripture and Theological Method: A Protestant Study in 'Sensus Plenior,' " *Catholic Bible Quarterly* 27:6-27.

———. "Theology as Translation," *Theology Today* 20:518-27.

Robinson, J. M., ed. *The Beginnings of Dialectic Theology,* vol. 1. Richmond, 1968.

Robinson, J. M. and Cobb, J. B., eds. *The New Hermeneutic.* New York, 1964 (New Frontiers in Theology II).

———. *Theology as History.* New York, 1967 (New Frontiers in Theology III).

Robertson, O. P. "The Outlook for Biblical Theology," in *Toward a Theology for the Future,* ed. D. F. Wells and C. H. Pinnock. Carol Stream, Ill., 1971. Pp. 65-91.

Rogers, J. B. *Scripture in the Westminster Confession.* Grand Rapids, 1967.

———. "Van Til and Warfield on Scripture in the Westminster Confession," in *Jerusalem and Athens,* ed. E. R. Geehan. Nutley, N. J., 1971. Pp. 154-71.

Rogers, J. B., ed. *Biblical Authority.* Waco, Texas, 1977.

Rowley, H. H. "The Authority of the Bible," in *From Moses to Qumran.* London, 1963. Pp. 3-31.

———. *The Relevance of the Bible.* London, 1941.

———. "The Relevance of Biblical Interpretation," *Interpretation* 1:3-19.

———. *The Unity of the Bible.* London, 1953.

———. "The Unity of the Old Testament," *Bulletin of the John Rylands Library* 29:326-58.

Runia, K. "The Authority of Scripture," *Calvin Theological Journal* 4:165-94.

———. *Karl Barth's Doctrine of Holy Scripture.* Grand Rapids, 1962.

Ryrie, C. C. "The Importance of Inerrancy," *Bibliotheca Sacra* 120:137-44.

Salomonsen, B. "Lingvistik og bibelsk teologi. En Praesentation af James Barr," *Dansk Teologisk Tidsskrift* 31:31-59.

Sanday, W. *Inspiration* (Bampton Lectures 1893). London, 1901.

⸻. *The Oracles of God.* London, 1902.

Sandeen, E. R. *The Roots of Fundamentalism.* Chicago, 1970.

Sanders, J. A. "Reopening Old Questions about Scripture," *Interpretation* 28:321-30.

⸻. *Torah and Canon.* Philadelphia, 1972.

Sasse, H. "Concerning the Nature of Inspiration," *Reformed Theological Review* 23:33-43.

⸻. "Inspiration and Inerrancy—Some Preliminary Thought," *Reformed Theological Review* 19:33-48.

Sawyer, J. F. A. *Semantics in Biblical Research.* London, 1972.

Schelkle, K. H. "Sacred Scripture and the Word of God," in *Dogmatic versus Biblical Theology.* Baltimore/Dublin, 1964.

Schicklberger, F. "Biblische Literarkritik und linguistische Texttheorie," *Theologische Zeitschrift* 34:65-82.

Schillebeeckx, E. *Revelation and Theology.* London, 1967.

Schippers, R. *Getuigen van Jezus Christus in het Nieuwe Testament.* Franeker, 1938.

Schökel, L. Alonso. "Hermeneutics in the Light of Language and Literature," *Catholic Bible Quarterly* 25: 371-86.

⸻. *La Parole Inspirée.* Paris, 1971.

Schweizer, E. "The Relation of Scripture, Church Tradition and Modern Interpretation," in *New Theology No. 1,* ed. M. E. Marty and D. G. Peerman. New York, 1964. Pp. 44-59.

Scroggs, R. "Tradition, Freedom and the Abyss," in *New Theology No. 8,* ed. M. E. Marty and D. G. Peerman. New York, 1971. Pp. 84-103.

Sekine, M. "Erwägungen zur hebräischen Zeitauffassung," *Supplement to Vetus Testamentum* 9:66-82.

Siertsema, B. "Language and World View (Semantics for Theologians)," *The Bible Translator* 20:3-21.

Simpson, C. A. "An Inquiry into the Biblical Theology of History," *Journal of Theological Studies* 12:1-13.

Skilton, J. H., ed. *Scripture and Confession.* Nutley, N. J., 1973.

Skydsgaard, K. E. "Scripture and Tradition," in *Challenge and Response,* ed. W. A. Quanbeck. Minneapolis, 1966. Pp. 25-59.

————. "Scripture and Tradition: Remarks on the Problem of Tradition in Theology Today," *Scottish Journal of Theology* 9:337-58.

————. "Tradition as an Issue in Contemporary Theology," in *The Old and the New in the Church,* ed. P. Minear. Minneapolis, 1961. Pp. 20-36.

Smart, J. D. *The Divided Mind of Modern Theology: Karl Barth and Rudolf Bultmann 1908–1933.* Philadelphia, 1967.

————. *The Interpretation of Scripture.* Philadelphia, 1961.

————. *The Old Testament in Dialogue with Modern Man.* London, 1965.

————. *The Strange Silence of the Bible in the Church.* Philadelphia, 1970.

————. "The Treacherousness of Tradition," *Interpretation* 30:18-25.

Smith, N. "Karl Barth on the Doctrine of the Inspiration of the Scriptures in the History of the Church," *Scottish Journal of Theology* 2:156-62.

Snaith, N. H. *The Inspiration and Authority of the Bible* (A. S. Peake Memorial Lecture, 1). London, 1956.

Soggin, J. A. "Geschichte, Historie und Heilsgeschichte im Alten Testament: Ein Beitrag zur heutigen theologisch—hermeneutischen Diskussion," *Theologische Literaturzeitung* 89:721-36.

Söhngen, G. *"Analogie und Metaphern." Kleine Philosophie und Theologie der Sprache.* München, 1962.

Spicq, C. "L'avènement de la Théologie biblique," *Revue de Sciences philosophiques et théologiques* 35:561-74.

Spivey, R. A. "Structuralism and Biblical Studies: The Uninvited Guest," *Interpretation* 28:133-45.

Spriggs, D. G. *Two Old Testament Theologies: A Comparative Evaluation of Eichrodt and von Rad to Our Understanding of the Nature of Old Testament Theology.* London, 1974.

Stek, J. H. "Biblical Typology Yesterday and Today," *Canadian Journal of Theology* 5:133-62.

Stendahl, K. "Biblical Theology, Contemporary," in *Interpreter's Dictionary of the Bible.* New York/Nashville, 1962.

————. "Method in the Study of Biblical Theology," in *The Bible in Modern Scholarship,* ed. J. P. Hyatt. Nashville-New York, 1965. Pp. 196-209.

Stibbs, A. M. "The Witness of Scripture to Its Inspiration," in *Revelation and the Bible*, ed. C. Henry. Grand Rapids, 1959.

Stonehouse, N. B. "The Authority of the New Testament," in *The Infallible Word*, ed. N. B. Stonehouse and P. Woolley. Philadelphia, 1946.

————. "Special Revelation as Scriptural" in *Revelation and the Bible*, ed. C. Henry. Grand Rapids, 1959.

Strimple, R. B. "The Relationship between Scripture and Tradition in Contemporary Roman Catholic Theology," *Westminster Theological Journal* 40:22-38.

Stuhlmacher, P. "Thesen zur Methodologie gegenwärtiger Exegese," *Zeitschrift fur die neutestamentliche Wissenschaft und die Kunde des Urchristentums* 63:18-26.

Sundberg, A. C. "The Bible Canon and the Christian Doctrine of Inspiration," *Interpretation* 29:352-71.

Tangberg, K. A. "Linguistics and Theology: An Attempt to Analyse and Evaluate James Barr's Argumentation in 'The Semantics of Biblical Language' and 'Biblical Words for Time,' " *The Bible Translator* 24:301-310.

Tasker, R. V. G. *The Old Testament in the New Testament*. London, 1954 (2).

Tenney, M. C., ed. *The Bible: The Living Word of Revelation*. Grand Rapids, 1968.

Thielicke, H. *Between Heaven and Earth*. New York, 1965.

Thiselton, A. C. "The Supposed Power of Words in the Biblical Writings," *Journal of Theological Studies* 25:283-99.

Thornton, L. S. *Revelation and the Modern World: Being the First Part of a Treatise on the Form of the Servant*. London, 1950.

Tilden, E. E. "The Study of Jesus' Interpretative Methods," *Interpretation* 7:45-61.

Tomes, R. "Exodus 14: The Mighty Acts of God: An Essay in Theological Criticism," *Scottish Journal of Theology* 22:454-78.

Torrance, T. F. *Karl Barth: An Introduction to His Early Theology, 1910–1931*. London, 1962.

————. *Space, Time and Incarnation*. London, 1969.

————. *Space, Time and Resurrection*. Grand Rapids, 1976.

Tracy, D. *Blessed Rage for Order: The New Pluralism in Theology*. New York, 1975.

Tresmontant, C. *A Study of Hebrew Thought.* New York, 1960.

Tucker, G. M. *Form Criticism and the Old Testament.* Philadelphia, 1971.

Van Ruler, A. A. *The Christian Church and the Old Testament.* Grand Rapids, 1966.

Van Til, C. *Christianity and Barthianism.* Philadelphia, 1965.

―――. *The New Modernism.* Philadelphia, 1946.

Vander Stelt, J. C. *Philosophy and Scripture. A Study in Old Princeton and Westminster Theology.* Marlton, N. J., 1978.

Vawter, B. *Biblical Inspiration.* London, 1972.

Veenhof, J. *Revelatie en inspiratie: de openbarings—en Schrift—beschouwing van Herman Bavinck in vergelijking met die der ethische theologie.* Amsterdam, 1968.

Verhaar, J. "Some Notes on Language and Theology," *Bijdragen* 30: 39-65.

Verhoef, P. A. "Some Thoughts on the Present-day Situation in Biblical Theology," *Westminster Theological Journal* 33:1-19.

Vaux, R. de. "God's Presence and Absence in History: The Old Testament View," *Concilium* 10:5-11.

―――. "Is It Possible to Write a Theology of the Old Testament?" in *The Bible and the Ancient Near East.* London, 1972. Pp. 49-62.

―――. "Method in the Study of Early Hebrew History," in *The Bible in Modern Scholarship*, ed. J. P. Hyatt. Nashville-New York, 1965.

Vischer, W. "La langue sainte source de la théologie," *Etudes Théologiques et religieuses* 21:318-26.

Vorgrimler, H., ed. *Dogmatic Versus Biblical Theology.* Baltimore/Dublin, 1964.

Vos, G. *Biblical Theology.* Edinburgh, 1975.

Wallace, D. H. "Biblical Theology: Past and Future," *Theologische Zeitschrift* 19:88-105.

Walvoord, J. W., ed. *Inspiration and Interpretation.* Grand Rapids, 1957.

Wand, J. W. C. *The Authority of the Scriptures.* London, 1949.

Warfield, B. B. *The Inspiration and Authority of the Bible.* Grand Rapids, 1967.

―――. *Limited Inspiration.* Philadelphia, n.d., reprinted from *Pres-*

byterian and Reformed Review, 1894: original title, "Professor Henry Preserved Smith on Inspiration."

Watson, P. S. "The Nature and Function of Biblical Theology," *Expository Times* 73:195-200.

Weber, O. "Inspiration. Dogmengeschichtlich," *Die Religion in Geschichte und Gegenwart,* 3rd ed. 3 (1959):775-79.

Weisengoff, J. P. "Inerrancy of the Old Testament in Religious Matters," *Catholic Bible Quarterly* 17: 128-37.

Wells, P. "James Barr et le fondamentalisme: faiblesse du 'fondamentalisme' et faiblesse du 'libéralisme'?" *Revue Réformée,* 29: 85-94.

———. "Révélation et Inspiration: Les options 'libérale' et 'fondamentaliste' sur l'Ecriture: James Barr contre Benjamin B. Warfield," *Hokhma* 8:39-64.

Wernberg-Möller, P. "Is There an Old Testament Theology," *The Hibbert Journal* 59:21-29.

Westermann, C., ed. *Essays in Old Testament Interpretation.* London, 1963.

Wilder, A. "Biblical Hermeneutic and American Scholarship," in *Neutestamentliche Studien für Rudolf Bultmann.* Berlin, 1957. Pp. 24-32.

Wingren, G. *Theology in Conflict.* Edinburgh, 1958.

Wirsching, J. *Was ist Schriftgemäss?* Gütersloh, 1971.

Wolff, H. W. "The Hermeneutics of the Old Testament," *Interpretation* 12:281-91.

Wolff, H. W., ed. *Probleme biblischer theologie: Gerhard Von Rad zum 70 Geburstag.* München, 1971.

World Council of Churches. "Tradition and Traditions" (Faith and Order Paper n° 40), in *Faith and Order Findings 1963.* Genève.

———. *New Directions in Faith and Order: Bristol 1967* (Faith and Order Paper n°. 50:32-41).

———. *Louvain 1971* (Faith and Order paper n° 59:212-15).

Wright, G. E. 'The Christian Interpreter as Biblical Critic: The Relevance of Valid Criticism," *Interpretation* 1:131-52.

———. "Exegesis and Eisegesis in the Interpretation of Scripture," *Expository Times* 48:353-57.

———. " Historical Knowledge and Revelation," in *Translating and Understanding the Old Testament: Essays in Honor of Herbert*

Gordon May, ed. H. T. Frank and W. L. Reed. Nashville, 1970. Pp. 279-303.

————. "History in the Old Testament: 'Old and New in Interpretation: A Study of the Two Testaments' by James Barr," *Interpretation* 22:83-89.

————. *The Old Testament and Theology.* New York, 1969.

————. "Reflections Concerning Old Testament Theology," *Studia Biblica et Semitica,* T. H. Vriesen Dedicata. Wageningen, 1966.

————. "The Unity of the Bible," *Scottish Journal of Theology* 8: 337-52.

Young, E. J. "The Authority of the Old Testament," in *The Infallible Word,* ed. N. B. Stonehouse and Paul Woolley. Philadelphia, 1946.

————. "The Canon of the Old Testament," in *Revelation and the Bible,* ed. C. Henry. Grand Rapids, 1959.

————. *Thy Word Is Truth.* Grand Rapids, 1957.

Young, W. "The Inspiration of Scripture in Reformation and in Barthian Theology," *Westminster Theological Journal* 8:1-38.

Zerafa, P. "The Limits of Biblical Inerrancy," *Angelicum* 39:92-119.